Britain Votes 2015

Edited by Andrew Geddes and Jonathan Tonge

UNIVERSITY PRESS

in association with

HANSARD SOCIETY SERIES IN POLITICS
AND GOVERNMENT

OXFORD

UNIVERSITY PRESS

Great Clarendon Street, Oxford OX2 6DP, UK

Oxford University Press is a department of the University of Oxford.
It furthers the University's objective of excellence in research, scholarship,
and education by publishing worldwide in

Oxford New York

Athens Auckland Bangkok Bagotá Buenos Aires
Cape Town Chennai Dar es Salaam Delhi Florence Hong Kong Istanbul
Karachi Kuala Lumpur Madrid Melbourne Mexico City Mumbai
Nairobi Paris São Paulo Shanghai Singapore Taipei Tokyo Toronto Warsaw

and associated companies in
Berlin Ibadan

Oxford is a registered trade mark of Oxford University Press
in the UK and in certain other countries

Published in the United States
by Oxford University Press Inc., New York

Database right Oxford University Press (maker)

First Published 2015

A catalogue for this book is available from the British Library

Library of Congress Cataloging in Publication Data

ISBN 978-0-19-874895-3

Typeset by Techset Composition Ltd, Salisbury, UK
Printed in Great Britain by Bell & Bain Ltd, Glasgow, UK

Acknowledgements

We wish to thank a number of people for their help in putting together this election volume. We are extremely grateful to all contributors for constructing, under draconian deadlines, detailed and thoughtful analyses of the election. They not only met deadlines but also adhered to the style guide, surely an unprecedented combination in academia. Most also managed to participate in the *Britain Votes 2015* conference in late May 2015, one of the first academic assessments of what took place at the election. That gathering included a number of practitioners whose contributions, candid and informative, further aided the insights in this volume. We particularly thank Labour's Vice Chair of the election campaign, Lucy Powell and parliamentary candidates Steve Woolfe MEP (UKIP) and Paula Keaveney (Liberal Democrats). On behalf of all contributors, we thank all party officials interviewed, on and off the record, for this volume. We also thank Chris Burgess of the People's History Museum, Manchester, for being our local host and are grateful to the Centre for British Politics at the University of Nottingham and the Departments of Politics at the universities of Liverpool and Sheffield respectively, along with the ESRC, for their co-sponsorship, alongside the main sponsor, the Hansard Society.

Dr Ruth Fox, Director and Head of Research at the Hansard Society, has been enormously helpful, not only in organising the *Britain Votes 2015* conference, but also in advising on this volume's contents and on the direction of *Parliamentary Affairs* more broadly, as the Hansard Society's journal. Luke Boga Mitchell, Communications and Digital Manager of the Society, also assisted greatly in setting up the *Britain Votes 2015* blog. Vanessa Lacey, Senior Publisher at Oxford University Press, has been very supportive on the publishing side. The same very much applies to Laura Buchan in terms of production, working on a hectic schedule taken over enthusiastically by Pete Rogers. Kelly Henwood has been very helpful in marketing.

We are also grateful to Arif Ansari and Michelle Mayman, at BBC North West, for organising a first-class conference two months prior to the election which helped crystallise some thoughts in advance of the contest – not least that Labour faced a very difficult task. Those ideas were greatly assisted by the considerable input from the Head of Politics at the University of Liverpool, Dr Stuart Wilks-Heeg.

Finally we wish to thank especially our families for their forbearance regarding the considerable amount of quality time forsaken in producing this volume.

Andrew Geddes and Jonathan Tonge
June 2015

Contributors

Tim Bale is Professor of Politics at Queen Mary University of London. He has published widely on political parties in the UK, Europe and further afield. Recent books include *The Conservatives since 1945: The Drivers of Party Change* (Oxford University Press, 2012) and *Five Year Mission: The Labour Party under Ed Miliband* (Oxford University Press, 2015). A new edition of his book *The Conservative Party from Thatcher to Cameron* will be published by Polity in 2016.

Jonathan Bradbury is Professor of Politics in the Department of Political and Cultural Studies at Swansea University. He researches and publishes on territorial politics and constitutional development, party approaches to governing the UK, and multi-level government and public policy. He is Convenor of the PSA Specialist Group on Territorial Politics and his most recent articles have been published in *Parliamentary Affairs* and *Regional and Federal Studies*.

Dr Rosie Campbell is a Reader in Politics at Birkbeck University of London. She has recently written on what voters want from their parliamentary candidates, attitudes to MPs' roles, the politics of diversity and gender and voting behaviour. She is the Principal Investigator of the ESRC funded Representative Audit of Britain, which surveyed all candidates standing in the 2015 British General Election, and co-investigator of a Leverhulme funded study of parliamentary candidates and MPs from 1945–2015 www.parliamentarycandidates.org.

Sarah Childs is Professor of Politics and Gender at the University of Bristol. She has published widely on women's political representation, with key pieces in *Political Studies, Politics and Gender, Government and Opposition, and Party Politics*. In 2015 she published two edited books *Gender, Conservatism and Representation*, and *Deeds and Words* with Karen Celis and Rosie Campbell respectively, both ECPR Press. Her most recent monograph is *Sex, Gender and the Conservative Party: From Iron Lady to Kitten Heels*, with Paul Webb, (Palgrave, 2012).

John Curtice is Professor of Politics at the University of Strathclyde. President of the British Polling Council, Professor Curtice has been running the exit poll for the last six General Elections. Amongst numerous publications, he has been co-author of several *British Social Attitudes* books and recently co-edited (with Marina Costa Lobo) *Personality Politics: The Role of Leader Evaluations in Democratic Elections* (Oxford University Press, 2014) whilst recent journal articles have included studies of the Alternative Vote and Scottish Independence referendums.

Dr David Cutts is Reader in Political Science at the University of Bath. He has published on a range of topics, including geographical and contextual effects in voting and attitudes, party campaigning, voter turnout, political engagement and electoral choice. He has also published widely on the Liberal Democrats.

David Denver is Emeritus Professor of Politics at Lancaster University. His most recent book (with Mark Garnett) is *British General Elections since 1964* (Oxford University Press, 2014) and he has analysed General Election results for each volume in this series since 1997.

James Dennison is a PhD Researcher at the European University Institute, Florence. He is also currently a Junior Visiting Scholar at Nuffield College, Oxford, and from 2015-2016 will be teaching at the University of Sheffield. His research interests include political participation, British and European politics and longitudinal methods. He is currently the Research Assistant on a British Academy funded project related to the 2015 General Election and the rise of UKIP.

Jocelyn Evans is Professor of Politics at the University of Leeds. He works on European voting behaviour and political parties, and is author of numerous articles on voting in France and Northern Ireland, as well as comparative work. He is the co-author of *The 2012 French Presidential Election: the Inevitable Alternation* (Palgrave, 2014).

Steven Fielding is Professor of Political History at the University of Nottingham. His latest book is *A State of Play: British Politics on Screen, Stage and Page, from Anthony Trollope to The Thick of It* (Bloomsbury, 2014).

Justin Fisher is Professor of Political Science and Head of the Department of Politics, History & the Brunel Law School at Brunel University London. He is Principal Investigator of the ESRC funded project examining constituency campaigning at the 2015 General Election.

Matthew Flinders is Professor of Politics and Director of the Sir Bernard Crick Centre for the Public Understanding of Politics at the University of Sheffield. He is Chair of the Political Studies Association of the UK.

Andrew Gamble is Professor of Politics at the University of Sheffield, having become Emeritus Professor of Politics at the University of Cambridge in 2014. Recent books include *Crisis without End? The Unravelling of Western Prosperity* (Palgrave Macmillan, 2014) and *The Spectre at the Feast: Capitalist Crisis and the Politics of Recession* (Palgrave Macmillan, 2009). Numerous recent articles on the financial crash and austerity include 'British Politics and the Financial Crisis', *British Politics* 4, 450–62 and 'Austerity as Statecraft', *Parliamentary Affairs*, 2015, 68.1, 42–57.

Andrew Geddes is a Professor of Politics at the University of Sheffield. He has published extensively on European and EU immigration politics and policy and on British relations with the EU, including (with Christina Boswell) *Migration and Mobility in the EU* (Palgrave Macmillan, 2010) and *Britain and the EU* (Palgrave Macmillan, 2011). For the period 2014–19 he has been awarded a European Research Council Advanced Grant for a five-year project entitled Prospects for International Migration Governance that analyses the drivers of global migration governance in Europe, North America, South America and Asia Pacific.

Matthew Goodwin is Professor of Political Science at the School of Politics and International Relations, at the University of Kent. He is also an Associate Fellow of the think-tank, Chatham House. He is most recently the co-author of *Revolt on the Right: Explaining Support for the Radical Right in Britain* (Routledge, 2014), and also of the forthcoming book with Oxford University Press, *UKIP: Inside the Campaign to Redraw British Politics*.

James Mitchell is Professor of Politics at the University of Edinburgh and Co-Director of Edinburgh University's Academy of Government and author of *The Scottish Question* (Oxford University Press, 2014). He is co-author of books and articles on Scottish elections in 2007 and 2011 and co-author of *The Scottish National Party; Transition to Power* (Oxford University Press, 2011).

Andrew Russell is Professor of Politics and Head of Department at the University of Manchester. He has written extensively on British parties and elections and has published several pieces on the Liberal Democrats including the 2005 book, *Neither Left Nor Right?* (Manchester University Press, with Ed Fieldhouse). He also is known for his research into the electoral engagement of hard-to-reach groups, especially young people. His media appearances during 2015 included a weekly summation of the campaign for BBC *Radio 5 live* which aired at the prime 3am Monday morning slot.

Jonathan Tonge is Professor of Politics at the University of Liverpool. He has published fifteen books and over fifty articles and chapters on British and Irish politics. Formerly Chair of the Political Studies Association of the UK and of the Youth Citizenship Commission, Professor Tonge was Director of the ESRC's 2010 and 2015 Northern Ireland General Election surveys. Recent books include *The Democratic Unionist Party; From Protest to Power* (Oxford University Press,

2014, with Braniff, McAuley, Hennessey and Whiting) and *Comparative Peace Processes* (Polity, 2014). He is co-editor of *Parliamentary Affairs*.

Dr Stephen Ward is a Reader in Politics at the University of Salford. He was previously a Research Fellow at the Oxford Internet Institute and has led a number of ESRC internet research projects. His research interests include: political participation, campaigns and elections online along with parties use of digital technologies. He has published widely in these areas in journals such as *Party Politics*, the *Australian Journal of Political Science*, the *Journal of Information Technology and Politics* and *New Media and Society*.

Paul Webb is Professor of Politics at the University of Sussex and co-editor of the journal *Party Politics*. He is author of numerous publications on party and electoral politics in the UK and abroad, and is currently working on a new survey of party members in Britain with Tim Bale.

Dominic Wring is Professor of Political Communication at Loughborough University. He is lead editor of *Political Communication in Britain: the Leader Debates, the Campaign and the Media in the 2010 General Election* and author of *The Politics of Marketing the Labour Party* (both Palgrave Macmillan).

CONTENTS

List of tables and figures

Figures

Tables

ANDREW GEDDES AND JONATHAN TONGE*

Introduction: Single Party Government in a Fragmented System

The 2015 General Election was, electors were told throughout the campaign, too close to call. The opinion polls all pointed to a contest that had the Conservatives and Labour almost inseparable. The BBC's eve of election poll of polls captured the uncertainty with the Conservatives on 34%, Labour on 33%, United Kingdom Independence Party (UKIP) on 12%, the Liberal Democrats on 8% and the Scottish National Party (SNP) expected to do very well in Scotland, winning almost all the Scottish seats. One thing was apparently clear: no party would get the 326 seats needed for a majority in the House of Commons. A hung Parliament would, as in 2010, be the outcome with party leaders and their emissaries then meeting in secret to work out the terms of a coalition deal or some other way of sustaining a government. The wider point was that Britain's socially and geographically fragmented political system seemed no longer capable of producing single party majority government. A telling image that captured this fragmentation had been provided in the supposed showpiece event of the campaign, the televised leaders' debate that saw seven party leaders from England, Scotland and Wales go head-to-head as a powerful representation of this new era of multi-party politics.

The opinion polls had powerful effects on the campaign and on some of the key assumptions informing election debate. David Cameron for the Conservatives and Ed Miliband for Labour claimed that their aim was single party majority government, but their manifestos were often reported as though they were mere bargaining chips as much as they were statements of governing intent. The real issue, or so it was reported, was trying to figure out the 'red lines', the issues on which the parties would not budge in any future negotiation. Perhaps then it did not really matter

*Andrew Geddes, Department of Politics, University of Sheffield, a.geddes@sheffield.ac.uk; Jonathan Tonge, Department of Politics, University of Liverpool, j.tonge@liv.ac.uk.

doi:10.1093/pa/gsv023

that the Conservatives were claiming that they would cut the welfare budget by £12 billion while finding another £8 billion to fund the NHS? These kinds of claims might not actually come to pass once a coalition deal or some kind of support agreement had been sorted out. Although expected to do very badly, Nick Clegg's Liberal Democrats were swift to position themselves once again as potential coalition partners for either of the two main UK parties, with Clegg, confident an incumbency effect would preserve many of his MPs, even offering to provide a heart for the Conservatives and a brain for Labour.

Meanwhile in Scotland, another key indicator of the fragmentation of the UK political system was that the SNP, emboldened and greatly strengthened by the closeness of the 2014 independence referendum, expected to make massive gains and potentially hold the balance of power in Westminster. The SNP leader, Nicola Sturgeon, claimed that her party could put Ed Miliband into government on an anti-austerity ticket and exclude the Conservatives. Horrified by this prospect, the *Daily Mail* asked if Sturgeon was the most dangerous woman in Britain.

The narrative created by opinion polls reinforced the idea that what mattered was the distribution of seats in a hung Parliament and the deal that would then be hammered out on the composition of the next government. At times, it appeared that fascination as to who might be shading a neck-and-neck race (in the separate Scottish contest the size of the walkover was more important) was threatening to overshadow policy debates. Yet potentially this was one of the most important elections of all. It was one which might ultimately contribute to the recasting of Britain's future in the European Union, whilst the future of the United—or disunited— Kingdom was also at stake.

Though only a singular sample of voters, the exit poll caused a bonfire of much of the previous 'informed' commentary. 'Very carefully calculated, not necessarily on the nail', as the BBC's election night presenter, David Dimbleby, put it, the exit poll had the Conservatives as the largest party (not a major surprise) but only just short of the seats needed to form a majority government (a very major surprise to many).

'Quite remarkable this exit poll' were Dimbleby's words, as he reported the finding of interviews at polling stations with more than 20,000 actual voters that the Conservatives would have 316 seats, Labour 239, the SNP 58, the Liberal Democrats 10 and UKIP 2. Former Liberal Democrat party leader, Lord Ashdown, responded by saying that he would eat his hat if the exit poll turned out to be anywhere near an accurate projection of Liberal Democrat performance. It understated the catastrophe engulfing Ashdown's party, reduced from 57 to eight seats, the lowest figure since 1970. The exit poll understated Conservative gains, as they secured 336 seats while Labour languished on a final tally of 232. UKIP held on to Douglas Carswell's Clacton seat, but lost the Rochester and Strood seat won by another Conservative defector, Mark Reckless, at a November 2014 by-election. Party leader Nigel Farage failed in his eighth attempt to secure a seat in the House of

Commons, this time in Thanet South. UKIP's paltry one seat represented a very poor return given the party's impressive 3.9 million votes, a 12.6% share. The most dramatic events occurred in Scotland, where the SNP almost swept the board, winning 56 of 59 seats, up from a mere six at the 2010 General Election. In sharp contrast to UKIP's fortunes, it took only 25,000 votes to elect an SNP MP. By the morning of May 8 both Ed Miliband and Nick Clegg, rather than working out the terms of a coalition deal, had resigned as party leaders. Nigel Farage resigned, as he said he would if he lost in Thanet South, but then swiftly un-resigned.

The election result confounded the expectations of almost all pollsters and most pundits. The dominant narrative was created by opinion polls that pointed to a hung Parliament, which in turn reflected the effects of a socially and geographically fragmented political system. The underlying diagnosis is correct. Socially, the ties that bind people to the main UK parties—the two party, Conservative versus Labour, system of years gone by—are becoming ever weaker. Even the distorting effects of Britain's non-proportional voting system were seen as insufficient to deliver single party majority government. Geographically, the four nations of the UK experience very different election contests with differing constellations of parties. Even within England, there are big differences between the south and north with the Conservatives becoming a party of southern England and Labour retreating into its northern heartlands.

Given such trends, how could one party ever hope to govern alone again? This begs the obvious question of how in 2015 this fragmented political system actually delivered single party majority government with the Conservatives governing alone for the first time since 1992? Analyses of the 2010 result suggested that fragmentation could mean that hung Parliaments with minority or coalition governments would be the standard future outcome.

Perhaps this affirms the wisdom of Danish Nobel prize-winning physicist Nils Bohr when he remarked that prediction is very difficult, especially about the future. Yet, if anything, developments after 2010 seemed to confirm rather than challenge the effects of this underlying diagnosis about the impacts of social and geographical fragmentation on future hung Parliaments. The rise of UKIP, which more than quadrupled its vote between 2010 and 2015, was a threat to Conservative and Labour support in England. Labour was also outflanked in Scotland on the anti-austerity left by the SNP. The Conservatives were seen as socially privileged bastions of the southern English shires. Indeed, initial criticism of Cameron's 2015 campaign performance was that he was simply too posh to roll up his sleeves and make the case for conservatism and the Conservatives. Perhaps stung by this criticism, roll up his sleeves is literally what he did.

The underlying assumption was that fragmentation worked in one direction, which was away from single party majority government. The 2015 General Election demonstrated otherwise. Fragmentation combined with the effects of a non-proportional electoral system delivered single party majority government. The Conservatives received 37% of the total vote but profited from Labour's failure to make major inroads in England and its wipe-out in Scotland. Labour saw its share of the vote increase marginally in England, but not by anywhere near enough to win enough key seats or to offset its Scottish losses. The oft-cited joke used to be that there were more pandas in Edinburgh zoo than there were Conservative MPs in Scotland. The 2015 General Election result meant that the same applied to Labour in Scotland too as only one MP clung on to his Westminster seat in the face of what London Mayor and new MP for Uxbridge, Boris Johnson, referred to as 'Ajockalypse Now'. Misery was heaped upon misery for the Liberal Democrats as they lost all but one of their Scottish seats, including those of ex-leader Charles Kennedy and ex-Chief Secretary to the Treasury, Danny Alexander.

While for many the return of single party government was a shock, the Conservative majority was only 12. The last time the Conservatives had won an election was when John Major secured 42.2% of the vote and a 21-seat majority in 1992. This was soon whittled down by by-election defeats while Major's Government suffered the corrosive effects of ratification of the Maastricht Treaty as the European issue ate away at the party and contributed to its landslide defeat at the 1997 General Election. It is easy to deploy this historical analogy and predict toil and trouble ahead for David Cameron as this Parliament too, or at least its beginning, is likely to be dominated by a referendum on Britain's EU membership. Yet the context is now very different; not least because Labour is considerably weaker than it was in 1992 with the decimation of its support in what were once its Scottish heartlands and a mountain to climb in England if it too were to aspire to form a single party government.

This collection explores the consequences for British electoral politics and the British political system of social and geographical fragmentation. The results and their implications are explored and assessed as too are the strategies of the main parties as well as the representativeness of the British political system and how the campaign was mediated. The importance of the economy to political fortunes is dissected, whilst there is wider consideration of the extent of engagement of electors, in an election in which there was only a very modest rise in turnout. Modern election analysis requires explorations of the distinctive campaigns and outcomes in different parts of the Kingdom and we duly devote significant space to Scotland (in particular) along with Wales and Northern Ireland. We also explore a series of key issues that were central to the campaign and will be fundamentally important components of debate in the years to come, such as the economy, immigration and British relations with the EU. We show how the 2015 General Election delivered a surprising result, but what it also delivered was single party government which has been the standard mode of government in Britain for the most of the last century. A surprising outcome was, in another sense, a very familiar one.

DAVID DENVER*

The Results: How Britain Voted

For many months before it happened, the overwhelming majority of media commentators and academic specialists were united in suggesting that the General Election in May 2015 was the most unpredictable in living memory. The reason for this
was the extraordinary evolution of party popularity after the 2010 election. The
days have long gone when inter-election cycles followed a fairly simple and familiar
pattern—the government would become unpopular and opposition parties more
popular until about the middle of the term and then the governing party would
gradually recover, while the others faded. Even by recent standards, however, the
course of opinion between 2010 and 2015 was remarkable.

1. The inter-election cycle of party support

Trends in General Election voting intentions over the period are shown in
Figure 1.1. As usual, the new government's honeymoon with the electorate was
short-lived. Despite falling behind Labour by the end of 2010, however,
Conservative support remained relatively buoyant until April 2012. The significant
slump in that month followed an ill-judged and poorly received Budget delivered by
the Chancellor, George Osborne, which was characterised by Ed Miliband as an
'omnishambles'. This was later named 'word of the year' by the *Oxford English Dic-
tionary* and began to be applied to various aspects of the government's performance. The electorate appeared to agree with Miliband. After the Budget,
according to Ipsos MORI, Osborne had the poorest satisfaction ratings (−30) of
any Chancellor since Kenneth Clarke in 1994. The effects were felt in the local elections in May, when the Conservatives lost over 400 seats and fell to 33% of the 'national equivalent' vote share, well behind Labour on 39%.

From April 2012 through to March 2015 support for the Conservatives varied
within very narrow limits. On these data, the party's share of voting intentions
fell (just) below 30% only once and never exceeded 33.6%. The reasons underlying

*David Denver, Lancaster University, d.denver@lancs.ac.uk

doi:10.1093/pa/gsv024

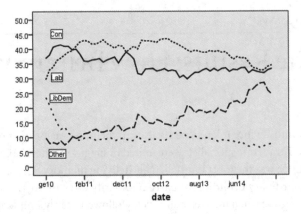

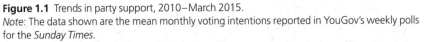

Figure 1.1 Trends in party support, 2010–March 2015.
Note: The data shown are the mean monthly voting intentions reported in YouGov's weekly polls for the *Sunday Times*.

the party's failure to move any higher in the public's estimation—even when there were clear signs of economic recovery and the next election approached—are explored elsewhere in this book but it is worth mentioning here that 'modernisers' at the top of the party appeared to go out of their way to alienate their own core supporters. Heavy cuts in expenditure on defence and the police combined with significantly increased spending on overseas aid were hardly likely to rally the Tory troops. The same applies to the withdrawal of child benefit from families paying the higher rate of income tax and the legalisation of same-sex marriage. These sorts of policies were intended, no doubt, to 'decontaminate' the Conservative brand and broaden the party's appeal. Upsetting core supporters is risky at the best of times, however. When there is a viable alternative party for the disaffected to turn to—and no evidence of new supporters being attracted—then the strategy looks distinctly unwise. In February 2013, just three weeks after the Commons vote on same-sex marriage, the Conservatives came third behind the Liberal Democrats and the UK Independence Party (UKIP) in a parliamentary by-election at Eastleigh, a seat which they initially had hopes of gaining. Nigel Farage, UKIP leader, subsequently highlighted the 'disconnect' between traditional Conservative supporters and their party in typically colourful terms: 'Tory voters are historically used to a party of free enterprise and wealth creation, but all it wants to talk about is gay marriage, wind turbines and metropolitan Notting Hill claptrap'.[1]

It is perhaps surprising that the 'omnishambolic' Conservatives were not even further behind Labour in the polls for most of the Parliament. The latter spent the first few months of opposition electing a new leader and Ed Miliband defeated

[1] *Daily Telegraph*, 16 March 2013.

the favourite—his elder brother David—to take the position, largely on the basis of the votes of affiliated trade unions. The younger Miliband struggled to make a positive impact with the electorate but for a time Labour was doing reasonably well in the popularity stakes. The party had a comfortable lead in the opinion polls, took the seat of Corby from the Conservatives in a by-election (November 2012) and made sweeping gains in the 2012 and 2013 local elections. On the other hand, Labour suffered a bad defeat in the 2011 Scottish Parliament election, falling from 46 to 37 seats and leaving the Scottish National Party (SNP) with an overall majority.

Labour support peaked in the latter half of 2012 but then drifted gradually downwards throughout 2013 and 2014 to a point where the two major parties were neck and neck as they entered the election year. It seems likely that this trend is explained by the increasingly negative view of Miliband held by the electorate. Whereas during 2011 his personal ratings according to YouGov (% satisfied with his performance minus % dissatisfied) had averaged −22.3, this fell to −29.8 in 2012, −30.7 in 2013 and −41.8 in 2014. In the latter year Labour's performance in the local elections was very modest and Miliband's reputation was not enhanced by a much-criticised speech at the party conference in which he failed to mention the deficit in public finances or immigration—two of the biggest issues worrying the electorate.

The big losers in this inter-election period, however, were the Liberal Democrats. As Figure 1.1 shows, their support plummeted as soon as they joined the Coalition—reflecting, no doubt, the disappointment of those who had voted for them as an anti-Conservative Party. Particularly damaging was the party leadership's agreement to the tripling of university tuition fees—breaking a clear campaign promise to oppose any move in that direction. From December 2010, the Liberal Democrats only occasionally exceeded 10% of voting intentions—less than half of their support in the 2010 election. In the last six months of 2014 they averaged only 7.2% and in December fell to fifth place behind both UKIP and the Green Party. The party leader, Nick Clegg, bore the brunt of the electorate's displeasure. Having risen dramatically in public estimation during the 2010 election campaign, his reputation then fell like a stone. Starting with a positive satisfaction rating of +40 in May 2010 he was in negative territory by the end of the year, averaged −42.8 during 2011 and thereafter never had an annual average score better than −50. For comparison, David Cameron's worst annual average was −19.5 in 2013.

The poor showing of Clegg and his party in the opinion polls was borne out in mid-term elections. The 2011 Scottish Parliament election was a disaster with only five seats won (compared with 16 in 2007). Local election results went from bad to worse. The party's national equivalent vote shares fell from 16 to 11% between 2011 and 2014, and more than 1700 council seats—over two-fifths of the number held in 2010—were lost. In parliamentary by-elections—in which they used to be the party to watch—the Liberal Democrats lost their deposit in 11 of the 19 contested.

Indeed, in Rotherham in November 2012, the party contrived to come eighth behind an assortment of other candidates while in Rochester and Strood in November 2014 their candidate failed to reach 1% of votes. In the European Parliament elections in May 2014 the Liberal Democrats won less than 7% of votes and lost 10 of their 11 seats. To add insult to injury, the pet project of the Liberal Democrats—to reform the electoral system used for Westminster elections—was dealt a severe blow when a proposal to adopt the Alternative Vote (AV) system was comprehensively rejected in a national referendum in May 2011 by 68–32%.

If the Liberal Democrats were the clear losers after the 2010 General Election, then the unmistakeable winners were the 'others'. By December 2010, the assorted other parties had overtaken the Liberal Democrats in the polls and the lead stretched as they maintained an unparalleled level of support.

Despite its success in the Scottish election, the SNP generally lagged behind Labour in voting intentions for Westminster until the aftermath of the independence referendum in September 2014. Independence was clearly rejected by the electorate, but there was then a surge in support (and in membership) for the SNP which led to talk of it all but sweeping the board in Scotland come the General Election—and thereby seriously damaging Labour's chances. In Wales, however, Plaid Cymru made little progress. The Green Party mustered only 1% of votes in the 2010 election (although it did win a seat) and for most of the inter-election period performed unimpressively, hovering around 2% in opinion polls and making no headway in by-elections or local elections. Things changed around the time of the 2014 European Parliament elections. In that contest, the Greens won almost 8% of the vote and increased their representation from two to three seats. Thereafter, their support in the polls remained steady at 7% by December, but during the first three months of 2015 it eased back to stand at 5% in March.

The main driver of variations in support for 'others', however, was UKIP. The party won 3.2% of the Great Britain vote in 2010 but afterwards, at first, appeared to make little progress. In a clutch of by-elections in November 2012, however, there were encouraging results. Increases in vote shares were generally larger than before, the Liberal Democrats were pushed into fourth place in two contests—Corby and Croydon North—while in another two (Middlesbrough and Rotherham) UKIP came second. The attendant publicity for the party helped to increase their poll ratings in late November and December. Another sharp improvement came in March 2013 following the Eastleigh by-election where an impressive second place ensured yet more valuable publicity for the party and Mr Farage.

Even better was to come, however. In the county council elections in England and Wales in May 2013, UKIP won almost 150 council seats and had a national equivalent vote share of 22%—an unheard of achievement for a 'fourth' party. Subsequently, UKIP rose to more than 17% of General Election voting intentions in June. A year later, the party came out top in the European Parliament election, winning 27.5% of votes and 24 seats. This was the first time in more than a century that a nationwide election did not result in either the Conservatives or Labour coming first in terms of popular support. There was a further sting in UKIP's tail, however. Late in 2014, two Conservative MPs resigned from the House of Commons, fought by-elections on behalf of UKIP and were comfortably re-elected. By January 2015, the party stood at 16.5% of voting intentions but then declined a little to end at 14.0% in March. Although both UKIP and the Greens had fallen back from their peak by the time that the election campaign was getting under way, there was certainly no sign of their support evaporating rapidly as had been the experience of minor parties in the past.

The unpredictability of the General Election outcome arose, then, not just from the fact that the two major parties were almost equal in (un)popularity by the first months of 2015. In addition, there was uncertainty surrounding the impact of a decline in Liberal Democrat support, as well as the prospects for the SNP, Greens and UKIP and how the performances of the latter would affect the votes of the big two.

2. Trends in party support during the 'short' campaign

Although parties nowadays engage in more or less continuous campaigning, there is clearly an increase in activity when an election is in the offing. Everything reaches a climax in the final few weeks of the 'short' campaign (which on this occasion was rather less 'short' than usual) since there always remains much to play for. In 2010, almost 40% of voters said that they made up their minds about which party to support during the campaign and the televised debates between the party leaders clearly had a dramatic impact on public opinion. In 2015, however, the parties and broadcasters found it difficult to agree on the timing and format of leaders' debates. In the end, there was only one debate in which both David Cameron and Nick Clegg participated (on April 2) and this was something of a farce since it involved the leaders of no fewer than seven parties.

Figure 1.2 charts the trend in voting intentions for the four leading parties from March 30 (the date of the dissolution of Parliament) on the basis of the (almost) daily polls undertaken by YouGov. As can be seen, apart from a slight improvement for the Liberal Democrats, little changed during a campaign which was variously described by commentators as 'turgid', 'antiseptic', 'sham', 'bloodless' and even 'sysiphean'.[2] On these data, after the first week, the Conservative share of voting intentions was always between 33 and 35% while Labour fell outside that range just once. Throughout, UKIP held steady at between 12 and 14% while, although

---

[2] Like Sisyphus in Greek mythology, the parties laboured mightily (during the campaign) only to end up where they started (according to the polls).

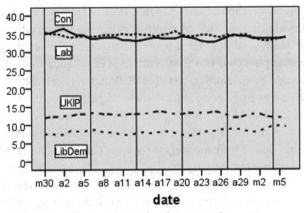

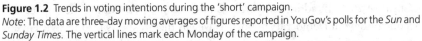

Figure 1.2 Trends in voting intentions during the 'short' campaign.
Note: The data are three-day moving averages of figures reported in YouGov's polls for the *Sun* and *Sunday Times*. The vertical lines mark each Monday of the campaign.

not shown in the figure, the percentage intending to vote Green also hardly changed, hovering around 5%. In Scotland, meanwhile, campaign polls continued to suggest that there would be a massive swing from Labour to the SNP.

The final predictions produced by the polling companies did nothing to dispel the widespread expectation that, in terms of votes at least, the election was too close to call. Five of them predicted a dead heat between the Conservatives and Labour; four gave the Conservatives a one point lead; two put Labour in a narrow lead. In the event, it did not turn out that way.

3. The national result

The shares of votes and the number of seats won by the major parties in 2015 (in Great Britain) and changes from 2010 are shown in Table 1.1. The electorate confounded the pollsters and pundits by giving the Conservatives a significant lead over Labour in the popular vote and, as a result, they emerged to general surprise with an overall majority in the House of Commons. Less unexpectedly, the Liberal Democrats slumped dramatically in popular appeal and were left with just eight seats. They were replaced as third party among the electorate by UKIP which advanced by almost ten points but won just one seat—a poor return for almost four million votes—while taking second place in 120 constituencies. The Green Party also improved its vote share, if less dramatically, but there were no additions to the single seat already held. In Scotland the SNP took 50% of the votes which yielded 56 of the 59 seats. Labour, having won 41 Scottish constituencies in 2010, was reduced to just one. This was an unparalleled thrashing for Labour in an election in Scotland.

Table 1.1 Share of votes and number of seats won (Great Britain) and changes from 2010

	Share of votes (%)	Change 2010–2015	Number of seats	Change 2010–2015
Conservative	37.7	+0.8	330	+24
Labour	31.2	+1.5	232	−26
Liberal Democrat	8.1	−15.5	8	−49
UKIP	12.9	+9.7	1	+1
Green	3.8	+2.8	1	0
SNP/Plaid Cymru	5.5	+3.2	59	+50
Other	0.9	−0.6	1	0

Note: The Speaker, who was not opposed by the Conservatives, Labour or Liberal Democrats, is treated as an 'other'.

3.1 Regional and constituency variations in changes in party support

Table 1.2 shows changes in party shares of votes across English regions and in Scotland and Wales. Outside Scotland, Labour increased its support everywhere, doing best in London (+7.1) and least well in Wales (+0.7). The Conservatives declined a little in the North West and Yorkshire/Humberside but managed to improve elsewhere. The Liberal Democrats, in contrast, experienced very steep falls across the country while UKIP achieved what would in normal political times be seen as spectacular improvements, even in London, the party's weakest 'region' in England. The election result in Scotland was clearly exceptional. In the face of the SNP onslaught, all three of the other major parties dropped back while the slightly increased share obtained by UKIP is largely explained by the fact that the number of candidates put forward by the party rose from 28 to 41.

Much greater variation in both the direction and extent of changes in party support would be expected at constituency level, since General Elections are more than simply national contests between party leaders (notwithstanding the impression conveyed by media reporting of the campaign). Local personalities, issues, events and traditions as well as constituency campaigning at the grass roots all have a part to play. There is, of course, an impressive level of continuity in the distribution of votes across constituencies. This is verified by the correlation coefficients measuring the strength of the association between the parties' shares of votes in 2010 and 2015. Excluding Scotland, these are 0.97 for the Conservatives, 0.96 for Labour and 0.89 for the Liberal Democrats ($N = 572$ in all cases). Support for UKIP and the Greens was rather less predictable on the basis of their performance in 2010, the relevant coefficients being 0.58 ($N = 529$) and 0.76 ($N = 306$), respectively.

Despite these strong relationships there remains considerable variation in the extent of change and, in some constituencies, its direction. Outside Scotland, Conservative support declined in 203 constituencies and rose in 369. Despite generally

Table 1.2 Changes in party shares of votes in regions

	Con	Lab	Lib Dem	UKIP	SNP/PC
North East	+1.6	+3.3	−17.1	+14.0	−
North West	−0.5	+5.3	−15.1	+10.5	−
Yorkshire/Humber	−0.2	+4.7	−15.8	+13.2	−
East Midlands	+2.3	+1.8	−15.2	+12.5	−
West Midlands	+2.3	+2.3	−15.0	+11.7	−
Eastern	+1.9	+2.4	−15.8	+11.9	−
London	+0.4	+7.1	−14.4	+6.4	−
South East	+1.5	+2.1	−16.8	+10.6	−
South West	+3.7	+2.3	−19.6	+9.1	−
Wales	+1.1	+0.7	−13.6	+11.2	+0.8
Scotland	−1.8	−17.7	−11.4	+0.9	+30.1

making progress, Labour's vote share fell in 101 English and 23 Welsh seats. There was no constituency where the Liberal Democrats managed an improvement, however, and none where UKIP declined. Nonetheless, even when changes were in the expected direction their magnitude varied hugely. Liberal Democrat decreases, for example, ranged from fewer than five percentage points in two cases (Cambridge and Bradford East) to more than 30 in three (Brent Central, Sheffield Central and Hereford and Herefordshire South). UKIP meanwhile rose by 20 points or more in 13 constituencies but by fewer than two points in four.

Although specifically local factors explain many constituency variations and thus make it difficult to generalise, it is worth looking for systematic patterns. A first step is to consider how changes in support for the various parties were inter-related and Table 1.3 reports the relevant correlation coefficients (again excluding Scotland). Negative coefficients indicate that where one of the parties concerned did better, the other had poorer results and *vice versa*. It can be seen that both the Conservatives and Labour benefited from the decline in Liberal Democrat support—the more the latter fell in a constituency, the better the major parties did. It was thought by many before the election that an advance by UKIP would be bound to hurt the Conservatives more than Labour. In fact, the figures suggest that although better UKIP performances were indeed associated with worse results for the Tories, the effect was actually stronger when changes in the UKIP and Labour vote shares are analysed. Changes in support for the Greens were not significantly related to Conservative performance and tended to mirror the pattern for Labour. It is striking, however, that the coefficient measuring the relationship between changes in vote shares for the Greens and the Liberal Democrats is the most strongly negative of all in the table. The collapse in Liberal Democrat support clearly helped the Green Party to its best ever General Election result.

It might reasonably be expected that the nature of party competition in different constituencies would affect changes in party support—as a consequence of tactical voting, for example. Table 1.4, which is restricted to England (due to the

Table 1.3 Correlations between changes in vote shares (England and Wales)

	Change % Con	Change % Lab	Change % Lib Dem	Change % UKIP
Change % Lab	−0.16	–	–	–
Change % Lib Dem	−0.38	−0.39	–	–
Change % UKIP	−0.30	−0.36	0.13	–
Change % Green	0.02	0.26	−0.53	−0.23

Note: The *N* for coefficients involving Conservatives Labour Liberal Democrats only is 572; for these parties and UKIP 529; for these and the Green Party it is 306 and for UKIP and Greens 280. All coefficients are statistically significant except that for the Conservatives and Green Party.

Table 1.4 Changes in overall vote shares in different electoral contexts (England only)

| | Top two parties in 2010 | | | | | |
	Con—Lab	Con—LDem	Lab—Con	Lab—LDem	LDem—Con	LDem—Lab
Con	+2.5	+2.8	−1.3	+0.4	+2.0	−2.9
Lab	+0.7	+3.0	+4.1	+8.3	+4.3	+12.5
Lib Dem	−13.7	−18.4	−13.2	−19.6	−16.7	−18.4
UKIP	+11.3	+10.2	+12.5	+9.5	+7.7	+7.0
Green	+2.1	+3.6	+2.5	+5.0	+3.5	+5.3
(N)	(129)	(166)	(127)	(63)	(33)	(10)

complexities of the party systems in Scotland and Wales), presents data enabling us to check this suggestion. The Liberal Democrats clearly lost most where they had more votes to lose—in constituencies where they had been in first or second place in 2010. Conversely, Labour did best where they were in competition with the Liberal Democrats while the Conservatives had above average increases in vote share where the Liberal Democrats were their main opponents. The Green Party improved most in Labour v Liberal Democrat seats. Presumably these constituencies would contain relatively large numbers of leftish-inclined voters who would be attracted to the Greens. For the same reason, UKIP had relatively poor results in these seats. The latter's advance in constituencies held by the Liberal Democrats from the Conservatives was below average, and this might suggest an element of tactical voting by potential UKIP voters.

As already noted, the election result in Scotland was spectacularly different from the outcome in the rest of Britain and the Scottish story is explored by James Mitchell in a later chapter. It is appropriate, nonetheless, to make a few comments here. First, despite the electoral upheaval, support for the 'British' parties was distributed across constituencies in much the same way that it had been in 2010. Correlating constituency shares in Scotland in 2010 and 2015 yields coefficients of 0.93 for the Conservatives, 0.90 for Labour and 0.86 for the Liberal Democrats ($N = 59$ in all cases). Strikingly, however, the figure for the SNP is only 0.57. So, although the geographical distribution of SNP support in this election was broadly similar to that in the previous one, the element of continuity was much weaker than is normal. This is mainly because the SNP recorded large votes in constituencies where it had previously been relatively weak.

Second, the increases in SNP vote shares varied widely—there were six constituencies (five of them SNP-held) where it was under 20 points; 23 where it was between 20 and 30 points; 27 where it was between 30 and 40 points and three Glasgow constituencies (South West, North and North East) where it was more than 40 points.

Third, when we inter-correlate the changes in the parties' vote shares there are only four statistically significant results. As elsewhere, both the Conservatives and Labour did better where the Liberal Democrats lost more (coefficients of −0.36 and −0.51, respectively). Also reflecting a trend in the rest of the country, the Green Party appears to have benefited from the Liberal Democrat collapse. Although only 16 seats are involved, the correlation between the changes in the two parties' vote shares is an impressive −0.75. The performances of the Conservatives and Liberal Democrats were unrelated to that of the SNP, but the rivalry between the latter and Labour as the leading parties in Scottish politics is underlined by the fact that changes in their vote shares were strongly negatively related (coefficient = −0.71). As even a cursory reading of the election results would reveal, the greater the gain by the SNP across the constituencies, the bigger was Labour's loss of support.

Finally, all elections throw up perplexing results and in the Scottish case this time it came from Edinburgh South. Here, the SNP increased its vote share by 26 points but quite how the incumbent Labour member managed to increase his share by four points and emerge from the wreckage as the sole Scottish Labour MP remains something of a mystery. It may be significant, however, that the SNP candidate received much adverse publicity for having referred to opponents of Scottish independence as 'Quislings' while, in the election itself, the slump in the Liberal Democrat vote (−30 points) was well above average (see also the later chapters by Curtice and Mitchell for brief discussions of this constituency).

4.   Patterns of party support in 2015

When we focus on variations in absolute levels of support for the parties rather than change between elections, we would usually be on territory that is much more familiar in that patterns are normally very similar from one election to the next. In this case, however, the rise of UKIP, the relative success of the Greens, the demise of the Liberal Democrats and, of course, what Alex Salmond called an 'electoral tsunami' in Scotland make matters somewhat less familiar than usual.

Nonetheless, regional variations in party support (Table 1.5) show that, with the exception of London, there remains a broad north–south division in England. Labour's strongest areas outside London remain the three northernmost English regions, although the party's lead over the Conservatives is now relatively slim in Yorkshire and Humberside. The three southern regions (Eastern, South East and South West) recorded very large leads for the Conservatives with Labour not even reaching 20% of votes in two of them. Scotland, of course, was a disaster area for Labour but even Wales can no longer be counted as particularly strong Labour territory. The north–south party division in England is even more apparent in terms of seats won. In the three northern regions the Conservatives won only 44 seats compared with 110 for Labour and 4 for the Liberal Democrats. In the Eastern, South East and South West regions, in contrast, the tally was 181 for the Conservatives, 12 for Labour, 5 for the Liberal Democrats and 3 for others (including the Speaker).

As usual, the Liberal Democrats had a relatively even spread of votes across regions but on this occasion it was at an abysmally low level. They failed to reach 10% of votes outside the South West—even in Scotland where they previously held 11 seats. In the South West itself—frequently referred to as a 'heartland' for the party—they scored 15.1% of votes but failed to win a single seat.

UKIP performed well everywhere—although less so in the South East and South West—except for London and Scotland. In the case of London, this is probably due to the cosmopolitan nature of the capital which contains large concentrations of recent immigrants. Finally, it is worth noting that the Green Party had stronger

Table 1.5 Party shares of votes and seats won in regions (row percent)

	Con	Lab	Lib Dem	UKIP	Green	SNP/PC	Other
North East	25.3	46.9	6.5	16.7	3.6	–	0.9
	3	26					
North West	31.2	44.7	6.5	13.7	3.2	–	0.7
	22	51	2				
Yorkshire/Humber	32.6	39.1	7.1	16.0	3.5	–	1.6
Seats	19	33	2				
East Midlands	43.5	31.6	5.6	15.8	3.0	–	0.6
Seats	32	14					
West Midlands	41.8	32.9	5.5	15.7	3.3	–	0.8
Seats	34	25					
Eastern	49.0	22.0	8.2	16.2	3.9	–	0.5
Seats	52	4	1	1			
London	34.9	43.7	7.7	8.1	4.9	–	0.8
Seats	27	45	1				
South East	50.8	18.3	9.4	14.7	5.2	–	1.5
Seats	78	4			1		1
South West	46.5	17.7	15.1	13.6	5.9	–	1.2
Seats	51	4					
Wales	27.2	36.9	6.5	13.6	2.6	12.1	1.0
Seats	11	25	1			3	
Scotland	14.9	24.3	7.5	1.6	1.3	50.0	0.3
Seats	1	1	1			56	

Note: The Speaker is counted as 'Other'.

results in the South of England (including London where they have a lengthy record of contesting local elections) than elsewhere.

In order to explore variations in party support across constituencies, Table 1.6 shows correlation coefficients measuring the associations between the shares of the vote obtained by the parties in constituencies in England and Wales and a standard set of socio-demographic variables drawn from the 2011 census. The data reveal no surprises in respect of the Conservatives and Labour. It is not exactly news to report that the former had larger shares of the vote in constituencies where there were more professional and managerial workers, owner occupiers, older voters, people with degrees and in more rural areas. They performed less well where there were more manual workers, social renters, younger people, those having no educational qualifications, students, those not owning a car, people belonging to ethnic minorities and in more urban areas. These patterns were clearly reversed in Labour's case.

The distribution of Liberal Democrat support is normally a paler reflection of that for the Conservatives in that the relationships tend to be in the same direction but weaker. Despite the slump in support for the former, in broad terms the same

Table 1.6 Bivariate correlations between party shares of vote in 2015 and constituency characteristics (England and Wales)

	Conservative	Labour	Liberal Democrat	UKIP	Green
% Professional/managerial	0.53	−0.43	0.31	−0.57	0.28
% Manual workers	−0.50	0.41	−0.30	0.57	−0.33
% Owner occupiers	0.58	−0.62	0.09*	0.34	−0.34
% Social renters	−0.65	0.69	−0.22	−0.07*	0.14
% Aged 18–24	−0.46	0.40	0.04*	−0.25	0.41
% Aged 65+	0.45	−0.60	0.17	0.37	−0.20
% In agriculture	0.31	−0.47	0.22	0.07*	0.03*
Persons per hectare	−0.42	0.53	−0.06*	−0.44	0.27
% With degrees	0.30	−0.22	0.31	−0.74	0.39
% No qualifications	−0.48	0.40	−0.34	0.65	−0.38
% Students	−0.40	0.36	0.09*	−0.41	0.45
% With no car	−0.70	0.75	−0.17	−0.26	0.24
% Ethnic minority	−0.35	0.52	0.12	−0.44	0.11*
(N)	(572)	(572)	(572)	(573)	(537)

Note: Coefficients not statistically significant at the 0.01 level are asterisked. The Speaker's seat is excluded in the case of the three 'major' parties.

still applies. Two points are worth noting however. First, in 2010 the Liberal Democrat vote tended to be slightly stronger the more students and young people there were in a constituency. This time, the correlation coefficients involving these variables are not statistically significant. Second, whereas the Conservatives have consistently done worse the larger the ethnic minority population in a seat, this was not true of the Liberal Democrats in 2015. If anything, indeed, they held up better (or lost less) where there were more ethnic minority voters.

The coefficients for UKIP and the Green Party are an unusual mixture but suggest that these two parties appeal to different sorts of communities. UKIP did best where there are more manual workers, older voters and people lacking educational qualifications but also, rather paradoxically, their vote share was positively related to the proportion of owner occupiers in a constituency. On the other hand, the party did worse in areas where there were more professionals, students, young people, residents with degrees, people with no car and ethnic minorities. Except for the ethnic minority variable, the relationships between the level of support for the Greens and these socio-demographic characteristics were the reverse of those for UKIP.

In sum, despite changes in the fortunes of the two major parties, the geographical and hence social bases of their support remained much as they have been in the past. The situation as far as the Liberal Democrats are concerned is a little more fluid

Table 1.7 Bivariate correlations between SNP share of vote in 2015 and constituency characteristics

% Professional/managerial	−0.68	% Social renters	0.67
% With degrees	−0.63	% No qualifications	0.57
% Owner occupiers	−0.41	% Manual workers	0.51
% In agriculture	−0.38	% With no car	0.41
% Aged 65+	−0.30		
% Church of Scotland	−0.24		

Note: N = 59. All coefficients are statistically significant at the 0.01 level.

while the profiles of the votes won by UKIP and the Greens suggest that the two find support in different sorts of areas. In interpreting the data in Table 1.6, however, it must be remembered that, on their own, these figures tell us nothing about the party choices of the people belonging to the various groups involved—for that, surveys and polls are required. Rather, correlations provide information about the relationship between the characteristics of *constituencies* and levels of party support in those constituencies.

Within Scotland, variations in Conservative and Labour strength were associated with the characteristics of constituencies in much the same way as in the rest of Britain. Interest centres, rather, on the SNP. Did that party's huge advance affect the socio-economic bases of its vote? The relevant data are shown in Table 1.7. In 2010, only five variables were significantly associated with SNP vote share—% professional and managerial (−0.40), % with degrees (−0.30), persons per hectare (−0.30), % manual workers (0.40) and % with no qualifications (0.29). Moreover, the strength of the correlations was modest. In 2015, the picture was somewhat different. As can be seen, the distribution of SNP support was much more clearly structured by occupational class and the class-related variables of education, housing and car ownership. In addition, the SNP did relatively less well where there were more older people and Church of Scotland adherents. In 2010, the five significant variables mentioned above accounted for 18% of the variation in SNP support; in 2015, the same five explained 65%. Despite winning 50% of Scottish votes, then, the SNP is no longer a 'catch all' party without a distinctive social base. Rather, in this election at least, it has taken over what were formerly the bases of Labour dominance in Scotland.

4.1 Turnout

Turnout in Britain is measured as the percentage of the eligible electorate which casts a ballot. Properly, therefore, it includes those who voted but whose ballots were rejected for one reason or another and that practice is followed here.[3] Although it might appear a rather obscure technical point, it is worth noting that before this election the system of electoral registration was altered. Rather than the appropriate form being completed by the 'Head of Household' on behalf of all residents at an address, each individual was required to register separately and also to provide proof of identity. Since those who were unwilling to undertake this slightly more complicated registration process—or simply never got round to it—are disproportionately likely to have been non-voters in any event, one might have expected that the new system would lead to slightly higher reported turnout figures.

On the day of the election, there was the usual wild speculation in the media about the level of turnout. In the next day's *Daily Telegraph*, for example, which was published after only a few results had been declared, it was reported that 'turnout was forecast to be at its highest for almost two decades'. It was also reported that a betting firm had already paid out on bets that turnout would exceed 68.5%. If true, this proved to be premature generosity on the part of Paddy Power since the overall British turnout was 66.6%. Despite the fact that the outcome was expected to be very close and claims that UKIP was able to mobilise previous non-voters, this was an increase of just 1.3 points on the figure for 2010. On the positive side, 2015 was the third General Election in succession that turnout has increased; on the other hand, it remains lower than at any election between 1950 and 1997.

Table 1.8 shows that, as with support for the main parties, there remains something of a north–south divide in England with respect to turnout. The three northern regions had relatively poor turnouts—worse, even, than the figure for London. Wales used to be a high turnout country but it is now a little worse than average. At 71.1%, an increase of more than seven points since 2010, the turnout in Scotland stands out as exceptional. The independence referendum in September 2014 clearly engaged the Scottish electorate to a remarkable degree and this carried over into the post-referendum period, as polls began to indicate the likelihood of a major improvement in the fortunes of the SNP and a sharp fall in Labour's popularity. Nonetheless, to keep matters in perspective and as with Britain as a whole, even in Scotland 2015 turnout failed to match the levels seen in elections between 1950 and 1997.

As usual, the level of turnout varied considerably across constituencies in 2015. At the bottom end, Stoke-on-Trent Central propped up the table with a turnout of 51.5%. At the other extreme, Scottish constituencies occupied the top three places. The highest turnout was in East Dunbartonshire (81.9%), which was the scene of a

---

[3]The constituency electorate figures used are from the House of Commons Library Briefing Paper number CBP7186.

Table 1.8 Regional turnout 2015

	Turnout 2015	Change 10–15
North East	62.0	+0.9
North West	64.4	+2.1
Yorkshire/Humber	63.3	+0.4
East Midlands	66.8	0.0
West Midlands	64.2	−0.5
Eastern	67.8	−0.2
London	65.6	+1.1
South East	68.8	+0.6
South West	69.7	+0.7
Wales	66.0	+1.2
Scotland	71.1	+7.3

Table 1.9 Bivariate correlations between turnout in 2015 and constituency characteristics (Great Britain)

% Professional/managerial	0.57	% Manual workers	−0.55
% Owner occupiers	0.54	% Social renters	−0.55
		% Private renters	−0.29
% In agriculture	0.35	Persons per hectare	−0.40
% With degrees	0.46	% No qualifications	−0.51
% Aged 65+	0.42	% Aged 18–24	−0.34
		% Ethnic minority	−0.35
		% With no car	−0.57
Constit. marginality 2010	0.05*		

Notes: All coefficients are significant at the 0.01 level except the one asterisked. $N = 632$.

very hard-fought battle between the incumbent Liberal Democrat (Jo Swinson) and the SNP, followed by East Renfrewshire (81.1%) and Stirling (77.7%).

As with the distribution of support for the major parties, in examining turnout variations across constituencies we encounter—for the most part—a highly predictable and familiar pattern. Table 1.9 shows correlations between the level of turnout in 2015 and census variables indicating the socio-economic characteristics of constituencies as well as their marginality (100—the winning party's percent majority) in 2010. In general—and it is nothing new—the coefficients for the social variables indicate that, despite the slight overall increase in turnout, Britain continues to be divided into relatively low turnout and relatively high turnout constituencies and the two are very different in social terms. The former are mainly urban, working class and poor; the latter rural and suburban, middle class and relatively affluent. As before, it is worth stressing that this analysis does not tell us the extent to which people in the various groups listed turned out to vote. Rather, it tells us that the more professionals, owner occupiers, people with degrees, people employed in agriculture and older people there are in a constituency, the higher was its turnout.

There is one unexpected result in Table 1.9, however. The closeness of the contest in a constituency in the previous election (marginality) has been regularly associated with turnout levels for many years. Parties put greater campaign efforts into more marginal seats (paying little attention to those that are either very safe or hopeless for them) and, unsurprisingly, these efforts usually bear fruit in higher turnouts. In 2015, indeed, there were frequent complaints that the parties were focusing more than ever on their target seats—and even on target voters within these seats. On this occasion, however, differential campaigning did not pay off in better turnouts—the relevant correlation coefficient is not statistically significant. There is no obvious reason for this surprise development. It may be that voters in marginal seats became so fed up with the constant stream of leaflets, direct mail, telephone calls and so on during the campaign that they turned off from the election altogether. In any event, this is clearly a question that requires further research.

5. Explaining the outcome

There is little difficulty in accounting for the poor performance of the Liberal Democrats in the election. This was merely the latest in a series of electoral disasters stemming from the decision to enter a coalition with the Conservatives and the subsequent evaporation of respect for the party leader, Nick Clegg. Explaining why the Conservatives defeated Labour so soundly is rather more difficult. In the immediate aftermath of the elections, politicians and media commentators put forward a variety of suggestions, including Labour's alleged move to the left over the previous five years, the 'innate conservatism' of the English electorate and the apparent arrogance of the SNP leadership in constantly claiming to be able to 'lock the Tories out of 10 Downing Street'. A full evidence-based account must await publication of the British Election Study report. But there are grounds for thinking that, to a considerable extent, the Conservative victory was a vindication of the 'valence voting' approach that has been emphasised by academic electoral analysts in recent years.

This suggests, first, that electors are concerned more about 'valence' issues—those on which there is general agreement on the ends to be pursued—than about ideology or the positions that parties take on more divisive issues. Second, electors make judgements about which party is likely to be more competent on the key valence issues. Third, as a shorthand way of determining the relative competence of the parties, they assess the relative merits of the party leaders and that judgement often determines which party they will support.

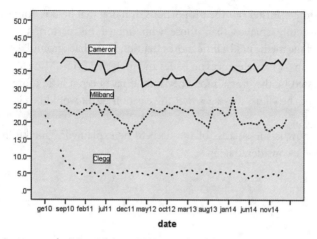

Figure 1.3 Best person for Prime Minister, 2010–March 2015.
Source: YouGov polls for *The Sunday Times*

According to YouGov, the three issues considered most important by the electorate in 2015 were the economy (mentioned by 52% of respondents), immigration
(51%) and the National Health Service (45%). These easily outstripped other issues
and can be defined as valence issues because everyone wants a healthy economy and
a first-class health service while the great majority of people favour controls on immigration. As to the party judged best to handle these issues, although Labour led
the Conservatives by 14 points on the National Health Service, the Conservatives
were ahead by 18 on the economy and 6 on immigration (an issue on which a significant proportion of respondents preferred UKIP). Overall, then, the Conservatives appear to have had the edge on the key valence issues in the election.

When it comes to assessments of the party leaders, however, there is no room for
doubt. David Cameron heavily outscored Ed Miliband. As Figure 1.3 shows, the
latter never once headed the former from the time he became Labour leader until
the start of the campaign. During the campaign itself, somewhat surprisingly,
YouGov asked the 'best Prime Minister' question only a few times and, although
there was some improvement in Miliband's position he still lagged well behind
Cameron. On the eve of poll, Ipsos MORI reported that Cameron was thought to
be the most capable Prime Minister by 42% of respondents compared with 27%
thinking this of Miliband. The last time that a General Election was not won by
the party of the leader preferred as Prime Minister was in 1979, when Margaret
Thatcher's Conservatives defeated Labour under James Callaghan. In that case,
however, although Callaghan was preferred by 44% to 33%, Thatcher nonetheless
received reasonably good personal ratings. Unhappily for Labour and Mr Miliband,
the latter not only lagged Mr Cameron in the electorate's estimation of who would be

the best Prime Minister but the proportions thinking that he was doing a good job were consistently smaller than those who judged his performance bad. Had pundits and the media paid a little more attention to the background data produced by the polls on party preferences on issues and preferred Prime Minister, rather than being obsessed by the 'horse race', they might have been a little more cautious in accepting the 'headline' messages that the election result would be close to a dead heat.

Finally, how is the success of the SNP to be explained? Thankfully that is a question to be considered later.

JOHN CURTICE*

A Return to Normality? How the Electoral System Operated

At first glance, the 2015 General Election heralded a return to normality. According to its advocates, the single-member plurality electoral system enables the electorate to choose directly between alternative governments by ensuring that whichever party comes first in votes secures an overall majority in seats, even though it may have won much less than half the vote.[1] For most of the post-war period that is precisely how it has operated. Now, after a hiatus in 2010, when no one party won an overall majority and the partisan colour of the government was determined by post-election coalition negotiations,[2] one party, the Conservatives, was returned with an overall majority despite winning just 37% of the UK-wide vote. Indeed, the party secured a majority even though, at 6.6 percentage points, its lead in votes over the Labour Party (in Great Britain) was 0.6 of a point less than it had been five years previously. The system can apparently be relied upon after all to reward the winning party with enough of a 'bonus' in seats to ensure that it wins an overall Commons majority.

However, a closer look at the result suggests in many respects the electoral system did not deliver what its advocates often claim as its merits. For a start, although the Conservatives won an overall majority, it was by historical standards a small one—just 12 seats—and certainly not one that can be guaranteed to withstand the potentially chilly winds of by-election losses and defections to which all governments tend to be subject. The party's majority is small even though the 6.6-point lead enjoyed by the Conservatives is larger than that secured by Tony Blair in 2005 and Edward

---

*John Curtice, University of Strathclyde, J.Curtice@strath.ac.uk

[1] Bingham Powell, G. Jr. (2000) *Elections as Instruments of Democracy: Majoritarian and Proportional Visions*, New Haven, Yale University Press; Norton, P. (1997) 'The Case for First Past the Post', *Representation*, **34**, 84–88.

[2] Adonis, A. (2013) *5 Days in May: The Coalition and Beyond*, London, Biteback; Laws, D. (2010) *22 Days in May: The Birth of the Lib Dem-Conservative Coalition*, London, Biteback.

doi:10.1093/pa/gsv025

Heath in 1970. Yet those two administrations enjoyed overall majorities of 66 and 31 respectively. The Tories' lead in votes is larger too than those enjoyed by the Conservatives in 1955 and 1959, yet those administrations also had more substantial parliamentary majorities of 59 and 99.

Meanwhile, apart from delivering a winner's bonus, another key feature of the way in which single-member plurality is meant to ensure elections are a choice between two alternative governments is by severely limiting the representation of third parties in the House of Commons.[3] Yet, despite a collapse in support for what had hitherto been Britain's principal third party, the Liberal Democrats, for the third time in a row more than 80 MPs were elected from parties other than Conservative or Labour. The new Parliament will be as fractured as its immediate predecessors.

Evidently the way in which the single-member plurality system worked in 2015 merits closer examination. This chapter assesses, first of all, how the system treated the two largest parties, the Conservatives and Labour, and explains why the majority it gave the Conservatives was so small. It then examines the way in which the system treated the smaller parties. Finally, the chapter considers the implications of what happened in 2015—and what might have happened if an alternative, more proportional system had been in place—for the debate about electoral reform.

1.   Conservatives and Labour

The degree to which the single-member plurality system rewards the winner of an election with a bonus in seats depends on two analytically separable aspects of the way in which it rewards the votes cast for the two largest parties.[4] The first is the degree to which the system exaggerates the lead in votes of the largest party over its principal rival, but does so in a manner that is independent of whichever party is the winner. The second is whether it treats one of the two largest parties more favourably than the other. The system may fail to deliver the winner a large majority either because it does not exaggerate the lead of any party to any significant degree, or because it treats the winning party less favourably than its principal competitor.

The presence or absence of both features depends on the way in which support for the two largest parties is distributed across constituencies. The system will only provide the winner with a substantial bonus if a relatively large number of seats are

---

[3] Duverger. M. (1954) *Political Parties: Their Organisation and Activity in the Modern State*, London, Methuen.

[4] Gudgin, G. and Taylor, P. (1979) *Seats, Votes and the Spatial Organisation of Elections*, London, Pion.

highly competitive (or 'marginal') between the two parties.[5] In those circumstances, seats readily change hands from one party to another, thereby making it likely that even a party with quite a small lead in votes will enjoy a substantial lead in seats. If, however, there are relatively few such seats, then a party might need a big lead in votes before it secures a majority of seats.

Meanwhile, the system will only treat the two largest parties equally if two conditions hold (or at least counterbalance each other).[6] First, the seats won by one party should on average contain just as many voters as those won by its principal opponents. If that condition does not hold, and a party is more successful in constituencies that have fewer voters, that party is likely to win more seats for any given share of the overall national vote. Second, one party's vote should not be geographically more efficiently distributed than that of its opponent. A party's vote is efficiently distributed if it wins a relatively large number of seats with small majorities and, conversely, loses relatively few seats narrowly. Efficiency also includes not registering high levels of votes in constituencies that are won by a third party.

Table 2.1 presents a variety of statistics that help us assess the ability of the single-member plurality system to exaggerate the voting lead of the largest party over the second party irrespective of which party has come first. On the right-hand side, the table reports two statistics that summarise how the division of the votes cast for Conservative and Labour alone (or the two-party vote) is distributed across constituencies. The first is the standard deviation; the bigger the number the more the two-party vote varies from one constituency to another. The second is the kurtosis, which provides an indication of whether there is a relatively large or small number of constituencies in which the two-party vote is relatively evenly divided. The more negative the number the fewer such constituencies there are.

On the left-hand side, two statistics bring out the implications of these two measures. These statistics are the number and the proportion of seats that can be considered marginal between Labour and the Conservatives. Marginal seats are defined here as those in which the Conservative share of the two-party vote would be between 45 and 55% if, as a result of a uniform shift of votes across all constituencies, the two parties were to enjoy exactly the same share of the vote across the country as a whole. They are in other words the seats that would be most competitive between the two

---

[5]Kendall, M. and Stuart, A. (1951) 'The Law of Cubic Proportions in Election Results', *British Journal of Sociology*, **1**, 183–197; Curtice, J. and Steed. M. (1982), 'Electoral Choice and the Production of Government: the Changing Operation of the Electoral System in the UK Since 1955', *British Journal of Political Science*, **12**, 249–298.

[6]Soper, C. and Rydon, J. (1958) 'Under-Representation and Electoral Prediction', *Australian Journal of Politics and History*, **4**, 94–106; Johnston, R., Pattie, C., Dorling, D. and Rossiter, D. (2001) *From Seats to Votes: the Operation of the UK Electoral System Since 1945*, Manchester, Manchester University Press.

Table 2.1 Changing distribution of the two-party vote, 1955–2015

	Marginals		Two-party vote	
	No.	Percent	Standard deviation	Kurtosis
1955	166	27.2	13.5	−0.25
1959	157	25.7	13.8	−0.29
1964	166	27.3	14.1	−0.45
1966	155	25.6	13.8	−0.46
1970	149	24.5	14.3	−0.27
1974 (Feb)	119	19.9	16.1	−0.68
1974 (Oct)	98	16.4	16.8	−0.82
1979	108	17.8	16.9	−0.87
1983	80	13.2	20.0	−1.05
1987	87	14.4	21.4	−1.03
1992	98	16.1	20.2	−1.03
1997	114	19.6	18.1	−0.85
2001	114	19.7	18.3	−0.82
2005	104	18.8	19.7	−0.96
2010	85	15.0	22.2	−1.08
2015	74	13.1	21.7	−1.19

Source: Curtice, J., 'So What Went Wrong with the Electoral System? The 2010 Election Result and the Debate about Electoral Reform', *Parliamentary Affairs*, **63**, 623–638, and author's calculations.
Marginal seat: Seat where Conservative share of two-party vote (overall Conservative share of two-party vote − 50%) lies within the range 45 − 55%.
Two-party vote: Votes cast for Conservative and Labour combined.
Table based only on seats won by Conservative or Labour at that election and contested by both parties.

largest parties in the event of a very close overall outcome. Inevitably, the fewer such seats there are, the less of a winner's bonus the electoral system is likely to generate.

The division of the two-party vote has long varied to a greater extent from one constituency to another than it did in the 1950s and 1960s. The kurtosis measure has also been more negative than it was during those decades. As a result, there have been fewer marginal seats. This decline was the result of a well-documented long-term drift towards Labour in the northern and more urban half of the country and a countervailing swing to the Conservatives in the southern and more rural half, a pattern that was only partially reversed in the wake of New Labour's electoral success.[7] However, it appears that the incidence of marginal seats has fallen once more and is now as low as it has ever been. Just 74 seats fall within our definition, lower than ever before, though as a proportion of all those seats won by either the Conservatives or Labour, the position now is much the

[7]Curtice, J. (2009) 'Neither Representative Nor Accountable: First Past the Post in Britain'. In Grofman, B., Blais, A. and Bowler, S. (eds) *Duverger's Law of Plurality Voting*, New York, Springer, pp. 27–46; Curtice, J. and Park, A. (1999) 'Region: New Labour, New Geography?' In Evans, G. and Norris, P. (eds) *Critical Elections: British Parties and Voters in Long-Term Perspective*, London, Sage, pp. 124–147.

same as it was in 1983.[8] Meanwhile, although the standard deviation of the two-party vote is little changed from 2010, the kurtosis is now at an all-time low.

This fall in the number of marginal seats reflects the fact that once again Britain delivered a less than uniform judgement on the merits of the two largest parties. Within England and Wales at least, Conservative support held up rather better in constituencies with relatively low levels of unemployment, perhaps because these were places that are more likely to have felt the fruits of the economic recovery. In any event, such places are disproportionately ones where the Conservatives were relatively strong in the first place. As a result, the Conservative share of the two-party vote fell, on average, by just 0.9 of a point in seats in England and Wales that the party won in 2010, but by 2.4 points in seats that Labour won last time around. If the country begins to pull in two different directions, then inevitably there will be fewer places where the outcome is reasonably balanced between the principal alternatives.

Still, this fall in the number of marginal seats makes it more rather than less surprising that the Conservatives should have managed to win an overall majority, however small. To understand why they were able to do so, we need to look at the second aspect of the way in which the electoral system treated the two largest parties, that is whether it treated one party more favourably than another. To help us ascertain what might have happened on that front, Table 2.2 reports two more statistics that summarise how the division of the two-party voted varied across constituencies.[9] The first is the difference between the average share of the two-party vote won by the Conservatives across all 632 seats in Great Britain and the overall share of the two-party vote won by the Conservatives across Britain as a whole. These two figures will diverge if one of the parties tends to perform better in constituencies where fewer people voted. In particular, if there tend to be more voters in constituencies where the Conservatives do relatively well, the mean share of the vote won by the Conservatives will be lower than the party's overall share.

The second measure is the difference between the median share of the two-party vote won by the Conservatives and the mean vote the party won across all 632 seats. The median is simply the share of the two-party vote that divides constituencies into two equal groups, with one half comprising those constituencies where the Conservative Party won more than the median vote and in the other where it won less. If a party's vote is efficiently distributed, its median vote will be higher

---

[8] In 1983, 606 seats were won by Conservative or Labour compared with 563 in 2015.

[9] Soper and Rydon, 'Under-Representation and Electoral Prediction'; for an alternative approach, see Johnston, R., Rossiter, D. and Pattie, C. (1999) 'Integrating and Decomposing the Sources of Partisan Bias: Brookes' Method and the Impact of Redistricting in Great Britain', *Electoral Studies*, **18**, 367–378.

Table 2.2 Measures of two-party bias, 1955–2015

	Conservative % two-party vote		
	Mean − overall	Median − mean	Median − overall
1955	+0.3	+0.6	+0.9
1959	+0.4	+0.8	+1.2
1964	+0.1	+0.4	+0.5
1966	−0.3	+0.2	−0.1
1970	−0.9	+0.8	−0.1
1970 (NT)	−0.1	+0.5	+0.4
1974 (Feb)	−0.1	−0.5	−0.5
1974 (Oct)	−0.3	+1.4	+1.1
1979	−0.7	−0.5	−1.2
1979 (NT)	−0.1	+0.9	+0.9
1983	−0.5	+1.7	+1.2
1987	−0.8	+1.4	+0.6
1992	−1.2	−0.0	−1.2
1992 (NT)	−0.2	−0.7	−0.9
1997	−0.4	−1.6	−2.0
2001	−1.4	−1.5	−2.9
2001 (NT)	−1.1	−1.4	−2.5
2005	−2.1	−1.1	−3.2
2005 (NT)	−1.5	−1.0	−2.5
2010	−1.3	−0.8	−2.1
2015	−1.6	+2.1	+0.5

Source: Author's calculations.
NT: Notional results based on estimates of what the outcome would have been if that election had been fought on the new constituency boundaries that were introduced at the subsequent election. The 2001 redistribution (together with a reduction in the number of seats) was confined to Scotland.
Two-party vote: Votes cast for Conservative and Labour combined.
Figures based on all seats in Great Britain. Northern Ireland excluded.

than its mean vote; if a party wins seats with relatively small majorities, this will tend to depress its mean vote while making little or no difference to its median level of support.

Table 2.2 reveals that the first potential source of bias has long tended to favour the Labour Party. For much of the post-war period, Britain's population has tended to move out of (predominantly Labour voting) urban areas (and the northern half of the country) into (more Conservative inclined) suburban and rural areas (in the southern half). Although the boundary commissions regularly redraw constituency boundaries in order to reflect that demographic change, inevitably they are always somewhat behind.[10] Meanwhile, Scotland and (especially) Wales, both

---

[10]Rossiter, D., Johnston, R. and Pattie, C. (1999) *The Boundary Commissions: Redrawing the United Kingdom's Map of Parliamentary Constituencies*, Manchester, Manchester University Press.

areas where the Conservatives generally perform less well, also tend to be over-represented relative to their share of the UK electorate. Thus throughout the last 50 years, the mean Conservative share of the two-party vote has tended to be below the overall share, but that after persistently widening the gap has narrowed each time the constituency boundaries have been redrawn.

The Conservatives had hoped that the parliamentary constituency boundaries would be redrawn once again before the 2015 election, and that this time the process would be speedier (and thus more up to date) as well as be conducted according to rules that would end the over-representation of Scotland and Wales. In this, however, their hopes were dashed when their coalition partners, the Liberal Democrats, voted with Labour to postpone the review (which by that time was already in progress) following the obstruction by Tory backbenchers of coalition proposals for reform of the House of Lords.[11]

In fact, the drift out of Britain's urban centres (and especially London) has become less marked in recent years.[12] Nevertheless, the difference between the average electorate in seats won by Labour (in 2015) and that in constituencies bagged by the Conservatives did grow from 3500 at the time of the 2010 election to 3850 now. However, differences between constituencies in the number of registered voters are not the only disparity that can bring about bias on account of differences in the sizes of constituencies; the phenomenon can also arise because of differences in the level of turnout. As at other recent elections, the turnout in constituencies won by Labour was lower than in those claimed by the Conservatives. However, the gap was a little less wide than it had been five years previously. This time, at 68.6%, the average turnout in seats won by the Conservatives was 6.8 points higher than the equivalent figure for constituencies won by Labour (61.8%). The equivalent gap in 2010 was 7.3 points. The net effect of these two countervailing trends was that, in 2015, around 7400 more votes were cast in the average constituency won by the Conservatives than in that won by Labour, the same difference as in 2010.

But if the difference in the average number of votes cast in Conservative and Labour constituencies was much the same as it had been in 2010, evidently the same was not true when it came to the relative efficiency of the distribution of the two parties' votes. Up until the 1980s, this source of bias had persistently advantaged the Conservatives, not least because Labour piled up huge majorities in constituencies with lots of heavy industry, including not least coal mining. But, since

[11]Curtice, J. (2015) 'The Coalition, Elections and Referendums'. In Seldon, A. and Finn, M. (eds) *The Coalition Effect, 2010–15*, Cambridge, Cambridge University Press, pp. 577–600.

[12]Champion, A. (2014) *People in Cities: The Numbers*, London, Government Office for Science.

1997, it has been Labour's vote that has been the more efficiently distributed.[13] Indeed, it was as a result of this development, together with the advantage that the party continued to draw from differences in the sizes of constituencies, that ensured that at recent elections the system treated Labour much more favourably than the Conservatives (as indicated by the third column of Table 2.2, which brings together the two potential sources of bias by comparing the median and the overall Conservative share of the two-party vote) enabling Labour in particular to win a comfortable overall majority of 66 in 2005, even though the party only enjoyed a three-point lead in terms of votes.

Now, however, this position has apparently been reversed once again. The median Conservative share of the two-party vote in 2015 was no less than 2.1 points higher than the mean share, a figure that, as the third column of Table 2.2 shows, is more than enough to counterbalance the impact of the difference between the size of Conservative and Labour held constituencies. There is one key reason for this change. The Conservatives performed particularly well in those seats that they won most narrowly in 2010, and which thus the party might have been expected to lose, given that across England and Wales as a whole there was overall a one-point swing[14] from Conservative to Labour. In fact in those seats that the Conservatives won most narrowly over Labour in 2010, there was typically a swing to the Conservatives; in seats that the party won with less than a five-point majority, this swing was of the order of 1.1 points in the opposite direction to that seen nationally. Not least of the reasons for this development is that, in line with the pattern at previous elections,[15] Conservative MPs who were elected for the first time in 2010 after ousting an incumbent Labour MP, and who had had the opportunity in the intervening five years to enhance their popularity locally, typically outperformed their party. On average, such new incumbent Conservative MPs enjoyed no less than a 4.5-point increase in their support.

As a result, the Conservatives suffered a net loss of just two seats to Labour instead of the loss of 11 seats that the party would have suffered if there had been a one-point swing to Labour in every seat in England and Wales—a pattern without which the Conservatives would not have won an overall majority. Meanwhile, the impact that this relative Conservative success in marginal seats had on the efficiency of the distribution of its vote is underlined by the fact that of the 74 seats that we previously defined

---

[13] Curtice, J. and Steed, M. (1997) 'Appendix 2: The Results Analysed'. In Butler, D. and Kavanagh, D. *The British General Election of 1997*, Basingstoke, Macmillan, pp. 295–325.

[14] Swing is defined as the change in the Conservative share of the vote less the change in Labour's share of the vote divided by two. In 2015, the Conservative share of the vote increased in England and Wales by 1.4 points, while Labour's did so by 3.4 points. (1.4–3.4)/2 thus equates to a one-point swing to Labour.

[15] Curtice, J., Fisher, S. and Steed, M. (2005) 'Appendix 2: The Results Analysed'. In Kavanagh, D. and Butler, D. *The British General Election of 2005*, Basingstoke, Macmillan, pp. 235–259.

as marginal, no fewer than 45 would be won by the Conservatives in the event of an even division of the GB-wide vote, while just 29 would be won by Labour. In short, the Conservatives are now clearly winning more seats with relatively small majorities.

However, there is one further important change in the distribution of Conservative and Labour support of which the statistics in Table 2.2 do not take proper account. This is the number of votes that each party 'wastes' in seats that are won by parties other than Conservative or Labour. Because, at recent elections, many more of the seats that the Liberal Democrats have won have been ones in which their principal competitors were the Conservatives rather than Labour, this has hitherto been a source of disadvantage for the Conservatives. But at this election, the collapse in Liberal Democrat support enabled the Conservatives to capture no fewer than 27 seats from the Liberal Democrats, more than twice as many as the 12 seats that Labour gained from that source—gains that were instrumental to the Conservatives' ability to win an overall majority despite enjoying a somewhat smaller lead in votes over Labour than in 2010. There are now just four seats left in which the Conservatives are second to a Liberal Democrat incumbent.

At the same time, Labour lost seats to the SNP in unprecedented fashion. No fewer than 40 of the 41 seats that the party was attempting to defend in Scotland were captured by the Nationalists. In combination, these two developments ensured that it was now Labour that was wasting more votes in constituencies that were won by third parties. On average, Labour won 23.3% of the vote in seats won by third parties, whereas the Conservatives secured just 15.6%— almost a complete reversal of the position in 2010 when the Conservatives on average won 28.4% in such seats, Labour just 16.6%.

The Conservatives were thus able to win a small overall majority for two main reasons. First, the party profited heavily from the decline in Liberal Democrat support, so that votes that had previously been wasted coming second to the Liberal Democrats were now used to elect Conservative MPs. Second, an above average performance in marginal seats, not least thanks to the local popularity of incumbent Conservative MPs defending their seats for the first time, ensured that the party's vote was more efficiently distributed and lost rather fewer seats to Labour than would otherwise have been the case. In short, the party won a majority not because the electoral system proved better able to exaggerate the lead of the largest party over the second party, but rather because of the elimination of some of the sources of bias that the party had hitherto suffered.

2. Third parties

Overall, support for parties other than Conservative or Labour fell from 33.4% (in Great Britain) to 31.0%, but this figure is still higher than at any election between 1922 and 2005 inclusive. Between them (including the entirely distinct parties in Northern Ireland) they won 87 seats in the House of Commons, a tally second only to the 92 seats won by such parties in 2005, and slightly up on the 85 such seats in 2010. However, whereas hitherto it has been the Liberal Democrats that have dominated such representation, their position as the third party in the House of Commons was usurped by the SNP.

So how do we understand the failure of the system once again to deny third parties representation? In fact, just as the ability of the single-member plurality system to provide the winner in votes with a bonus in seats is contingent on the geographical distribution of party support, so also is the extent to which the system fails to reward smaller parties.[16] If a party's vote is relatively evenly spread, the system will indeed reward a smaller party with few if any seats, as it means it will secure a relatively small share of the vote everywhere. On the other hand, if a smaller party's vote is concentrated in particular constituencies, then it may be rewarded quite handsomely by the system.

The contingent and thus potentially very varied way in which the system treats smaller parties was amply illustrated by the 2015 election. The system did more or less exclude some parties. UKIP, which came third in votes across the UK as a whole, ended up (along with the sixth placed Greens) coming equal 10th (behind four Northern Irish parties as well as the SNP, Plaid Cymru and the Liberal Democrats) in terms of seats. It was the party that came fifth in votes, the SNP, that succeeded in becoming the third largest party in the House of Commons. The crucial difference between the two parties was that UKIP's vote was for the most part relatively evenly spread, whereas support for the SNP was, of course, confined to constituencies in Scotland.

UKIP's success in winning nearly 13% of the vote in Great Britain was truly remarkable. It was the first time since the advent of the Conservative–Labour duopoly in 1922 that the Liberal Democrats (and before them the Liberal party) had been usurped in a UK General Election from their position as the third most popular party in terms of votes. It confirmed UKIP's position as the most significant wholly independent fourth-party challenge in English politics.[17] But the party was rewarded with just one seat, the Clacton berth of the locally popular defector from the Conservative Party, Douglas Carswell. At 6.2, the standard deviation of its support across constituencies was noticeably much less than that of the Liberal Democrats (8.4). The party only managed to win more than a quarter of the vote in 16 constituencies, and came a close second (i.e., within 10% of the winner) in just two.

Although the SNP's vote is wholly confined to and thus concentrated within Scotland, in fact within that part of the UK its vote is geographically quite evenly

[16] Gudgin and Taylor, *Seats, Votes and the Spatial Organisation of Elections*.

[17] Curtice, J. (2014) 'Messages from the Voters: The 2014 Local and European Elections', *Juncture*, **21**, 77–81.

Table 2.3 Change in Labour and SNP support between 2010 and 2015 in Scotland, by the level of Labour support 2010

Labour % share 2010	Mean change in % Labour support 2010–2015	Mean change in % SNP support 2010–2015	(No. of seats)
Less than 20%	−7.7	+21.6	(9)
20–30%	−14.5	+27.1	(6)
30–40%	−8.6	+23.7	(7)
40–50%	−18.3	+31.0	(17)
More than 50%	−26.0	+35.9	(20)
All seats	−17.8	+30.0	(59)

Source: Author's calculations.

spread. In 2010, for example, the standard deviation of Nationalist support was just 8.7; in contrast that for the Labour Party in Scotland was no less than 16.3, while the equivalent figure for the Liberal Democrats north of the border was, at 13.5, also much higher. Despite winning a slightly bigger share of the vote than the Liberal Democrats, the party won just six seats compared with the Liberal Democrats' tally of 11. But while an evenly spread vote is disadvantageous for a party when it is relatively small, it becomes an advantage when it is well ahead nationally— which is the position in which the SNP found itself in 2015 in winning almost exactly half of the vote in Scotland. Indeed, the SNP's vote proved to be even more evenly spread this time around with the standard deviation falling to 7.0.

This change was in part at least the result of a crucial, if arithmetically almost inevitable, pattern given the scale of Labour's losses north of the border. Labour's vote fell by almost 18 points across Scotland as a whole. But in nine constituencies, Labour did not win as much as 18% of the vote in 2010. This meant that to some extent at least Labour's vote must fall more heavily in seats where the party was previously relatively strong (and thus often the SNP relatively weak). This is indeed precisely what happened. As Table 2.3 illustrates, for the most part Labour's vote fell more heavily—and the SNP's vote increased more substantially—the stronger Labour had been in 2010. The only exception to this pattern was in seats where Labour won between 30 and 40% of the vote in 2010, among whom are included the seat of Edinburgh South where uniquely Labour managed to increase its share of the vote, thanks in all probability to a high level of tactical switching to Labour by Conservative and Liberal Democrat voters.[18]

---

[18] As we might anticipate, SNP support also increased less where the party had previously been strongest. In the six seats that the party won in 2010, for example, support for the party rose on average by 14.1 points, less than half the equivalent figure for Scotland as a whole.

As a result of this pattern, Labour's vote in Scotland became much more evenly distributed; the standard deviation of its support fell to just 10.4. And now that it was by a long way only the second most popular party in Scotland, this evenness helped to ensure that the party's losses and the SNP's gains were almost as high as they could possibly be. True, if the fall in Labour support and the rise in the SNP vote had been uniform across the whole of Scotland, Labour would still have lost as many as 38 of its existing 41 seats to the SNP, but in the event its tally of losses proved to be as many as 40.

The almost inevitable consequences of what happens to the geographical distribution of a party's vote when it loses ground very heavily are also apparent in the case of the Liberal Democrats. The party's vote fell almost as heavily across Britain as a whole—by 15.5 points—as Labour's did within Scotland. But there were 170 constituencies where the party did not manage to win as much as 16% of the vote in 2010. In this case too, it was thus inevitable that to some degree at least support for the party should fall more heavily in places where it had previously been stronger, thereby reducing the extent to which its vote varied from one constituency to another.

This, indeed, is what happened. In those seats where the party won less than 16% of the vote in 2010, the party's support fell on average by 10.4 points. On the other hand, it fell by 15.8 points in those places where it secured between 16 and 28%, while in those constituencies where it had started off with more than 28% of the vote last time, its vote fell on average by as much as 19.8 points. One of the features of the party's performance at recent elections had been a measure of success in developing areas of local strength, thereby ensuring a more geographically varied vote that proved more rewarding when it came to winning seats.[19] Most of that increased variation was now lost. At 8.4 not only was the standard deviation of party support well down on the equivalent figure of 10.4 in 2010, but in fact it was lower than at any previous election since 1983.

Not that the party lost all of its concentrations of local strength. It has often been remarked that Liberal Democrat MPs are typically especially dependent on their local popularity in order to win and retain their constituencies. Indeed, the party hoped that this local popularity would on this occasion enable some of its MPs to defend their seats successfully against the national tide. They were not wholly mistaken in that expectation. In those 47 seats where the local Liberal Democrat MP was attempting to defend his or her seat, the party's vote fell on average by just under 14.5 points, well below the near 20 point drop that the party generally

---

[19]Russell, A. and Fieldhouse, E. (2005) *Neither Left nor Right? Liberal Democrats and the Electorate*, Manchester, Manchester University Press.

suffered in seats where it was relatively strong.[20] But all that this simply meant was that the vote for the typical Liberal Democrat MP fell by more or less as much as the party's support did across the country as a whole. Indeed, the party's eventual tally of eight seats, its lowest since 1970, was still two seats fewer than it would have been if the change in support for the party had been uniform across the country.[21]

Despite increasing its average share of the vote in the seats it fought (568 in Great Britain) from 1.8% in 2010 to a record 4.2% in 2015, the Greens could do no more than retain the Brighton Pavilion seat that Caroline Lucas first won in 2010. The party's vote remained very evenly spread with a standard deviation of just 2.8. Apart from Ms Lucas' seat, the party managed to win over 20% of the vote in just one other constituency. The party was left still looking some way apart from having the level, and distribution, of support needed to make a substantial parliamentary breakthrough. Like UKIP, its vote was much less concentrated than that for Plaid Cymru in Wales, who managed to retain the three heavily Welsh-speaking seats it already held, or that for the four principal parties that exclusively fought seats in Northern Ireland, all of whom won more seats than either the Greens or UKIP.

As a result of the collapse in the Liberal Democrat vote and the sharp differences in the way the electoral system treated the smaller parties, the 2015 election has occasioned a fundamental change in the character of third-party representation in the House of Commons. Hitherto it was dominated by a party, the Liberal Democrats, that had a substantial GB-wide vote, albeit one that had become somewhat more geographically variegated than previously. Now, third-party representation is largely the preserve of parties that only contest elections in Scotland, Wales or Northern Ireland, and which are primarily concerned to represent the distinctive interests and identities of those parts of the UK. That is the inevitable consequence of using an electoral system that is responsive to the geography as well as the level of a party's support.

3. Prospects and implications

Critics of the single-member plurality system often focus on the disproportionality of the results that the system can produce. Indeed, on one measure, the sum of the differences between the parties' shares of the vote and their shares of the seats

---

[20] And, indeed, the average drop of 21.6 points that the party suffered in the 10 seats where the incumbent MP stood down.

[21] Or, more accurately, if the change in party support across England and Wales as a whole had applied uniformly across constituencies there, while the change in support in Scotland had occurred in every constituency there.

Table 2.4 Projected outcome of the 2015 election under regional proportional representation

	Projected seats	% Share of seats	% Seats − % votes
Conservatives	252	38.8	+1.9
Labour	211	32.5	+2.1
UKIP	81	12.5	−0.1
Liberal Democrats	49	7.5	−0.4
SNP	30	4.6	−0.1
Green	6	0.9	−2.9
PC	4	0.6	0.0
Others (NI)	17	2.6	−

Source: Author's calculations.
Seats allocated by Government Region. Total number of seats in each region, proportional to current electorate, using St Lague divisor. Division of seats within each region determined by D'Hondt divisor, but confined to those parties in a region that won at least 5% of the vote.

(divided by two)[22] at least, the outcome of the 2015 election was almost as dispro-portional as that of any previous post-war election—only the outcome in 1983 was slightly more disproportional.[23] Certainly if some form of proportional represen-tation had been in place, such as the regional party list system used in elections to the European Parliament,[24] the Conservatives would not have had an overall majority, though David Cameron might have still have been Prime Minister (and the UK facing a prospect of a referendum on its membership of the European Union) if he had been able to come to an agreement on forming a government with UKIP (Table 2.4).

However, this criticism of the electoral system arguably misses the point. It is not meant to produce results that are proportional. Rather, as noted earlier, it is meant to be systematically disproportional such that the winner secures an overall major-ity and smaller parties reap little reward. And despite the success of the

---

[22] Loosemore, J. and Hanby, V. (1971) 'The Theoretical Limits of Maximum Distortion: Some Analytic Expressions for Electoral Systems', *British Journal of Political Science*, 1, 467–477.

[23] Measured across the UK as a whole, this index of disproportionality was 24.3 in 1983 and 24.0 in 2015, though if the calculation is confined to Great Britain the two elections are equally disproportional, with an index value of 23.9 in both cases. However, on another measure, the Gallagher least-squares index [see Gallagher, M. (1991) 'Proportionality, Disproportionality and Electoral Systems' *Electoral Studies*, 10.1, 33–61] that places greater weight on large differences between a party's share of the vote, the 2015 result was, in fact, no more disproportional (with an index score of 15.0) than that in 2010 (15.1) and indeed was less so than at any election since and including 1997. I am very grateful to Dr Stuart Wilks-Heeg for his assistance on this point.

[24] But assuming that a party would have to win at least 5% of the vote in a region to be entitled to any seats in that region.

Table 2.5 The relationship between seats and votes following the 2015 General Election

Con lead over Lab (% GB vote)	Seats (UK)		
	Con	Lab	Others
5.8	327	236	87
0.0	302	256	92
−3.7	279	278	93
−12.5	229	326	95

Source: Author's calculations.

Conservatives in winning a small overall majority, it is whether the system can be relied upon to achieve those objectives that the question marks still arise.

As already noted, the Conservatives were able to win an overall majority not because the system proved more effective at generating a 'winner's bonus' but rather because some of the ways in which the party was treated less favourably than Labour were no longer present. Indeed, there are actually fewer marginal seats than ever before. Meanwhile, the number of third-party MPs is more or less as high as it has ever been. This does not sound like a recipe for ensuring that future elections will necessarily produce an overall majority—and certainly not ones of the size that until recently were commonplace for most of the post-war period.

That this, indeed, is the case becomes apparent when we examine how many seats each party might win under certain hypothetical conditions. Table 2.5 presents what the outcome would be if the level and distribution of support for third parties remains as it was in 2015, but the Conservative lead over Labour varies as a result of movements of support from the outcome in 2015 that occur uniformly in each and every constituency. Thus, for example, the first row of the table shows what would happen if, as a result of a 0.4-point swing of support from Conservative to Labour that occurred in each and every constituency, the Conservative lead fell from the 6.6-point lead the party actually enjoyed in 2015 to one of 5.8 points. The remaining rows show the consequences of larger uniform swings, that is the 3.3-point swing that would result in Conservative and Labour having the same share of the overall vote, the just over 5-point swing that put Labour 3.7 points ahead of the Conservatives, and the 9.5-point swing that would mean the party was 12.5 points ahead.

Two key points emerge from this table. First of all, the system now does indeed treat the Conservatives more favourably than it does Labour. On these assumptions, Labour would still have 46 fewer seats than the Conservatives if the two parties were to win the same share of the vote and would need to be 3.7 points ahead before it won the same number of seats. Moreover, whereas Labour would need to be as much as 12.5 points ahead of the Conservatives to win a bare overall majority, the Conservatives need a lead of only 5.8 points in order to achieve the same objective. Not least of the reasons for this bias are the continued losses that Labour would still suffer in Scotland on these assumptions. Even the 9.5-point swing projected in the final column would result in Labour recapturing just one seat from the SNP.

Second, the range of results that would result in a hung Parliament in which no one party would have an overall majority is wide indeed. Any outcome between a Labour lead of 12.5 points and a Conservative one of 5.8 points would result in no single party winning an overall majority. This range is wider than it has been after any previous election.[25] In short, it would appear that there are still considerable doubts about the ability of the electoral system to generate an overall majority in the event that either the Conservatives or Labour only enjoy a narrow lead.

In practice, the next election will not be fought under the current parliamentary boundaries. Now that they have a parliamentary majority it can be anticipated that the Conservatives will succeed in pursuing a redrawing of the boundaries to a successful conclusion. As the law and the Conservative manifesto currently stand, that redrawing will also be accompanied by a reduction in the number of MPs from 650 to 600.[26]

On its own, redrawing the boundaries is likely to ensure that the electoral system treats Labour even less favourably that it does at present, primarily by substantially reducing the difference between the average number of registered voters in Conservative and Labour constituencies. That though will clearly not necessarily ensure that the system is equitable in its relative treatment of the two largest parties. However, reducing the size of the Commons to 600 can be expected to restore to a degree at least the extent to which the system produces a 'winner's bonus'. Other things being equal, larger constituencies are more likely to be heterogeneous in their social and political character and thus more likely to be competitive between Conservative and Labour. It seems unlikely, however, that this change will be sufficient to ensure that the electoral system reacquires the ability to produce an overall majority in all but the rarest of circumstances, not least because it will do little to diminish the substantial phalanx of SNP MPs. The UK may have narrowly avoided having another hung Parliament this time around, but it could still well find itself at continued risk of one occurring in future, even if single-member plurality remains in place.

---

[25]The previous record was the 13.9 range between a Conservative lead of 11.2 points and a Labour lead of 2.7 points produced by the equivalent calculation after the 2010 election. See Curtice, J., Fisher, S. and Ford, R. (2010) 'Appendix 2: An Analysis of the Results' In Kavanagh, D. and Cowley, P. *The British General Election of 2010*, Basingstoke, Palgrave Macmillan, pp. 385–426.

[26]Curtice, 'The Coalition, Elections and Referendums'.

Britain Votes (2015) 41–53

TIM BALE AND PAUL WEBB*

The Conservatives: Their Sweetest Victory?

Virtually nobody standing for, or working for, the Conservative Party at the General Election of 2015 expected it to win an overall majority. True, there were those who were more bullish about the party's prospects than many of the pundits and pollsters who published their predictions in the week running up to the poll—but in most cases only to the extent that they believed that the Tories would emerge not just as the largest party (the consensus view of the forecasters) but would do so with enough seats to mean they could put together a minority government or else renew the coalition with the Liberal Democrats that had governed the country since May 2010.

Both Jim Messina, the veteran of the Obama campaign who David Cameron had brought in to advise the Tories on voter identification and mobilisation, and Lynton Crosby, the Australian consultant who was in overall charge of the Conservative campaign, were quietly confident by polling day itself that the party would win more than 300 seats. They were not overly surprised by the exit poll. Even then, they did not breathe easy until the result from the marginal constituency of Nuneaton came in at 1.50 am, showing that the Conservatives had increased their share of the vote by four percentage points, while Labour's had actually dropped. As more and more results came in, it became clear that the exit poll's projection had actually understated the Conservatives' margin of victory: Mr Cameron would be back as Prime Minister, but more than that—he would be heading a Tory Government which, with 12 seats more than all the other parties in Parliament put together, would not need to rely on anyone else's help to run the country.

This, then, was a historic victory, achieved against expectations and in some ways in defiance of what are sometimes presented as the laws of political gravity. David Cameron is the first Prime Minister since Margaret Thatcher in 1983 to increase the number of Tory MPs in Parliament from one election to the next and the first Tory PM since Anthony Eden in 1955 to increase the party's share of the vote.

*Tim Bale, Queen Mary University of London, t.bale@qmul.ac.uk; Paul Webb, University of Sussex, p.webb@sussex.ac.uk

doi:10.1093/pa/gsv026

The Tories won 330 seats (51% of the total) on a vote-share of 37% (just under one percentage point up from 2010). Just as encouragingly, albeit under the radar, they picked up around 500 additional seats in local government and assumed control of 30 more councils, which, given how often party activists these days are either elected representatives or their friends and relations, may help them at the next General Election, currently scheduled for 2020. They will also be advantaged at that election by boundary reforms which, according to some projections, could effectively give the Conservatives an extra 20 seats or so and mean Labour will need a swing as big as those achieved by Herbert Asquith in 1906 and by Clement Attlee in 1945 to win an overall majority next time around.

The Conservatives' improved performance was down in no small measure to what we might call 'the black widow effect': after mating with their Liberal Democrat coalition partners, they gobbled them up, taking 27 of their seats. The Tories lost only two seats, net, to Labour, helped by an incumbency effect favouring Conservative MPs who won their seats in 2010, and, as we shall go on to suggest below, by being well ahead of Her Majesty's Official Opposition when it came to voters' views on which party would best manage the economy and which had the best leader. In this, they were almost certainly helped by their campaign, which much like the work done by *Better Together* before the Scottish independence referendum, could hardly be called pretty but turned out to be highly effective. Not only did it manage to focus relentlessly on Labour's negatives and neutralise any of its positives, it may also, via its emphasis on the 'chaos' inherent in some sort of Labour–SNP 'deal', have persuaded some who might otherwise have wavered ultimately to vote Tory. Possibly (although only partially) as a result, UKIP, contrary to most people's expectations before the election, may well have done as much, if not more, damage to Labour than to the Conservatives in some crucial English marginals.

1.   The long-term context: Conservative development, 1992–2010

David Cameron, along with George Osborne, has taken the Tories a long way in the ten years since he became leader towards restoring their reputation as Britain's (or at least England's) 'natural party of government'. Indeed, it is easy to forget just how bad things had become back then. After presiding over the country's embarrassing and expensive exit from the Exchange Rate Mechanism (ERM) in 1992, thereby forfeiting public trust in its ability to run the economy, the Conservative Party turned in on itself over Europe and was subsequently swept away in the 1997 Labour landslide. Rather than coming to their senses, however, the Tories headed for the ideological hills, selecting a series of frankly unelectable leaders and pursuing policies (or at least, adopting a rhetoric and tone) that looked a long way out of step with where most of the electorate located themselves.[1] By their third defeat in a

---

[1] Quinn, T. (2008) 'The Conservative Party and the centre ground of British Politics', *Journal of Elections, Public Opinion and Parties*, **18**, 179–199.

row in 2005, it had become obvious, even to many die-hard right-wingers, that things would have to change—or at least be made to look as if they had changed.

Cameron, who offered himself as the proverbial 'change candidate' appeared to many (even to some of those who could not bear his incipient sense of entitlement and his claim to stand on the pragmatic centre-ground) to be the answer to the party's prayers: Eurosceptic without being obsessive, Thatcherite without being a zealot, and a gifted communicator—a politician not only able to convey genuine enthusiasm for national treasures like the NHS but to look like he was at home in the more socially liberal, ethnically diverse country that twenty-first century Britain had become. His game plan, however, was rather more complex than some of his right-wing detractors and some of his left-wing and socially liberal admirers gave him credit for. He and other 'modernisers' clearly believed that the Conservatives must do all those things that Conservative oppositions (including the one led by Margaret Thatcher between 1975 and 1979) had done to put the party back in contention. Rather than obsessing over issues which fired up the party faithful but put off large numbers of voters—especially many liberal middle-class voters who ought otherwise to be Tory supporters—the party should focus counter-intuitively on topics, such as the environment, that would symbolise a shift away from its past. And it should insist that those parts of the welfare state which (like it or not) enjoyed overwhelming public backing, such as the NHS, education and pensions, were completely safe in the new leadership's hands.

'Team Cameron', however, did believe in a smaller role for the state and that the public could be convinced, *pace* New Labour, that tax cuts and spending reductions would not automatically lead to reductions in public services. They just believed that the place to persuade people was in government rather than out of it. Unfortunately for them, however, things did not go entirely according to plan. Gordon Brown's decision not to call a snap election in the summer of 2007 was followed by a chapter of accidents and then the global financial crisis. All of this boosted Tory fortunes but effectively put the brand decontamination operation on ice, meaning that the lead which the Conservatives had built up over the next year or two was more fragile than it looked. By May 2010, as the economy began to recover and doubts about the Conservatives' good intentions began to resurface now that Cameron and Osborne were talking about 'an age of austerity', a double digit Tory lead at the end of 2009 had dropped into single figures—so narrow that even a brilliant short campaign would have had trouble getting Cameron over the line—around 323 seats—for an overall majority. And sadly for him, the Tory campaign, although incredibly well financed and equipped (at the national level at least) with what was then state-of-the-art technology, turned out to be anything but brilliant. Little wonder perhaps that the British Election Study's panel study found that the Tories ended up with less support at the end of the short campaign than they had at the beginning.[2]

As a result, the Tories had fallen short—their lead on 'instrumental' evaluations associated with 'valence politics', namely relative judgements about leadership, credibility and competence, was enough to make them the largest party in a hung Parliament but was insufficient, given lingering concerns about their real intentions towards public services and how much they had really changed, to afford the party the overall majority that some Conservative MPs had assumed would be theirs.[3] Some of those MPs were even more alarmed at what happened next. Faced with a Liberal Democrat leadership which was some way to the right of the majority of their party, but who clearly were not going to be content with simply supporting a Conservative minority Government, Cameron offered Clegg a full-blown majority coalition. Given that Labour could not match that offer, it is understandable that it was accepted. But what defies understanding is the Liberal Democrats' failure to negotiate an agreement, be it on policy or on portfolios, which might have given them a sporting chance of claiming credit for what the government they had joined would go on to do. Little wonder that William Hague, former Tory leader and future Foreign Secretary returned from the negotiations and declared, 'I think I've just killed the Liberal Democrats'.[4]

2. The permanent campaign: 2010–2015

Having effectively captured and neutered their coalition partners, the Conservative leadership immediately co-opted them into what was a ruthless and highly effective campaign to re-write history and, in so doing, destroy Labour's reputation for economic competence. Years of uninterrupted growth after 1997 had allowed Labour to build up a big lead on the issue and, while that lead been lost during the banking crisis, the party had been closing on the Conservatives again as the economy began to recover in the months leading up to the election. Now, however, it was involved in a leadership contest in which even the most Blairite of the candidates spent most of their time insisting on the need to move beyond New Labour rather than the

---

[2]For a detailed look at 2010 based in part on BES findings, see Green, J. (2010) 'Strategic Recovery? The Conservatives under David Cameron', *Parliamentary Affairs*, **63**, 667–688.

[3]See Bale, T. and Webb, P. (2010) 'The Conservative Party'. In Allen, N. and Bartle, J. (eds) *Britain at the Polls 2010*, London, Sage, pp. 37–62.

[4]Quoted in G. Parker, 'Highs and Lows of the UK's Coalition Government', *Financial Times*, 26 March 2015. The most comprehensive sources on the coalition include D'Ancona, M. (2014) *In It Together: The Inside Story of the Coalition Government*, London, Penguin; Seldon, A. and Finn, M. (eds) (2015) *The Coalition Effect, 2010–2015*, Cambridge, Cambridge University Press, 2015; Beech, M. and Lee, S. (2015) *The Conservative–Liberal Coalition: Examining the Cameron–Clegg Government*, Basingstoke, Palgrave.

importance of defending its record and its achievements. Seizing the opportunity provided by this hiatus—and by an emergency budget supposedly designed to ensure that Britain did not go the way of Greece—Osborne and Cameron (assisted by Liberal Democrat politicians desperate to persuade their erstwhile supporters that they had gone into coalition to protect what they insisted was 'the national interest'), rammed home the message that Labour had, in their words, 'maxed out the nation's credit card' and 'failed to fix the roof while the sun was shining', thereby giving the impression that 'the mess' they were having to clear up was due not so much to a global crash as to Blair's and Brown's supposed profligacy and mismanagement. This was enough to ensure that even when, as Shadow Chancellor Ed Balls predicted, the Coalition's austerity programme damaged (or at least delayed) the recovery, Labour was unable to capitalise on its temporary distress. Labour's difficulties in turn meant that when the economy at last began to grow again, after Osborne quietly took his foot off the brake, the Conservatives were able to contrast the Coalition's performance with a deeply-embedded caricature of what had happened between 1997 and 2010, namely the idea—hotly disputed by many economists, who point out that the sums involved were inconsequential, both in relative and absolute terms—that Labour had 'overspent' and run a deficit even when the economy was doing well. That narrative, and of course the recovery itself—even though it was not accompanied by the kind of sustained rise in real wages needed to generate a 'feelgood factor'—ensured that, by the time the 2015 election came round, the Tories led Labour as the best party to handle the economy by some 20 percentage points.

Cameron and Osborne were also ruthless, perhaps even more so, in exploiting Labour's other big weakness—the widespread perception that it was a soft touch on welfare. Given the hyperbole that characterised tabloid newspapers' coverage of the issue, their readers could be forgiven for thinking that almost everybody claiming benefits was either doing so fraudulently or as a foreigner, or both—when, that was, in the very worst tabloid case, they're weren't busy breeding and then killing their own children.[5] Naturally, official statements or ghosted columns put out in the name of government ministers were generally more careful and coded, with Osborne's headline-grabbing response to the Mick Philpott case perhaps the paradigmatic example.[6] They nonetheless constituted a concerted

---

[5]This was essentially the implication of the coverage of the genuinely shocking trial of one benefit claimant who, with two accomplices, was found to have burnt down his house with some of his children still inside. See 'Vile product of welfare UK', *Daily Mail*, accessed at http://www.dailymail.co.uk/news/article-2303120/Mick-Philpott-vile-product-Welfare-UK-Derby-man-bred-17-babies-milk-benefits-GUILTY-killing-six.html on 3 April 2013.

[6]For Osborne's reaction when quizzed by a reporter about Philpott, see http://www.bbc.co.uk/news/uk-22024061, accessed on 4 April 2013.

and effective effort, exploiting long-established and popularly held distinctions between the 'undeserving' and the 'deserving' poor, to justify money-saving policy changes by giving the impression that the only losers would be people currently getting 'something for nothing'—the shirkers and skivers rather than the workers and the strivers. Labour, because it was almost bound to stick up for those who stood to lose out, could then be portrayed as a budget-busting friend of the feckless, with any outrage expressed on its part at the shocking unfairness of the stereotypes involved simply playing into Osborne's hands by giving legs to all the stories that helped reinforce those stereotypes in the first place. And when Labour belatedly tried to go the other way and attempted to 'out-Osborne Osborne' by making some supposedly 'tough choices' of its own on welfare, it was too late to convince voters it was sincere and probably did no more than legitimise and perpetuate the myths that played so well for the Conservatives in the first place.

Of course, the Conservatives did not have everything their own way. They failed, because of a bust-up with the Liberal Democrats over Lords reform, to achieve a reduction in the size of the Commons that would have prompted a boundary review estimated to be worth around 20 additional Tory seats. And on one issue, immigration, which, since the mid-1960s, has been one of their most reliable weapons in their electoral battles with Labour, they struggled to maintain credibility. A rash pledge in the run up to the 2010 election that a Tory Government would reduce annual net immigration from the hundreds to the tens of thousands backfired when, despite legislation and rule changes designed to 'crack down', the figure actually rose markedly over the course of the Parliament. True, it was UKIP rather than Labour which benefited most from this all-too-obvious failure, despite Miliband shifting his party's stance on the issue to a more restrictive one from 2011 onwards.[7] Nevertheless, the Tories' lead over their main opponent shrank, according to YouGov's tracker on best party to handle immigration and asylum, from 28 percentage points (45 vs 17) in May 2010 to just six points (22 vs 16) on the eve of the General Election in May 2015.

Meanwhile, on Europe—where Conservatives have also come to assume that they enjoy an advantage over Labour in these increasingly Eurosceptic times—their position was far from strong: certainly any hope that Miliband's decision not to match Cameron's offer to hold an in-out referendum would damage him proved forlorn—possibly because it was obvious to the electorate that the offer was only made in order to appease Eurosceptic backbenchers worried about UKIP. The story on health (traditionally Labour's strong suit) was not quite as bad, but the issue nonetheless remained a problem—and was made worse when the government went ahead with legislation in 2011–2012 that totally contradicted

---

[7]Bale, T. (2014) 'Putting It Right? The Labour Party's Big Shift on Immigration Since 2010', *Political Quarterly*, **85**, 296–303.

their pre-election promise to avoid a 'top-down reorganisation' of the NHS. Prior to the legislation being announced, the Tories had actually reduced Labour's lead on the issue to one or two percentage points. After the announcement, Labour's lead went back into double figures and, prompted, too, by rising waiting times, hospital deficits, and local closures, pretty well stayed there until polling day in 2015.

3. The short campaign: March–May 2015

To understand why the Conservatives fought the campaign of 2015 the way they did, one has to go back to the Conservative campaigns of 2005 and 2010. The latter was widely perceived, not least by those working at Conservative Campaign Headquarters (CCHQ), as a bit of a mess. Its untested main theme—the big society—not only failed to impress, but was a distraction. Meanwhile nobody was ever quite sure exactly to whom they were reporting and who had the final word. What a contrast with 2005, when at least everyone knew who was running the show—the so-called Wizard of Oz, Lynton Crosby—and the result, while dire, was a marked improvement in terms of seats, on the two previous contests.

Campaign 2015, then, would be the safe if dull one in which Cameron looked and sounded like a Prime Minister sticking to the game plan devised by the fabled Australian who was supposed to know what he was doing. Cameron, having decided, along with George Osborne, on the basic strategy—banging on about fears on the part of 'business' about a Labour Government; donning hi-viz jackets and hard-hats to emphasise their 'long term economic plan' for 'hard-working families'; counterposing Conservative 'competence' with Labour 'chaos'; talking up the SNP 'threat' while simultaneously portraying them as bullies and blackmailers; and badmouthing Miliband as a weak and weird individual whose only decisive act had been to shaft his own brother—left the tactics to the hired help. This, along with the fact that Cameron refused to risk a one-on-one television debate with Labour's leader and confined his public appearances to carefully crafted pseudo-events, attracted more brickbats than plaudits—and some serious reservations even within the Prime Minister's own camp. The Tory leader's response to such criticisms, however, was essentially limited to rolling up his sleeves at his photo-ops to show how 'pumped' he was and how hard he was working. Other than that he simply stuck with the programme, reminding journalists that this was the 'most organised, disciplined, clear campaign I have ever been involved in'.

There were few surprises, then, but there were some raised eyebrows. In particular, the decision to declare at the same time as continuing to pound away at Labour's purported profligacy, that a Conservative Government would guarantee billions of additional spending on the NHS, without actually identifying where the money would come from, was seen as a rather desperate move to prevent Labour from getting as much traction on health as it hoped. Desperate or not, it may well have done the trick. And the fact that it could be defended on the grounds that the Tories were good for the money because, unlike Labour, they could be trusted to grow the economy, was testimony to the unassailable lead they had built up on the latter—one that meant they felt able to ignore suggestions that they should somehow match Labour's promise to tax 'non-doms' and raise the top rate of income tax to 50p, both policies being intended to tap into the widespread feeling (reinforced by the so-called omnishambles budget of 2012) that the Conservatives were 'out of touch' and 'the party of the rich'.

Clearly, the Tory leadership decided there was little point in wasting time trying directly to counter such deeply held prejudices. Instead they countered with some prejudices of their own, using highly supportive newspapers—especially the *Sun* ('This is the pig's ear Ed made of a helpless sarnie. In 48 hours, he could be doing the same to Britain'), the *Mail* ('For sanity's sake don't let a class-war zealot and the SNP destroy our economy—and our very nation'), and (to the embarrassment of some of their staff) the *Telegraph* ('Nightmare on Downing Street') and the *Times*—to ramp up fears of a Miliband–Sturgeon deal and to remind the public (if they needed reminding) of Ed Miliband's shortcomings as a leader.[8] The party also used the press, especially in the last week of a campaign when it, like everyone else, firmly believed that the country was heading for another hung Parliament, to question the legitimacy of any possible attempt by Labour, if it finished behind the Conservatives in terms of seats, to form a government.

Perhaps the least-noticed aspect of the Conservative campaign, however, was the decision, taken late in 2014, that, rather than focusing solely on the constituencies they needed either to defend or snatch from Labour while going easy on their Co-alition partners, the Conservatives would throw a significant proportion of their considerable financial resources at trying to unseat Liberal Democrats—an effort that gathered pace during the campaign when frontbenchers were dispatched to seats few had imagined were in play. Even then, the Tories' target seats coordinator, Stephen Gilbert, forecast that the Liberal Democrats would win around 15 seats—which was way below most pundits' guesses but, as it turned out, was almost twice as many as the eight that Nick Clegg's party finally ended up with. Clearly, the fact that the Conservatives took 27 seats from their erstwhile partners was due mostly to the Liberal Democrats losing an average 21 percentage points in seats they held by less than ten points from the Tories in 2010. But it also had something to do with the fact that Tory candidates in those seats managed to add an average of nearly four percentage points to the vote the party received at the previous election.

---

[8] See Jewell, J. 'Election Coverage: Sweet Victory or a New Low for UK Press?', accessed at https://theconversation.com/election-coverage-sweet-victory-or-a-new-low-for-uk-press-41569 on 9 May 2015.

This points to the main reason (apart of course from winning all those Liberal Democrat seats) why the Conservatives were able to win an overall majority in spite of the fact that Labour actually managed to improve its share of the vote marginally more than they did. For the first time in a long time, the Tories managed better than their opponents to concentrate their vote in exactly the right places. In both safe Conservative and safe Labour seats, the Tories actually slipped by an average of two percentage points compared with 2010. In those marginal seats they were defending against Labour, however, they increased their average share by two points, while Labour managed to increase its share by, on average, less than two points. That said, given that Conservative candidates in Labour-held marginals did not in the main significantly increase their share of the vote, the main reason they were able to make eight gains from Labour (to offset their ten losses) may well have been down to some of the Labour vote going to UKIP. The fact that the nearly fourfold increase in the share of the vote won by Nigel Farage's party did not damage the Conservatives as much as expected, especially given that far more of its voters had previously supported the Tories than Labour, was remarkable. It is perhaps a testament to the effectiveness of the 'coalition of chaos' strategy that many of them seem to have ended up sticking with the Conservatives for fear of letting in Miliband and/or the SNP. In any case, the SNP surge played an obviously important role in decimating Labour representation north of the border, while inflicting no damage on the Tories there—a major advantage for the Tories, although in the event they would have won an overall majority had Labour maintained its habitual dominance over the Scottish seats.

4.　Why the Conservatives won: post-election polling evidence

Although the Conservatives enjoyed a remarkable victory, one thing seems fairly clear: it was not because of any great love on the part of the British electorate for the party or an affinity with its perceived values or ideology. According to British Election Study data gathered shortly before the campaign started,[9] Labour just about retained its place as the most popular party in terms of partisan identification, with 27.8% of respondents claiming to identify with it (down from 31% in 2010), compared with 26.1% for the Conservatives (down from 27.1%) and 6.2% for the Liberal Democrats (15.9% in 2010). Neither was the Conservative Party especially well liked, with an average score of just 3.77 on a scale running from 0 ('dislike') to 10 ('like'), compared with 4.12 for Labour and 3.02 for the Liberal Democrats; UKIP (5.10), SNP (3.94) and the Greens (3.98) all scored more highly than the Tories on this scale. Moreover, BES data show that

---

[9]We are grateful to the directors of the BES for making Wave Four of their panel data available for this analysis.

the Conservatives were regarded as being more ideologically remote from the average voter than most other parties: the mean position of voters on a scale running from 0 ('very left-wing') to 10 ('very right-wing) was almost exactly in the centre, at 4.99, while the Tories and UKIP were both perceived as being well to the right of this position (at +2.93 and +2.94, respectively), whereas the other main parties were all regarded as being to the left of the average voter— and all were seen as closer than the two right-wing parties; the Liberal Democrats were closest (at −0.21), followed by SNP (−1.42), Plaid Cymru (−1.69), Labour (−1.87) and the Greens (−2.06).

The limited post-election polling evidence available at the time of writing suggests that precisely the same factors that ushered the Conservatives into government in 2010 counted in their favour once again in 2015: perceived economic and leadership competence.[10] Interestingly, post-election data published by Lord Ashcroft show that the modal response to the question of which was the most important issue in 2015 was the NHS rather than the economy—and this held regardless of whether or not respondents were asked to consider their own family's position (58%) or the country's position as a whole (55%).[11] One would normally expect the relative salience of the NHS to favour Labour—and indeed, there was some mileage for the party on this issue, as 76% of those voting Labour cited health as the most important issue for the UK, whereas only 39% of those voting Conservative did so. Even so, close behind the NHS in terms of salience was the need to 'get the economy growing and creating jobs' (51%), and 61% of those citing this as one of the three most important issues voted Conservative, while only 50% voted Labour. More directly telling, perhaps, is the fact that 46% of respondents (a plurality) agreed with the statement that 'the national economy is not yet fully fixed, so we will need to continue with austerity and cuts in government spending over the next five years', including 84% of those who voted Conservative; in contrast, only 17% of Labour supporters saw things this way, as did 45% of Liberal Democrat supporters.

Further support for the argument that valence considerations weighed decisively in the balance is provided by a Greenberg Quinlan Rosler (GQR) post-election poll that was commissioned by the TUC.[12] This shows that the top three reasons for supporting the Conservatives were the feeling that the economy was recovering (39%), that progress that had been made with deficit-reduction (29%) and the belief that David Cameron would make a better Prime Minister than Ed Miliband (18%). It is not

---

[10] Bale and Webb, 'The Conservative Party'.

[11] See http://lordashcroftpolls.com/wp-content/uploads/2015/05/LORD-ASHCROFT-POLLS-Post-vote-poll-summary1.pdf, accessed on 29 May 2015.

[12] See http://www.gqrr.com/uk-post-election-3, accessed on 30 May 2015.

necessarily that voters were entirely sold on the detail of economic policy: the GQR poll showed that fewer people agreed with the Conservative position that the best way to get the economy growing would be to get the deficit under control and cut taxes and red tape (43%) than with Labour's emphasis on ensuring that 'working people feel better off and more comfortable spending' (48%). Nevertheless, 40% felt that Labour would 'spend too much and can't be trusted with the economy', and 25% felt they would make it 'too easy for people to live off benefits'. A quarter also felt that Labour in government would be 'bossed around by Nicola Sturgeon and the Scottish Nationalists', which suggests that the Tories' negative campaigning on the theme of a Labour–SNP 'threat' may have resonated with a significant number of voters. More generally, far more respondents saw the Tories as competent (53%) and having a good track record in government (50%) than Labour, for whom the respective figures were only 29% and 25%.

For the second election running David Cameron proved a huge asset to his party's electoral prospects. The Ashcroft poll showed that some 71% of Tory voters cited the leader as one of the three most important reasons for voting for the party, compared with just 39% of Labour voters. This is a very striking differ- ence, which is consistent with the possibility that more and more voters are coming to rely on leadership evaluations as a heuristic simplification to guide their decision at a time when policy debates are becoming increasingly complex and almost impossible for non-experts to adjudicate on.[13]

While these valence considerations certainly mattered at the level of the individ- ual voter, one other thing should not be overlooked in seeking to understand the unexpected Tory majority in 2015: the paradoxical impact of Liberal Democrat losses to Labour, of which the Tories were a serendipitous beneficiary. While dis- gruntled Liberal Democrat voters from 2010 probably shifted predominantly to Labour, this almost certainly ended up helping the Conservatives in terms of overall seat gains. The last BES pre-election panel showed 27% of the 2010 Liberal Democrats saying that they were intending to shift to Labour at the General Election, while only 11.2% were planning to vote Conservative. Moreover, in the seats that the Liberal Democrats were defending in 2015, the Conservatives lost 0.5% of their vote on average, while Labour increased by 2.7%. However, this profited Labour relatively little, given that in 33 of the 57 seats that the Liberal Democrats were defending, their nearest challengers were the Tories, compared with only 17 in which Labour were the main opponents. Thus, by taking Liberal

---

[13] See Bittner, A. (2011) *Platform or Personality? The Role of Party Leaders in Elections*, Oxford, Oxford University Press; Evans, G. and Andersen, R. (2005) 'The Impact of Party Leaders: How Blair Lost Labour votes'. In Norris, P. and Wlezien, C. (eds) *Britain Votes 2005*, Oxford, Oxford University Press; Costa Lobo, M. and Curtice, J. (eds) (2014) *Personality Politics? The Role of Leader Evaluations in Democratic Elections*. Oxford, Oxford University Press.

Democrat votes, Labour's electoral progress in such seats more often than not only served to let the Conservatives win.

One final observation about the electoral standing of the Tories should be made, which takes us back to the point about the party not being especially loved by voters, notwithstanding the majority it secured in the Commons. It is clear that the Conservatives continue to have some significant image problems, which may hinder them in the next Parliament. The GQR poll shows that the number one 'doubt' voters have about the Tories is that 'they are for the rich and powerful, not ordinary people' (36% expressing this view). Not far behind (32%) is the feeling that 'they can't be trusted with the NHS' (the most salient issue at the election, remember), while a mere 29% of voters regarded them as 'honest'. This suggests a picture in which the nation has entrusted the government of the country to the Conservatives while having their eyes wide open as to the deficiencies of the party. To put it differently, the Tories may not have a strong bank of political capital on which to draw when the going gets tough in the years leading up to 2020—as it almost certainly will, given the challenges to be faced over continuing economic recovery, and the UK's political relationships both internally and with the EU.

5. Conclusion

Speaking just after he realised he had won, David Cameron called 2015 his 'sweetest victory'. But, as many commentators rushed to remind him, it has the potential to turn very sour very quickly. His narrow, 12-seat majority is smaller, it is worth recalling, than the 21 seat majority won by John Major (on 42% of the vote) back in 1992. Moreover, anyone old enough to remember that time will recall how that victory soon turned to ashes as Britain's 'Black Wednesday' exit from the ERM, the announcement of massive job losses in the coal industry and parliamentary rebellions over the Maastricht Treaty, turned Major from hero to zero practically overnight. It is difficult at present to foresee anything on the immediate economic horizon that could do such dramatic damage to the Tories' valuable reputation for competence in that sphere, although the severity of the expenditure cuts promised by George Osborne certainly has the potential to tip the economy into recession yet again. However, an arguably chronic tendency towards ideological overreach and internal strife over Europe means that whoever succeeds Mr Cameron, presuming he makes good on his promise not to seek another term, needs to be careful not to assume that he or she has the next General Election in the bag. Cameron has laid the foundations, but they need to be built on—and, given the cagey and contingent nature of the support given to the Conservatives by many of those who voted for them in May 2015, that building will have to be erected on the centre-ground of British politics rather than the cloud-cuckoo land inhabited by some of the PM's less pragmatic colleagues. Still, for all the dangers coming down the line, we should acknowledge

Cameron's achievement. As the respected political commentator, John Rentoul, put it a few days after the election, 'Overnight, he has transformed from the one-term mechanic called round to fix the deficit, who couldn't even do that, into a 10-year prime minister who can stamp his personality on the nation.'[14]

Cameron may be helped to do that by a Conservative Party that is at last beginning to look a little bit more like the country it governs. The willingness of at least some constituency associations to pick (without being pressured to do so) less conventional Conservative candidates in safe or at least winnable seats means that the Tory benches in the Commons now contain the party's highest ever proportion of women, the 68 female MPs who sit there making up 21% of the party's contingent in the lower house. The Tories also have the largest number of non-white MPs they have ever had: a total of 17, seven of whom are new entrants to the Commons. In addition, 'only' 48% of Tory MPs went to independent schools (with 34% having been to comprehensives and 18% to grammars). Although this hardly constitutes proportional representation, given that only 7% of pupils currently go to schools outside the maintained sector, it is a drop from the 54% who had been privately educated in 2010 and continues a long-term trend towards more state-educated Tory MPs. That said, a disproportionate share of the majority of Tory MPs who are graduates attended elite universities: some 34% of Conservatives in the Commons were educated at Oxford or Cambridge. If David Cameron was serious when he talked in the wake of his victory about the Tories becoming 'the party of working people', then, in this respect at least, he still has a long way to go.

---

[14]Rentoul, J. 'Is No One Going to Give Cameron Any Credit?' *Independent on Sunday*, 10 May 2015.

STEVEN FIELDING*

'Hell, No!' Labour's Campaign: The Correct Diagnosis but the Wrong Doctor?[1]

As Britons cast their votes, public opinion surveys suggested that Ed Miliband had a fair chance of emerging as the head of a Labour minority administration, even if the Conservatives held more seats in the Commons than Labour. So, when the broadcasters announced their exit poll, Miliband was not alone in being shocked by the size of the Conservative lead over Labour and the near-certainty of a Conservative Government the poll represented. For, if Labour's horrible performance in Scotland was widely anticipated, the party's failure to take more than a handful of Conservative-held English marginal constituencies was not. And it was in England, not just Scotland, where Labour lost this election: even had Miliband won all 59 seats north of the border, David Cameron would still have been re-elected Prime Minister.

Scotland did, however, play a crucial role in England. The false prediction of a hung Parliament meant the prospect of a minority Miliband government supported by an 'anti-austerity' Scottish National Party (SNP) came to dominate English voters' minds. According to Conservative propaganda this would be a 'coalition of chaos'. Dominated by SNP leader Nicola Sturgeon, a Miliband government would destroy the economy while breaking up Britain. This grim prospect

---

*Steven Fielding, School of Politics and International Relations, University of Nottingham, steven.fielding@nottingham.ac.uk

[1]This chapter was informed by insights drawn from 15 confidential interviews with Labour members drawn from Miliband's team of advisors, national officials, regional organisers, candidates, agents, managers and campaigners—as well as a member of the Lobby. It has benefited from the sight of Goes, E. (forthcoming) *The Labour Party under Ed Miliband: Trying but Failing to Renew Social Democracy*, Manchester, Manchester University Press while Bale, T. (2015) *Five Year Mission. The Labour Party under Ed Miliband*, Oxford, Oxford University Press was an invaluable guide to the period 2010–2015.

doi:10.1093/pa/gsv027

persuaded more than a few English voters to support Cameron's party rather than UKIP, the Liberal Democrats—or Labour.

The success of the 'coalition of chaos' narrative was however a symptom of a deeper problem: Labour's failure to evoke a positive response amongst the kinds of voters whose support the party needed most if it was to return to office. Many had doubts about the Conservatives and some saw merit in parts of Labour's approach. But most nonetheless considered Britain would be better led and the economy managed more ably under Cameron rather than Miliband. On these critical issues of 'statecraft'—in effect the art of governing competently—Labour had trailed the Conservatives since well before 2010.[2] Given that, and irrespective of what the opinion polls said, the result should not have been such a bolt from the blue.

1. The Blairite version

In the wake of Labour's defeat, commentators and party figures offered their explanations. As Miliband was elected leader in 2010 arguing the party had 'to move beyond New Labour', it was no surprise that those associated with Tony Blair were the first to point the finger. After all, Peter Mandelson, one of the architects of New Labour, had warned Miliband even before he became leader that if he wanted 'to create a pre-New Labour future for the party, then he . . . will quickly find that it is an electoral cul-de-sac.'[3] With less than six months to go before polling, Blair himself predicted that Miliband's embrace of a 'traditional left-wing' agenda meant Labour would lose.[4]

Veteran New Labour hands launched a media offensive that ensured they set the tone for how many would explain the defeat. Three days after the election, former minister Alan Milburn, described Miliband's strategy as a 'hideous and ghastly experiment', which had defied 'the fundamentals of winning elections'.[5] Preeminent Blair biographer, John Rentoul, bluntly claimed 2015 'was an election that Labour could have won, and David Miliband could have won it'. For Ed had discarded what Rentoul called 'the eternal verities of the Blairite truth', something his brother would never have done.[6] According to Rentoul, a Blairite 'wants to win as broad as possible

---

[2] For an outline of the concept, Bulpitt, J. (1986) 'The Discipline of the New Democracy: Mrs Thatcher's Domestic Statecraft', *Political Studies*, **34**, 19–39.

[3] Anonymous (2010) 'Miliband Hits Back at Criticism', accessed at http://www.bbc.co.uk/news/uk-politics-11127658 on 2 January 2015.

[4] *The Economist*, 3 January 2015, 'Don't Go that Way'.

[5] *The Sunday Times*, 10 May 2015, 'Keep the Red Knives Flying Here'.

[6] Rentoul, J. (2015) 'David Miliband Could Have Won It for Labour', accessed at http://www.independent.co.uk/voices/comment/election-2015-david-miliband-could-have-won-it-for-labour-10234473.html on 10 May 2015.

a coalition of support on the centre and left to make the country fairer, whereas the non-Blairite left think you can go faster towards equality without the centre because such change will generate its own support'.[7] For Rentoul and others, keeping hold of the centre ground meant Miliband admitting Labour had contributed to the deficit by spending too much in office, and supporting much of the Cameron government's austerity measures. Instead, by opposing many of the government's cuts and attacking business, Miliband embraced a 'core vote strategy'.

Those seeking the party leadership after Miliband's resignation embraced much of this argument. According to Liz Kendall, Labour focused too much on issues of concern only to the poorest voters, failing to indicate it understood middle-class 'aspirations and ambitions'.[8] As a result, Mary Creagh argued, Labour lost 'Middle England', that body of voters Blair is credited with bringing to the party in 1997. Small business owners were especially afraid of Labour, she claimed.[9] Indeed, Yvette Cooper claimed Miliband promoted an 'anti-business, anti-growth and ultimately anti-worker' agenda.[10] Even the trade union-backed Andy Burnham claimed Labour should have admitted it had spent too much in government.[11]

Adding just 1.5% to Labour's 2010 vote share was certainly a pathetic achievement; and, thanks to the Scottish disaster, the party held 26 fewer seats than in the previous election. But was this the inevitable result of Miliband's attempt to move on from New Labour? In 1852 Karl Marx claimed: 'Men make their own history, but they do not make it as they please; they do not make it under self-selected circumstances, but under circumstances existing already, given and transmitted from the past'.[12] Political scientists have subsequently explained change through the 'structure-agency' dichotomy, one that questions how far any agent, such as a party leader, can transform the context in which they exist.[13] This

---

[7] Rentoul, J. (2013) 'What Is a Blairite?', accessed at http://blogs.independent.co.uk/2013/10/09/what-is-a-blairite/ on 3 February 2015.

[8] *The Sunday Times*, 10 May 2015, 'Blairite Liz in Race to be Labour Leader'.

[9] Chapman, J. (2015) 'Mary Creagh Launches Leadership Bid', accessed at http://www.dailymail.co.uk/news/article-3081985/Mary-Creagh-launches-Labour-leadership-bid.html#ixzz3aI1xpIfr on 14 May 2015.

[10] Dathan, M. (2015) 'Yvette Cooper's Epiphany', accessed at http://www.independent.co.uk/news/uk/politics/yvette-coopers-epiphany-ed-miliband-was-too-antibusiness-10260650.html on 19 May 2015.

[11] Gosden, E. (2015) 'Andy Burnham: Deficit Was "Too Large"', accessed at http://www.telegraph.co.uk/news/politics/labour/11610165/Andy-Burnham-Deficit-was-too-large-when-Labour-was-in-Government.html on 4 June 2015.

[12] Marx, K. (1852) The Eighteenth Brumaire of Louis Bonaparte', accessed at https://www.marxists.org/archive/marx/works/download/pdf/18th-Brumaire.pdf on 9 May 2015.

[13] Hay, C. (2002) *Political Analysis. A Critical Introduction*, Basingstoke, Palgrave, pp. 89–134.

prism is especially relevant to an explanation of the failure of Labour's 2015 campaign, which effectively began when Ed Miliband decided to stand as leader: for Miliband wanted to change how his party did politics.

Miliband believed the 2008 banking collapse had transformed politics to such an extent, if it were ever to win office again Labour had to campaign on a different platform to the one established by New Labour in 1997. But many in the party disagreed. To many MPs and officials as well as some members, the majority of whom had been schooled in 'the eternal verities of the Blairite truth', Miliband's strategy was wrong. To many of them, Miliband sought to turn it back into a 'traditional left-wing' party, one dominated by the unions and led by figures wanting to 'tax and spend' with no thought to its impact. But not only was this a grotesque distortion of the pre-Blair Labour Party, it bore little relation to what Miliband offered.

Yet, whatever was the character of the party he sought to lead, Miliband indisputably did not persuade enough voters to support it. This chapter explores how far that failure was due to his shortcomings, be they strategic or presentational, or to the 'circumstances existing already'. For it was never going to be easy for Labour to bounce back from its 2010 defeat, especially as it had been largely due to a recession for which many held the New Labour years responsible. This allowed the Coalition to blame its austerity programme on Labour mismanagement while reaping credit for any signs of recovery. Moreover, Labour was no longer the sole repository for voters alienated by the government of the day: mid-way through the Parliament, the SNP in Scotland and UKIP in England claimed the support of many who might otherwise have voted Labour in 2015. In these circumstances, any leader would have found it tricky mapping a route back to power.

2. A new leader for a new era

Even before 2010 many in the party wanted, as the Blairite James Purnell put it after resigning from Gordon Brown's Cabinet in 2009, 'to open up New Labour, reinvent it and then eventually move beyond it'.[14] Having won two landslides the party's 2005 re-election was more difficult—but Blair's departure two years later was unaccompanied by any rethinking. Moreover, even before the 2008 crisis, growth had been slowing and voters were less keen on public spending. It was, however, the banking collapse that did for New Labour, the moment at which the Conservatives resumed their traditional place as the party most trusted to manage the economy.

Defeat convinced all but the most recidivistic Blairite that a critical eye needed to be cast over the period 1997–2010. For New Labour had emerged amidst a time of economic buoyancy in which Blair claimed Labour could make Britain fairer but within the free market and without increasing taxes. If the Blair–Brown governments modestly reduced poverty and inequality, the fiscal crisis—and the system

---

[14]*Guardian*, 18 July 2009, 'James Purnell: I Lost Faith in Gordon Brown Months Ago'.

of deregulation that made it possible—threw this achievement into reverse. Britons now had to deal with austerity, job insecurity and falling real incomes—and many blamed Labour for all three. Having been forced to raise the top rate of tax to 50%, to help pay for the billions needed to bail out the banks, in 2009 Labour also lost the support of an important media ally, Rupert Murdoch, who controlled the *Sun*.

Most Labour members therefore looked on the first leadership election since 1994 as their chance to choose someone who could set a new course.[15] David Miliband was the most experienced figure in the field of five. Despite being Blair's preferred candidate he was not uncritical of the Blair legacy, even proposing a 'mansion tax' on homes valued at £2 million or more. Most, however, still saw David—for good or ill—as a creature of the New Labour establishment. The former minister for Climate Change, David's younger brother Ed, believed only he could 'decisively move the Labour Party on from the Blair–Brown era'. Sensing the mood for change in the party he stressed more than did his brother New Labour's shortcomings.[16]

While a YouGov poll suggested David was the choice of 47% of voters to Ed's 19%, Labour's electoral college thought differently: by a margin of just 1.3%, Ed won. Divided into three equal parts, in this college of MPs and MEPs, party members and trade union levy payers, David's support was concentrated amongst the first two, Ed's in the third. Yet Ed's union support was on such a scale it compensated for his minority position amongst MPs and members. This led some to claim that leaders of the largest unions had 'fixed' the contest in Ed's favour, although none produced evidence of fraud. The truth many found hard to swallow was that the party had elected someone promising to take the party in a radically different direction to the one mapped out by Blair.

How much of a change Miliband offered will be analysed below, but his narrow victory meant he was, as an advisor put it, always conscious of the 'thinness of his mandate'. Indicating his desire for conciliation, he twice asked his brother to be Shadow Chancellor. For even if Miliband had wanted to, he could not base his leadership in the unions: while their votes helped him become leader, he feared that too close an association would harm him in many voters' eyes. Only a minority of MPs were convinced supporters and most of the Shadow Cabinet supported David, as had those at Labour's London HQ, some of them being reduced to tears when they heard he'd lost.[17] Ed Miliband was consequently said to cut an isolated figure in his own party. At best the new leader could expect passive acquiescence from the Labour machine for his change of course.

---

[15] See Dorey, P. and Denham, P. (2011) '"O, brother, Where Art Thou?" The Labour Party Leadership Election of 2010', *British Politics*, **6**, 286–316; Hasan, M. and MacIntyre, D. (eds) (2011) *The Milibands and the Making of a Labour Leader*, London, Biteback, pp. 191–254.

[16] Hasan and MacIntyre, *The Milibands and the Making of a Labour Leader*, pp. 177, 181, 184.

[17] Hasan and MacIntyre, *The Milibands and the Making of a Labour Leader*, pp. 238–239.

3. A post-New Labour strategy

Miliband's victory did not end the debate over Labour's new course. If advocates of 'Blue Labour' wanted the party to drop its unquestioned embrace of the free market, members of Progress supported a modified Blairism. Miliband even initiated a policy review, although it is questionable how seriously he took that enterprise. For Miliband already knew his own mind. He sought not a 'pre-New Labour future' but a recalibration of Blair's approach, not to abandon the centre ground but to talk to it in a different way.

During the leadership campaign Miliband had praised New Labour's ability to unite lower and middle-income voters around its ability to speak to 'people's aspirations'.[18] But if Blair claimed he could help voters achieve their individual 'aspirations' in an era of affluence, Miliband believed he had to address their collective 'anxieties' in an era of insecurity. If Blair spoke for 'Middle England', Miliband aimed to represent the 'Squeezed Middle', a term mooted by John Healey while still a minister in the Brown government, and which signified that large part of the population whose living standards were predicted to remain below what they had been before the fiscal crisis for years to come.[19]

In setting his course Miliband left unresolved one vital matter from New Labour's past. Various polls suggested that while a majority considered the banks to blame for the crash at least one-third believed responsibility lay with the Blair–Brown governments. Conservatives certainly claimed their Coalition was merely clearing up the mess left by Labour, an accusation made with ever-greater vehemence in the short campaign. Labour's own research suggested this assertion resonated strongly with those whom the party needed to win back. If unclear how Labour was to blame for the deficit, many voters were confident it had mismanaged the country's finances and so could not be again trusted to run the economy.

During the first months of Miliband's leadership, arguments raged over whether the party should defend the late government's record or concede mistakes were made.[20] It was, however, unknowable if either tactic would change minds or reinforce existing views. In any case, Ed Balls, the Shadow Chancellor, did not believe Labour had anything for which to apologise, as spending levels had not been especially high. If many economists endorsed his view, leading Blairites believed Brown (but not Blair) had been culpable, although even they were divided over the issue. With his Shadow Cabinet also split, Miliband believed he

---

[18]Fabian Society (2010) *The Labour Leadership*, London, Fabian Society, p. 56.

[19]Anonymous (2010) 'John Healey's Fight for the "Squeezed Middle"', accessed at http://leftfootforward. org/2010/09/john-healeys-fight-for-the-squeezed-middle/ on 19 May 2015; The Resolution Foundation (2013) *Squeezed Britain 2013*, London, Resolution Foundation.

[20]*Guardian*, 4 June 2015, 'The Undoing of Ed Miliband'.

should leave this matter to History, confident he could concentrate voters' attention on his message for the future.

Right from the start Miliband believed, as an adviser put it, that 'taking on vested interests would be his calling card'. He cast himself as a tribune of the people, standing up to the powerful to ensure fair treatment for the 'hard-working majority'. It was this ambition that informed his support for: the curbing of energy prices; an investigation into invasions of privacy committed by News International journalists and challenging tax avoiders. Miliband outlined his new course during Labour's 2011 annual conference. Surprisingly, given his reputation, Miliband told those assembled that Margaret Thatcher had introduced necessary reforms, such as selling council houses to tenants, cutting punitive income tax rates and reforming trade union laws. More conventionally, he praised New Labour for building schools and hospitals, introducing a minimum wage and reducing child poverty. But both, he argued, had left unchanged 'the values of our economy'. This meant that even before the banking collapse, 'the grafters, the hard-working majority who do the right thing', stopped being adequately rewarded for their efforts. Their ambitions were frustrated as those at the top took what they wanted and it was this pursuit of the 'fast buck', Miliband, argued, that had caused the financial crisis.

Miliband believed the banking crisis proved Britain needed, not 'traditional left-wing' policies, but a different kind of capitalism, one that looked beyond the short-term. He wanted to promote a fairer and *therefore* more efficient economy, believing that if workers were treated better they would become more productive and contribute more effectively to an expanding economy. For inspiration, Miliband and his team looked to Germany but also the United States and President Theodore Roosevelt who broke up abusive monopolies. This was because, Miliband argued, parts of the economy no longer served consumers' interests. In announcing plans to establish an Annual Competition Audit to challenge monopolies such as was found amongst energy suppliers he even declared: 'It's Labour that is the party of competition'.[21]

If Miliband claimed that 'all parties must be pro-business today', he distinguished between business leaders such as Fred Goodwin, who ran the Royal Bank of Scotland into the ground while making millions for himself and the likes of John Rose, of Rolls Royce, a man who created wealth and jobs. Miliband said he would support those emulating Rose, entrepreneurs, he termed the 'producers' who 'train, invest, invent, sell' rather than 'predators' like Goodwin just interested in 'taking what they can'. This would be achieved through measures the modesty of which belied Miliband's radical rhetoric, including helping small businesses more

---

[21] *Independent on Sunday*, 19 January 2014, 'President Theodore Roosevelt Provides Ed Miliband with an Unlikely Role Model'.

easily access credit and giving government contracts only to firms with adequate apprenticeship schemes.

There was an unresolved timidity at the heart of Miliband's readjustment of the New Labour approach. Blair pursued an ostensibly 'preference accommodation' strategy, one that listened to what voters said they wanted and presented the appearance of giving it to them.[22] New Labour therefore did not directly challenge the public's preconceptions but, having won their support, covertly tackled core Labour issues, notably inequality. Miliband's biggest criticism of New Labour was, however, that its leaders were relatively uninterested in equality, something Blair conceded.[23] He therefore wanted equality put at the heart of Labour's message, even though according to Ipsos MORI it was an issue of concern to no more than one-sixth of voters. This meant Miliband—unlike Blair—needed to adopt a 'preference shaping' strategy, one designed to persuade voters of the issue's importance. Yet, while his 2011 speech argued that a more equal society would create a more productive economy, the imperative for equality remained an underdeveloped rhetorical theme during Miliband's leadership.

4. Mis-communicating the message

It is one thing for a party leader to have a strategy and quite another to successfully convey it to the public. His 2011 address illustrated some of Miliband's difficulties with regard to communication. The annual conference speech is one of the few times a Leader of the Opposition has more media attention than the Prime Minister. Yet, instead of being seen as outlining a vision of an economy productive and fair the meaning of his speech was subverted to such an extent some saw it as 'anti-business'.

Miliband's inept delivery did not help: that allowed his shortcomings to become the story of the speech. More fatally, Miliband did not appreciate how far journalists needed help navigating his unfamiliar 'predator/producer' distinction. In briefing the press, Labour's communications team could not give examples of which kinds of businesses were 'predators' and those that were 'producers'. Miliband's Front Bench colleagues had also not been informed, so they gave journalists inconsistent answers. Confusion abounded. Even sympathisers found it difficult to know how to interpret the speech: one even wondered if the 'predators' section was padding.[24] With the right-wing media already keen to depict him as 'Red Ed', according to

---

[22] Fielding, S. (2002) *The Labour Party. Change and Continuity in the Making of 'New' Labour*, Basingstoke, Palgrave, pp. 85–115.

[23] *Observer*, 10 May 2015, 'Blair Tells Labour: Return to the Centre Ground to Win Again'.

[24] Ferguson, M. (2011) 'Do the Public Agree with Ed After All?', accessed at http://labourlist.org/2011/10/do-the-public-agree-with-ed-after-all/ on 1 June 2015.

one journalist the speech was 'very easy pickings for the press'. Some New Labour 'spin' might have helped Miliband get his message to the public: but that was something he ostentatiously disavowed.

Miliband's team was taken aback by the media reaction so they quickly dispensed with 'predators and producers'. Ironically, a YouGov poll suggested 55% of the public agreed with Miliband's assertion that 'predators, not producers' dominated the economy. Indeed, his call for a 'responsible capitalism' was subsequently echoed—although not acknowledged—by David Cameron. This suggested Miliband had identified an important issue. But instead of expanding on his strategic message Labour retreated behind a series of 'retail offers' that exploited people's immediate sense that their standards of living were declining under austerity. The most successful of these offers was Miliband's 2013 pledge to freeze energy prices. Yet while making an impressive impact, it was not part of a sustained attempt to reshape how voters thought about the economy as a whole and left Labour vulnerable when energy prices fell. It also did nothing to address the party's poor economic record, meaning that while voters believed Labour was broadly on their side, tea and sympathy notwithstanding, it was not the best party to get the economy moving again.

Moreover, when explaining his message arguably Miliband's biggest problem was Miliband himself—or rather the 'Ed Miliband' constructed by the media. All politicians have to tackle the gap between who they are and how they are perceived, and there was some substance to this 'Miliband'. When running for leader—the moment he first came to public notice—one member of the Lobby claimed: 'he looked like a dweeb'. Miliband was certainly not the most adept public speaker and his adenoidal voice was not an asset. As further evidence of the bitter legacy of the leadership contest, it was members of David's campaign who suggested these attributes made Ed 'weird'; they were also the first to compare him with the animated character 'Wallace'.[25]

Miliband initially did not care about such seemingly superficial matters. But over time he was persuaded otherwise: by the short campaign he dressed better and his public addresses were more competently delivered. Miliband even—allegedly—had his adenoids removed. Yet, throughout his leadership the Labour leader was dogged by questions about why so many thought him 'weird' or a 'geek'. With less than 12 months before polling day, he was forced to confront the issue head-on, stating: 'If you want the politician from central casting, it's not me; it's the other guy. . . . I want to offer something different'.[26] But many voters did not want something 'different' and while claiming to be the candidate of

---

[25] Hasan and MacIntyre, *The Milibands and the Making of a Labour Leader*, p. 200.

[26] *Observer*, 26 July 2014, 'Mocking Ed Miliband's Image Would Be Bad Electoral Strategy'.

'substance' many did not know of what substance Miliband was made. For a public ignorant about policy, how a party leader looks is their guide to what the person is like. Physical attractiveness does play a part in political success: the superficial *is* the substance.[27]

An important influence on how the public regarded Miliband was the tabloid press, all but one title of which backed the Conservatives in 2010. With the *Sun*'s daily circulation halving to two million between 1997 and 2015, Miliband's advisors believed the press was less important than in the 1990s. Labour's communications team knew, however, that the press influenced what appeared on radio and television: BBC journalists, in particular, often let their peers in print dictate what they reported as 'news'.

Miliband's media problems intensified in 2011 when he supported an investigation into the phone hacking activities of News International journalists and backed the resulting Leveson Inquiry's proposals to regulate the press. Considered by a Labour HQ insider to be a 'brave and principled stand' they also saw this stance as a 'mistake'. For the return of a Labour Government now threatened Murdoch's commercial interests, as well as those other media magnates. As a result most tabloids, other than the *Daily Mirror*, repeatedly drew readers' attention to the Labour leader's 'weirdness'. Miliband's 'alien' character was subtly indicated through references to his North London, intellectual and, more slyly, Jewish origin—or more crudely by exploiting his late father's Marxism so as to imply the Labour leader 'hated Britain'. A favoured tactic was publishing photographs that made Miliband look odd, most notoriously one taken in 2014 in which he unskilfully tackled a large bacon sandwich. That particular shot was reproduced many times, on television quiz and comedy programmes as well as across the front page of the *Sun* just before polling day, replete with the headline: 'Save Our Bacon'.

Added to this mix was that Miliband became party leader by beating his older brother. Labour's own research revealed that one of the few things voters ever knew about Miliband was that he had 'stabbed his brother in the back'. In an era when politics means so little but family so much, this soap opera narrative resonated, evoking as it did the Bible's Cain and Abel. Reactions to Ed's temerity went beyond politics: the left-wing MP John Cruddas supported David largely because of the visceral 'brother thing'.[28]

As a result of this brew, Miliband—who aspired to stand up to the powerful on behalf of the people—was more like a broken reed than a tribune. He actively harmed Labour's electoral prospects such that a May 2014 ComRes poll indicated that 40% of Britons were less likely to vote Labour while Miliband remained leader.

---

[27] Berggren, N., Jordahl, H. and Poutvaara, P. (2010), 'The Looks of a Winner: Beauty and Electoral Success', *Journal of Public Economics*, **94**, 8–15.

[28] Hasan and MacIntyre, *The Milibands and the Making of a Labour Leader*, pp. 210–11.

This would not have surprised party workers across the country. According to one who fought many by-elections held after 2010, it was not unusual for voters to state: 'I'm always Labour, but'—as their preface to an attack on Miliband. The Labour candidate for Warrington South claimed the 'Ed issue never stopped coming up on the doorstep—too many people just did not see him as an alternative prime minister'.[29] According to one Midlands organiser, as 'Ed wasn't doing the business as leader' party workers stopped talking about him. Things were so bad, when a voter was reported as saying something positive about their leader, campaigners cheered. As they put it, the problem was 'intangible', the reasons given so 'flimsy': mention of Miliband's name often provoked a shrug and a sigh, no explanation considered necessary. As another Labour worker in the Midlands reported, to most people, 'he just didn't look right'.

5.   The party on the ground

One way to counteract media influence and convince people of Miliband's message was to reinvigorate party membership. During the New Labour years this had declined by 40% to below 200,000. But even before then, constituencies in Labour heartlands—especially Scotland and the north of England—were run by small bands of activists few of who made contact with voters. By 2010 the situation was as bad as it had ever been: indeed, advocates of 'Blue Labour' believed, the party's disconnection from ordinary people was an important reason for its defeat.

As part of moving on from New Labour, Miliband wanted Labour to become 'a community organisation', one that could reach out to those millions for whom party politics had become an anathema.[30] But, according to Arnie Graf, the US community activist Miliband employed to give the initiative impetus, this meant Labour transforming itself from being a top-down organisation.[31] Graf ran seminars with officials and activists to persuade them to embrace change but his reception was mixed. If the MP Tom Watson became a fan, one regional organiser claimed Graf's vision was 'not geared to a political party that needs to win an election'. To prove the effectiveness of his approach Graf focused his work in Preston but when Labour made little headway there during local elections the sceptics prevailed. With a General Election encroaching, they argued, Labour should refocus on

---

[29] Bent, N. (2015) 'Five Years on the Frontline', accessed at http://www.progressonline.org.uk/2015/05/15/five-years-on-the-frontline-and-six-tests-for-our-new-leader/ on 16 May 2015.

[30] Hasan and MacIntyre, *The Milibands and the Making of a Labour Leader*, p. 198.

[31] Graf, A. (2014) 'The Culture of Politics Has to Change', accessed at http://labourlist.org/2014/12/the-culture-of-politics-needs-to-change-from-command-and-control-to-a-culture-of-engagement/ on 2 April 2015.

conventional methods.[32] As a result, one Miliband advisor regretfully noted, Graf's was 'a road not taken.'

If Labour had to make the most of what little it had, the party actually enjoyed a good record of doing just that. Thanks to local efforts, in 2010 the party retained a number of unlikely seats, notably Birmingham Edgbaston. To promote such efforts in 2015, the party's limited resources were distributed to constituencies where they were needed most. This formed the basis for what was by all accounts a successful campaign, at least when measured in terms of voters contacted, volunteers and leaflets delivered. From Scotland to Kent candidates and organisers described 2015 as the best constituency campaign they had ever fought. According to one Midlands candidate in a marginal Conservative seat 'we had the money, we had the resources . . . in terms of the machine the party delivered'. By the time polling day approached Labour claimed its members had held over four million 'conversations' with voters.

Yet, however good was the effort in the constituencies to make sure those identified as Labour supporters turned out to vote, it was the responsibility of the national campaign to inspire people to want to vote for the party. And, many complained, *that* was where lay Labour's biggest problem.

6. The short campaign

Just as the transformation of Labour into a 'community' organisation made way for conventional electioneering, as May 2015 approached Miliband's ambitious policy review was sidelined for a vote-maximising approach. Indeed—especially after UKIP's strong performance in the May 2014 European elections—Labour became more conservative, aiming to accommodate voters' preconceptions.

It fell further back on a variety of 'retail offers' to targeted groups. These were, however, no substitute for a compelling overall case that might persuade voters from diverse backgrounds to support the party. Miliband's 2012 leader's speech had advanced such a theme, in the shape of 'One Nation Labour', although he regarded it as just a temporary rhetorical device. It nonetheless cleverly appropriated a traditional Conservative concept, one also adopted by New Labour prior to 1997 and, in a way Miliband's 2011 speech had not, allowed him to claim the centre ground at the same time as advancing his post-New Labour course while also isolating the Conservatives as the party of the privileged elite. Miliband even won media praise for his efforts. For a time everything the party said or did was branded 'One Nation'. Despite this, a September 2013 ComRes

---

[32] Sen, H. (2013) 'Why I'd Sack Arnie Graf', accessed at http://hopisen.com/2013/why-id-sack-arnie-graf/ on 4 March 2015.

survey found that only 25% of voters felt they knew what 'One Nation Labour' meant, an opinion shared by some Labour MPs. It was quietly dropped and by 2014 had all but disappeared.[33]

Lacking a persuasive theme, during the first weeks of the official campaign Labour did its best to address its main shortcomings while trying to focus voters' attention on the Conservative threat to the NHS, that being Labour's one strong point. Miliband had always believed he could overturn his off-putting image, expecting a series of televised leadership debates would allow viewers to see him as he truly was. Labour had therefore fought strongly for holding the debates along the lines of the three broadcast in 2010. The Conservatives, for the same reason, sought to avoid them and ensured Miliband would only share the stage with Cameron in just one debate—and then with five other leaders. Even so, when Miliband did appear in front of millions of viewers he was not the weird-looking geek of tabloid repute. But perceptions built over the years were too strong to be transformed in a few weeks.

Labour used its manifesto launch to establish as strongly as it might that the party could be trusted with the economy. Challenging voters' perceptions, Miliband made a virtue of the modesty of the party's spending commitments, promising that every Budget would cut the deficit until it had disappeared. Indeed, Labour's pledge to increase spending on the NHS by £2.5 billion was exceeded by the Conservatives' undertaking to raise it by £8 billion. Such was the switch-around Labour appeared to have become the more fiscally prudent of the two main parties, an impression that did the party in Scotland only harm given it was fighting the 'anti-austerity' SNP.

Despite such caution, Labour retained policies that ensured the rich paid their share in reducing the deficit. It promised to reinstate the 50p top rate of tax and abolish the 'non-dom' tax status while reviewing other tax avoidance schemes. The party's extra NHS spending was moreover to be partly paid for by a tax on domestic properties worth over £2 million. Echoing Miliband's earlier pledge to stand up for the 'Squeezed Middle', the manifesto confirmed energy bills would be frozen under a Labour Government, as would train fares, while the minimum wage would be raised to £8 an hour and the 'bedroom tax' abolished.

To counter accusations it was 'anti-business' the party launched a separate business manifesto. This restated Labour's opposition to an EU referendum due to the uncertainty it would create amongst those considering investing in Britain. The party also committed itself to building up the country's infrastructure through high quality apprenticeships and a British Investment Bank. Labour similarly promised to lower business rates for small companies. Scepticism nonetheless

---

[33] *New Statesman*, 23 September 2014, 'So Long, Slogan: Whatever Happened to One Nation?'

remained on the doorstep. As with Miliband's image, Labour needed more time to tackle ingrained doubts about its economic trustworthiness.

In any case, during the last two weeks of the campaign, Labour's damage-limitation strategy was blown off-course by the 'coalition of chaos' narrative. With opinion polls showing Labour neck-and-neck with the Conservatives, Cameron's party decided to frighten voters with the prospect of a minority Miliband government dependent on the SNP. In this way Labour's collapse in Scotland made its decisive contribution to the campaign. Exploiting unappeased concerns that Miliband was unfit to be Prime Minister and incapable of running the economy, the Conservatives claimed the SNP would force Labour to increase spending while unravelling the Union.

That which a member of Miliband's team called the Conservatives' 'Goebbels-like' demonisation of the SNP was loyally echoed in the press and translated into lead items on radio and television news.[34] This forced Miliband to answer hypothetical questions about how he would handle the SNP if he led a minority government. As a result, Labour found it hard to win airtime for its actual policies, such that officials complained to the BBC about its journalists' obsession with 'the Scottish line'. As a prominent Labour insider conceded, the party just 'didn't have a narrative strand to challenge it'.

Party workers across England reported the success of the purported SNP threat with few voters believing a 'weak' Miliband could stand up to a 'strong' Sturgeon. Even someone intending to vote Labour in an East London constituency was reported as saying: 'I'm not having England run by Jocks'. In the Midlands, the 'coalition of chaos' was said to have firmed up Conservative support, drawn UKIP supporters to Cameron's party and caused the hitherto undecided to 'break to the Tories in a big way' in the last days.

7.   An absence of statecraft

In essence, Labour lost the General Election because it was led by someone unable to convince a sufficient number of English voters he possessed the skills necessary to be Prime Minister and that his party could manage the economy.

Since 2008 Labour had trailed the Conservatives as to which party people thought best able to run the economy. That lead varied but from 2013 it grew as the economy recovered, such that by April 2015 Ipsos MORI had Cameron's party 18% ahead. When pollsters GQR asked voters why they had not supported Labour on May 7, at 40% concern about its economic competence was by far the biggest overall reason. Fatally for Labour, middle-class

---

[34] *The Sunday Times*, 10 May 2015, 'Keep the Red Knives Flying Here'.

voters and those over 55 years of age—the groups that turned out to vote in the greatest numbers—cited the issue more than the rest.[35]

The GQR survey also revealed that the third and fourth most cited motive for not voting Labour was the view that it would have been 'bossed around by the SNP' (24%) and a preference for Cameron over Miliband as Prime Minister (17%). The richest and oldest voting cohorts expressed some of the greatest concerns about Miliband's statecraft. But, even more importantly, amongst those who considered voting Labour but ultimately supported the Conservatives these reasons were respectively cited 30 and 32% of times. At 42%, the concerns such important swing voters held about Labour's economic ability were a little higher than voters overall. It was, however, their negative perception of Miliband that played a disproportionate role in determining why they rejected his party.

The Labour leader had correctly diagnosed the country's illness: the reality of declining standards of living for the many while the rich grew ever richer was empirically hard to deny. But he failed to convince the patient that he was the right doctor to administer the cure. Voters found elements of Labour's programme attractive, but Miliband's overall post-New Labour course remained counter-intuitive to most. He failed to appreciate the extent to which his modest challenge to neo-liberal orthodoxy had to be justified in clear and popularly understandable terms. For, the argument that austerity was the only solution to the deficit was something deeply ingrained in the minds of those middle-income voters whose support Labour required.[36] Too often, Miliband's attitude to communication was inconsistent and while he had improved by the short campaign, it was by then too late. Yet even had he been as skilled a communicator as the Tony Blair of legend, Miliband would have struggled, given perceptions of his party's responsibility for the deficit, and the distortions to which he was personally subject. Flawed, naïve agency conspired with an implacable, unforgiving structure to defeat him. Miliband attempted to reassure the nation that he had prime ministerial capabilities and in the first television showpiece event of the campaign declared that, 'Hell yes', he was tough enough to govern, but failed to convince.

In the absence of a broad, confident and comprehensible appeal, by 2015 Labour hid behind a series of 'retail offers'. This did it no good. For many voters, its enemies had defined what they took to be the character of Miliband's Labour; to others it remained just unclear. According to the General Secretary of Unite, Len McCluskey, one of those said to have 'fixed' Miliband's election as leader: 'Labour had no central

---

[35]Greenberg Quinlan Rosner Research (2015) 'UK Post Election Poll for the TUC', accessed at http://www.gqrr.com/uk-post-election-6 on 20 May 2015.

[36]Stanley, L. (2014) '"We're Reaping What We Sowed": Everyday Crisis Narratives and the Acquiescence to the Age of Austerity', *New Political Economy*, **19**, 895–917.

theme, defining what it stood for'.[37] Nick Bent, Labour's candidate for Warrington South had voted for David Miliband, but also felt it was 'the lack of a clear and consistent Labour narrative' that did for the party. This widely held view was best summed up by a Midlands' party worker who stated: 'If you asked people what the Conservatives stood for they could easily tell you but they would have struggled to say what Labour stood for'.

Conceding this lack of clarity, a member of Miliband's team of advisors believes the Labour leader should have made a more self-assured and earlier break with the New Labour years. Whether this was possible, and would have succeeded, given the constraints within which Miliband operated remains a moot point. But, in the absence of a credible leader articulating a coherent message, one that addressed the failures of the past and outlined a convincing programme for the future, it is no wonder many English voters preferred a Conservative Party led by a *relatively* credible leader promising *comparative* competence. In other words, Labour lost because, despite the multiplication of party choice, in what remained a two-horse race to become Prime Minister, Miliband *looked* to be the less safe choice.

---

[37] *The Guardian*, 14 May 2015, 'Labour Did Not Lose Election Because It Was Too Leftwing'.

DAVID CUTTS AND ANDREW RUSSELL*

From Coalition to Catastrophe: The Electoral Meltdown of the Liberal Democrats

On the coalition negotiations in May 2010, William Hague is reported to have told his wife, Ffion: 'I think I've just killed the Liberal Democrats.'[1] The final agreement was signed off on 20 May 2010. It seems the fate of the Liberal Democrats might have been sealed. After barely one month in coalition, the party's poll rating had fallen by 8%. Three months on and three weeks before Lord Browne's report on Higher Education and Student Finance, it had more than halved to 11%.

By the seven month anniversary of the coalition agreement, a YouGov poll in the *Sun*[2] had the Liberal Democrats languishing at 8%. It was never to recover. The party's collapse was complete. Four and half years later it polled 8%, its worst UK- wide share of the vote for 45 years. Even on election night party grandees were in denial. In reaction to the BBC/ITN/SKY exit poll suggesting that the number of Liberal Democrat MPs will be reduced from 57 to 10, Lord Ashdown retorted: 'I can tell you—that is wrong. If these exit polls are right, I'll publicly eat my hat'. The exit poll was wrong, but actually understated the Conservative march into Liberal Democrat territory. Only eight Liberal Democrats survived; the party's MPs, once described as the 'cockroaches of UK politics' by former Party President Tim Farron, proved to be far from resilient in face of a Labour on-slaught and a brutal Conservative micro-targeting blitz. The morning after the

*David Cutts, University of Bath, D.J.Cutts@bath.ac.uk; Andrew Russell, University of Manchester, andrew.russell@manchester.ac.uk

[1]Quoted in G. Parker, 'Highs and Lows of the UK's Coalition Government', *Financial Times*, 26 March 2015, accessed at http://www.ft.com/cms/s/2/45f73818-d17e-11e4-ad3a-00144feab7de.html#axzz3c6wBCIeu on 26 March 2015.

[2]*Sun*, 20 December 2010.

doi:10.1093/pa/gsv028

night before, Nick Clegg resigned as leader having taken the party's representation in Westminster backwards at two successive General Elections. The fall from the heights of Cleggmania to meltdown is the focus of this analysis, which examines whether the Liberal Democrats' position was ever salvageable? Did the Liberal Democrats compound mistakes which made matters worse? Can the party survive long-term? We assess what happened, why it happened and evaluate whether the party has a long-term future in British Politics.

1.   What happened? The collapse in facts and figures

1.1.   The impending disaster

Within six months of entering coalition with the Conservatives, there is evidence that the electorate may have already made up its mind. With poll ratings as low as 8% by the close of 2010, the Liberal Democrats had surrendered their mantle as the party of protest and were now the main focus of public anger and distrust. Over the four and half years, the party's poll rating remained static with little sign of it ever reaching the dizzy heights of double figures for a sustained period of time. By the early part of 2015, the party was threatened by the rise of the Greens. Indeed, at one point, the Liberal Democrats polled as low as 5% (YouGov, 3 March 2015) and, rather than fighting UKIP for third-party status, they were regularly battling the Greens for fourth place in Britain, while in Scotland the SNP seemed set to eclipse the Liberal Democrats.

Unsurprisingly, the party suffered at the ballot box throughout the life of the Coalition government. The erstwhile 'by-election kings' turned paupers, with lost deposits in 11 of the 19 British by-elections over the Parliament. In November 2014, the Liberal Democrats' 0.9% of the vote in Rochester and Strood was the worst in any by-election in the party's history and the lowest poll ever by a party in government. The loss of 10 MEPs at the 2014 European election was a 'new low' and followed seat losses in the devolved elections in Wales and Scotland earlier in the Parliament. Of greater importance, given its reliance on community-based grassroots politics, was the severe reduction in its local councillor base.[3] The decline was almost immediate. One year on from entering government, the party suffered heavy local election defeats losing nearly 40% of the council seats they were defending and control of nine councils. The scale of the decline in the Midlands and the northern metropolitan areas undid overnight much of the Liberal Democrats' long-term targeting efforts pre-2010 and the positioning of the party as the main competitor to Labour in its city strongholds. It also marked the party's lowest share of the vote in English local elections for three decades.

---

[3] Cutts, D. (2014) 'Local Elections as a Stepping Stone: Does Winning Council Seats Boost the Liberal Democrats' Performance in General Elections?', *Political Studies*, **62**, 361–380.

Nevertheless, the local collapse did not end there; in the 2012 local elections, the party's councillor base dropped below 3000 for the first time since the Liberal Democrats were formed, while in 2014 the party lost a further 310 council seats, 130 in London. Between the 2010 and 2015 General Elections, the local councillor base stood at just over 2200, a loss of more than 1300.

1.2.   Unpopular Clegg: from hero to villain

The 2010 campaign mantra, 'I agree with Nick', and the ensuing Cleggmania was a fading memory. The party leader's road from hero to villain was almost instantaneous. Just entering coalition government alienated most left of centre voters, but as Deputy Prime Minister, Clegg himself seemed increasingly toxic. The tuition fees issue rather than being the source of the problem became a symbol of his personal failure. It was well known that as leader he had doubted the policy in the run-up to 2010 but in that campaign the party had orchestrated public pledges signed by candidates against any increase in fees. In the coalition negotiation the party dropped the pledge, but did manage to get agreement allowing Liberal Democrats to abstain on the vote. However, with concessions for poorer students and higher education policy falling under the remit of the Department for Business Innovation and Skills—and under a Liberal Democrat Cabinet Minister Vince Cable—many Liberal Democrat MPs voted for the bill which instigated a tripling of tuition fees in England and Wales. Crucially, it was not David Cameron and the Conservatives that were blamed by those who did not like the policy but Nick Clegg and his party who were castigated and held responsible. Cast as the pantomime villain, the man who had personally highlighted the 'broken promises' of others became just like the rest—even his apology in September 2012 was lampooned rather than accepted. It seemed the public had stopped listening.

However, tuition fees were only a partial explanation for the leader's and party's lack of popularity. In May 2011, the public, by more than two to one, voted in a referendum against replacing first-past-the-post with the Alternative Vote electoral system. Even amongst stalwarts within his own party, Clegg came under attack for his 'complete failure to devise and lead an effective campaign . . . and allowing it to be positioned so that the public perception was that this was all about furthering Liberal Democrat interests.'[4] In the face of poor leadership ratings and electoral setbacks, Clegg came under mounting pressure. Prior to the 2014 European Elections, Clegg's attempts to be the man to stand up for Europe in two televised debates with the UKIP leader, Nigel Farage, backfired badly. The party suffered near wipe-out in the European Elections prompting activists to call for Clegg's

---

[4] *Daily Mail*, 'I'm Sorry to Report the Political Death of My Disastrous Leader, Nick Clegg', accessed at http://www.dailymail.co.uk/debate/article-2638398/Im-sorry-report-political-death-disastrous-leader-Nick-Clegg-A-damning-critique-Deputy-PM-DES-WILSON-founder-Lib-Dems.html on 25 May 2014.

resignation. Lord Oakeshott, a former Treasury spokesman for the party, resigned after commissioning and publicising four constituency polls, including one in Clegg's Sheffield Hallam seat, in order to suggest that the party would do better without Clegg as leader. If this was a coup designed to replace Clegg with Vince Cable it failed spectacularly but Oakeshott did not go quietly. Under Clegg, the party had become a 'split-the-difference centre party, with no roots, no principles and no values'[5] rather than a 'radical, progressive party', he argued, and reiterated his central claim that 'we must change the leader to give Liberal Democrat MPs their best chance to win in 2015'.[6] Oakeshott was ostracised within the party and Clegg continued to lead the party into the election.

Once in government, Nick Clegg's approval ratings as party leader regularly trailed his competitors. Throughout the Parliament, Clegg's standing was for the most part adrift from the other leaders (see Figure 5.1). For the Liberal Democrats this was unfamiliar territory[7] and posed difficult questions. Given the party's low social and partisan base, placing itself as the party of protest and stressing the virtues of its leader when in opposition proved to be relatively effective in enhancing the party's credibility as an electoral force worth voting for. With both options largely redundant in 2015, the party turned once again to its safety net of the local, in order: to focus on the local popularity of incumbents; to work hard in constituencies with a strong local platform; and to intensify local party activism. Many in the party hoped that these local factors that would save the Liberal Democrats from disaster in 2015. In truth it was the party's only hope.

1.3. Did they/we see it coming or not?

In the aftermath of the election result, Ryan Coetzee (Liberal Democrat Chief Election Strategist) stated that: 'The moment "316" flashed on to the TV screens at Lib Dem party headquarters I knew election night was going to be bad.'[8] Given

---

[5] 'Clegg—A Very Botched Coup', accessed at http://www.bbc.co.uk/news/uk-politics-27611002 on 28 May 2014.

[6] 'Clegg—A Very Botched Coup', accessed at http://www.bbc.co.uk/news/uk-politics-27611002 on 28 May 2014.

[7] Russell, A. and Fieldhouse, E. (2005) *Neither Left nor Right? The Liberal Democrats and the Electorate*, Manchester, Manchester University Press; Cutts, D. Fieldhouse, E. and Russell, A. (2010) 'The Campaign That Changed Everything and Still Didn't Matter? The Liberal Democrat Campaign and Performance'. In Geddes, A and Tonge, J. (eds) *Britain Votes 2010*, Oxford, Oxford University Press, pp. 107–124.

[8] *The Guardian*, 'The Liberal Democrats Must Reunite, Rebuild or Remain in Opposition', accessed at http://www.theguardian.com/commentisfree/2015/may/22/liberal-democrats-opposition-labour-government on 22 May 2015.

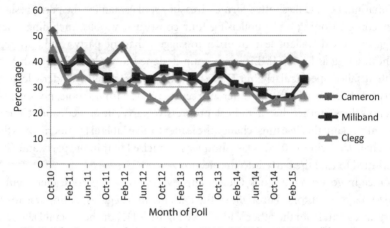

Figure 5.1 Satisfaction ratings for party leaders, 2010–2015 (Ipsos MORI polls)

persistently low opinion poll ratings, poor performances at the ballot box and the unpopularity of Clegg, it seems in hindsight unfathomable why the result was so unexpected. Two schools of thought emerged during the course of the Parliament regarding the fate of the Liberal Democrats.

The first, using British Election Survey (BES) data, provided strong evidence that the Liberal Democrats would lose most of its support in seats where they started from a strong position and lose least in their weaker seats—in other words mirroring changes in other elections over the cycle where their decline in support had been broadly proportional to prior strength.[9] It cautioned that the Liberal Democrats faced the possibility of being wiped out, although even it conceded that party incumbency was likely to play a factor and could dilute some haemorrhage of Liberal Democrat support. During the election campaign, further evidence of a Liberal Democrat collapse also fitted this narrative. A ComRes/ITV news poll in 14 Liberal Democrat strongholds in the South West of England found a 13% swing from the Liberal Democrats to the Conservatives. The key conclusion: under uniform swing the party would lose all its seats in the South West.

The second school of thought rubbished the prospect of uniform swing against the Liberal Democrats in party held seats where the sitting MP sought another term in office. It stressed: the importance of the incumbent candidate and his or her ability to build a personal vote (after all, there was evidence that incumbency

---

[9]The British Election Study (BES), 'What the BES Suggests About Constituency Variation in Party Performance', accessed at http://www.britishelectionstudy.com/bes-resources/what-the-bes-suggests-about-constituency-variation-in-party-performance-by-stephen-fisher-university-of-oxford/#.VXCuX MZN05Q on 7 December 2014.

bonuses were greater for the Liberal Democrats than for other parties);[10] the local platform in sustaining party activity over the non-regulatory campaign period; and the effectiveness of the local ground campaign. Where these factors occur in unison it was argued, the Liberal Democrats would buck the national swing against them and hold on to far more seats than expected. Proponents pointed to evidence from previous elections but also to two other indicators.

First, there was the Eastleigh by-election in February 2013, where ironically the incumbent Chris Huhne resigned, and the new Liberal Democrat candidate Mike Thornton retained the seat, fighting off a determined threat from UKIP and the Conservatives. The result, the Liberal Democrats' only by-election win under Nick Clegg's leadership, fuelled hope that the party could fight an incumbency election and survive. Notwithstanding such optimism, the result actually told a different story. Despite throwing the 'kitchen sink' at the seat, the Liberal Democrats scraped home by just over 1700 votes. They polled 32% of the constituency vote and were undoubtedly helped by a split opposition. The 14.4% drop in vote share mirrored the national poll rating fall since 2010.

Second, for the first time during the electoral cycle, there was constituency polling. Even though Lord Ashcroft's constituency polls were only snapshots at a particular point in time, the polls themselves were followed with much interest. Furthermore, they had a special relevance for the Liberal Democrats. Lord Ashcroft asked a two-stage question; first a standard voting intention question and then one asking respondents to think about their specific constituency (alternative vote intention question). The latter was designed to capture any personal vote and local constituency factors from which Liberal Democrat MPs seeking re-election were perceived to benefit. Lord Ashcroft found that the difference between the two questions was indeed greatest in Liberal Democrat held seats. The findings also revealed just how much the Liberal Democrats performance varied by constituency. In some seats—Eastbourne, Sutton and Cheam, Thornbury and Yate, Carshalton and Wallington and Eastleigh—the party seemed to bucking the national trend, while elsewhere—Chippenham, Taunton Deane, Berwick upon Tweed and Bristol West—it was not. Lord Ashcroft polled 39 of the 46 Liberal Democrat held seats in England and Wales. With 11 of the seats outside the margin of error—and predicted to be held—and eight seats too close to call but with the Liberal Democrats narrowly ahead, Lord Ashcroft's constituency polls gave credence to the party's claims that the Liberal Democrats could retain around half of their seats. This was backed up by BES evidence which found support for the Liberal Democrats was 10 percentage points higher when respondents were asked the second Ashcroft question—and with the Liberal Democrats' own internal polling suggesting that some seats were

---

[10] Hallam Smith, T. (2013) 'Are You Sitting Comfortably? Estimating Incumbency Advantage in the UK 1983–2010', *Electoral Studies*, **32**, 167–173.

even closer than Lord Ashcroft was indicating (Hornsey and Wood Green; East Dunbartonshire) the narrative of the second school of thought reigned supreme.

2.   The electoral outcome

The Liberal Democrats entered the 2015 General Election with 57 seats and on the basis of the 2010 General Election results were second in 243 seats: 167 to the Conservatives and 76 to Labour. Given the low poll ratings, the Liberal Democrats knew that they faced a difficult fight to hold on to all their seats and were prepared for some losses. However, the party felt that the personal standing of its local MPs would see them defy any possible meltdown. It therefore adopted a strongly defensive targeting strategy with resources concentrated in incumbent seats, primarily those that had sitting MPs and where the local party had remained active for a sustained period during the electoral cycle. The performance of the local party in second-order elections was also a consideration with resources switched away from the seats if they had experienced a catastrophic drop in their local representation. As a consequence, a number of seats held by the Liberal Democrats, particularly those where the current MP had stood down and/or only required a small swing to the main challenger, were not the subject of major defensive operations, e.g. Brent Central, Norwich South, Redcar, Dorset Mid and Poole North. Even though the party ran an 'incumbency election' targeting strategy, it was hopeful of pulling off a possible surprise in a small number of seats it didn't hold, with Watford, Montgomeryshire and Maidstone and the Weald regarded as the three with the most potential. As polling day neared, rumours began to surface in a number of seats that support was ebbing away. Publicly at least the party was defiant—'we will do a lot better than people think' said Clegg, just 24 hours before election day.

2.1.   The national and regional breakdown

The final result makes for grim reading. The Liberal Democrats retained only 8 of their 57 seats; 6 of the 46 held in England—Carshalton and Wallington, Leeds North West, Norfolk North, Sheffield Hallam, Southport and Westmorland and Lonsdale—one of the three held in Wales—Ceredigion—and one of the 11 seats held in Scotland—Orkney and Shetland. The cull saw many of the Liberal Democrats' senior figures lose their seats, including the former Chief Secretary to the Treasury, Danny Alexander, Business Secretary Vince Cable, Energy and Climate Change Minister Ed Davey, Pensions Minister Steve Webb and the former party leader Charles Kennedy. Unsurprisingly, this was the party's worst seat haul since 1970. Nationally, the party polled 7.9% of the total vote, a drop in excess of 15% (see Table 5.1). In terms of votes cast, the Liberal Democrats lost just over 4.4 million votes since

Table 5.1 2015 Liberal Democrat performance across the UK and by country

Country	Seats	Net loss	2015 Votes	Vote share (%)	Net change (%)
UK	8	−49	2,415,862	7.9	−15.2
England	6	−37	2,098,404	8.2	−16.0
Scotland	1	−10	219,675	7.5	−11.3
Wales	1	−2	97,783	6.5	−13.6

2010. The party's share of the vote fell most in England and least in Scotland. In Wales, the drop in Liberal Democrat vote share was less than the national swing mainly because of floor effects. In simple terms, the party's vote across Wales is concentrated in particular constituencies and in many others it was arithmetically not possible to drop by the national swing. In the United Kingdom as a whole, 335 Liberal Democrat candidates lost their deposit as their vote collapsed across the board.

The scale of the meltdown in England is further evident across the different regions (see Table 5.2). In the South West, their traditional heartland, the party lost all 15 of its parliamentary seats and saw its vote drop by just under 20%. It did not fare much better elsewhere. In the North East, the Liberal Democrat vote fell by more than 17% with the loss of two seats and a similar sizeable drop in support occurred in the South East where the party lost all four of its sitting MPs. It performed marginally better in London than elsewhere but still haemorrhaged seats to both the Conservatives and Labour.

2.2. Did incumbency matter?

Table 5.3 examines the Liberal Democrats' 2015 performance by seat type. The first thing to note is that the party did not perform considerably better in its traditional heartland seats (those seats that the party held both in 1992 and 2010) than breakthrough or post-1997 seats. Indeed, the decline in vote share is pretty similar across both these seat types. Of greater interest is the party's performance in incumbent seats, and where a sitting MP stood for re-election. In the 57 incumbent seats, the Liberal Democrats' vote share dropped by 15.7%, marginally above the national mean change in its vote share since 2010. There was a clear difference in performance according to whether the sitting MP stood for election and where the incumbent had retired. Where an incumbent Liberal Democrat stood for re-election, their vote share, on average, fell by 14.1% compared with 21.7% in those seats where the sitting MPs had stepped down. In simple terms, there clearly was an incumbent effect; the Liberal Democrats did better in those incumbent seats where incumbent candidates were seeking re-election than where they were not. However, generally

Table 5.2 2015 Liberal Democrat performance by region

Region	Mean 2015, % LD, vote	Mean 2010, % LD, vote	Mean change, ± 10–15	Seats 2015	Seats 2010	Change 10–15
East Midlands	5.5%	20.8%	−15.3%	0	0	0
Eastern	8.0%	24.1%	−16.1%	1	4	−3
London	7.3%	22.1%	−14.8%	1	7	−6
North East	6.4%	23.6%	−17.2%	0	2	−2
North West	6.4%	21.6%	−15.2%	2	6	−4
South East	9.4%	26.2%	−16.8%	0	4	−4
South West	15.0%	34.7%	−19.7%	0	15	−15
West Midlands	5.3%	20.5%	−15.2%	0	2	−2
Yorkshire and The Humber	6.9%	22.9%	−16.0%	2	3	−1

Table 5.3 2015 Liberal Democrat performance by historical base, incumbency, first time incumbency and new candidates

Seats	Mean 2015, % LD, vote	Mean 2010, % LD, vote	Mean change ± 10–15
Heartland Seats (15)	31.7%	47.0%	−15.3%
Breakthrough Seats (42)	29.7%	45.6%	−15.9%
LD Incumbent Seats (57)	30.2%	46.0%	−15.7%
LD Incumbent Candidates (45)	31.8%	45.9%	−14.1%
LD New Candidates (12)	24.4%	46.1%	−21.7%
LD FT Incumbents (9)	29.4%	39.3%	−9.8%
LD Held (Scotland Only) (11)	31.4%	42.5%	−11.1%
LD-Con Seats (Eng & Wales) (33)	31.7%	48.7%	−17.0%
LD-Lab Seats (Eng & Wales) (12)	24.7%	41.3%	−16.6%
LD Non-Held Seats (573)	5.6%	20.9%	−15.2%

Note: Ceredigion was a LD-Nat seat. All LD-Con/LD-Lab seats are based on 2010 results (excludes Eastleigh by-election). Mike Thornton in Eastleigh is classified as a new candidate.

speaking, any incumbency advantage—just over 1% when compared with the national drop in vote share—was in the same ball park as the main parties would be expected to achieve in similar circumstances. The expectation that Liberal Democrat incumbent candidates would be immune from any national swing against them because of their personal standing in the area, hard work and local activism proved to be misconceived and simply wrong. Interestingly though, and confirming previous evidence,[11] first time Liberal Democrat incumbents (i.e. those who only

---

[11]Cutts, D. (2012) 'Yet Another False Dawn? An Examination of the Liberal Democrats' Performance in the 2010 General Election', *British Journal of Politics and International Relations*, **14**, 96–114.

won the seat in 2010) did buck the trend given that their performance was slightly less disastrous than longstanding incumbents albeit they were starting from a lower base of support. In Scotland the party did better than anywhere else in the UK; in the face of the SNP tidal wave, the Liberal Democrats always knew they would be up against it and during the campaign there was a strong push in a number of Scottish seats—Dunbartonshire East, Edinburgh West, Caithness, Sutherland and Easter Ross—to position themselves as the main opposition to the SNP. As a consequence, in a number of these seats their vote held up, albeit this was insufficient to secure them any successes bar Orkney and Shetland.

Turning to England and Wales, of the 46 seats that the Liberal Democrats held going into the election, the Conservatives were the main challengers in 33 and Labour in 12. Plaid Cymru was the main threat to the Liberal Democrats in Ceredigion. As expected, the Liberal Democrats haemorrhaged votes to Labour in the 12 Liberal Democrat–Labour battlegrounds. The Liberal Democrat vote collapsed by around 17% in these seats, while the mean increase from 2010 in the Labour vote was 12.3%. Apart from Cambridge, where incumbent Julian Huppert narrowly lost by 599 votes, the other Liberal Democrats (both sitting MPs and new candidates) were comfortably beaten. However, it was in the Liberal Democrat–Conservative battlegrounds where the real damage was done. With the Conservatives actively seeking a majority, and requiring 23 further seats to achieve this goal, Conservative election strategists Lynton Crosby and Jim Messina openly targeted these Liberal Democrat key seats. A key part of this plan was the 'decapitation strategy' in the South West, where 14 Liberal Democrat seats were up for grabs. Conservative strategists micro-targeted potential switchers from the Liberal Democrats to the Conservatives, ruthlessly contacting them through the combination of centralised targeting messages, at the cost of considerable amounts of money over a sustained period of time, and personal contact from their local team on the ground.

The Conservatives' strategy proved to be highly effective not only in the South West but elsewhere in these battleground seats. For the Liberal Democrats, the key was to keep its coalition of left of centre voters, soft Conservatives and traditional Liberal voters together in order to fight off any opposition advance. The results show that the Liberal Democrats indeed suffered from a tactical unwind of its left of centre vote in these seats. The mean combined Labour and Green vote increased by nearly 8%, as did the vote for UKIP. The latter reflects socially conservative traditional Labour voters in regions such as the South West who left Labour during the Blair–Brown era and saw the Liberal Democrats in 2010 as a vehicle for protest but five years later now regarded their natural home as UKIP. Crucially in these battleground seats, the Liberal Democrats faced a pincer effect, with those on the left leaving in droves and Liberal Democrat–Conservative waverers jumping ship to support the Conservatives. On average, the Conservatives increased their share of the vote in these 33 seats by 2.3%. Closer inspection of the results also reveals that in all six English seats the Liberal Democrats held, the Conservative vote actually fell. In the 27 seats they lost, only three seats—Eastbourne −1.1%, Sutton and Cheam −0.9% and St Ives −0.7%—saw a drop in support for the Conservatives. The Liberal Democrats won seats in England where the opposition vote split more evenly and the Conservative vote failed to rise. Given the large swings against the Liberal Democrats in Southport and Carshalton and Wallington, any increase in the Conservative vote would have resulted in losses there too. Put simply, it could have been even worse.

Finally the Liberal Democrats performance in their incumbent seats varied considerably. There were huge swings against the party in some seats—18.7% swing to Labour in Bristol West and 16.1% to the Conservatives in Yeovil—but in others it was much smaller—4% and 4.4% to the Conservatives in Eastbourne and St Ives, respectively. Generally speaking though, the Liberal Democrats lost more support in seats where they started from a strong base. For instance, in the 155 seats where the Liberal Democrats polled less in 2010 than the national swing against them in 2015, it was arithmetically impossible for them to lose any more support. So those seats where the party polled 15.5% or less in 2010 saw a drop of 10.2% in Liberal Democrat support. In the 340 seats where the party polled between 15.5 and 30% five years previously, their vote fell by 15.8%. In those 136 seats where the Liberal Democrat vote was more than 30% in 2010, the party's share of the vote, declined by an average of 19.9%.

3.   Causes and consequences

As has already been alluded to, the collapse in the Liberal Democrat vote took hold almost immediately after entering coalition. After the first six months, the party's poll rating then remained low and fairly stable throughout the 2010–2015 Parliament. Those voters from the centre-left of the political spectrum who had supported the Liberal Democrats, often tactically, to keep the Conservatives out were left angry and betrayed. In the first 12 months, the Liberal Democrats' vocal support for Conservative austerity measures and their high profile u-turns on policy, most prominently on student finance and backing increases in VAT, sealed their fate amongst this group of the electorate. Initially, this seemed salvageable. The party hierarchy's decision to have Liberal Democrats in different portfolios across government was a grave error of judgement. The party failed to learn the lessons from elsewhere that in coalition 'the little party always gets smashed'.[12]

In fact, the little party does not need to get smashed. The Liberal Democrats themselves fared well from being the junior partner with Labour in the Scottish

---

[12] *New Statesman*, 'What Merkel Told Cameron about Coalitions', 23 January 2013.

government for two terms in Holyrood, while an even bigger example of the junior coalition partner thriving in British politics has seemingly been forgotten by many. All serious accounts of the success of Labour in the landslide victory of the 1945 Election put Labour's record in government as the junior partner in the war-time coalition as central to the party's success. Labour held the office of Deputy Prime Minister (Attlee), the Home Office and Minister of Labour and used their record in government to successfully convince a large section of the British public that the party could be trusted with their plans to rebuild the UK economy after the War and institute the modern welfare state based on the workings of Keynes and Beveridge.[13]

To offset this, the Liberal Democrats might have negotiated complete control of departments such as Education and the Environment to enhance issue ownership.[14] As in countries like New Zealand, they could have also occupied ministerial positions outside cabinet allowing them to develop both a distinctive policy platform but also a separate voice from the Conservatives on policies over which they would have no influence. Instead, the party 'put the interests of the nation first', arguing that strong government was necessary to turn Britain's economic fortunes around. They also gambled that they would reap the rewards along with the Conservatives for their role in the economic recovery; but even here, a relatively incoherent presentation of the coalition undermined and weakened their attempts to take credit for government policies. In truth, the Liberal Democrats coalition strategy spectacularly misfired becoming increasingly diluted and damaged by errors of judgement and repeated compounding errors.

3.1. Presentation of the coalition

The Liberal Democrats' presentation of the coalition and their role in it became more confused as the Parliament proceeded. Unsurprisingly voters soon became sceptical of the party's actual role. By April 2011, a YouGov poll for the *Sunday Times* found that 74% of ex-Liberal Democrat supporters felt that the party had little or no influence on decisions taken in government. Of course, Clegg and his fellow Liberal Democrat ministers were hamstrung by the coalition deal. They needed to walk the tightrope as both defender and critic of coalition policies and to work as colleagues but remain bitter rivals to the Conservatives. This proved increasingly unsustainable over the long term.

Early on the Liberal Democrats were overly supportive, perhaps reflecting their perceived gains from the coalition agreement: commitment for a referendum on

---

[13] Hennessey, P. (1992) *Never Again Britain 1945–51*, London, Penguin.

[14] Russell, A. (2010) 'Inclusion, Exclusion or Obscurity? The 2010 General Election and the Implications of the Con–Lib Coalition for Third-Party Politics in Britain', *British Politics*, **5**, 506–524.

changing the voting system; House of Lords reform; pupil premium; and increasing the tax threshold. Vince Cable's attack on Cameron's immigration remarks in April 2011 was the sign of things to come. After losing the Alternative Vote referendum, the Liberal Democrats then became embroiled in row with the Conservatives over a wholly or partially elected House of Lords, accusing its coalition partners of 'not honouring their commitment . . . and breaking the coalition agreement'. The compounding effect of poor poll ratings and increasingly bad election results ratcheted up the pressure on Clegg and party ministers. By September 2013, the tone had become increasingly more negative and there were clear signs that the party was attempting to differentiate itself from the Conservatives and end its pro-coalition stance. First, Cable attacked Conservative policies on immigration, the economy and Europe, accusing their coalition partners of, in reference to the nasty party, 'reverting to type'. Then Clegg claimed that the Liberal Democrats had been the moderating influence in coalition, blocking policies from inheritance tax cuts for millionaires to scrapping housing benefit for young people. However, it was on the economy where the tone became increasingly adversarial. In January 2014, Clegg attacked Conservative plans for £12 billion more welfare cuts, accusing his coalition partners of being chameleons on tax priorities and stating that only the Liberal Democrats could tackle the deficit fairly. The increasingly negative tone on the economy sent out a confused picture to the electorate. The party that had supported austerity measures was now distancing itself from the Conservatives and risked not gaining the full credit for its role just when the coalition's economic policies were bearing fruit. This culminated in Danny Alexander's alternative Liberal Democrat 'Yellow budget' less than two months before polling day, which clearly laid out these differences and seems to have misfired.

There were a number of consequences of the Liberal Democrats' incoherent presentation of the coalition and their role in it. First, despite the longstanding narrative that the Liberal Democrats were blamed for the coalition failures and not credited for the successes, the evidence suggests that this was far from the truth. Survey evidence from Wave 4 of the BES suggests that on issues ranging from the economy to education, only 20% ascribed any credit or blame to the Liberal Democrats. The majority either blamed the Conservatives for the coalition's failures—on the NHS—or credited it for its successes—the economy. Put simply, the Liberal Democrats' role for most of the electorate was largely irrelevant.

Second, alongside issues of trust and competence following the broken promises on tuition fees, the backtracking on VAT and support for austerity measures, there was also a clear sense that the electorate did not know what the party stood for. In October 2014, PR firm Edelman found that only 25% voters correctly linked the Liberal Democrats' key policies with the party. For instance, 35% of voters thought that the policy of increasing the tax threshold to £12,500 was a Conservative policy, 21% a Labour initiative, with only 19% correctly associating it with the

Liberal Democrats.[15] More fundamentally, the majority of voters felt that the Liberal Democrats did not own any of the key issues and lacked policy direction. From the economy to schools, only around a quarter of those polled by the BES felt that these were Liberal Democrat priorities. When compared against the other parties, it is was clear that many of the issues that the Liberal Democrats pursued—pupil premium, raising the tax threshold etc.—despite support from the public were either incorrectly associated with the Conservatives, or simply lacked salience amongst the electorate in the heat of a General Election.

Third, the decision to portray the party as a moderating force in government simply played into the Conservatives' hands. The Conservative parliamentary party, some of whom had been highly critical of Cameron's modernising agenda, largely backed the leadership as the Prime Minister successfully deflected any blame for moderate positions on both domestic and foreign policy on the interference of the Liberal Democrats. Any prospect of the Conservative parliamentary party splintering on controversial issues such as Europe was allayed by the Liberal Democrats seeking to take credit for blocking and amending coalition policy.

3.2.   *The folly of equidistance*

Part of the Liberal Democrats' appeal since 1992 had been their ability to develop a distinctive political niche in the electoral market, in order to simultaneously maximise their support in different geographical areas and from a range of social groups, whilst at the same time retaining their ideological integrity.[16] Rather than purely fighting over the competitive centre ground, the party has sought to maintain a radical edge with distinctive policies to sell to the electorate. Central to its success post 1992 was its abandonment of equidistance. After spending much of the last 20 years or so convincing the electorate that they were not merely a half-way house between Labour and the Conservatives and selling themselves as a distinctive political voice, the Liberal Democrats both in government and in the run-up to polling day reverted back to the policy. Despite warnings from some that the Liberal Democrats risked being in a political 'no-man's land',[17] the party persisted in defining themselves at the midpoint between the Conservatives and Labour. Campaign slogans such as the Liberal Democrats will 'act as the heart of a Conservative led government and the head of a Labour one' seemed to confirm that the party had lost its radical, distinctive edge. Of course, traditional

---

[15] *Huffington Post*, 'Barely Anyone Knows What the Liberal Democrats' Policies Are', 13 October 2014.

[16] Russell, A. and Fieldhouse, E. (2005) *Neither Left nor Right? The Liberal Democrats and the Electorate*, Manchester, Manchester University Press.

[17] *The Independent*, 'Former Nick Clegg ally Jeremy Browne blasts "insipid" Liberal Democrats leader', 12 February 2015.

proximity models of voting suggest that if left and right parties converge to the middle ground then the third party would get their vote squeezed and that any third-party squeeze is far more likely in a majoritarian system. So electorally, the strategy was always fraught with danger, but politically the equidistant stance risked blurring the party's policy distinctiveness as the party defined itself in terms of how others behaved, something which seems to be evident from the BES data highlighted above.

The equidistance stance also inadvertently proved to be a gift for the Conservatives. With the SNP on the march in Scotland, the prospect of a Labour minority government propped up by the SNP was ruthlessly exploited by the Conservatives during the campaign. Not only did the Conservatives warn of a possible coalition of chaos involving Labour the SNP and the Liberal Democrats, it also stressed the virtue of decisive leadership and government which it said could only be achieved with a majority Conservative Government. This narrative was much easier to sell given the Liberal Democrats' increasingly adversarial position, as the party of protest in government during their later years in coalition. Rather than a force to stop unadulterated conservatism, the Liberal Democrats' message of moderation and adopting the middle position was painted as a recipe for chaos and uncertainty. Fewer Conservative MPs, the narrative went, risked the possibility of the SNP holding Britain to ransom.

3.3.   The campaign

It remains debatable whether the campaign could have made a significant difference to the Liberal Democrat performance in the 2015 General Election given their evident collapse around six months after signing the coalition agreement. Nonetheless, it is certainly possible that some seats could have been saved and the party could be rebuilding from a stronger base than it currently has. As we have shown, entering coalition led to serious errors of judgement which only amplified the problem. The loss of trust and competence, the failings of leadership, the focus on issues which lacked salience with voters, the incoherent presentation of the party's role in the coalition and the party's attempts to rectify the problems by adopting the failed equidistance stance of the early 1990s all contributed to the party's woeful performance in 2015. Mistakes made during the campaign added to this.

The SNP rout of Labour in a post-referendum Scotland was hardly a shock. The problems for Labour and the possible influence of the SNP in a Labour-led Westminster administration was the talk of the media in the run-up to the election campaign. Yet the Liberal Democrats dithered on the issue, believing that it would not affect them. The party resolutely stuck to its equidistance stance when clarity over their position from the outset would have lanced the boil. As a consequence, instead of placing themselves in a position to manage the issue they were forced to react to events. With the Conservatives now actively using the Labour-SNP threat as a wedge to split its opponent's (including the Liberal Democrats') voters, the Liberal Democrats decided to 'punch back' through warnings of a right-wing coalition, which it termed BluKip. This proved to be another strategic error. First, the prospects of such a coalition were highly unlikely with UKIP at best predicted to pick up only a handful of seats. Second, it reinforced the Conservative message that the only way to get decisive government and eliminate the risk of coalitions driven by the right or left was to vote Conservative. For those Liberal Democrat–Conservative waverers in Liberal Democrat battleground seats, the fear of both those eventualities made the decision much easier, to the detriment of many sitting Liberal Democrat MPs.

Strategically, the party should have foreseen this course of events. It was not as if the Scottish problem emerged after the seven-strong party leaders' debate. Perhaps the party was hamstrung by internal difficulties. Ruling out a coalition with the Conservatives could have persuaded left of centre voters to swing back to the Liberal Democrats, particularly in the constituency face-offs with the Conservatives. However, this was unlikely given the entrenched levels of distrust with the party within this cohort. Put simply, this section of the 2010 Liberal Democrat vote had moved on, whatever the position of the party.

A more plausible option was to rule out any coalition with Labour. This would have weakened the Conservatives' argument in Liberal Democrat–Conservative battlegrounds and may have persuaded centre-right waverers to stay with the Liberal Democrats and thus secured a number of seats but might have been difficult to sell given the Liberal Democrats' disassociation from the Conservatives in the latter years of the coalition. Furthermore it is not clear that it would have been popular with the party rank and file, begging the question whether this was ruled out for fears of splitting the party? It is possible. If this was the case, one could plausibly assume that party strategists were placed in a no-win situation: hold the middle ground and face becoming a party with a small rump of MPs; or have slightly more MPs but risk opening up wounds that could lead to a split down 'Orange book' lines.

Aside from errors on political message, it was always questionable whether the party could run the kind of intensive incumbency election campaign across 50 seats. In an era where central funding is increasingly influencing the intensity of party campaigns, the Liberal Democrats were ill advised to spread scarce resources so evenly. Given the disastrous election results throughout the electoral cycle, exceptionally low poll ratings and an extremely well-funded Conservative electoral machine, the party's targeting plans needed to be far more ruthless than it was. In truth, the party was fighting on three fronts—against Labour, the Conservatives and the SNP—which in reality was always going to be a difficult balancing act to pull off. Moreover, there is anecdotal evidence that on the ground the level of activism had varied considerably both between and within safe seats. The sporadic nature of local activism during the electoral cycle undoubtedly reflected the losses to its councillor base but low morale amongst its remaining activists was also a factor. In the face of crushing local election, by-election and European election defeats, it became increasingly difficult to motivate people to work the ground and show the flag. This also had another important consequence. Without the continued activism, the base of support in these key seats dropped making it much more difficult to persuade and retain voters in the run-up to and at election time. Whether this made a difference to the result in some seats is difficult to tell, but it certainly did not help in extremely close contests.

4. Conclusion: where does the party go now?

The Liberal Democrats now find themselves at a political crossroads. They are back to the levels of the 1970s and face a huge rebuilding process to restore public trust, party competence and credibility. They face a real battle to re-establish themselves as a political force in a crowded market, something which conceivably could take decades to achieve. As a political party, they need to re-discover their purpose and niche: their radical distinctiveness and cause, and a longstanding appeal to a wider audience than just their core supporters. But the scale of this task is vast. On the basis of no redistricting from now until 2020—which is highly unlikely and could be detrimental to the Liberal Democrats—the party is second in only 62 seats. It is less than 5% behind the incumbent in only seven of these seats and less than 10% behind in a further nine. They also face a battle in Labour strongholds where UKIP has replaced them in many of these seats as the best placed to unseat Labour incumbents. Meanwhile in Conservative safe seats they have fallen down the pecking order with both UKIP and Labour sharing second place hauls. At the local level, their councillor base has been seriously weakened following further losses on election day.

Restoring credibility is likely to come from the ground upwards with the party initially focusing on its grassroots to build momentum. Nevertheless, numerous questions remain here. What the 2015 General Election illustrated was the weakness of the Liberal Democrats' social and partisan base. Building support in an area around the person is based on quicksand, given previous evidence that it ebbs away when the incumbent retires and, from 2015, that it fails as a safety net when nationally the party is in trouble. Moreover, the party's comparative advantage in terms of campaign activism, targeting and party tactics have gone with other parties copying what works and then taking it to another level. The whole essence of community level politics and how the party operates as a grassroots organisation should be up for debate and serious questions about whether in electoral terms it really works and how it can work against powerful central–local party machines should now form an important part of any internal assessment.

Over the coming years, the party could face a rocky ride. Yet record increases in party membership in the immediate aftermath of the election are positive, signalling that the party retains goodwill and a purpose for many in British politics. This remains though a critical point in the party's history. A failure to learn the lessons of this catastrophic defeat could result in the Liberal Democrats' slow death and ultimately electoral obscurity.

JAMES MITCHELL*

Sea Change in Scotland

1. Background

The 2010 General Election saw a 5% swing from Labour to Conservative, yet Scotland recorded a swing in the opposite direction. The assumption was that this was a 'favourite son' effect, with Scots supporting Gordon Brown and his party. Labour had won another emphatic victory with a highly efficient 42% share of the vote translated into 41 seats, almost 70% of Scotland's 59 constituencies. By-election gains for the Liberal Democrats and SNP during the previous Parliament were easily won back by Labour. Two Edinburgh Labour MPs looked vulnerable to a Liberal Democrat challenge, but the rapid decline in Liberal Democrat support after 2010 made these seats look much less vulnerable. The most marginal seat was Edinburgh South—the only seat Labour was to hold in 2015. The next two most marginal seats were held by the SNP (Dundee East) and the Liberal Democrats (Dunbartonshire East) with Labour the apparent challenger. Scotland's sole Tory MP looked vulnerable to a Labour challenge. The Electoral Reform Society was not alone in assuming that there seemed 'little prospect of Labour's grip on Scottish representation at Westminster being broken even if its vote falls considerably from its relatively high level in 2010'.[1] If anything, Labour looked likely to have more MPs at the next UK election.

Normality had been restored. In 2007, the SNP had formed a minority government in the Scottish Parliament after it narrowly defeated Labour. Polls following the Holyrood election suggested that the SNP would do well in 2010 but voters returned to Labour as the UK election drew closer. A sizeable element of Labour's support, evident at least from the late 1980s, saw the SNP as second choice and vice versa.[2] A pattern appeared to have been established. Labour and

*James Mitchell, School of Social and Political Sciences, Edinburgh University, James.Mitchell@ed.ac.uk

[1] Electoral Reform Society (2010) 'The UK General Election In-depth Report', accessed at http://www.electoral-reform.org.uk/images/dynamicImages/file4e3ff1393b87a.pdf, p. 15.

[2] Brand, J., Mitchell, J. and Surridge, P. (1994) 'Will Scotland come to the Aid of the Party?', In Heath, A., Jowell, R. and Curtice, J. (eds) *Labour's Last Chance? The 1992 Election and Beyond?* Aldershot, Dartmouth, p. 224.

© The Author 2015. Published by Oxford University Press on behalf of the Hansard Society; all rights reserved.
For permissions, please e-mail: journals.permissions@oup.com
doi:10.1093/pa/gsv029

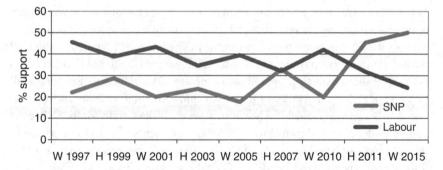

Figure 6.1 Labour and SNP support at Westminster and Holyrood elections, 1997–2015.

SNP would compete to become Scotland's largest party in Holyrood but Labour continued to have an apparently impregnable Scottish lead in elections to the Commons. The explanation appeared simple. Voters focused on which party they wanted to form a government. The SNP were a credible alternative to Labour at Holyrood but the battle for Westminster was between Labour and the Conservatives, leaving the SNP largely irrelevant. Sartori had long ago identified two sources of relevance for a party: governing and blackmail potential.[3] Devolution gave the SNP governing potential in Edinburgh, but it only had blackmail potential in Westminster.

Polls reflected the impact of whichever electoral contest was uppermost in the minds of the electorate at any given time. There might be an overhang following a Holyrood or Westminster election, but voters would shift focus by polling day. At different times, Labour and the SNP each assumed (or hoped) that the overhang effect from one electoral contest would carry through to the next. After the SNP breakthrough at Holyrood in 2007, the SNP assumed that its support would carry over to the 2010 UK election. Labour, in turn, assumed its support in 2010 would carry it to victory at Holyrood in 2011. In the event, the SNP extended its lead in 2011 and bucked the electoral system to gain an overall majority in Holyrood just a year after Labour's Scottish victory in 2010. The pattern looked set to continue in the 2015 election but as Figure 6.1 graphically shows, this was decidedly not the case.

2. The independence referendum

There was one event that played havoc with the seemingly established post-devolution pattern. For a long time, the extent and manner in which the Scottish independence referendum would affect the 2015 General Election was unclear.

---

[3]Sartori, G. (1976) *Parties and Party Systems: A Framework for Analysis*, Cambridge, Cambridge University Press.

The SNP's referendum policy had allowed it to appeal to voters who were either opposed to or at least unconvinced by the case for independence but inclined to support the SNP as a competent government.[4] Between 2007 and 2011, the SNP formed a minority government in Holyrood but were unable to hold a referendum as the opposition majority opposed such a measure. When the SNP won an overall majority in Holyrood in 2011, its manifesto commitment to an independence referendum became unavoidable. There was, however, little comfort for the SNP in the polling evidence on independence. The SNP's opponents expected an easy win in the referendum, based on polls suggesting that only between a quarter and a third of Scots favoured independence. They also assumed this would have dire consequences for a demoralised and divided SNP facing difficulty, even annihilation, at the 2015 UK General Election and 2016 Scottish elections. Alex Salmond, SNP leader and Scottish First Minister, sought to include a third option—more powers—on the ballot paper. This was rejected by the Prime Minister, resulting in a polarised debate in which those who supported the middle ground option would determine the result.

The referendum witnessed unforeseen levels of public engagement over two years and was framed in broad terms. The Scottish Question had never simply been about national identity, nor constitutional status but was also about the kind of state and society people envisaged for Scotland. Public policy concerns and party politics mix with constitutional preferences and identities.[5] The referendum saw Labour and Conservatives in an uncomfortable alliance under the umbrella of *Better Together*. The image of this alliance would linger. In the event, the polls narrowed and for a brief period independence looked within sight. The victory for the union was unambiguous—by 55–45%—but post-referendum politics was not as expected due to earlier expectations, the exceptional levels of public engagement and the awkward union of Labour and the Tories. As two seasoned campaigners noted over 20 years ago, politics is an expectations game, 'Success is not measured by actual results, but by preconceived expectations'.[6] Within days of the referendum it had become clear that the SNP would not adopt the political equivalent of the foetal position common after a traumatic defeat. Instead of damaging introspection, supporters of independence celebrated progress in the belief that independence was within sight.

Within hours of the result being declared, Alex Salmond took responsibility for the defeat and announced he would resign as SNP leader and First Minister of Scotland. He

---

[4]Carman, C., Johns, R. and Mitchell, J. (2014) *More Scottish than British: The 2011 Scottish Parliament Election*, Basingstoke, Palgrave Macmillan.

[5]Mitchell, J. (2014) *The Scottish Question*, Oxford, Oxford University Press.

[6]Matalin, M. and Carville, J. (1995) *All's Fair: Love, War, and Running for President*, New York, Random House, pp. 142–143.

had been at the centre of the campaign and the main focus of *Better Together* attacks. His resignation helped the SNP move on from defeat and removed the main focus of opposition ire. SNP membership soared from around 26,000 at the time of the referendum to over 100,000 by March 2015. There was little doubt as to who would succeed him. His deputy, Nicola Sturgeon, was second only to Salmond in popularity in a survey of party members conducted after the 2007 Holyrood election.[7] No-one else was nominated and the new leader embarked on a 'tour', culminating in a rally in Glasgow's Hydro arena in November addressing 12,000 people.

The energy and excitement generated by the referendum passed to the SNP despite defeat. SNP strategists were keen to channel this energy into the UK General Election but did not want to be accused of treating the election as a re-run of the referendum. The leadership considered allowing pro-independence activists, including a proportion of SNP members, to stand in the General Election under a 'Yes' banner rather than as SNP candidates in the General Election. This was opposed by the new leader as it might suggest that the SNP had not accepted the referendum result. In the event, the SNP conference in November 2014 endorsed a less radical approach, proposed by the new leader, that non-members could stand under the SNP banner, allowing 'Yes' activists who had not been party members to stand. It sought to take advantage of the post-referendum mood but avoid the accusation of treating the General Election as either a re-run or continuation of the referendum.

The main criterion for selection of SNP candidates appears to have been the level of activity of applicants during the referendum, allowing some candidates to emerge who had not been socialised into SNP internal politics and creating potential challenges for group cohesion amongst those who would be elected. The process of candidate selection occurred over December 2014 and into early 2015, so that there was little respite for those who had been engaged in the referendum but ensured that engagement and momentum was maintained. A number of new SNP MPs only came to prominence in their local areas during the referendum.

While the SNP successfully made the transition from referendum defeat to campaigning in the 2015 election, its opponents struggled to move on from success in the referendum. *Better Together* had been an uncomfortable alliance consisting of Labour, Conservatives and Liberal Democrats. When polls suggested that there might be a majority for independence, the three British party leaders promised to deliver more powers, having made strenuous efforts throughout the campaign to avoid making any such commitment. The Prime Minister put a formal end to the alliance when he spoke in Downing Street shortly after the official referendum result was declared. Mr Cameron announced the establishment of a Commission under Lord Smith, who had chaired the Organising Committee for the Glasgow

---

[7] Mitchell, J., Bennie, L. and Johns, J. (2012) *The Scottish National Party: Transition to Power*, Oxford, Oxford University Press, p. 162.

Commonwealth Games in 2014, to consider further devolution and insisted that the voice of Scotland had been heard and 'now the millions of voices of England must also be heard. The question of English votes for English laws—the so-called West Lothian question—requires a decisive answer'.[8] This signalled the next phase in debate on the Scottish Question, not its final resolution and the end of the Tory-Labour alliance.

Johann Lamont, Labour's Scottish leader and a Member of the Scottish Parliament, resigned a month after the referendum, suggesting that the Scottish Labour Party was 'just a branch office of a party based in London'.[9] She was succeeded by Jim Murphy, MP for East Renfrewshire, who resigned from Labour's Shadow Cabinet at Westminster and committed himself to standing for the Scottish Parliament in 2016. It was unclear at first whether he would stand again for the House of Commons but announced his decision to do so three months before the General Election. There had been tensions between Labour's elected representatives in Westminster and Holyrood since devolution. Jim Murphy was closely associated with Tony Blair and stood against Neil Findlay and Sarah Boyack, both Members of the Scottish Parliament. Mr Murphy won most votes in the elected members' section and amongst the wider membership but Neil Findlay came top in the affiliated section. The deputy leader position was also contested, with Kezia Dugdale MSP defeating Katy Clark MP with the same, though more emphatic, pattern in each of the three sections of Labour's electoral college. As the new leader did not have a seat in Holyrood, his deputy led the party in the Scottish Parliament following the pattern established by Alex Salmond when he became SNP Leader in 2004 while still an MP without a Holyrood seat and Nicola Sturgeon led the SNP group of MSPs until the 2007 Scottish elections.

While polls following the referendum suggested that the SNP would make significant gains, Labour strategists expected that many voters who had supported independence would return to Labour at the General Election. The devolution pattern of voting was expected to reassert itself. On being elected leader, Mr Murphy had insisted that Labour would not lose a single seat to the SNP in 'the fairest nation on the planet'.[10] He was 'astonished' at how easy it was to take on the 'sluggish, lethargic and off the pace' SNP,[11] comments interpreted as a criticism of Johann Lamont as much as of the SNP.

---

[8] Cameron, D. (2014) 'Scottish Independence Referendum: Statement by the Prime Minister', accessed at https://www.gov.uk/government/news/scottish-independence-referendum-statement-by-the-prime-minister on 20 June 2015.

[9] *Daily Record*, 25 October 2014.

[10] *Observer*, 14 December 2014.

[11] Buzzfeed (2015) accessed at http://www.buzzfeed.com/jamieross/its-been-easy-its-been-to-outdo-the-snp on 20 June 2015.

3. The Scottish Question in the election

No single one of the elements of the Scottish Question[12] alone explains the rise of the SNP or support for autonomy but the concatenation of identity, constitutional politics and everyday concerns. The perception that Scotland is a distinct political entity may be a necessary condition for demands for autonomy, but other factors are important. Devolution had been established following a referendum in 1997 in which the interplay of national identity and opposition to the Conservatives proved key in explaining why three-quarters of voters supported the establishment of a Scottish Parliament.[13] National identity has proved an insufficient guide as to voting behaviour. More people who saw themselves as British and not Scottish voted SNP than voted Conservative in 2011's Holyrood elections.[14]

There can be little doubt that the referendum had a significant impact on the General Election, but this was not straightforward. Support for independence and the SNP has never been the same. There had always been people who supported independence who did not vote SNP and SNP voters (and even some members) who did not support independence. But increased support for independence and the excitement generated by the referendum assisted the SNP. Labour's challenge was to break any potential link between supporting independence and voting SNP, but it struggled to find a consistent message.

Jim Murphy said that he would employ a Yes supporter in his team[15] and insisted that Labour was 'open' to Yes supporters. Yes voters, he maintained, were 'the most important voters in the UK'.[16] The SNP took a similar view, seeing the 45% Yes vote as its target in the General Election but aware of the danger of treating the election as a continuation of the referendum. Two months after the referendum, Gordon Brown argued that 'Scottish politics has got to be reset and Labour is pressing the reset button' arguing that Scots had to stop 'obsessing about the constitution' and 'focus on improving people's lives'.[17] There were problems with the call for reset. Scotland's constitutional status had been intimately linked to everyday public policy by Brown and Labour for over a generation in making the case for devolution. Voters had experienced a referendum in which constitutional and everyday public policies had been intertwined in debates on Scotland's future. The reset

---

[12] Mitchell, *The Scottish Question*.

[13] Denver, D., Mitchell, J., Pattie, C. and Bochel, H. (2000) *Scotland Decides: The Devolution Issue and the Scottish Referendum*, London, Cass.

[14] Carman *et al.*, 'More Scottish than British', p. 36.

[15] *The Herald*, 7 December 2014.

[16] *The Herald*, 8 February 2015.

[17] BBC News, 'Gordon Brown Calls for Scottish Politics 'Reset', accessed at http://www.bbc.co.uk/news/uk-scotland-scotland-politics-30256101, on 29 November 2014.

button would have to take Scotland back not just to before the referendum but before devolution. But there was a more fundamental problem. Labour's Scottish leader focused heavily on the prospect of a second referendum if the SNP did well, constantly reminding voters about an event that Mr Brown had been keen to move on from. Jim Murphy's message was that voting SNP would lead to another referendum. Labour never resolved the dilemma of how to respond to what many people regarded as the most important Scottish political event in recent history. The SNP leadership maintained that they were not seeking a mandate to call for another referendum but that they hoped to be part of a 'progressive alliance' in the Commons.

The 2010 coalition agreement had promised to implement the proposals of the Calman Commission on devolution, established in response to the SNP's Holyrood election victory in 2007. Calman was supported by the three Unionist parties, a forerunner of *Better Together*, and was given legislative form in the 2012 Scotland Act, increasing Holyrood's powers to alter income tax, raise revenues with some other taxes, devolve the power to borrow and other responsibilities previously retained at Westminster. It was sold to Scottish voters as an extension of Holyrood's powers and to English voters as making Holyrood more fiscally responsible,[18] a classic example of the confluence of disparate but complementary interests. Calman had still not been fully implemented by the time of the referendum or the 2015 General Election and had been overtaken by the referendum and Smith Commission. The Smith Commission reported in late November 2014 recommending further extensions in Holyrood's powers. All Holyrood parties, including the SNP and Greens, were involved in the Smith Commission. The Commission claimed to recommend the 'biggest transfer of power to the Scottish Parliament since its establishment'.[19] In January 2015, the Coalition published its response to Smith, *Scotland in the United Kingdom: an enduring settlement*.[20] There ensued a debate on whether the UK Government's white paper had addressed or diluted the Smith recommendations. The details became lost in the election campaign, but there was little doubt that all political parties represented in the Commons in Scotland were proposing to devolve more powers. This was an agenda that had proved to work to the advantage of the SNP since the 1970s. In February 2015, Gordon Brown abandoned his demand that Scotland press the rest button when

---

[18] Gallagher, J. 'Why the Scotland Bill Is Good News for England', *Daily Telegraph*, 30 November 2010.

[19] Smith, L. (2014) 'Report on the Smith Commission for Further Devolution of Powers to the Scottish Parliament', accessed at https://www.smith-commission.scot/wp-content/uploads/2014/11/The_Smith_Commission_Report-1.pdf on 20 June 2015, p. 4.

[20] Secretary of State for Scotland (2015) 'Scotland in the United Kingdom: An Enduring Settlement', Cm.8990, accessed at https://www.gov.uk/government/uploads/system/uploads/attachment_data/file/397079/Scotland_EnduringSettlement_acc.pdf on 20 June 2015.

he criticised the 'weaker' Coalition plans for more powers and promised to go further than the Smith Commission with more powers over welfare. The former Prime Minster argued that the Smith Commission plans were too restrictive and accused the Coalition of taking a 'narrow' approach in a change in strategy from his call to 'reset' Scottish politics. The SNP's opponents were competing amongst themselves on the SNP's preferred agenda.

4. Shibboleths, others and austerity

The Conservatives have been portrayed by opponents as 'anti-Scottish' since the days of Margaret Thatcher's premiership. The Conservatives are the 'other' for a large section of the Scottish electorate and have struggled to remove this image in Scotland.[21] It has been standard for over 30 years in Scottish elections for Labour and the SNP to compete to define themselves as more anti-Tory than the other. Being perceived to be aligned with the Conservatives is very damaging for other parties in Scotland. Distance from and opposition to the Conservatives have become shibboleths (or substitutes) for radicalism in Scottish politics. During the election, Labour made much of the anniversary of the 1979 vote when SNP MPs voted no confidence in James Callaghan's Labour Government that precipitated the General Election that year. The SNP highlighted Labour's cooperation with the Conservatives in *Better Together*, linking this to the rise of New Labour.

The belief that there would be a hung Parliament worked to the SNP's advantage. It gave the SNP potential governing relevance[22] for the first time ever. The SNP could never before credibly claim to be able to influence the formation of the UK Government during an election (though that is indeed what happened in the latter part of the 1974–1979 Parliament). Nicola Sturgeon insisted that the SNP would 'lock the Tories' out of power and repeatedly offered to work with Ed Miliband in a 'progressive alliance'. Aiding the sense of the SNP's relevance was the decision by broadcasters to include the SNP leader, along with the leaders of Plaid Cymru and the Green Party, to take part in televised leadership debates. The SNP was given more media coverage than at any previous UK election. Polls taken immediately after the debates and media commentary suggested that the SNP leader had performed well.

The SNP articulated an anti-austerity message throughout the campaign, as they had during the referendum. This further added to Labour's difficulties in Scotland. The Conservatives may have long been the 'other' in Scottish politics, but the SNP

---

[21] Convery, A. (2014) 'The 2011 Scottish Conservative Party Leadership Election: Dilemmas for Statewide Parties in Regional Contexts', *Parliamentary Affairs*, **67**, 306–327.

[22] Sartori, 'Parties and Party Systems'.

became the 'other' in English politics. The prospect of a hung Parliament may have worked to the SNP's advantage but was used to convey the impression that a minority Labour Government would be controlled by the SNP. As a party largely unknown outside Scotland, the SNP could be easily caricatured and presented as a bogeyman. The portrayal of the SNP in the General Election by the Conservatives mirrored the portrayal of the Conservative Party in Scotland by its opponents in the past, as a party with limited territorial interest and at the opposite end of the spectrum from most voters. Labour was left in the invidious situation of having to respond to questions about working with the SNP in the event of a hung Parliament. The initial response was to rule out a coalition with the SNP though the SNP itself had already stated that this was not its preference and eventually to dismiss any working arrangement with the SNP. Labour's uneasy balance in opposing Conservative austerity policies while avoiding resurrecting images of 'fiscal incontinence' was made more difficult by SNP demands to take sides in a progressive alliance.

5. Frenchgate, tactical voting and the press

On April 4th, the *Daily Telegraph* carried a story based on a leaked UK Government memo that purported to record a conversation between Nicola Sturgeon and the French Ambassador in which the former reportedly had 'confessed that she'd rather see David Cameron remain as PM (and didn't see Ed Miliband as PM material)'. There were two issues: whether the First Minister had been accurately reported and who had leaked the document. Both the Scottish First Minister and the French Ambassador denied that this had been said and indeed the author of the memo went on to note, 'I have to admit that I'm not sure that the FM's tongue would be quite so loose on that kind of thing in a meeting like that, so it might well be a case of something being lost in translation'[23] but the latter part was given less prominence. An enquiry established by the Cabinet Secretary reported after the election and found that Alastair Carmichael, Secretary of State for Scotland, had given his Special Adviser permission to leak the document and discuss it with a journalist at the *Telegraph*, a newspaper that was hostile to the SNP. Mr Carmichael denied this at the time. Mr Carmichael was the only Scottish Liberal Democrat returned at the General Election and there were inevitable calls for his resignation and a by-election in Orkney and Shetland.

This episode invites speculation as to its impact on the outcome of the election, as did another feature that attracted less attention during the campaign. As in previous General Elections, party activists and others have called for tactical voting. One well-known political website suggested that charts proposing an anti-SNP tactical

---

[23] *Guardian*, 3 April 2015, accessed at http://www.theguardian.com/politics/2015/apr/03/nicola-sturgeon-denies-saying-she-wanted-david-cameron-to-win-election on 20 June 2015.

voting were 'going the rounds on social media' and looked 'set to play a big part at GE15'.[24] There were a number of problems with this expectation. First, competing advice was available with voters in some constituencies given conflicting advice should they wish to tactically vote against the SNP. Second, the impact of social media looks likely to have been overstated and third, there is an underlying assumption that voters can be guided in this way or indeed there might be much appetite to vote tactically. Indeed, there is reason to believe that such advice backfires amongst those voters who have gravitated between Labour and the SNP and who might have found the advice to vote Conservative or Liberal Democrat unpalatable. Reminding voters of any link with the Conservatives was unlikely to have served Labour well.

In recent elections, the SNP has had support in sections of the Scottish press that was entirely absent before 2007. Newspaper readership in Scotland, as elsewhere, has been in long-term decline. In April 2015, the largest selling newspaper in Scotland was the *Sun* (223,745) followed by the *Daily Record* (189,439). On election day, the former offered readers in Scotland and England very different messages: its English edition urged a Tory vote to 'Stop the SNP running the country' amongst other reasons while its Scottish edition headlined 'why it's time to vote SNP'. But more significant was the *Daily Record*, a paper that has loyally supported Labour for generations. Its front page had a picture of David Cameron with the headline 'Come on England Kick Him', though the paper had very few sales in England, and its back page carried photographs and statements from both Ed Miliband and Nicola Sturgeon.

6. The result

At one point during the 1979 General Election, Jim Callaghan was optimistic that Labour would win 'unless there has been one of those sea changes in public opinion towards Thatcher. If people really decided they want a change of government, there is nothing you can do.'[25] Hubris, rather than optimism, was in plentiful supply in Scottish Labour in the months leading up to the 2015 General Election. The SNP victory was emphatic and was frequently referred to as a tsunami. A landslide might be a more appropriate metaphor. Slow movement has been evident for some time, but the pace of change had noticeably sped up until the deluge which finally drew the attention of those observing from a distance.

Two veteran Liberal Democrats—Malcolm Bruce and Menzies Campbell—retired at the election as did seven Labour MPs—including Gordon Brown and Alistair Darling. But just as these leading members were bowing out, Alex Salmond was seeking his return to the Commons (having been an MP from 1987 to 2010). The SNP won 56 of Scotland's 59 constituencies on 50% of the vote.

---

[24] Accessed at https://www.politicalbetting.com on 20 June 2015.

[25] Donoughue, B. (2008) *Downing Street Diary*, vol. 2, London, Jonathan Cape, pp. 483–484.

Table 6.1 Westminster election party votes and seats in Scotland, 2010–2015

	Share of vote % (2010 in brackets)	Number of seats (2010 in brackets)
SNP	50.0 (19.9)	56 (6)
Labour	24.3 (42.0)	1 (41)
Conservatives	14.9 (16.7)	1 (1)
Liberal Democrat	7.6 (18.9)	1 (11)
Others	3.2 (2.5)	0 (0)
Turnout	71.7 (63.8)	–

This was the highest share of the vote since the Scottish Unionist Party and Liberal Nationals combined (41.5 + 8.6%) to win 50.1% in 1955. With 1,454,436 votes, the SNP won more votes than any party in Scotland since mass enfranchisement. Turnout in Scotland was 71.7%, up from 63.8% in 2010, reversing the normal trend that has seen lower turnouts in Scotland compared with the UK as a whole, suggesting that the exceptional turnout recorded in the September 2014 Scottish independence referendum had an impact. Labour's share of the vote was lower than at any election since 1918, having to reach back before then to the pre-full enfranchisement time of 1900. The scale of Labour's defeat has overshadowed the weakness of the Scottish Conservatives. The Conservatives retained their only seat but with their lowest ever share of the vote. The Liberal Democrats only have to go back 50 years to find a similar share of the vote and a further five years back to when it had only one MP. Table 6.1 shows the full scale of the SNP's triumph and the poor performance of all the other parties in 2015.

The swing from Labour to the SNP, if such is meaningful in multi-party politics, was 26.1% across Scotland. The largest swing was recorded in Glasgow North East where Anne McLaughlin took the seat for the SNP from Labour on a swing of 39.3%. The SNP benefited from both the highest share of the vote for a single party in the age of mass enfranchisement (the Tory share of the vote in 1955 is often mistakenly cited but, as noted above, was in fact an alliance of Scottish Unionist Party and National Liberal votes) but also a highly efficient vote. The SNP won under 40% in only four seats. The lowest share of SNP vote was in Edinburgh South with 33.8%, retained by Labour largely due to a poor SNP candidate, who may have provoked tactical voting in affluent areas and made voters in traditional Labour parts of the constituency stay with Labour. Even in Orkney and Shetland, a seat that has historically been poor for it, the SNP won 37.8%. The SNP won 50% or over in 35 seats. The Liberal Democrats came second in eight seats they had previously held but were behind UKIP in 17 seats and Greens in 10 seats. In the seats it contested, UKIP averaged 3.0% of the vote with its best result on Orkney and Shetland where it won 4.8%. The Greens averaged 2.6% in

Table 6.2 Party performance in Scottish constituencies, 2015

Party (no. of seats contested)	First placed	Second	Third	Fourth	Fifth	Sixth	Seventh
SNP (59)	56	3					
Labour (59)	1	38	12	8			
Cons (59)	1	7	47	4			
Lib Dem (59)	1	8	2	21	26	1	
UKIP (38)	–	–	–	15	10	13	
Green (31)	–	–	–	10	14	6	1

seats they contested but managed to save three deposits. Party placements in constituencies are indicated in Table 6.2.

Turnout across Scotland was higher than the UK as a whole for the first time since
1983. The highest turnout was in East Dunbartonshire (81.9%) followed by East
Renfrewshire (81.1%), the latter having recorded the highest turnout in the UK
in 2010. Scotland has traditionally included a number of constituencies with the
lowest turnouts, but there were only two seats with under 60% turnout: Glasgow
Central with 55.4% and Glasgow North East with 56.8%. This suggests some spill-
over effect from the independence referendum when turnout was 85%.

Labour had long been the beneficiary and the SNP had lost out under the simple
plurality electoral system in Scotland but in 2015 this was reversed. In 2010,
Labour's 42% share of the vote translated into just under 70% of seats. In 2015,
the SNP became a major beneficiary of the electoral system, winning 95% of
seats with 50% of the vote and easily breaking previous records for deviation
from proportionality. This was the kind of result Labour had feared might
happen with devolution under this electoral system but had not expected this in
elections to the Commons. The SNP's vote was highly efficient, with only two
seats with over 60% of the vote but 54 with over 40%. In contrast, in 2010,
Labour had nine seats with over 60% of the vote and another nine with under 20%.

The new contingent of SNP MPs was more diverse than any previous grouping
returned from Scotland. Twenty (36%) of the 56 SNP MPs are women, seven are gay
or lesbian, the youngest is 20 years old (and second youngest is 24) and one is an
Asian Scot. None was educated at Oxbridge (though one was educated at
Harvard), the average age is 44 and only two were privately educated. Sixteen
were or had previously been councillors and three previously worked as party
researchers or special advisers.

7. Conclusion

As ever, many factors explain the outcome of the election in Scotland. The referendum's impact has inevitably assumed prominence in much commentary. This is

understandable but the referendum may have been more epiphenomenal than explanatory; that is the referendum may have been the culmination of other factors long brewing in Scottish politics but now given the chance of expression. These longer term factors include the complex relationship between Labour and SNP voting evident in elections to Holyrood and Westminster since devolution, aided by party dealignment. The persistence of an anti-Conservative mood amongst a significant part of the Scottish electorate remains important. There were also some immediate factors at work. The perception that there would be a hung Parliament and Labour's difficulties in addressing the Scottish dimension of this along with difficulties in knowing how to consistently address the referendum played to the SNP's advantage. Overall, the key to the SNP's success lies in it becoming relevant as never previously in a UK General Election.

Britain Votes (2015) 101–116

JONATHAN BRADBURY*

Wales: Still a Labour Stronghold but Under Threat?

As analysed elsewhere in this volume, it was not only the Conservative Party, but also territorially-based parties in the UK periphery, that played highly significant roles in preventing the Labour Party from winning the 2015 General Election. The purpose of this chapter is to address what happened to Labour's challenge in Wales, another of their strongholds, and what role was played, respectively, by territorial politics and competition with the Conservatives in this case. In considering these questions, interest immediately focuses on the extent to which Plaid Cymru offered the possibility of following the SNP's example and eclipsing a Labour Party dominant in Wales since the First World War.

Prospects of change always appeared more limited. Prior to 2015 Labour dominated General Elections in Wales and also appeared to have successfully adapted to devolution with a clear Welsh Labour brand and a commitment to clear red water with British Labour, so as to better represent both class and nation. While Scottish Labour at the devolved level lost power in 2007, Welsh Labour had continued to hold office in the National Assembly. Even in the 2010 General Election defeat, Labour in Wales still achieved the highest vote share at 36%. This was Labour's lowest vote share since the First World War, but the party still took the lion's share of the seats with 26 out of 40 seats. The Conservatives rose to eight seats and both the Liberal Democrats and Plaid Cymru had three seats each. Throughout the run up to the 2015 election it was expected that Labour's vote and seat share would simply rise again from the 2010 low point. This would mean that territorial electoral politics in Wales would deliver no Scottish-style expression of regional tension, the most dramatic form of territorial political mobilisation as conceptualised by Rokkan and Urwin, but rather deliver momentum for Labour's bid to govern again at the centre.[1]

---

*Jonathan Bradbury, Department of Political and Cultural Studies, Swansea University, j.p.bradbury@swansea.ac.uk

[1] Rokkan, S. and Urwin, D. (1982) 'Introduction: Centres and Peripheries in Western Europe'. In Rokkan, S and Urwin, D. (eds) *The Politics of Territorial Identity, Studies in European Regionalism*, London, Sage, p. 10.

doi:10.1093/pa/gsv030

An issue that was also important, but rather less focused upon, was the extent to which the rise in the UKIP share of the vote in Wales also offered the possibility of Wales experiencing electoral change more comparable to trends in England. In the 2014 European elections in Wales, UKIP came second behind Labour. Yet, the evidence of a robust trend of support for UKIP remained limited and it was unclear what support UKIP would receive in a First-Past-The-Post Westminster election, much less whether it could actually win any seats. Equally, there had been a trend of small but continuous improvements in the Conservatives' vote and seat share at both Westminster and Assembly elections in Wales since 1999 but this had largely been in the context of Labour being in government at both levels. The main Westminster gains had been in 2010 against the background of the unpopular Brown Government, and the expectation in 2015 was that Labour's gains would be at the expense of the Conservatives. Hence, it appeared that there might be some evidence of English-style anti-centre political sentiment, a weaker but still important form of territorial political mobilisation as conceptualised by Rokkan and Urwin, but it would be limited in extent and marginal in significance, and a further rise in support for the Conservatives was unlikely.[2] Overall it was not expected in the case of Wales that any of nationalism or anti-centre politics as different forms of territorial politics, or conservatism would progress; instead it was presumed that Labour would do rather better at being supported as both an effective party of the periphery as well as a plausible governing party of the centre than elsewhere in the UK.

The chapter is organised in two sections to explore the extent to which such expectations were borne out by events. Section 1 considers the 2015 election results and party performance in Wales, and Section 2 considers how the campaign was contested in Wales and what debates about party strategies were conducted immediately following the election. The conclusion assesses how we might then broadly interpret the nature of party competition in the 2015 election in Wales as well as its implications for the future.

1.   Election results and party performance

The election results in 2015 delivered some surprises. Labour achieved a vote share of 36.9%, just 0.7% higher than their 2010 performance. This was their second worst electoral performance since the First World War, not quite as bad as 2010 but still worse than 1983 (see Table 7.1). On this basis Labour may still have hoped to retain all the seats won in 2010 but the party not only failed to win back seats it had lost to the Conservatives in 2010—Cardiff North, Vale of Glamorgan, Carmarthen West and Pembrokeshire South and Aberconwy—but it lost two

---

[2]Ibid, pp. 9–10.

Table 7.1 UK General Election results in Wales, 1979–2015

	Con	Lab	Lib Dem (formerly Lib and Lib-SDP)	Plaid Cymru	Others (inc UKIP and Green)
1979					
Vote share	32.2%	47.0%	10.6%	8.1%	2.2%
Seats	11	21	1	2	1
1983					
Vote share	31.0%	37.5%	23.2%	7.8%	0.4%
Seats	14	20	2	2	0
1987					
Vote share	29.5%	45.1%	17.9%	7.3%	0.2%
Seats	8	24	3	3	0
1992					
Vote share	28.6%	49.5%	12.4%	8.8%	0.7%
Seats	6	27	1	4	0
1997					
Vote share	19.6%	54.7%	12.4%	9.9%	3.4%
Seats	0	34	2	4	0
2001					
Vote share	21.0%	48.6%	13.8%	14.3%	2.3%
Seats	0	34	2	4	0
2005					
Vote share	21.4%	42.7%	18.4%	12.6%	4.9%
Seats	3	29	4	3	1
2010					
Vote share	26.1%	36.2%	20.1%	11.3%	6.2%
Seats	8	26	3	3	0
2015					
Vote share	27.2%	36.9%	6.5%	12.1%	17.3%
Seats	11	25	1	3	0

Turnout: 1979: 79.4%; 1983: 76.1%; 1987: 78.9%; 1992: 79.7%; 1997: 73.6%; 2001: 60.6%; 2005: 62.4%; 2010: 64.9%; and 2015: 65.6%.

more—Gower and Vale of Clwyd. Both were lost narrowly, by 27 and 237 votes, respectively, with Gower proving the biggest shock, as it had been represented by a Labour MP since 1910. Labour did win Cardiff Central, their key target seat against the Liberal Democrats, obtaining a majority of nearly 5000. But overall, Labour's failure to make real progress on vote share was reflected in the net *loss* of one seat.

Plaid Cymru, who may have been presumed to be Labour's main challenger, fared little better. They saw their vote share rise marginally from 11.3 to 12.1%, their third best Westminster performance. Nevertheless, they simply retained the same three seat share won in 2005 and 2010. Their big disappointment came in failing to take Ynys Mon from Labour, losing by 229 votes. Much more dramatic was the sharp rise of UKIP and the equally sharp decline of the Liberal Democrats. The Liberal Democrats collapsed from 20.1% in 2010 to 6.5% in 2015, and as well as losing Cardiff Central to Labour they lost Brecon and Radnorshire to the Conservatives. They retained just one seat, Ceredigion. The 2015 result was the worst since the 1970 General Election, when the former Liberal party won 6.8% of the vote share in Wales and similarly had just one MP. The party moved on from the election from a base of second place in just three other constituencies and no third place finishes. Meanwhile, UKIP rose from 2.4% of the vote in 2010 to 13.6% in 2015. This made them the third largest party in Wales by vote share, eclipsing even Plaid Cymru on vote share, though because of the mediating effects of the First-Past-The-Post electoral system they still won no seats.

Against all expectations, the Conservatives made a net small gain on their vote share from 2010 of 1.2% and in contrast to Labour were able to convert this into increased seats, two from Labour and one from the Liberal Democrats, without losing any of their own. This meant that Labour still won 25 of the 40 seats, but the Conservatives' haul of 11 seats (a net gain of three) meant that the only clear gainers in the election in Wales were not Labour, but the Conservatives. Overall, there was a swing from Labour to Plaid Cymru in six seats, from Labour to UKIP in six seats and from Labour to the Conservatives in 16 seats. Labour achieved a swing from the Conservatives in only six seats and the remaining six seats witnessed a swing from the Liberal Democrats to one of the other parties in four seats and from Plaid Cymru in two.

One should not get carried away. While Labour in Wales stagnated compared with its own previous achievements it still clearly outperformed Labour overall both in England and Scotland in 2015. It remained the largest party by some way both in vote and seat share. Even in another bad election Wales held comparatively firm for Labour. Nevertheless, the election results provided a shock for the Party. Polling conducted prior to the election had fairly consistently placed Labour at around 40% of the vote in Wales, suggesting that they would retain all their seats won in 2010 and add victories in Cardiff North as well as Cardiff Central, to take 28 seats in all. The issue had not been whether Labour in Wales would advance but whether they would advance sufficiently to help the Party to win an overall majority at Westminster.[3]

The results also stored up multiple threats for the future, though they varied in apparent immediacy. The threats from Plaid Cymru and UKIP were important but looked least immediate. Labour have taken the potential threat from Plaid Cymru to replace Labour as the party representing both class and nation in Wales very seriously ever since Plaid's dramatic advances in the 1999 Assembly election, yet only in Ynys Mon did Plaid finish a close second to Labour. UKIP came second to Labour in six seats which were geographically concentrated in the South Wales valleys. Since the appearance of People's Voice and independent candidates in the mid-2000s, there has been the potential for the vote in these traditional Labour voting communities to fracture off to other parties purporting to better represent the interests of

---

[3]Welsh Political Barometer, accessed at http://blogs.cardiff.ac.uk/electionsinwales/ on 9 June 2015.

localities and the post-industrial working class. UKIP is the strongest organisational player yet to emerge to mobilise this disaffection. They also had 25 third place finishes across Wales. Even so, in all the seats where UKIP came second in 2015 it was still a distant second. In contrast, the most immediate threats appeared to lie in the 13 Labour-held seats where the Conservatives achieved second place in 2015. In six of these across the more urbanised North and South Wales coasts Labour had majorities of less than 4000 against the Conservatives, who had every right to consider them potentially winnable in 2020.

Notwithstanding the Liberal Democrats' collapse and UKIP's unrewarded rise, overall the 2015 General Election in Wales is ultimately most notable for Labour not increasing in representation again and the Conservatives consolidating their competitiveness as a trend. Even in the context of being in office at the UK level they increased their majorities in the seats that they held; and they won two seats from Labour that were not actually among the top target seats of the party at a UK level, both requiring a swing of around 4%. It was the Conservatives' best vote share performance since 1992 and their best seat haul since 1983. It was the first UK election in a generation in which Labour had not been in government at the UK level, trying to defend its record; rather it was in opposition and able potentially to capitalise on opposition to the government. Labour failed to take its opportunity, and the Conservatives continued their gradual rise in Welsh politics whilst maintaining power at the UK level. Labour representation also continued to be flattered by the distortions of a simple plurality electoral system that gave the Party 62.5% of the seats in Wales on 36.9% of the votes.

Labour still appears resilient when one considers the knock-on implications of the 2015 General Election result for the 2016 Assembly elections but here again there are signs of electoral change. Since the first National Assembly elections there has been clear evidence of differential voting patterns between UK and Welsh elections, marked by Plaid Cymru consistently polling better in Assembly elections and Labour polling worse in Assembly elections when in office at Westminster and better in the one Assembly election thus far when not.[4] This pattern may be repeated in the 2016 Assembly elections with again Plaid Cymru and Labour doing better. However, the 2015 General Election result, coupled with National Assembly opinion polls taken during the election period, while showing continuity in Plaid Cymru's differential voting performance, appears to suggest a flattening out in the electoral performances of the main British-wide parties across institutions and the further growth of Other parties at the Assembly level (see Tables 7.2 and 7.3). The main potential loser of vote share in this analysis is Labour, which according

---

[4]Scully, R. and Wyn Jones, R. (2006) 'Devolution and electoral politics in Scotland and Wales', *Publius: The Journal of Federalism*, **36**, 135–152; Bradbury, J. (2010) 'Wales and the 2010 General Election'. In Geddes, A. and Tonge, J. (eds) *Britain Votes 2010*, Oxford, Oxford University Press, pp. 143–157.

to recent polls will decline by over 5% in their Assembly vote share between 2011 and 2016 to mirror their 2015 Westminster performance. Current predictions see it as unlikely that Labour will be dislodged from power at the Assembly level; it should still be comfortably the largest party. However, it is predicted that the breakthrough to six-party representation that was not possible under the First-Past-The-Post electoral system in the 2015 election is likely to occur under the mixed member proportional representation electoral system used by the Assembly. As Table 7.3 suggests, at this stage in the Assembly election cycle, both UKIP and the Greens are likely to gain Assembly Members, although even if the polls are reliable, much can happen in the interim.

When one turns to other features of the 2015 election results in Wales, there were both similarities with and differences from British-wide trends. Turnout at 65.6% was slightly below the UK average. The highest turnout was seen in the Conservative hold of Cardiff North (76.13%), and the lowest in the safe Labour seat of Merthyr Tydfil (53.01%). Patterns of turnout generally confirmed the previous British-wide experience that in Wales many more Conservative votes than Labour votes are wasted in their parties respective safe seats, and that it takes more votes to get a Conservative elected. This of course was not the case in England in 2015. Overall, the election saw a 30% turnover in MPs; among the experienced Labour MPs standing down were Peter Hain in Neath and Paul Murphy in Torfaen, and among the newcomers were Stephen Kinnock, son of Neil Kinnock, the former Labour Leader, who won in Aberavon. The number of women MPs went up by two to nine (22.5%). This included Liz Saville Roberts in Dwyfor Meirionnydd, Plaid Cymru's first ever woman MP. The other eight female MPs were all Labour, reflecting Labour's continued usage of all women shortlists to select candidates. On these figures Wales' female representation was 6.9% lower than for the UK as a whole, and Wales still had no black and minority ethnic MPs in 2015.

Overall, electoral politics in Wales at the 2015 General Election were significant for establishing that trends were interesting for their comparability to those in England rather than to those in Scotland. Of course, the performance of Plaid Cymru is still a factor in ensuring that we continue to consider electoral politics in Wales in terms of who represents Wales territorially at Westminster. Yet, the 2015 result was more notable first, because UKIP's rise means that Welsh voters have clearly joined the trend seen in England towards giving a platform for UKIP to express anti-centre protest politics against the three main British-wide parties. Second, and ultimately more importantly, the result was important for showing that Welsh politics still principally revolves around two-party competition in terms of UK politics, between Labour and the Conservatives, in which Labour is the largest party, but in which in this election the Conservatives continued to make gains.

This should not actually particularly surprise us. While a clear majority of voters in Wales assert some form of Welsh identity and support devolution, support for

Table 7.2 Distribution of votes and seats in National Assembly for Wales, 1999–2011

	Constituency		Regional lists		Total seats
	Vote share (%)	Seats won	Vote share (%)	Seats won	
1999					
Conservative	15.9	1	16.5	8	9
Labour	37.6	27	35.5	1	28
Lib Dem	13.5	3	12.5	3	6
Plaid Cymru	28.4	9	30.5	8	17
Others	4.7	0	5.1	0	0
2003					
Conservative	19.9	1	19.2	10	11
Labour	40.0	30	36.6	0	30
Lib Dem	14.1	3	12.7	3	6
Plaid Cymru	21.2	5	19.7	7	12
Others	4.8	1	11.8	0	1
2007					
Conservative	22.4	5	21.5	7	12
Labour	32.2	24	29.6	2	26
Lib Dem	14.8	3	11.7	3	6
Plaid Cymru	22.4	7	21.0	8	15
Others	8.3	1	16.2	0	1
2011					
Conservative	25.0	6	22.5	8	14
Labour	42.3	28	36.9	2	30
Lib Dem	10.6	1	8.0	4	5
Plaid Cymru	19.3	5	17.9	6	11
Others	2.7	0	14.6	0	0

Table 7.3 Predicted vote shares and seats, 2016 National Assembly for Wales election

	Conservative	Labour	Lib Dem	Plaid Cymru	UKIP	Greens	Others
Vote share constituency	22%	37%	7%	19%	12%	3%	1%
Vote share list	21%	34%	5%	20%	12%	6%	2%
Predicted seats	13	28	2	11	5	1	0

Source: http://blogs.cardiff.ac.uk/electionsinwales/2015/05/06/final-welsh-political-barometer-poll-of-the-election/, 6 May 2015, accessed on 9 June 2015.

independence remains very low. This is usually around the 10% level although opinion polls during the period of the Scottish referendum debate suggested that it dropped below 5%. The natural constituency for Plaid Cymru, based on Nationalist aspirations, appears to be much lower than that for the SNP in Scotland, and accordingly there is greater space for Labour or indeed any of the other British-wide parties to seek to represent Welsh interests in a British context. Overall, Welsh politics remains to a large extent domesticated to British politics and in that context UKIP's new appeal and the Conservative Party's performance in 2015 were the key potent factors in shaping political change in Wales as they were in England. While Welsh politicians can never ignore the Scottish comparison, the dynamics of Welsh electoral politics has a good deal in common with northern English regions where Labour also were principally threatened by UKIP and the Conservatives and largely held on, but could not provide anything like the intended springboard for success that Labour had hoped.

2. The election campaign and party strategies

The meaning of the results and perceptions of party performances nevertheless still had to be filtered through analyses of how the campaign was conducted and post-election debate about party strategies. It is to be expected that the nature of the campaign would be similar to other parts of the UK, particularly in respect of how the British-wide parties presented their case. Nevertheless, there were three distinct elements of a Welsh dimension to the campaign. First, there was the potential for reference to each party's approach at the Welsh level in the National Assembly; second, the possibility of participation by political actors from the Welsh level who were not actually standing in the election; and third the importance of substantive debate about the constitutional development of devolution itself between the parties. In making their case to Welsh voters it is noteworthy that, after complaints of being excluded from UK-wide leaders' debates in 2010, Plaid Cymru were included in both the seven leaders' debate and five leaders' opposition debate. As a result Leanne Wood, as leader of Plaid Cymru, received unprecedented television coverage and was the only specifically Welsh party leader appearing in British-wide televised debates. In the Welsh leaders' debates, representatives for the Conservatives, Labour, the Liberal Democrats and Plaid Cymru were now also joined by those for UKIP and the Green Party. The sum of these elements was that Plaid Cymru was given the biggest opportunity to make its case afresh to Welsh voters.

In making their cases, all parties had a Welsh dimension to their campaign. The Conservative Party, led by Stephen Crabb, the Secretary of State for Wales, emphasised the extent to which the Welsh economy was on its knees in 2010 and how under the coalition government Wales had become the fastest growing part of the British economy.[5] They also emphasised the failures of Labour in running the National Health Service in Wales, highlighting the contrast between the coalition's

---

[5]Welsh Conservatives, *Ambitious For Wales, Delivering For Wales*, Election Manifesto 2015, Cardiff, Welsh Conservatives.

maintenance of NHS spending in England in real terms while in Wales Labour had in real terms cut the Budget. As part of their commitment to moving towards an increase of £8 billion per annum funding of the NHS in the 2015–2020 Parliament, the Welsh budget would also receive an additional £450 million, a commitment Labour did not match. The Conservatives criticised Welsh Labour's centralised vice-like grip on the NHS; Welsh Labour's failure to introduce a cancer drugs fund in contrast to England and the length of waiting lists in Wales, describing one in seven people as languishing on waiting lists.

Crabb accused politicians in the Cardiff bubble of being over-focused on seeking powers for the Assembly; in his experience it was a low saliency issue on the doorstep. Even so, the Conservatives had concluded the distribution of powers was unclear and unstable, and the Assembly needed to be fiscally account-able for the spending powers and responsibilities it held. Consequently, the Conser-vatives would implement the recent 2015 St David's Day agreement, which provided for moving to a reserved powers model, making some enhancements of the legislative powers of the assembly and providing for a referendum to be held on introducing an income tax varying power. To guarantee the Assembly against financial loss through fiscal devolution and corresponding loss of block grant allocation they would introduce a funding floor to the block grant. Crabb cam-paigned positively for fiscal devolution as a precursor to a more fiscally aware Welsh political culture that would be keener on supporting wealth creation and less focused on regulation.

Labour sought again to draw a contrast between the Conservatives as being the party for the few and Labour as the party for the many.[6] They attacked the way in which Conservative policies on the economy had left 83,000 people using food banks across Wales and increased the number working below the living wage, whilst promising to abolish zero hours contracts. Labour also defended their ap-proach to the NHS in Wales, stating that overall the block grant had received a 10% cut in real terms for Wales. Labour in Wales had decided to view the NHS and social care together, allocating additional spending to the social care budget. They highlighted that the Conservative £8 billion NHS funding pledge was not costed. In contrast, Labour's pledge to increase NHS funding by £2.5 billion would be introduced from the start of the Parliament, specifically funded by the proceeds from new taxes, and would release funds for the Welsh budget that would fund 1000 extra medical staff in Wales. Labour's Shadow Secretary of State for Wales, Owen Smith, claimed that between 1997 and 2010 Labour had rescued the NHS and suggested that even after just five years of the Coalition they would have to do so again.

---

[6]Welsh Labour, *Britain Can Be Better*, Election Manifesto 2015, Cardiff, Labour Party.

Labour supported further legislative powers for the Assembly and the introduction of a funding floor for the block grant, although the Party remained sceptical about the devolution of an income tax varying power. Labour preferred instead to emphasise that the specific taxes that the Party would introduce at the UK level, such as the mansion tax, would deliver over £1 billion over the next Parliament to Wales via the block grant. Where the Conservatives pointed towards a vision of fiscal devolution that encouraged fiscal economy and a focus on the economy, Labour maintained its support for essentially governmental and legislative devolution, backed by an expansion of funding through the block grant to support public services: redistributive fair federalism against fiscal competitive federalism.

The Liberal Democrat campaign fronted by Kirsty Williams, the leader of the party in the Assembly, promoted relatively few distinctive Welsh policies.[7] They championed a cross party commission on the NHS in Wales and sought to portray themselves as the real authors of the St David's Day Agreement, the long-term champions of home rule dragging the Conservatives and Labour behind them. But the Liberal Democrats' position as the party that might restrain the worst aspects of either the Conservatives or Labour in a possible coalition government did not give them a clear positive definition with Welsh voters, and their potential to be a repository of protest voting was lost to two other parties who marked out much more distinct positions.

On the left Plaid Cymru provided a critique of austerity policies, principally focusing on their detrimental social effects as they related to problems faced in Wales.[8] They advocated cutting the deficit over a much longer period and favoured loan financed public works programmes to stimulate economic growth. They advocated a Team Wales approach to campaigning for parity with Scotland in its provision through the Barnett formula in the Block grant which would yield an additional £1.2 billion per annum. This would pay for improved public services and help the development both of the living wage and an end to zero hours contracts throughout the public sector in Wales. Leanne Wood used her platforms both in UK-wide and Welsh leaders' debates to provide a post-austerity vision for Wales, focusing on people as Wales' greatest asset and stressing the need for ambition. She too critiqued Labour's centralisation of the NHS in Wales and sought to champion trade union rights in the workplace. It was a position which echoed that of the SNP in Scotland that sought to outflank Labour in providing an alternative focus for standing up for Wales against the Conservatives, portraying Labour as a failed party that would deliver simply austerity-light policies. They accepted that Labour might be the largest party in a hung Parliament at Westminster; in which

---

[7] Welsh Liberal Democrats, *Stronger Economy, Fairer Society, Opportunity For Everyone*, Election Manifesto 2015, Cardiff, Liberal Democrats.

[8] Plaid Cymru, *Working for Wales*, Election Manifesto 2015, Cardiff, Plaid Cymru.

context Plaid Cymru pledged to influence a minority Labour Government to prevent Wales being treated unfairly by government cuts and to push for an extension of devolved powers.

Conversely, on the right, UKIP sought to raise the profile of immigration and EU membership as issues in Wales.[9] UKIP's policies of favouring an Australian-style points system for all potential immigrants and leaving the EU, meaning that such a system would apply to all Europeans as well, contrasted sharply with all the other parties. Specifically Wales-related debate mainly highlighted the extent to which both Plaid Cymru and the Greens were the most enthusiastic for both immigration and continued EU membership, but otherwise it simply reinforced how distinctive UKIP's position was to all of the other British-wide parties. Otherwise, UKIP provided a distinctively sceptical approach to devolution in opposing any new powers for the Assembly; instead requiring it to perform better on the responsibilities it already had. Ultimately, UKIP sought to tap into electoral sentiment that the established Westminster parties had let the people down; UKIP would restore British sovereignty and re-empower people to govern themselves.

The multi-party nature of the campaign therefore brought to the fore quite diverse strategies. How effective were the party's campaigns perceived to be in relation to Wales and what lessons did they draw coming out of the election? Plaid Cymru's campaign received a somewhat underwhelming response. The party's official position was to talk up their success in staving off Labour's efforts to win seats from them, the achievement of six second places as well as the retention of their three seats. A solid basis had been laid for the future. However, on the BBC TV election night broadcast, Laura McAllister, the political commentator and previously a Plaid Cymru nominee on the Richard Commission, described Plaid Cymru's performance as lacking in ambition and average in achievement when compared with the colossal advances made by the SNP. Leanne Wood had personally failed to turn her increased public profile as a result of the Leaders' debates into momentum for winning votes at the 2016 Assembly elections. The public debate on Plaid Cymru went quiet very quickly, so it was not clear whether critical reflections would change campaign strategy for the future.

In contrast the Liberal Democrat result inspired ready admissions of failure. Kirsty Williams, the Welsh Leader, who had opposed the UK party going into coalition with the Conservatives, acknowledged that her party had failed to explain why they had done this and had then also failed to demonstrate the benefits of their role in government. The Party had focused many of its resources on last ditch efforts to save its existing seats. This proved a forlorn effort, the party's problems exemplified in Cardiff Central, where the u-turn on student finance policy when in government was widely considered to have lost the large student vote.

---

[9] UKIP, *Believe in Wales*, Election Manifesto 2015, Cardiff, UKIP.

Williams described the collapse in vote share and loss of all but one seat as 'truly devastating' and a massive re-building effort lay ahead.

In contrast, UKIP were upbeat about their performance. As their Welsh Leader, Nathan Gill, put it, 'We lost every single deposit five years ago—we are now the third party in Wales'.[10] UKIP were in expansionist mood in considering their prospects in the Assembly elections and were confident of a sustained vote for the 2020 General Election. If UKIP turns opinion poll ratings into votes at the 2016 Assembly elections, the party will get representation through the list seats. UKIP also could look forward to the potential added advantage of the higher saliency of their core issues during 2016, due to the debate on EU membership and associated issues of immigration and British citizens' rights ahead of a referendum that could occur by late 2016 and certainly no later than 2017. Even if an EU referendum vote were lost, the No vote could be expected to be a significant one and UKIP would remain as its carrier.

For the Conservatives, there was the most satisfaction of all with the success of their campaign. At a fundamental level the Conservatives appeared to have aligned their pro-enterprise economy message with being pro- rather than anti-Welsh. Their critique of Welsh Labour and the NHS was seen as a key factor in winning the Vale of Clwyd seat, where the Conservative candidate was a GP who had campaigned against the local effects of NHS policy. In leaders' debates, Crabb emphasised that concern about the NHS in Wales was the number one issue on the doorstep during the campaign. It was a campaign strategy that could bear repetition across Wales in the 2016 National Assembly elections. The Conservatives' pro fiscal devolution proposals also had the potential to wrong-foot Labour; for the Conservatives could now claim it was they who were taking devolution forward against Labour scepticism. It was also apparent that Labour's scepticism could only prove persuasive if you were pessimistic about Wales' economic prospects. Craig Williams, victorious candidate in Cardiff North, described the election as 'a game changer for the Conservative Party in Wales'.[11]

In Wales, as in the UK as a whole, much of the focus of post-election analysis of party strategy fell on the Labour Party. The initial response of Carwyn Jones, the Labour First Minister for Wales, was to acknowledge that 'it was not the result we were hoping for' and that Labour needed 'to do much more to win back support from people across the country'.[12] He was also quick to acknowledge that Labour needed to develop a more pro-business message, although he believed Welsh Labour had done that and simply needed to publicise it more.[13] Party sources

---

[10] *Western Mail*, 9 May 2015.

[11] *Western Mail*, 9 May 2015.

[12] *Western Mail*, 9 May 2015.

[13] *Wales on Sunday*, 10 May 2015.

laid more emphasis on problems in party campaign organisation. They indicated that Labour had incorrectly felt that they were winning Cardiff North and therefore ambitiously refocused resources to Vale of Glamorgan and diverted resources from Vale of Clwyd to Arfon for the same reasons. They did not appreciate they might lose Gower until the election count itself. In the event they lost all five seats.[14] In looking forward, Carwyn Jones placed his principal focus upon competition with Plaid Cymru and the need to stay ahead of them in future elections. He took much heart from the fact that Labour had yet again beaten Plaid Cymru and his key lesson was the need to strengthen the Welsh Labour brand. One option was to seek a federal relationship with the British Labour Party as a means to 'improve effectiveness as a campaigning and policy development organisation'.[15]

In contrast, former Labour Minister and MP for Pontypridd, Kim Howells, in a series of interviews, described Labour's campaign as a 'disgrace' and 'dull'. The party had become devoid of positive ideas and needed a major overhaul.[16] David Taylor, who had previously worked as a special advisor for Peter Hain, and now worked as a political consultant, commented specifically on Carwyn Jones' less self-critical re-action in two tweets on social media after the election that 'this level of denial does not bode well for Welsh Labour' and 'Carwyn complacency after appalling campaign & dire results somewhat alarming, needs to start taking some responsibility & show some humility'. The *Western Mail* quoted a Labour source as saying 'David is right to highlight the alarming complacency within the party and unless the hierarchy pulls it socks up, we face a disastrous Assembly election'.[17]

Alun Davies, the Labour Assembly Member for Blaenau Gwent, also broke cover to say that 'the UKIP vote across large parts of Wales, including in my own constituency of Blaenau Gwent, wasn't simply an anti-immigrant vote; it was in large part an anti-Labour vote as well and an anti-political vote'. He also argued that Labour had 'fundamentally and completely lost the argument on the economy' and 'comprehensively lost the argument on the National Health Service' in Wales against a Conservative campaign which had been 'brutally effective'. He suggested Welsh Labour needed to appreciate the 'perception of failure in delivery of key policy areas such as health and education that is affecting the support of the wider Labour Party in Wales' and that if 'we walk in to the Assembly elections next year simply believing that seats across Wales are going to fall into our laps then we will have the shock of our lives and we will quite deserve to have the shock of our lives'.[18]

---

[14] *Western Mail*, 9 May 2015.

[15] *Wales on Sunday*, 10 May 2015.

[16] Accessed at www.bbc.co.uk/news/uk-wales-32863936/ on 9 June 2015.

[17] *Western Mail*, 9 May 2015.

[18] *Western Mail*, 11 May 2015.

It is likely that Labour will remain cautious in any post-election rethink, keen to hold its ground as the party representing class and nation against Plaid Cymru competition. An energetic approach to campaigning and mobilising their vote may be sufficient to turn still favourable opinion polls into seats in the 2016 Assembly elections and renewed success in 2020. Yet, it is apparent that there were strongly held views in the Party that it was not simply the Nationalist threat that Welsh Labour needed to counter but the competition on different flanks from the Conservatives and UKIP, and the problems they may encounter in defending their record in government. This brought to mind problems perceived in Welsh Labour's campaign after the very poor Assembly election result in 2007 that Welsh Labour lacked a broad appeal beyond those perceived as core Labour voters and lacked clarity in what its practical social democratic achievements might be for people from traditional Labour voting communities.

The issue of Conservative warnings of a minority Labour Government being unduly influenced by the SNP did not form much part of the post-election analysis in Wales. However, there was anecdotal evidence of some candidates believing it was a factor. Byron Davies, the victorious Conservative candidate in Gower, said that 'the thought of a pact between the SNP and Labour was a worrying thought in the back of people's minds'.[19] The five YOUGOV/ITV Wales/Cardiff University polls on Welsh political opinion in Wales suggested very little movement in the polls between 27 April and 6 May. Yet, in the actual vote, Labour were 2.1% lower than their 6 May poll result of 39% and the Conservatives 2.2% higher than their last poll result of 25%.[20] Possibly the polls were consistently misleading, but equally a late switch to the Conservatives may also explain the failure of the Labour campaign to recognise the seats where it might be vulnerable to defeat. If more analysis reveals that the SNP fear factor influenced this late switch then this rather reinforces the idea of Labour's vulnerability in Wales, not simply to the contest with Plaid Cymru over representing Wales, but also to the contest with the Conservatives for providing credible reassurance of the UK's stability.

Overall, the manner in which the campaign was conducted reflected a battle between the Conservatives and Labour and then a battle between Labour and other opposition parties to represent opposition to Conservative Government. At the heart of that latter battle lay a presumed core contest between Labour and Plaid Cymru to represent Wales. In the interpretation of the results these presumptions remained strong, particularly in official Labour responses. In this sense electoral politics in Wales continued to be read in a manner quite strongly comparable to Scotland; the key difference being that Welsh Labour had in the past fought off Plaid Cymru's efforts to emulate the SNP by stealing their clothes and taking their vote,

---

[19] *Western Mail*, 9 May 2015.

[20] Welsh Political Barometer, accessed at http://blogs.cardiff.ac.uk/electionsinwales/ on 9 June 2015.

and they had done so again. Carwyn Jones appeared most anxious to re-invest in Welsh Labour's Welshness to ensure they continued to win this contest. Plaid Cymru joined in this interpretation as it effectively kept the contest they ultimately wanted to win as the central lens through which Welsh politics was viewed.

However, most of the other parties' post-mortems of the election read Welsh politics rather differently and emphasised the plural strands of political debate in Wales, including how voting behaviour might be affected by views of the economy, governmental competence at the devolved level and territorial state stability. At the same time Labour critics read the challenges to Labour as coming diversely from the anti-centre protest vote behind UKIP, which was also an anti-Welsh centre vote, and Conservative campaigns on the problems of Welsh Government under Labour, as well as from Plaid Cymru. It may well be that strategic thinkers at the heart of Welsh Labour have been astute in continuing to combat nationalism but as well as a lack of distinct Scottish party identity the other key factor that led to the decay of Scottish Labour was a perception of its failure in government. In Scotland the SNP was able to capitalise on that. In Wales it is the Conservatives that could largely capitalise on this, especially in the absence of an effective Nationalist party. While Labour ascendancy continues and its resilience should never be underestimated, the 2015 election may well be remembered most for signalling the arrival of cogent party competition from all sides, not just or even from the Nationalist side, which may yet transform Welsh electoral politics along lines more familiar to England than to Scotland.

3. Conclusion

Competition from territorially-based parties as well as the Conservatives did in practice play a significant role in the 2015 General Election in Wales as elsewhere in the UK. As expected this did not take the form of a vote for bloc representation by the ethno-regionalist Nationalist party, Plaid Cymru. More surprisingly, it took the form of a substantial new minority vote for UKIP. At the same time the election witnessed the consolidation of the Conservative Party as a significant representative of Welsh opinion, and of the interest among Welsh voters as well to support the Conservatives as a credible party of centre government. Viewed in Rokkan and Urwin's terms, Nationalist expression of regional tension did not progress but anti-centre politics did to some extent, and conservatism continued to gradually prosper. While Labour maintained dominance in vote and seat share, it lost rather than gained momentum both as an effective party of the periphery to re-present Welsh interests and as a plausible alternative governing party of the centre.[21]

Discussion of the campaign and party strategies indicates that in the minds of politicians the latent potential for Plaid Cymru to carry regional dissent

[21]Rokkan and Urwin, 'Introduction: Centres and Peripheries in Western Europe', p. 10.

Britain Votes (2015) 117–132

JONATHAN TONGE AND JOCELYN EVANS*

Another Communal Headcount: The Election in Northern Ireland

1. Introduction

The Westminster election in Northern Ireland attracted more interest beyond the region than is normally the case. This was not because of healthy new attention being paid to the polity's regular communal (to critics, sectarian) bloc headcount. Rather, it was because the contest's outcome might influence the formation of a minority government at Westminster. This possibility was actively discussed even into election night results programmes, after the exit poll predicted the Conservatives to fall just short of an overall majority, with 316 seats. As that seat tally rose, Northern Ireland's election slid back to its default positions of obscurity and parochial communalism. Religious community background remained easily the most important voting determinant. Unionist electoral pacts in four constituencies heightened the prevailing sense of a traditional Orange versus Green contest, one in which the Alliance Party, aligned to neither bloc, lost its solitary representative. Turnout was a very modest 58%, well below the UK average. Only Sinn Fein, the Social Democratic and Labour Party (SDLP) and Alliance contested all 18 constituencies. Nonetheless, the contest was not entirely bereft of interest. There were significant arguments over a disparate array of topics ranging from welfare reform to that of same-sex marriage, still banned in Northern Ireland. Four seats changed hands and the once-dominant Ulster Unionist Party (UUP) recovered some recent lost ground to regain Westminster representation.

*Jonathan Tonge, Department of Politics, University of Liverpool, j.tonge@liv.ac.uk; Jocelyn Evans, Department of Politics and International Studies, University of Leeds, j.a.j.evans@leeds.ac.uk

doi:10.1093/pa/gsv031

Table 8.1 Party vote and seat shares in Northern Ireland, 2015 Westminster election

	Seats	Change in seats	Votes	% of votes	Change in % share from 2010
DUP	8	0	184,260	25.7	+0.7
Sinn Fein	4	− 1	176,232	24.5	− 1.0
SDLP	3	0	99,809	13.9	− 2.6
UUP	2	+2	114,935	16.0	+0.8
Independent	1	0	17,689	2.5	− 0.1
Alliance	0	− 1	61,556	8.6	+2.2
TUV	0	0	16,538	2.3	− 1.6
Conservative	0	0	9,055	1.3	N/A[a]
Green	0	0	6,822	1.0	+0.5

[a]The Conservatives held an electoral alliance with the Ulster Unionist Party in 2010.

2.   The results

Table 8.1 indicates party fortunes in the contest. As has been the case since the 2001 election, Sinn Fein dominated the Nationalist bloc vote, the party's share being 63.8%, compared with the SDLP's 36.2%. Equally predictably, the Democratic Unionist Party (DUP) maintained its lead over the UUP evident at the previous two Westminster elections, this time by 61.6% to 38.4%.

As can be seen, changes in party vote shares were modest. As might be expected, there was a very strong relationship between party performance in 2010 and that in 2015 as Table 8.2 shows.

The results marked a significant upturn in fortunes for the UUP, a 'positive joy' for the leader since 2012, Mike Nesbitt, who had prioritised a return of his party to Westminster.[1] The UUP had suffered catastrophic reverses to the DUP in 2005 and its only MP, Lady Sylvia Hermon, quit in disgust prior to the 2010 election over the bizarre alliance with the Conservatives. Tentative signs of revival emerged in the 2014 local elections and the capture of two parliamentary seats in 2015 exceeded expectations. The party's hopes centred mainly upon taking ultra-marginal Fermanagh and South Tyrone from Sinn Fein, one of four constituencies where electoral pacts between the DUP and UUP were agreed. The DUP stood aside for the UUP in Fermanagh and South Tyrone and Newry and Armagh, a deal reciprocated by the UUP in Belfast East and Belfast North. The pact arrangement was derided as bad politics that turned off or disenfranchised the electorate. Yet turnout increased in all four constituencies in which the pacts operated, by an average of 3.5%. Only four of the other 14 constituencies recorded an increase in turnout. The electoral arrangement was also criticised as a skewed deal favouring the DUP; or as a pact which would not work,

---

[1] *Irish Times*, 9 May 2015, 'Revitalised UUP Get Most from Night of Mixed Fortunes', p. 5.

Table 8.2 Correlations between 2010 and 2015 Westminster election vote at constituency level

2015	DUP (2010)	UCUNF (2010)	Alliance (2010)	SDLP (2010)	SF (2010)
DUP (16)	.942 (17)				
UUP (15)		.736 (17)			
Alliance (18)			.957 (18)		
SDLP (18)				.931 (18)	
SF (18)					.959 (17)

The figures in brackets represent the number of constituencies contested.

although more perceptive commentators acknowledged the potential for both parties.[2]

The deal worked extremely well for both forces, allowing the DUP to recapture East Belfast and retain the key seat of North Belfast. Had the UUP polled at its 2010 level in East Belfast, rather than stepping aside, Alliance would have retained the seat. If the DUP had lost votes to the UUP in North Belfast and the SDLP had stood aside for its Nationalist rival, the seat would have been taken by Sinn Fein. A unified communal headcount worked for the DUP in North Belfast amid what its victorious candidate, Nigel Dodds, claimed was 'one of the nastiest campaigns I have been involved in'.[3] From fearing the elimination of parliamentary representation in Belfast, Unionists again held half of the city's four seats. In Fermanagh and South Tyrone in 2010, although a solitary Unionist candidate (standing, oddly and nominally, as an independent) had stood, the Unionist campaign had been lacklustre. Amid greater Unionist unity, a more prominent candidate (Tom Elliot was a former UUP leader) and weaknesses in Sinn Fein's defence of the seat, the UUP defied expectations and overturned the slender republican majority of four. The UUP's other gain was not pact-dependent, a 3% swing in South Antrim allowing the party to recapture a seat lost to the DUP in the calamitous election of 2005. Whilst the UUP's revival should not be exaggerated, in that its vote share rose by less than 1% in both the 2014 local and 2015 General Elections, the party had restored its credibility as an alternative for relatively moderate Unionists still somewhat DUP-adverse. Table 8.3 provides the party vote shares in individual constituencies.

Average turnout in majority Protestant constituencies was 55.7% and in majority Catholic constituencies 60.5%, maintaining a differential, but one that has been reduced in recent elections, having been as high as 11% as recently as 2005 (North and South Belfast are excluded from the 2015 tallies as their populations are almost

---

[2] See as an example of a more judicious analysis, Alex Kane's view at http://www.newsletter.co.uk/news/analysis-great-deal-for-the-dup-but-nesbitt-could-still-be-a-winner-1-6641211 on 19 March 2015.

[3] *Irish Times*, 9 May 2015, p. 5.

Table 8.3 Northern Ireland constituency results, 2015 Westminster election (% of vote)

	Result	DUP	UUP	Alliance	Sinn Fein	SDLP	Oth	Turnout	Turnout change from 2010	% Swing from 2010
Belfast E	DUP gain from Alliance	49.3	–	42.8	2.1	0.3	2.7	62.8	+3.9	5.5 Alliance to DUP
Belfast N	DUP hold	47.0	–	7.2	33.9	8.2	3.6	59.2	+2.7	1.6 SDLP to SF
Belfast S	SDLP hold	22.2	9.1	17.2	13.9	24.5	13.0	60.0	+2.6	3.4 UUP to DUP
Belfast W	SF hold	7.9	3.1	1.8	54.2	9.8	23.2	56.4	+2.4	–
East Antrim	DUP hold	36.1	18.8	15.0	6.9	4.9	18.3	53.3	+2.7	2.5 DUP to UUP
East Londonderry	DUP hold	42.2	15.4	7.6	19.8	12.3	2.7	51.9	−3.4	4.0 UUP to DUP
Fermanagh & S Tyrone	UUP gain from SF	–	46.4	1.3	45.4	5.4	1.5	72.6	+3.6	1.1 SDLP to SF
Foyle	SDLP hold	12.4	3.3	2.3	31.6	47.9	2.6	52.8	−4.7	1.8 SF to SDLP
Lagan Valley	DUP hold	47.9	15.2	13.9	2.9	6.3	13.8	55.9	−0.5	2.0 UUP to DUP
Mid Ulster	SF hold	13.4	15.4	1.9	48.7	12.4	8.2	60.3	−2.9	0.7 SF to SDLP
Newry & Armagh	SF hold	–	32.7	1.7	41.1	24.1	0.4	64.3	+3.8	0.8 SF to SDLP
North Antrim	DUP hold	43.2	12.1	5.6	12.3	7.0	19.9	55.2	−2.6	–
North Down	IND hold	23.6	–	8.6	0.8	1.0	IND 49.2, OTH, 16.8	56.0	−0.8	–
South Antrim	UUP gain from DUP	30.1	32.7	9.8	12.9	8.2	6.3	54.2	+0.2	3.0 DUP to UUP
South Down	SDLP hold	8.2	9.3	3.8	28.5	42.3	7.9	56.8	−3.4	2.0 SDLP to SF
Strangford	DUP hold	44.4	14.4	13.8	2.6	6.9	18.0	52.8	−0.9	6.0 UUP to DUP
Upper Bann	DUP hold	32.7	27.9	3.8	24.5	9.0	2.1	59.0	+3.6	1.7 DUP to UUP
West Tyrone	SF hold	17.5	15.9	2.2	43.5	16.7	4.3	60.5	−0.4	3.8 SF to SDLP

Note: The strong second places for People Before Profit, with 19.2% of the vote in West Belfast and Traditional Unionist Voice (TUV), with 15.7% of the vote in North Antrim, render the concept of swing nebulous in those constituencies. In North Down, the DUP did not contest the seat in 2010, so, again, swing is meaningless.

equally religiously mixed). There was little indication of an appetite for Westminster parties to field election candidates if the performance of the Conservative Party is any guide. Although they contested every seat except Fermanagh and South Tyrone and Belfast North, the Conservatives averaged only 1.3% of the vote and even their best performance, 4.4% in North Down, was deposit-losing.

Sectarian headcounting, for so long the dominant theme of Northern Ireland's elections, showed no sign of dissipating. Table 8.4 indicates the Unionist and Nationalist bloc voting figures. The relationship in each constituency between Protestant and Catholic community background percentages and Unionist or Nationalist bloc voting is then depicted in Figures 8.1 and 8.2.

Figures 8.1 and 8.2 plot the relationships between the percentage of Protestants in a constituency and the Unionist vote and likewise between the percentage of Catholics and the Nationalist vote. On the Unionist side, a plethora of parties make up that combined vote; the DUP, UUP, TUV, UKIP and the Conservatives, plus the support for the Independent Unionist, Sylvia Hermon. On the Nationalist side, the position is much more straightforward, a simple aggregate of the votes for Sinn Fein and the SDLP.

The correlations between the percentage Protestant population and Unionist vote and between the percentage Catholic population and Nationalist vote remain remarkably strong, virtually unchanged from the previous election. They are shown in Table 8.5.

Only East Belfast provided a significant outlier in terms of Unionist bloc voting, with a strong Alliance performance in an overwhelmingly Protestant constituency. If this outlier is removed, the Protestant–Unionist correlation moves to 0.980. West Belfast provides something of an outlier on the Nationalist side, given the strong performance of People Before Profit, which diminished the overall Nationalist vote by nearly one-quarter from 2010 and helped to ensure that the Nationalist bloc vote was less than two-thirds of votes cast, in a four-fifths Catholic constituency.

3.   The campaign within Unionism

The DUP's campaign focused upon retaking East Belfast from Alliance. Considerable hostility from the DUP towards its centrist rival had been evident since Naomi Long's success in 2010 over the DUP leader, Peter Robinson, in a seat held by the DUP since 1979. This opprobrium increased markedly after Alliance's decision in December 2012 to support the Nationalist parties on Belfast city council in preventing the Union flag being flown permanently from the city hall, in favour of its display only on designated days. Alliance came under considerable pressure from loyalist groups beyond the control of the DUP from thereon, with its East Belfast office (and others) firebombed during the following 18 months. Alliance's

Table 8.4 Unionist, Nationalist and Non-Unionist/Non-Nationalist vote shares, 2015 Westminster election

Constituency	Protestants	Protestant %	Total Unionist Vote	Total Unionist %	R. Catholics	R. Catholic %	Nationalist vote	Nationalist %	No religion	Turnout %
Belfast E	69,533	75.4	19,575	49.3	11,712	12.7	950	2.4	10.5	62.8
Belfast N	46,821	45.7	19,096	47.0	48,126	46.9	17,637	43.4	6.4	59.2
Belfast S	48,630	43.7	14,685	35.7	49,025	44.0	14,962	38.4	9.5	60.0
Belfast W	15,645	16.7	4660	13.2	75,263	80.1	22,638	64.1	2.7	56.4
East Antrim	63,148	70.1	24,523	73.2	18,362	20.4	3953	11.8	8.5	53.3
East Londonderry	53,097	53.3	20,418	58.8	41,564	41.7	11,127	32.1	4.4	51.9
Fermanagh & S Tyrone	40,100	39.1	23,608	46.4	59,159	57.7	25,810	50.7	2.6	72.6
Foyle	22,193	22.0	6763	18.3	75,731	75.1	29,404	79.5	2.1	52.8
Lagan Valley	73,158	71.9	30,451	75.0	19,346	19.0	3644	9.2	8.1	55.9
Mid Ulster	30,522	30.8	14,658	35.8	66,152	66.7	24,990	61.1	2.1	60.3
Newry & Armagh	34,380	30.6	16,522	33.1	74,591	66.4	32,514	65.2	2.5	64.3
North Antrim	71,446	66.0	31,431	75.0	30,723	28.4	8068	19.3	4.8	55.2
North Down	66,618	74.4	28,344	83.3	11,269	12.6	628	1.8	11.8	56.0
South Antrim	59,349	59.8	25,258	69.6	31,619	31.9	7689	21.1	7.5	54.2
South Down	29,224	26.9	10,812	25.3	75,384	69.3	30,363	70.9	3.4	56.8
Strangford	65,353	73.1	26,026	76.7	15,447	17.3	3211	9.5	8.7	52.8
Upper Bann	58,998	50.0	28,797	61.0	51,919	44.0	15,831	33.5	5.1	59.0
West Tyrone	27,502	30.2	13,060	33.8	61,993	68.0	23,251	60.2	1.5	60.5

North Down's MP, Sylvia Hermon, was re-elected as an Independent (she stood on the same label in 2010) but can be regarded as Unionist. She was formerly a UUP MP and was not opposed by the UUP.

Source for religious composition of constituencies: Russell, R. (2013) *Census 2011: Key Statistics at Assembly Area Level*, Northern Ireland Research and Information Service Information Paper NIAR 161-13, accessed at http://www.niassembly.gov.uk/globalassets/documents/raise/publications/2012/general/7013.pdf, on 17 May 2015.

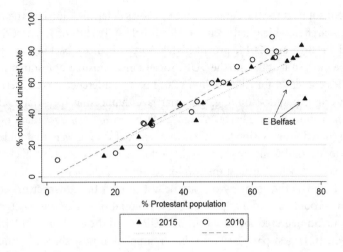

Figure 8.1 Unionist constituency vote by Protestant population, 2010–2015

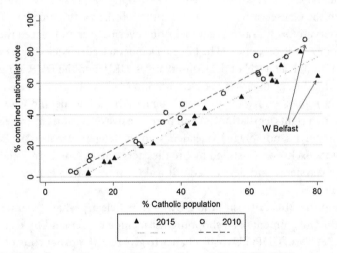

Figure 8.2 Nationalist constituency vote by Catholic population, 2010–2015

Table 8.5 Correlations between religious community background and Unionist or Nationalist bloc vote, 2005–2015

	2005	**2010**	**2015**
Catholic-Nationalist	0.975	0.987	0.985
Protestant-Unionist	0.974	0.943	0.919

consistent support for the Parades Commission's determinations on the routes of Orange marches, which had seen the North Belfast Twelfth of July return parade stopped in 2013 and 2014, provoked DUP ire. Alliance's backing for same-sex marriage was also at odds with the DUP's social conservatism. Robinson summarised the DUP's contempt for Alliance in his 2014 party conference speech, deriding the 'flag-lowering, parade-stopping, gay marriage supporting, pro-water charging, holier-than-thou Alliance Party'.[4] Alliance's *Step Forward Not Back* manifesto[5] contained a shared future vision (numbers in integrated schools were to double to 20% by 2020 for example) but the party, whilst performing well, was always likely to struggle to hold East Belfast against the combined forces of Unionism.

For the DUP, the recovery of East Belfast offered the prospect of additional strength through size in any post-election negotiations. The unexpected loss of South Antrim neutered the gain but the DUP ended the election as it had begun, as the fourth largest party at Westminster, a position now shared by the much-reduced Liberal Democrats. In anticipation of a possible role of kingmaker in government formation, the DUP, unlike the other smaller parties (with the exception of the Liberal Democrats), was careful to keep open the possibility of doing business with the Conservatives or Labour, although the party's members favoured the Conservatives by a ratio of seven-to-one over Labour and placed themselves considerably right-of-centre.[6] The Liberal Democrat leader, Nick Clegg, cautioned against a 'Blukip alliance' of the Conservatives, UKIP and the DUP, a 'right-wing alliance that brings together people who don't believe in climate change; who reject gay rights; who want the death penalty back and people who want to scrap human rights legislation'.[7] Amid the extensive television coverage afforded to smaller parties, notably in the leaders' and challengers' debates, the DUP protested at its exclusion (justified by broadcasters due to Northern Ireland's distinct party system) and demanded a Royal Commission to explore the future of the BBC.

Beyond the BBC criticism, the DUP outlined clearly what it wanted from a future UK Government. The shopping list included a demand to keep defence spending at 2% of GDP; EU treaty change to give the UK greater control over immigration and the removal of the 'spare room subsidy', more commonly known as

---

[4] Peter Robinson, Speech to DUP party conference, La Mon Hotel Belfast, 22 November 2014, accessed at http://www.mydup.com/news/article/conference-2014-leaders-speech-rt-hon-peter-robinson-mla on 22 May 2015.

[5] Alliance Party (2015) *Step Forward Not Back: Alliance Party 2015 Westminster election manifesto*, Belfast, Alliance Party.

[6] Tonge, J., Braniff, M., Hennessey, T., McAuley, J. and Whiting, S. (2014) *The Democratic Unionist Party: From Protest to Power*, Oxford, Oxford University Press.

[7] 'DUP Part of Right-wing Threat Warns Clegg', *Irish News*, 17 April 2015, p. 10.

the 'bedroom tax', even though it had not been extended to Northern Ireland anyway. The DUP's traditional line on being right-wing on security and constitutional issues but, cognisant of a working-class support base, more centre-left on economic issues, was a useful outlook in promoting equidistance between the main Westminster parties. Local issues of importance, such as parade routes and flags, were kept hidden from view in terms of possible leverage.

Similar to the DUP, the UUP did not offer preferment for the Conservatives or Labour. The UUP manifesto also bore many similarities to that offered by the DUP, particularly regarding a reduction in corporation tax and greater local financial control, adding demands for VAT cuts for property repairs and the hospitality industry and extra funding for mental health.[8] The party claimed the extra economic activity engendered by its tax reductions would be worth £1.4 billion against a diminished take of £500 million. The UUP's proposals for integrated education from the age of four did not differ markedly from those of Alliance.

4. The campaign within nationalism

With the party's focus seemingly upon the elections to the Irish Parliament and the Northern Ireland Assembly in 2016, the centenary of the Easter Rising, Sinn Fein's Westminster campaign was lacklustre. It was even marked by very unusual public criticism from within, following the publication of an election leaflet promoting Gerry Kelly's candidature in marginal North Belfast. This was the constituency where most Troubles killings occurred (577) and where sectarianism remained rawest.[9] Attempting to unseat the DUP's Westminster leader, Nigel Dodds, Kelly's leaflet lacked subtlety, in deploying a pie chart showing the percentage of Catholics (46.94) and Protestants (45.67) in the constituency, taken from the 2011 census. Voters were urged, on the basis of the Catholic majority, to elect the Sinn Fein candidate to 'Make the Change, Make History'. The figures represented the entire constituency population, but the adult demography was somewhat different, with Protestant adults still holding a slight majority. Aided by the Unionist electoral pact and splitting of the Nationalist vote between Kelly and the SDLP candidate, the DUP comfortably held the seat. Whilst any Unionist outrage might be dismissed as faux and synthetic, given Northern Ireland's existence on the basis of a similar headcount, more significant criticism of Sinn Fein's leaflet came from an unlikely source—two of its own members, who publicly denounced the leaflet as an

---

[8] Ulster Unionist Party (2015) *One Day, One Vote, One Chance for Change: Ulster Unionist Party Election Manifesto*, Belfast: UUP accessed at http://uup.org/assets/images/uup%20ge%20manifesto.pdf, on 22 May 2015.

[9] Accessed at http://www.belfasttelegraph.co.uk/news/general-election-2015/battle-for-north-belfast-getting-vote-out-is-key-to-dodds-reelection-for-dup-31148874.html on 12 May 2015.

'absolute disgrace' and the 'very antithesis of what republicanism represents at its core'.[10]

Beyond the communal counting, the main thrust of Sinn Fein's election campaign lay in the opposition to the welfare reforms being introduced at Stormont. The party had appeared to accept the UK Government's financial package offered in the Stormont House Agreement in December 2014 and supported the subsequent preliminary legislation. The deal comprised '£650 m of new and additional funding; flexibilities that protect £900 m of resource spending (normally ring fenced for capital) and additional capital borrowing of up to £350 m' with the promise that a £114 million 'fine' for the failure to complete welfare reform on time be reduced if completed during 2015–2016.[11] It was lauded in the Conservative Party manifesto as 'a deal to help ensure that politics works, the economy grows and society is more cohesive and united'.[12]

Having appeared to acquiesce to the arrangements, Sinn Fein followed its March 2015 ard-fheis in Derry, at which the proposals had attracted minimal disquiet, by rejecting the plans and then continuing to oppose proposed Conservative welfare and service cuts during and beyond the campaign, voting down the passage of the welfare reform bill three weeks after the election and reviving uncertainty over the political institutions. The party demanded the reinstatement of £1.5 billion which it claimed had been cut from Northern Ireland's block grant whilst advocating the devolution of powers of income tax, national insurance to the region and capital gains tax, as well as the power to set the minimum wage and end zero hours contracts. Whilst the precise timing of Sinn Fein's apparent u-turn was odd, the party was keen to establish its anti-austerity credentials. Critics had accused Sinn Fein of opposing austerity in the Irish Republic at the same time as presiding over its implementation in the North. By now moving against welfare cuts in Northern Ireland, Sinn Fein diminished the legitimacy of the charge.

Beyond the financial issues, Sinn Fein reiterated longstanding demands for a bill of rights and an Irish Language Act remained, whilst the party also advocated gender quotas for election candidates.[13] Sinn Fein's advocacy of a united Ireland was expressed via a continuing commitment to a border poll on Irish unity although it remained unclear whether it would be a North only plebiscite—in

---

[10] Accessed at http://www.newsletter.co.uk/news/regional/election-diary-sf-rising-star-savages-kelly-s-sectarian-leaflet-1-6723815 on 4 May 2015.

[11] HM Government, 'UK Government Financial Package to Northern Ireland', accessed at https://www.gov.uk/government/uploads/system/uploads/attachment_data/file/390673/Stormont_House_Agreement_Financial_Annex.pdf on 21 May 2015, p. 1.

[12] Conservative Party (2015) *Strong Leadership: A Clear Economic Plan: A Brighter, More Secure Future: The Conservative Party Manifesto 2015*, London, Conservative Party, p. 69.

[13] Martin McGuinness, 'Standing up to the Tories', *Irish News*, 28 April 2015, p. 11.

the gift of the British Secretary of State, certain to result in a no vote and more likely to harm the republican cause—or an all-island vote via the two jurisdictions, the latter a potentially interesting expression of sentiment regardless of the seeming impossibility of implementation. Amid talk of a hung Westminster Parliament, Sinn Fein's policy of abstention came under scrutiny. Any possibility of the party taking their seats in a British Parliament was robustly denied by Sinn Fein's Deputy First Minister and by the national chairman, Declan Kearney, the former adamant that it remained a matter of 'principle' and the latter stating that Sinn Fein would 'never' take their seats. Given the denials, which preceded entry into Dail Eireann and the Northern Ireland Assembly, the degree of credence to be afforded such protestations was open to debate, but nonetheless it was apparent that there was no movement on the subject at the present time within Sinn Fein.

The eclectic range of 'dissident' republicans long disillusioned with Sinn Fein's compromises may have been particularly sceptical about Sinn Fein's abstentionist pledge. The political dissidents had enjoyed a few modest local election successes in 2014, one even topping the poll in Derry. The paramilitary aspect of dissidence remained active and was evident in attempted bombings and death threats during the General Election campaign. The dissidents were regarded as 'still a threat' even if their campaign was dismissed as 'going nowhere' by the main Nationalist newspaper.[14] The year prior to the beginning of the election campaign had witnessed three deaths related to the security situation, 73 shootings and 36 bombing incidents, with 35 people charged (from 227 arrests) under the Prevention of Terrorism Act.[15] Over the five years since the last Westminster election campaign, there had been 634 shooting and bombing incidents and eight deaths. This was small-scale compared with the Troubles, but the peace remained imperfect.

SDLP policy for Northern Ireland did not differ markedly from that offered by Sinn Fein, nor did the campaign, which was also 'anti-austerity'. The SDLP emphasised how it had regularly tabled amendments to bills in the Northern Ireland Assembly that had been defeated by the DUP and Sinn Fein. Yet, whilst going into formal opposition in the Assembly remained an option for the SDLP, it was difficult to see how this alone could restore the party's fortunes. The SDLP supported greater devolution of fiscal powers and placed particular emphasis upon the need for tourism VAT to be reduced to 5% to grow the number of visitors. In pledging to form a 'Celtic coalition' with the SNP and Plaid Cymru, the SDLP

---

[14]See, for example, the editorials in the *Irish News*: 'Dissidents Still a Threat', *Irish News*, 23 April 2015 and 'Dissidents Put Lives At Risk', *Irish News*, 29 April 2015.

[15]Police Service of Northern Ireland (2015) 'Security Situation Statistics 2014–15', Belfast, PSNI, accessed at http://www.psni.police.uk/annual_security_situation_statistics_report_2014-15.pdf on 22 May 2015, pp. 2–4.

criticised the 'silent partners' of Sinn Fein, absent from Westminster.[16] Only four months after supporting the Stormont House Agreement, the SDLP grandly pledged to negotiate a 'New Economic Accord with Westminster'.[17] The party's comfortable defence of its three seats did not assuage the desire for a change of personnel at the helm. Within one week of the election, the former leader Mark Durkan and former deputy leaders Seamus Mallon and Brid Rodgers had called for Alasdair McDonnell to stand down.[18] Amid geographical confinement, another shrunken vote share and the perception of better ideas, days and leaders behind it, the SDLP's long slow decline continued.

5. Social conservatism and the moral agenda

A feature of the election campaign was the debate over social conservatism. Same-sex marriage became one of the most discussed topics. The referendum campaign in the Irish Republic on the issue, which saw a decisive endorsement (by a near two-to-one margin) of same-sex marriage, was already underway when the election in Northern Ireland took place. The DUP remained firmly opposed to revising the traditional terms of marriage. The party had already blocked the attempted introduction of same-sex marriage three times via the introduction of Petitions of Concern in the Northern Ireland Assembly. In addition, DUP ministers had opposed blood donations from gays and adoption by gay couples.

After the election the DUP leader allowed his Assembly members (MLAs) to vote with their conscience rather than a party whip on issues such as gay marriage and abortion, but the net effect would be the same. The UUP already allowed its MLAs a free vote on same-sex marriage, but only one voted in favour of the change, although he (Danny Kinahan) found it no barrier to his election to Westminster in 2015. The DUP was also prominent in backing the Christian bakery, Ashers, which had declined to bake a cake with a slogan supporting gay marriage. Shortly after the election the bakery lost the case, being found to have discriminated against its customer. The DUP promised a 'conscience clause' bill protecting individuals against having to act against their religious beliefs, although any legislative proposals appeared certain to flounder against the requirement for cross-community support.

For some within the DUP (but not the leadership) social conservatism offers the prospect of electoral outreach to Catholic conservatives.[19] Yet this seems unlikely to

---

[16] Alasdair McDonnell, 'Time to Choose a Better Way', *Irish News*, 29 April 2015.

[17] Social Democratic and Labour Party (2015) *Prosperity Not Austerity: Westminster Manifesto 2015*, Belfast, SDLP.

[18] *Irish News*, 'Durkan; SDLP Needs Change in Leadership', *Irish News*, 15 May 2015, p. 4.

[19] See, for example, the comments of the former minister, Edwin Poots, in Tonge et al, *The Democratic Unionist Party*, op cit. p. 182.

yield much dividend amid an electorate still polarised amid by communal division in terms of voting patterns. Moreover, that conservative Catholic constituency is diminishing in size as liberal views spread and it is doubtful that even less socially liberal older Catholics, having endured decades of anti-Catholicism from the DUP's founder, could ever be persuaded to consider the DUP as a viable voting proposition. During the election campaign, the DUP leadership was keener to show the party as a modern force than an organisation rooted in biblical certainties. As the Unionist newspaper, the *News Letter* noted of the DUP's view of homosexuality, the party's strategy was to avoid the question altogether.[20] Same-sex marriage and abortion were subjects entirely omitted from the DUP's 32-page election manifesto. The DUP leadership also took care to also omit any mention of such items from its requirements of a future British Government. Obviously these 'moral' issues were devolved items (as re-affirmed at the time of the 2006 St Andrews Agreement when many members insisted the regional opt-out was crucial), so there was no particular reason for the DUP to raise them as bargaining chips. However, their omission was also a product of the DUP leadership's desire to do nothing to deter the potential suitors of its own 'civil partnership'—the Conservative or Labour leaderships—from courtship in the event of a hung Parliament. David Cameron made his distaste clear: 'I totally disagree with the DUP about this issue',[21] whilst not closing off any post-election deal options.

The DUP leadership's desire to keep same-sex marriage discussions off topic was soon blown off course by the comments of the party's Northern Ireland Executive Health Minister, Jim Wells, at a hustings three weeks before the election. Located very much within the religiously devoted Free Presbyterian wing of the party, Wells allegedly claimed that the children of gay couples were far more likely to be abused or neglected.[22] Although he subsequently apologised, Wells was also involved in controversy over alleged criticism of a lesbian couple's lifestyle and he resigned from office. Debates over same-sex marriage featured in the subsequent televised debates between the party leaders.

Yet despite the furore, Wells' comments were unlikely to dissuade the DUP vote. Of more significance was the gradually changing internal party dynamic, imperceptible to those unwilling to take a closer look. One perceptive commentator was correct in arguing, against the flow, that 'just beneath the surface, the DUP is

---

[20] Sam McBride, 'Analysis: DUP Strategy to Avoid Moral Issues in Disarray, accessed at http://www.newsletter.co.uk/news/regional/analysis-dup-strategy-to-avoid-moral-issues-in-disarray-1-6712551 on 28 April 2015.

[21] *Irish News*, 'Cameron Refuses to Rule Out a DUP coalition', 23 April 2015, p. 8.

[22] Accessed at http://www.newsletter.co.uk/news/regional/health-minister-apologises-for-gay-marriage-child-abuse-remark-1-6707479 on 24 April 2015.

changing'.[23] Whilst the Free Presbyterians, for whom the DUP was a vehicle for politicised Protestantism, remain the largest single denomination within the party, very few have joined in the last two decades and the party will gradually come to reflect a more 'normal' distribution of Protestant denominations. This change will also be facilitated by the influx of more socially liberal former UUP members who entered the party after the Good Friday Agreement. The DUP will hardly overnight become a liberal and secular entity—the current leader believes strongly in faith-derived politics informing his party.[24] The legacy of Paisleyism remains strong even if the influence of Paisley's Free Presbyterian Church wanes. Nonetheless, the party is undergoing change and has come some distance from the views of, for example, former senior DUP figures such as the Reverend Ivan Foster, who, in April 2015, criticised the DUP for softening its stance on the 'vile sin' of homosexuality since the days when the party was at the forefront of the 'Save Ulster from Sodomy' campaign of the 1970s.[25]

Sinn Fein had brought proposals for marriage equality before the Assembly on three occasions prior to the election and pledged to continue reform the existing law in the party's manifesto.[26] During the Westminster election the party was campaigning simultaneously and successfully for a Yes vote for same-sex marriage in the Irish Republic. The SDLP also offered support for same-sex marriage, although five of the party's 14 Assembly members did not vote in the 2015 debate on the issue. The SDLP could fairly point out it was not alone in its divisions, given that Alliance, which strongly trumpeted its support for change, found three of its eight members abstaining on the same-sex marriage bill. The SDLP also took a hard line on abortion, party leader McDonnell opposing a softening of the law even in cases of lethal foetal abnormality.

Overall, the debate over social conservatism amounted to a political contest which did not replace the old Orange versus Green paradigm, but, on same-sex marriage at least, tended to replicate divisions. The Protestant and Unionist wing continued to advocate traditional social values, still more overtly on the DUP side, although even that party will thaw in due course. Both of the main Unionist

---

[23] Sam McBride, 'Analysis: It Might Not Look Like It But the DUP is Changing', accessed at http://www.newsletter.co.uk/news/regional/analysis-it-might-not-look-like-it-but-the-dup-is-changing-1-6709299 on 25 April 2015.

[24] The current leader, Peter Robinson, insists that on a 0–10 scale where 0 equals no faith influence and 10 equals the maximum influence upon a party, faith should equal 10, but should not be derived from a particular church. See Tonge, J. et al. *The Democratic Unionist Party*, op cit.

[25] Accessed at http://www.newsletter.co.uk/news/regional/dup-soft-on-vile-sin-of-homosexuality-foster-1-6712547 on 12 May 2015.

[26] Sinn Fein (2015) *Equality Not Austerity. 2015 Westminster Election Manifesto*, Belfast: Sinn Fein, accessed at http://www.sinnfein.ie/contents/34582 on 5 May 2015.

parties regarded the issues as matters of conscience rather than formal party positions by 2015, although the DUP was still seen as a party hostile to change. In the centre, Alliance's support for same-sex marriage offered a clear choice for liberal Unionists who rejected the DUP's fusion of politics with a particular moral view. The Green Nationalist side also retained some of its longstanding social conservatism (which even Sinn Fein's left turn of the 1980s had not entirely sidelined) but this was largely on the abortion issue, with neither of the two Nationalist parties advocating a loosening of abortion legislation on the scale of the 1967 Abortion Act elsewhere in the UK, even allowing for Sinn Fein's avowed 'pro-choice' stance. However, Sinn Fein's strong support for same-sex marriage, a position backed by most of the SDLP, marked a significant contrast with Unionist positions.

6. Conclusion

The election amply demonstrated how the linkage between religious community background and voting patterns remains the strongest in Europe. For all that successive surveys indicate that the largest category of electors is that eschewing Unionist or Nationalist labels, this category is very much a minority voter species at election time. Although enjoying a modest vote rise in this contest, the main party declining alignment to either bloc, Alliance, has never achieved a percentage vote share in double figures at any Westminster election—and it was fighting its eleventh such contest. One assessment of the election asserted that 'there are a lot of shy Unionists and pro-Union supporters out there . . . maybe a bit embarrassed by some aspects and manifestations of unionism and loyalism'.[27] Nonetheless, it is Unionists and Nationalists who show up at the polls, to cast votes for 'their' ideological parties.

Other issues beyond the old inter-communal attachments were important in the election, although how Northern Ireland's representation might affect the parliamentary arithmetic at Westminster often overshadowed local policy discussions. Welfare reform figured prominently and the extent of devolution to Northern Ireland, particularly in respect of its (lack of) fiscal autonomy, was also a concern. There was consensus across the divide on the need for improved public services and strong support for harmonisation of corporation tax across Ireland, meaning a substantial reduction in the North.

Religiously derived issues featured in the campaign to an unusual extent. Amongst the main parties, support for same-sex marriage was offered by Sinn Fein, Alliance and the SDLP and opposed by the DUP (the UUP remained neutral although most of its elected representatives opposed the idea). Whilst moral issues such as same-sex marriage and abortion potentially provide electoral

---

[27] Alex Kane, 'Unionism Was Overall Winner in the Election', *Irish News*, 15 May 2015, p. 21.

reconfigurations and new divides between social conservatives and 'progressives', the old Orange versus Green affiliations remain paramount and, if anything tend to be replicated via a Unionist social conservatism versus a Nationalist greater progressivism or liberalism faultline, although this division is far from absolute. There is likely to be considerable pressure placed upon the DUP and UUP on the same-sex marriage over the next few years, provoking arguments on different aspects of the issue. These go beyond the actual merit of rival positions on the issue and into consideration of, first, the isolation of Northern Ireland in comparison to the Irish Republic and the remainder of the UK, versus respect for the principles of devolved self-government and second, the relative merits of any court challenge against the democratic mandate of the DUP and UUP to resist change. Cultural wars have been dominated by the Orange-Green contests of parades and symbols since the Good Friday Agreement, but over the next few years the socio-moral arena will also be significant.

A large swathe of the electorate remains unattached to traditional Unionist or Nationalist labels and declares as non-aligned. However, this sizeable section remains less likely to vote than the ideological identifiers, making Northern Ireland elections continuing contests of mainly true believers. As for the intra-bloc contests, they merely highlighted what these election volumes have been previously asserting. There is electoral space, in the form of a substantial mildly Protestant and moderately Unionist middle-class, for the UUP to revive, as the party continues its organisational improvements. Re-entry to Westminster fulfilled one of the UUP's immediate strategic objectives. For the SDLP, there is less electoral space to recover and the crises of leadership and organisation meant a further loss of vote share, even in an election in which a somewhat distracted Sinn Fein did not perform particularly well.

Acknowledgements

The authors acknowledge with thanks the support of the Economic and Social Research Council for award ES/L007320/1, The Northern Ireland 2015 General Election Survey.

JUSTIN FISHER*

Party Finance: The Death of the National Campaign?

Party finance in 2015 in many ways marked a continuation of previous trends. First, and most obviously, the position of the Conservatives as the 'wealthy party' was firmly re-established. The party was financially dominant in 2010 as well, but this election demonstrated clearly that this had not been a blip. Second, in the conclusion to the article on the 2010 election, I suggested that national campaign spending might be slipping behind constituency-focused campaigning.[1] The evidence from this election was that not only had this trend continued, but that it might not be too much of an exaggeration to say that national campaign expenditure as we have traditionally understood it may well now effectively be dead, or at least in terminal decline at Great Britain (GB) level. As we will see, the vast majority of spending by the Conservatives, Labour and Liberal Democrats was not on large scale nationally-focused campaigns, but on supporting constituency efforts through ever more precise micro-targeting of key voters in target seats. Third, if 2010 had proved to be hyperbolic in terms of digital campaigning without any great evidence of its importance or impact, expenditure in 2015 suggested that digital campaigning may now be becoming more significant.[2] But critically, some digital methods (such as Facebook) were more significant than others. And perhaps most importantly, old-fashioned direct mail still dominated.

1. Long-term trends in income and expenditure

Until the period of Tony Blair's leadership, Labour's electoral record could reasonably be described as 'patchy' at best. No Labour Government had ever won a full

---

*Justin Fisher, Magna Carta Institute, Brunel University London, justin.fisher@brunel.ac.uk

[1] Fisher, J. (2010) 'Party Finance—Normal Service Resumed?', *Parliamentary Affairs*, **63**, 778–801.

[2] Fisher, J., Cutts, D. and Fieldhouse, E. (2011) 'Constituency Campaigning in 2010'. In D. Wring, R. Mortimore and S. Atkinson (eds) *Political Communication in Britain: TV Debates, the Media and the Election*. Basingstoke, Palgrave, pp. 198–217.

doi:10.1093/pa/gsv032

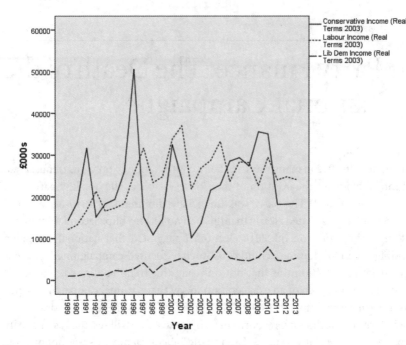

Figure 9.1 Central party income, 1989–2013 (at 2003 prices)

second term. Under Blair, Labour won three full-terms. Equally, Labour's financial dominance under Tony Blair now looks increasingly like being an historical anomaly. As I wrote in 2010, in party finance terms, at least, the post-Blair period appeared to represent the resumption of normal service, with the Conservatives restoring their traditional financial dominance.[3] And yet, over the course of the first part of the 2010–2015 Parliament, Labour actually managed to generate most income. As Figure 9.1 shows, up to and including the latest available accounts ending in 2013, Labour started to attract more income than the Conservatives.[4] This is captured well in Figure 9.2, which examines Labour central income as a percentage of that of the Conservatives. Yet, it also shows that by 2013, the financial gap between Labour and the Conservatives was closing. Conservative income after 2010 dropped off fairly sharply and though Labour's income was swelled by the receipt of public funds (such as Short money) by virtue of being in opposition, its voluntary income still exceeded that of the Conservatives following the 2010 General Election. Yet it would be a mistake to characterise this as a Labour financial resurgence. The key pattern in the post-2010 period in respect of the Conservatives

---

[3] Fisher, J. 'Party Finance—Normal Service Resumed?'

[4] Data for national party income and expenditure come from the individual parties' accounts.

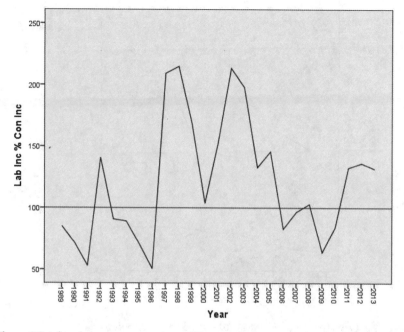

Figure 9.2 Labour income as a percentage of Conservative income, 1989–2013

was the familiar cycle of voluntary donations that are tied so strongly to the General Election cycle.[5] Rather than Labour's income growing, it fell immediately after the 2010 election and then remained reasonably constant (actually declining slightly), as a result of more steady income from trade union affiliation fees and public funds, whereas the Conservatives' income, largely now dependent on voluntary income, dipped more dramatically at first. This is captured in Figure 9.3, where the data are smoothed and show how Labour's income since the early 2000s has been in general decline. As we will see, as the election approached, a more familiar upturn in Conservative income occurred.

Not surprisingly, levels of income are associated with levels of expenditure. As Figure 9.4 shows, expenditure cycles strongly around the timing of General Elections with significant falls in the immediate aftermath. The post-2010 period was no different, with Labour spending most in the period up to end of 2013. However, as the smoothed data in Figure 9.5 show, this was more a function of a drop in Conservative spending than a significant rise in Labour expenditure, which remained fairly constant and well below the party's spending in the early 2000s. Part of the reason for this was the greater financial prudence demonstrated by the larger two parties in recent years. A previous trend for parties is that they

---

[5]Fisher, J. (2000) 'Economic Evaluation or Electoral Necessity? Evaluating the System of Voluntary Income to Political Parties', *British Journal of Politics & International Relations*, **2**, 179–204.

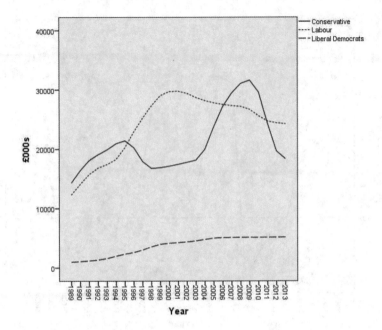

Figure 9.3 Central party income, 1989–2013 (smoothed. 2003 prices)

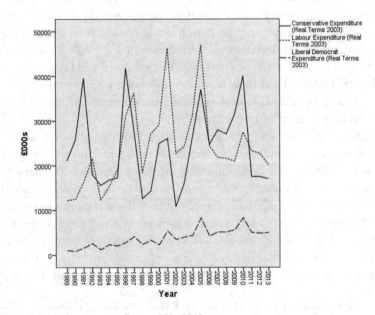

Figure 9.4 Central party expenditure, 1989–2013

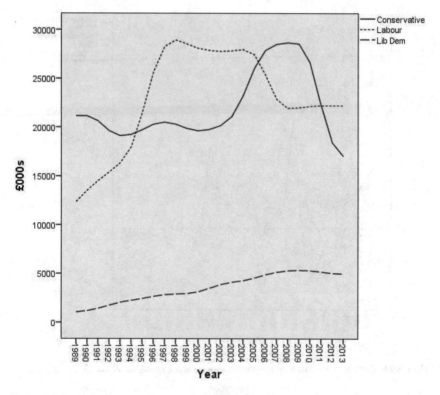

Figure 9.5 Central party expenditure, 1989–2013 (smoothed. 2003 prices)

have often spent much more than their income in any one year. Since 2007, however, that particular habit appears to have been broken. Since then, both Labour and the Conservatives have generally been able to contain their spending, and while the reverse has been true for the Liberal Democrats, the latest accounts (2013) indicate that they too have been able to spend less than they've generated (Figure 9.6). These trends are demonstrated even more starkly in Figure 9.7. The result for the largest two parties is that their liabilities have fallen sharply.

2.   Another party finance Parliament

The 2005–2010 Parliament was one where the issue of party finance reform loomed large following the 'loans for peerages' episode, the Hayden Phillips review and the *Political Parties and Elections Act 2009*.[6] And this Parliament did at one stage look as though the same would occur. In the end, it was not so prominent, but in the long-term, the events of 2010–2015 may have much more significant

---

[6] Fisher, J. 'Party Finance—Normal Service Resumed?'

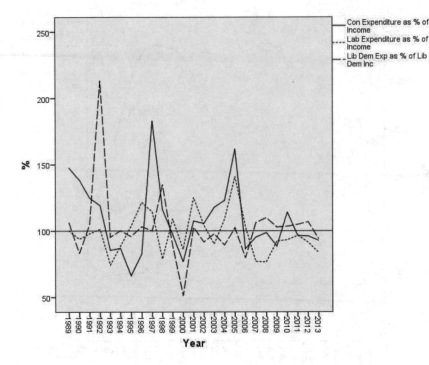

Figure 9.6 Central expenditure as a percentage of central income, 1989–2013

implications for party finance regulation in the UK. Soon after the 2010 General Election, the Deputy Prime Minister, Nick Clegg—a champion of radical party finance reform—asked the Committee on Standards in Public Life (CSPL) to once again review the whole area of party finance. The Committee's previous report on party finance, published 1998 had resulted in the introduction of extensive reform through the *Political Parties, Elections & Referendums Act 2000*. The Committee reported in November 2011 and focused on trying to remove 'big money' from politics.[7] The report made two important points early on: first, political parties play an essential role in the country's democracy; and, second, that there was potentially a difficult choice because any desire to remove large donations would require donation caps. If caps were imposed then an extension of public funding was the only realistic way of ensuring that parties survive. So there was a choice—donation caps and an extension of public funding or the status quo— the CSPL favoured the former.

---

[7]Committee on Standards in Public Life (2011) *Political Party Finance: Ending the Big Donor Culture*. London, HMSO.

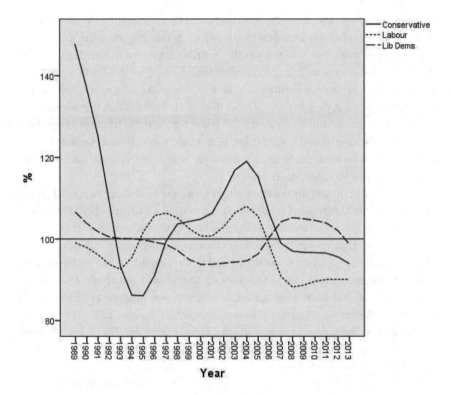

Figure 9.7 Central party expenditure as a percentage of central party income, 1989–2013 (smoothed)

The report made 24 detailed recommendations, the most significant of which were capping donations, extending state funding and cutting election expenditure limits. This was radical—going further than the Phillips review in the previous Parliament and like that report, very much outside the British tradition of party finance which has evolved in a very different way from other European and North American countries, focusing not on state support, but on expenditure caps as a key policy instrument.[8] As with the Phillips report, the CSPL recommended donation caps. But the Committee went further. Where the Phillips report recommended a £50,000 cap, the CSPL went for £10,000, arguing that such a cap would not advantage any party to the extent that would a £50,000 cap. Critically, the CSPL report also tried to deal with the trade union question in respect of caps in a more coherent way than the Phillips report had done.

---

[8]See Phillips, H (2007) *Strengthening Democracy: Fair and Sustainable Funding of Political Parties. The Review of the Funding of Political Parties.* London, HMSO; Fisher, J. (2009) 'Hayden Phillips and Jack Straw: The Continuation of British Exceptionalism in Party Finance?' *Parliamentary Affairs*, **62**, 298–317.

Capping individual and company donations is relatively straightforward. But trade union donations (which include affiliations) are potentially more difficult as they are made up of individual trade unionists' contributions to an affiliated union's political fund. Defenders of this arrangement therefore argue that trade union payments should be regarded differently and not capped. As a result, Labour has objected to previous proposals for donation caps on the basis that these would also capture trade union affiliation payments.[9] Politically, however, this has always been a very difficult case to make. And it has been made more difficult by the fact that as unions have merged, much of Labour's trade union income now comes from a small number of so-called 'super unions'.

Coupled with that, many trade unionists no longer necessarily support Labour, but still pay into the political fund, which is also used for other political purposes. The CSPL's proposal was that for affiliated unions not to be caught by the cap, they should demonstrate that they were in fact making a collection of individual donations by requiring members to both 'contract in' to the political levy and then make a positive decision that some of that levy should be paid to Labour. Historically, 'contracting-in' had been a 'no-go area'—while it was proposed in green paper from the Thatcher Government (*Democracy in Trade Unions*, 1983) the idea was abandoned in the subsequent legislation (*Trade Union Act 1984*). Interestingly, however, it has re-surfaced in the first Queen's speech of the new Conservative Government in the Trade Union Bill.

The CSPL's plan for the parties if caps were introduced was an extension of public funding, proposing an allocation from the public purse based on votes not only at Westminster level, but also in devolved elections. This was a sensible move given the growing importance of the devolved institutions and would have helped to deal with the disadvantage that some parties traditionally have in respect of vote share under the majoritarian system used for the Commons compared with the semi-proportional electoral system used for Scottish Parliament and Welsh Assembly elections. Such a scheme was calculated by the Report as costing around 50 pence per elector per year—a very small sum.

The final key proposals were in respect of election spending. The Committee proposed a 15% reduction in spending limits. However, this failed to acknowledge that the cost of elections is actually falling. The figure of £30,000 per constituency contested introduced by the *Political Parties, Elections & Referendums Act 2000* to calculate the national spending limit has never been adjusted for inflation. The result is that the amount the parties are permitted to spend in real terms has been steadily falling: the limit of around £19 million set in 2000 equates in 2015 to around £13 million at 2000 prices. Over time, elections have actually been costing less by virtue of inflation—a trend that would have been accelerated

---

[9] Fisher, J. 'Party Finance—Normal Service Resumed', p. 200.

further had the Conservative plans to reduce the number of seats in the House of Commons been successful in the 2010 Parliament.

Yet, despite the report costing nearly half a million pounds to produce, its recommendations were effectively buried on the morning of its publication. There is rarely a good time to propose more extensive public funding (though in truth, polls suggests that opinion is very volatile on this issue[10]), and a proposal in the depths of an economic crisis was even more difficult. The CSPL acknowledged this and proposed that nothing should be done until after the 2015 election. Speaking for the Conservatives as the party's then Chair, Baroness Warsi announced that 'the public will simply not accept a plan to hand over almost £100 m of taxpayers' money to politicians'.[11] And, Nick Clegg—a previous champion of radical reform who had commissioned the report—distanced himself from the report's conclusions very rapidly, saying 'the government believes that the case cannot be made for greater state funding of political parties at a time when budgets are being squeezed and economic recovery remains the highest priority'.[12] Labour, too, notably failed to support the report. All-party talks were attempted to seek to strike some kind of deal, but they explicitly excluded the possibility of an extension of state funding and drew to a close without any proposals for reform in the spring of 2013.[13]

An unsuccessful attempt in April of 2013 was made to revive the debate. Three backbench politicians from the largest three parties in Britain proposed a draft Bill to reform party funding. Arguing that there 'is widespread agreement that our representative democracy in the UK is vulnerable to the influence of well-financed interest groups and wealthy individuals', the proposals were firmly rooted in the Phillips Review and that of the CSPL.[14] To that end, very similar reforms were put forward, namely donation caps, a reduction in campaign expenditure and the introduction of more extensive state funding. However, there were some notable innovations in the proposals. First, while the CSPL report had proposed delaying implementation until after the 2015 General Election, this report favoured a phasing in of donation caps and increased public funding. It proposed a donation cap of £50,000 should be introduced by January 2014 and that the cap should be

---

[10]van Heerde-Hudson, J., and Fisher, J. (2013) 'Parties Heed (with Caution): Public Knowledge of and Attitudes Towards Party Finance in Britain', *Party Politics*, **19**, 41–60.

[11]Accessed at http://www.theguardian.com/politics/2011/nov/22/party-funding-reforms-kelly-report on 24 April 2014.

[12]Accessed at http://www.bbc.co.uk/news/uk-politics-15822333 on 24 April 2014.

[13]Accessed at http://www.bbc.co.uk/news/uk-politics-23177856 on 24 April 2014.

[14]Funding Democracy (2013) *Funding Democracy: Breaking the Deadlock*. London, Funding Democracy, accessed at www.fundingukdemocracy.org on 2 July 2013.

reduced incrementally to £10,000 by January 2023. To compensate for the loss of income, the report proposed introducing enhanced state funding along the same lines as the CSPL, but again in a phased manner, inverse to the reduction in the cap on donations. And again, just as with the CSPL Report, it is envisaged that campaign spending would be reduced by 15%.

The report also advocated imposing expenditure limits on an annual basis (rather than just in the year before a General Election) and imposing far stricter controls on third-party spending. This desire to further regulate third-party spending was rooted in a purely hypothetical problem. *The Political Parties, Elections and Referendums Act 2000* (PPERA) introduced third-party spending controls for the first time at national level (previously only constituency-level activity had been covered). Yet since the introduction of PPERA, this aspect of legislation has not been tested as third-party activity has been at a much lower level that many expected. The report was effectively ignored, however, although one aspiration was achieved entirely by coincidence—the *Transparency of Lobbying, Non-Party Campaigning and Trade Union Administration Act* 2014, placed further restrictions on third-party spending despite the apparent absence of a need for such enhanced regulation.

Yet perhaps the most significant party finance act of the Parliament was one that had no roots in the principles of party finance reform. Rather, it came about indirectly as a result of a brawl in the House of Commons bar. After a series of incidents, the Labour MP for Falkirk, Eric Joyce, resigned from the Labour Party and later declared that he would not stand in the 2015 election. What followed had implications both for Labour's election campaign and for possible reforms of party funding in the future. Amidst accusations that the process of candidate selection to replace Joyce were being abused by the Unite union, Labour leader Ed Miliband announced surprisingly radical proposals for reforming the relationship between affiliated trade union members and the Labour Party, which effectively endorsed the CSPL proposals in respect of members of affiliated trade unions. Not only would members now have to 'contract in' to the political levy, they would also have to consent to a proportion being paid to Labour.

To understand why these proposals were so radical, it is necessary to summarise part of the Labour Party's historical development. From the outset, Labour's structure as a party was different from that of others. It was not, for example, until 1918 that members could join on an individual basis—previously membership came through the affiliated nature of trade unions or socialist societies. This collective element of trade union affiliation remained as a result of the principles entrenched in the *Trade Union Act 1913*, which established that for trade unions to engage in political activity, they must create a separate political find. This covered all political activity—not just that with the Labour Party—and trade union members were required to actively 'contract out' if they wanted to avoid paying the additional fee.

The 1913 Act laid the ground rules for an important aspect of Labour funding for much of the next 100 years. Political activity through the Labour Party would be expressed collectively through a union's decision to affiliate to the party. And for many in the Labour movement, this principle remains of key importance. It has faced challenges in the past. In the aftermath of the General Strike, the then Conservative Government sought revenge on the unions by changing the law such that trade union members must now 'contract in'—that is, make the decision to pay into the fund rather than opt out. The result was quite predictable—around a quarter fewer trade unionists opted in to the political levy, though the impact on Labour's finances was mitigated in part by unions' raising the affiliation fee for those who continued to pay into the political fund. Soon after the end of the war, however, Labour restored the practice of 'contracting out' and that has remained in place ever since.[15]

In that context, Ed Miliband's proposals went right to the heart of Labour's relationship with affiliated unions in two dramatic ways. First, it moved away from presumed consent to contribute to the political fund. Second, it required members of affiliated unions to positively declare that they wish part of the political fund to be paid to Labour in affiliation fees. Both fundamentally challenged the principle of the collective action through unions and moved membership to a far more individualised basis. Critically, these reforms were approved by the party at a special conference in the Spring of 2014.[16] Most attention at the time was paid to Labour's longer-term relations with trade unions, but the implications of the decision went much deeper, since in effect, the principal stumbling block to party finance reform from Labour's perspective had now been removed. Should donation caps be proposed again in any future review of party finance, Labour would be able to accept them because they could genuinely classify trade union affiliation payments as being a collection of small individual payments made positively by members, just as the CSPL had proposed. Following the 2015 election, new reform proposals on party finance are not presently in the offing and are perhaps less likely to be so with a Conservative majority government (given the push for reform in the last Parliament came from the deputy Prime Minister, Nick Clegg). But should proposals come about, Labour would have an advantage in any future discussions about reform, having made significant changes, which could enable reform to take place. In that context, objections to reforms from other parties would seem much more difficult to justify.

---

[15]Pinto Duschinsky, M. (1981) *British Political Finance 1830–1980*, Washington, DC, American Enterprise Institute.

[16]Accessed at http://www.theguardian.com/politics/blog/2014/mar/01/labour-votes-on-membership union-reforms-at-special-conference politics-live-blog on 24 April 2014.

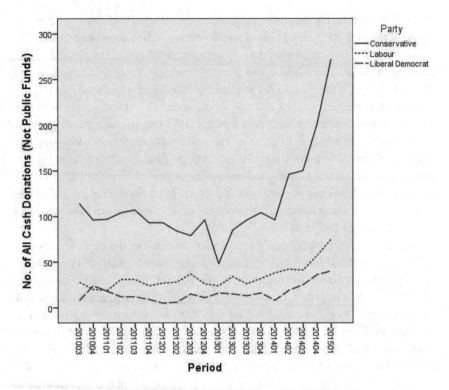

Figure 9.8 Number of declared donations to central party 2010 Q3 to 2015 Q1.

3. Donations 2010–2015

If Labour looked like it might have a financial advantage at the end of 2013, subsequent trends revealed that to be a significant false dawn. Figure 9.8 shows clearly how the number of declared cash donations (those in excess of £7500) to the central Conservative Party increased very significantly from the final quarter of 2013 onwards.[17] The Conservatives, for example, received 593 declared donations in 2014 (compared with 333 in 2013). Of course, the number of donations only tells us so much. What is also critical is the volume, which, as Figure 9.9 shows, also increased significantly in 2014, while the volume of Labour donations initially fell, putting the Conservatives at a significant financial advantage in a period where investment in the election campaign was especially critical. During 2014, the Conservatives received £24.5 million in declared donations centrally, compared with Labour's £10.4 million, and the Liberal Democrats' £4.8 million. Over the whole period from the last quarter of 2013 to dissolution of Parliament in 2015,

---

[17]The source of the data for Figures 9.8 and 9.9 is the Electoral Commission.

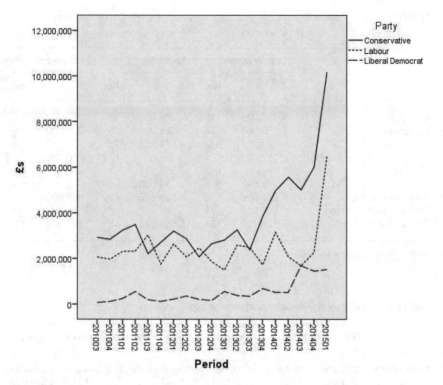

Figure 9.9 Declared cash donations 2010 Q3 to 2015 Q1 (real terms)

the Conservatives secured £40.5 million in declared donations; Labour, £19.8 million and the Liberal Democrats, £7.3 million.

3.1 Election period donations

The *Political Parties, Elections and Referendums Act 2000* requires donation declarations to be made weekly during the period between dissolution and polling day. Although well intentioned and delivering more in the way of transparency than the regular quarterly donations, they tell us comparatively little about the impact of party finance on the election as the money arrives too late to do that much which is substantial. Nonetheless, the more regularly declared donations provide at least a picture of party popularity during the campaign, as well as, of course, welcome income for the parties. Table 9.1 details the sums received by parties in declared donations over the six declaration points from dissolution in late March to polling day, while Table 9.2 illustrates when in this period donations were received.

First, the Conservatives received the most in voluntary declared donations. Of Labour's total, some £551,811 was from public funds as an opposition party. Second, just as in 2010, the sums received were significantly larger than in 2001

Table 9.1 Source of election-period declared cash donations and levels of declared non-cash donations

	Conservative		Labour		Lib Dems	
	£	No.	£	No.	£	No.
Individual	4,758,025	119	808,000	19	275,000	11
Company	1,150,563	38	465,000	6	316,000	7
Trade union	n/a	n/a	4,674,862	18	n/a	n/a
Unincorporated associations	192,000	4	n/a	n/a	10,000	1
Public funds	n/a	n/a	551,811	1	n/a	n/a
Other	19,542	2	10,000	1	n/a	n/a
Total cash donations	5,987,926	149	6,509,673	45	601,000	19
Total non-cash donations	132,203	14	n/a	n/a	n/a	n/a
Total all donations	6,120,129	163	6,509,673	45	601,000	19

Source: The Electoral Commission.

Table 9.2 Timing of weekly declared cash and non-cash donations

£s	Week 1	Week 2	Week 3	Week 4	Week 5	Week 6	Total
Conservative	501,850	492,512	1,093,206	1,368,450	2,359,170	304,941	6,120,129
Labour	1,887,312	1,109,946	1,530,000	131,242	1,841,173	10,000	6,509,673
Lib Dems	20,000	50,000	75,000	89,000	137,000	230,000	601,000

Source: The Electoral Commission.

and 2005, even though both the Conservative and Liberal Democrat sums dipped a little compared with 2010. Third, while the balance between individual and company donations increased a little (from a factor of 3.0 to 4.1) for the Conservatives compared with 2010, Labour's reliance on trade union money for larger donations became more pronounced. In 2010, the volume of income from trade unions was larger than that from individuals in terms of declared donations by a factor of 2.7. In 2015, it was 5.8. For example, Labour's central party received £1,617,000 from Unite and £1,100,000 from the GMB during this six-week period. They also received £20,000 from Eddie Izzard and two donations of £10,000 from Lord David Owen. Looking at the timing of payments, the Conservatives generated more week on week (with the exception of the final week where they still raised more than half of the Liberal Democrats' overall total). This included nine non-cash donations totalling £81,688 from Sovereign Business Jets Ltd. Finally, while both the Conservatives and Labour received the least in the last week of the campaign, the reverse was true for the Liberal Democrats, following a final week donation of £200,000 from Brompton Capital Ltd.

4. Election period expenditure

4.1   Conservatives

As in the 2010 election, the Conservatives found themselves at a significant financial advantage in terms of campaign expenditure. As Figure 9.9 shows, the party was able to raise substantial sums of money from late 2013 onwards, meaning that there was sufficient income to plan and execute a campaign some time in advance of polling day. As we will see with Labour, while the overall level of expenditure made by the two main parties during the regulated 365 days before polling day was ultimately of a similar level, the point at which it was spent differed (and perhaps critically so). A second similarity with 2010 was that the Conservatives' healthier financial position meant that the party could engage in a wider variety of campaigning techniques. For example, unlike Labour and the Liberal Democrats, the Conservatives did make use of some fixed billboard advertising. Equally, the party took out a very limited number of national press advertisements. However, with both techniques, this represented a significant reduction compared with 2010 and continued the decline of the use of these techniques that have been observed over successive elections. Fixed billboards were far fewer in number and far less significant in terms of expenditure compared with 2010. The small numbers that were erected were principally—though not exclusively—in target seats; the reasoning being that not all targets actually have poster sites. Similarly, the vast majority of newspaper advertising was placed in local newspapers—again focused on target seats. For example, the 30 April edition of the *Northampton Chronicle & Echo* featured a 'wrap' advert covering the front page, back page and inside front and back covers.

Beyond these techniques, the Conservatives' national expenditure reflected a pattern that was also true for Labour and the Liberal Democrats; namely that the bulk of spending was focussed on target seats—and specifically, key voters within those seats. A significant proportion of this involved telephone voter identification, direct mail and social media. Telephone voter identification took place principally from a phone bank at the party's central headquarters, as well as from a small phone bank in the Midlands. Volunteers were also able to call from home.

This activity was enhanced by a more developed computer system. In 2010, for example, the Conservatives were behind Labour in as much as feedback from canvass returns needed to be entered centrally. This time, the data were uploaded 'in real time', enhancing the parties' responsiveness with direct mail. A significant innovation in this campaign was the way in which data were collected in respect of propensity to vote for a particular party. A 1–10 scale was used to capture this, as well as voters' preferred leader, which party was seen as being best on the economy, and their previous vote. These voters were then categorised into eight different voter types. By using the 1–10 scale for each party, the Conservatives were able to estimate, for example, the likelihood of someone moving from the Conservatives to Labour, the Liberal Democrats or UKIP. Individualised, micro-targeted direct mail reflecting the voter type with messages 'relevant to them' followed.

The party also directed further resources at target seats. It had 100 paid campaign organisers in place in key seats and produced standardised campaigning templates for each local party, reflecting the new canvassing approach described above. The leader's tour was also focused strongly on target seats as well as seeking to generate coverage in regional media. Digital campaigning was integrated into the target voter campaign and mainly focused on Facebook and email—again focused principally on key voters in key seats. Targeted personalised Facebook posts often had links to specific videos on the party's YouTube channel, which would appeal to a particular voter, and these videos reportedly had high open rates. In terms of email, the central party paid particular attention to seeking to ensure that emails were opened, by extensive piloting of subject headers, reflecting concerns in 2010 that many emails went unread.[18] This strategy appeared to have been successful, with a claimed open rate of 40–50%. In addition to these activities, opinion polling took place in target seats prior to 2015, with expenditure on national polling after that, in part because of a concern that naming the candidate in a seat poll during the regulated period for constituencies could count against the candidate's rather than the national expenditure limit. In general, the parties' own polling reflected the voting propensity questions that had been used in campaigning and was seen as being more informative than top-line voting intention as featured in published polls.

4.2 Labour

Labour's campaign spending priorities largely reflected practice in the 2010 election and suggested that the national and constituency campaigns were now largely integrated, with the emphasis strongly on the constituencies and key voters within them. As in 2010, there were no billboard advertisements. Instead, there were a few poster vans. And again, reflecting practice in 2010, there were no advertisements in the national press. Instead, the bulk of Labour's national campaign expenditure was on the targeted use of telephone voter identification, direct mail, the leader's tour (and Woman to Woman tour), staff in key strategic seats and some expenditure on digital campaigning via Facebook and geo-targeting through cookies.

---

[18] Fisher, Cutts and Fieldhouse, 'Constituency Campaigning in 2010', p. 213.

There were further similarities with 2010. Once again, Labour's campaigning priorities were driven in part by finances. The difference was that in total, Labour spent far closer to the national limit this time. However, a significant proportion of that spend came in the last four months of the campaign, thereby reducing its effectiveness. As in 2010, Labour had its sophisticated Contact Creator infrastructure in place. However, in part because of the row over the Falkirk candidate selection, and Ed Miliband's subsequent changing of Labour's rules in respect of affiliated trade unions, the party had virtually no budget to spend on direct mail and election campaigns more generally in 2013 and 2014. Unite, the GMB and UNISON all withdrew significant sums following the episode, and while the money was eventually pledged, it meant that the direct mail campaign was not as well planned as necessary. No budget was made available for direct mail until January 2015, meaning that voters received large amounts repeatedly over a short period of time. This upsurge in income late in the cycle is clearly evident in Figure 9.9 and shows how far behind was Labour relative to the Conservatives in terms of pre-campaign fundraising. Before early 2015, Labour had to rely on a new Royal Mail service (Door Drop), whereby postcodes and sectors can be specified. At a cost of 4p per item, this was cost-effective, though less targeted than personalised direct mail. In effect, however, the withdrawal of funds following the Falkirk row diminished the significance of the core campaigning technique and in general made it extremely difficult to plan the campaign with any continuity, marking this campaign out as being very different from previous ones.

This lack of available budget until the last four months also affected other aspects of Labour's campaign. For example, in 2014, Labour's headquarters became concerned that a numbers of candidates' election materials were substandard compared with those of the Conservatives. However, it became difficult to intervene in any substantial way as the party was unable to fund replacement materials. This also prevented the national party assisting candidates in producing monthly newspapers in the 18 months before the election. However, the party did have some success in positioning staff in key strategic seats from 2012 onwards. All target seats had at least two paid staff, and some had up to six. This was made possible by the use of other budgets from the national party (such as that for the European elections), which did not rely so closely on discretionary spend.

Spending on digital campaign methods was still significantly smaller than more traditional ones such as direct mail. However, it had developed since 2010. The principal digital campaign platform was Facebook, which permitted targeting of key groups through postcodes for example. This technique was focused most on young and liberal groups—older voters were approached more through the phone banks. By way of contrast, no investment of any consequence was made in Twitter campaigning; Twitter being regarded as 'a Westminster bubble thing' and being too untargeted. The national party did, however, use the NationBuilder

number of voter contacts required some three years before the election, and these data, gathered through CONNECT, helped to determine the target status of a seat. Through CONNECT, the party was able to run a national telephone voter identification programme, which then helped inform direct mail and Facebook activity. The bulk of the telephone voter identification was undertaken at the party's headquarters, together with some limited commercial phone-banking.

The telephone voter identification was supported by opinion polling in key seats to help inform the party about the necessary clarity required for its messages. Taken together, the CONNECT system allowed the Liberal Democrats to engage in data modelling to estimate the propensity to support the party, and direct mail and Facebook were then used to micro-target key voters in the key seats. Direct mail would also be tailored depending on the type of electoral contest in individual constituencies.

In addition to the extensive use of telephone voter identification and direct mail, the other principal aspects of campaign expenditure were also focused on key seats. The party employed regional organisers from 2012, and Nick Clegg's tour was focused solely on target seats. Connectedly, all the party's media activity was conducted in these strategic seats. All of this activity was further supported by NationBuilder, which was used both nationally and in 60 key seats. This proved to be a successful means by which the party could raise funds, both through conventional means and through crowdfunding. In addition, it provided website templates for local parties. The principal digital expense, however, was on Facebook, regarded as being particularly useful for micro-targeting as well as targeted advertisements. By way of comparison, Twitter was seen as being less useful in terms of campaign expenditure, seen mainly as 'fast reaction for the Westminster intelligentsia'. Like Labour, the Liberal Democrats spent no money on fixed billboards. Nor was there any expenditure on national newspaper advertising—only a few local newspaper advertisements were taken out.

5. Conclusion

Party finance in 2015 represented further continuation of patterns observed in previous elections. The Conservatives' return to being the 'wealthy party' was confirmed and any impact of this was exacerbated by Labour's inability to raise and spend significant sums until relatively close to the election. But perhaps the most interesting continuation was the apparent death of traditional national campaign expenditure at GB level. Barring the Conservatives' minor forays into billboards and national press advertisements, national campaign spending is now a highly targeted effort supporting constituency campaigns. And, in spending terms at least, it may now make little sense to speak of air and ground wars as though they are equal partners. What is clear from the 2015 election is that for major parties campaigning across Britain, the vast bulk of campaign expenditure is aimed at key voters in key seats. In effect, the GB level parties have moved in terms of expenditure from the broadcast national campaigns of the past to narrowcast targeted expenditure. And the reasons for this are both strategic and financial. Strategically, all three main GB level parties have arrived at similar conclusions—highly targeted campaigning is most effective in terms of delivering electoral payoffs. Financially, national spending limits have introduced opportunity costs for Labour and the Conservatives—parties must decide which campaign methods deliver most return, since what is spent on x cannot be spent on y. For the Liberal Democrats, the financial considerations are slightly different. Their much more limited resources also introduce opportunity costs in terms of spending, but on account of their limited finances rather than spending limits. For all three parties, it makes most financial sense to spend their money in a highly selective and targeted way. For all this, however, more traditional campaign expenditure can still survive in defined geographic areas. The SNP, for example, used both billboards and press advertisements (albeit in more regionally focused newspapers in parts of Scotland) to a significant degree alongside some more targeted approaches, in part because the party was not only in good political shape, but also in a better financial shape. So the broadcast methods are not necessarily dead at the level of the smaller nations within the UK, but at GB level, they are evidently disappearing.

But 2015 was not just about continuation. Two developments were of particular note. First of all, digital campaigning is now clearly growing in significance, both in terms of use and expenditure. 2010 may have (wrongly) been hailed as a digital election, but 2015 was when it started to be a meaningful aspect. Inevitably, however, there are caveats. First, only some digital techniques attract investment, notably Facebook rather than Twitter. Second, this does not represent a revolution in campaigning, but an evolution—digital techniques complemented more traditional modes of contact, expanding rather than fundamentally changing the means by which parties interact with the electorate. Third, direct mail is still the dominant form of expenditure. The second development of note was the change in Labour's financial relationship with its affiliated unions. This may have profound implications on the likelihood of party finance reform being introduced at some point in the future, perhaps an end to the 'stop-go' approach that has previously characterised British attempts at reform.[19] In the meantime, Labour may face some future financial uncertainty with the possibility that income from trade unions will fall significantly, not least because some members of affiliated unions may not positively state their preference for their union's political fund to

---

[19]Fisher, J. (Forthcoming, 2015) 'Britain's Stop-Go Approach to Party Finance Reform'. In Boatright, R. (ed) *The Deregulatory Moment? A Comparative Perspective on Changing Campaign Finance Laws,* Michigan, University of Michigan Press.

support the Labour Party. Such concerns may be exacerbated by the fact that Labour's fundraising prowess from non-union sources which developed so strongly under Neil Kinnock, John Smith and Tony Blair, has declined so significantly in recent years.

The final issue is the continuing utility of legislation on campaign expenditure. As things stand, party (national level) and candidate (constituency level) expenditure are regulated separately. There has always been a blurred line between the two, but this election in particular suggested that the difference was becoming increasingly cosmetic, prompting the question of whether campaign spending regulations are still fit for purpose. One solution would be to combine candidate and party spend to remove any ambiguity. Yet, the result of that would surely be a negative one, with all likely spend being focused only on a minority of seats (and indeed, key voters within them). This suggests that there may be no ready solution without a great deal more thought. Yet, perhaps there need not be. Instead, we might simply note that rather than being wasteful as many have previously accused them of being, parties are actually increasingly skilled at spending their relatively limited resources.

Britain Votes (2015) 154–167

ANDREW GAMBLE[*]

The Economy

Until the exit poll was announced at 10 pm on the night of the General Election it seemed that one of the iron verities of British General Elections was about to be overturned. Despite the Conservatives being a long way ahead of Labour in terms of economic competence and the best leadership team for managing the economy, and despite a series of good news stories about the economy, the polls still appeared to show that their message was not being translated into a substantial poll lead. This was not for want of trying. The Conservative campaign orchestrated by Lynton Crosby played to the Conservatives' advantages, making the handling of the economy and the party leader best qualified to be Prime Minister the two key strands of the Conservative attack upon Labour. The party relentlessly focused on these two issues. Only when these two did not appear to be having sufficient traction did the party emphasise a third strand, the threat of a minority Labour administration being propped up by the SNP. But even this strand aimed to reinforce the key messages on the economy and on leadership—that only the Conservatives could be trusted not to endanger the economic recovery. A favourite Tory slogan was 'Don't give the keys back to the guys that crashed the car', and the image of a weak Labour Government propped up by the SNP whose interests were opposed to those of Middle England was used to target voters in England who were worried about economic stability. In this sense the Conservatives ran a very conventional campaign, one which had served them well in many previous elections, such as 1959, when the party's main message was 'Life's better with the Conservatives; don't let Labour ruin it', complete with the image of an aspirational family busy washing their car on the drive of their suburban home.[1]

In 2015 the message was essentially the same, although this time the Conservative promise was that Life *will* be better with the Conservatives if the electorate would only stick with them. The 2015 General Election was the second in a row where the majority of voters were worse off than they had been five years previously.

---

[*]Andrew Gamble, Department of Politics, University of Sheffield, a.m.gamble@sheffield.ac.uk

[1]Butler, D. and Rose, R. (1960) *The British General Election of 1959*, London, Macmillan.

© The Author 2015. Published by Oxford University Press on behalf of the Hansard Society; all rights reserved. For permissions, please e-mail: journals.permissions@oup.com
doi:10.1093/pa/gsv033

George Osborne had used this as a stick to beat Labour in 2010, and in 2015 tried in his budget speech to deny that the same thing had happened under his watch, but figures from the Institute of Fiscal Studies (IFS) and the Resolution Foundation suggested otherwise.[2] The continued stagnation of living standards in the 2010 Parliament may explain why the Conservatives found it difficult to translate their perceived lead on economic competence into votes. In the previous five years they had worked hard to win the argument on the economy and re-establish themselves as the party of economic competence and Labour as the party of economic incompetence. In George Osborne the Conservatives possessed a highly political Chancellor, who was also the key political strategist for the Conservatives within the Coalition Government. He was determined from the outset that the Conservatives should win the political argument about the economy and regain their reputation as the safe choice for voters worried about the security of their houses, their jobs and their savings. After the disaster of Black Wednesday in 1992 when the pound was forced out of the Exchange Rate Mechanism, and the Conservatives were forced to impose steep tax rises to stabilise the economy, the Labour Party under Tony Blair and Gordon Brown had overtaken the Conservatives as the party the electorate most trusted with the economy, and this reputation for economic competence was further consolidated by the first 10 years of Labour Government after 1997 when the economy grew steadily and the public finances were managed prudently, in line with the growth in the economy, until the small structural deficit which emerged after 2005.

The 2008 financial crash changed everything and forms the essential backdrop for understanding the 2015 General Election. Prior to the crash in 2008 the Conservatives had accepted Labour's spending plans, including the small structural deficit. Party disagreement on the economy focused firstly on financial regulation, with the Conservatives urging that it should be further relaxed, so that the City of London could remain competitive with financial centres elsewhere, and secondly on the distribution of the proceeds of growth. The Conservatives favoured devoting more of the 'growth dividend' to tax cuts than to higher public spending. The UK economy had grown continuously since Black Wednesday, the longest period of uninterrupted domestic growth in the previous 200 years and even if many were sceptical of Gordon Brown's boast that boom and bust had been permanently overcome, there were very few in the political class who sensed the cataclysm about to unfold. Some fiscal tightening was expected in 2007 and some slow-down in growth, but the general view was that there would be a soft landing for the economy, and that growth would quickly rebound.

---

[2]Institute for Fiscal Studies (2015) 'Living Standards Have Been Through a Prolonged and Severe Squeeze', accessed at http://election2015.ifs.org.uk/living-standards on 1 April 2015; Resolution Foundation (2014) 'The State of Living Standards', accessed at http://www.resolutionfoundation. org/publications/state-living-standards/ on 11 February 2014.

Once the crash had happened, however, the political situation changed irrevocably. Financial meltdown was avoided, if only narrowly, by prompt action coordinated by the US and UK governments and central banks, but it could not prevent the deepest recession in the western economies since 1945 (UK output dropped by 6% in 2009), leaving governments with big challenges of dealing with yawning fiscal deficits and finding a path to economy recovery. Before the 2010 General Election sharp differences of emphasis emerged between the main Westminster parties. Neither party disputed the Treasury's orthodox diagnosis that a major fiscal stabilisation and austerity package would be necessary at some point, but there was a serious disagreement over the timing. Gordon Brown insisted that the choice was between Labour investment and Tory cuts and argued that no cuts in front-line spending were either necessary or desirable until the economic recovery was firmly established. The Liberal Democrats broadly took this line as well, warning against too rapid fiscal stabilisation and a plunge into austerity. The Conservatives on the other hand changed their position and now became fiscal hawks, arguing that reducing the deficit was the only way to lay the foundations for economic recovery. Fiscal stabilisation could not wait for the recovery to begin. No one seriously challenged the policy orthodoxy that stabilisation would be needed at some stage, and before the election there was some convergence of view between the Conservatives and some members of the Government, notably Labour's then Business Secretary Peter Mandelson and Chancellor, Alastair Darling, who accepted that the Government had to set out plans to bring down the deficit over the lifetime of the next Parliament. They still wanted to do so in a way which would not jeopardise the capacity of the economy to recover. Gordon Brown was reluctant at first to concede this, and when in September 2009 he finally did admit the need for some cuts, he insisted that they would not affect front-line services.

After the 2010 General Election the Conservatives were the largest single party and seized the opportunity to form a Coalition Government with the Liberal Democrats which gave them a stable majority. Although some were sceptical that the coalition could last a full Parliament, even with the new fixed term Parliament Act, the Coalition proved resilient. Dealing with the aftermath of the financial crash and securing the economic recovery became the shared rationale for forming and sustaining the Coalition, although from the outset economic policy was shaped mainly by the Conservatives.

1.   The framing of the crisis

The Coalition set out its plans for the economy in the emergency June Budget of 2010 and the Autumn Statement later that year. These were highly political documents, designed to frame the financial crisis and the required policy response in a particular way, marking a distinct shift from the previous Government, even if the underlying diagnosis was similar. The key problem was identified as the deficit, which was preventing recovery and leading to an inexorable rise in debt and interest payments. Gordon Brown's dividing lines between the parties of investment and cuts were replaced with dividing lines between sound finance and bankruptcy. Osborne had already marked out this territory before the election, but now he significantly hardened his fiscal stance. Seizing on the sovereign debt crises which were beginning to engulf several states in the Eurozone, he declared that the situation he had inherited was much worse than he had expected, there was now a pressing financial emergency, and urgent action needed to be taken to bring the public finances under control, otherwise Britain would suffer the fate of other highly indebted countries like Greece, lose its credit rating in international financial markets and control over its economy. Osborne therefore proposed to go beyond Alastair Darling's last budget and pre-budget report which had set out a path of fiscal adjustment to cut the deficit by half by 2014–2015 and put debt on a declining trajectory. Osborne set out a new target, to eliminate the deficit entirely by 2014–2015, and to do so primarily by cuts in spending (85%) and increases in taxes (15%). The main tax increase was VAT, which the Conservatives had ruled out before the election, but now justified on the ground of the financial emergency. The Conservatives had inherited Labour's plans for spending cuts, which Departments had prepared before the election, and these it implemented but at an accelerated pace.

Osborne's great achievement in 2010 was to frame the main policy problem in the aftermath of the financial crash as a problem of the deficit and the debt.[3] In the early months of the Coalition Government, he constructed a narrative around Labour overspending, which was blamed for the economic situation which the Coalition had inherited. Labour had not fixed the roof while the sun was shining, and as a result Osborne claimed that the economic situation was far more serious than for most other countries. Government ministers for the next five years and particularly during the 2015 election talked about Labour's Great Recession, Labour's financial crisis and Labour's economic mess. They pounced on the note which Liam Byrne, the Chief Secretary to the Treasury had left behind for David Laws, his successor, which laconically pronounced; 'I'm afraid there is no money'. Although obviously intended as a joke, it was used by Coalition ministers as confirmation of their narrative that Labour had overspent and had been profligate with the public finances. David Cameron brandished an enlarged reproduction of the note in the 2015 election campaign. It became as famous as Norman Lamont's laconic remark 'Je ne regrette rien' in 1993 and echoed the note which Reginald Maudling the Chancellor of the Exchequer left for his successor, James Callaghan, in 1964: 'Good luck old cock. Sorry to leave it in such a mess'.

---

[3]Craig, M. (2015) 'An Analysis of Crisis Construction in the British Post-2008 Context', Unpublished PhD Thesis, University of Sheffield.

The message which Osborne and other Ministers emphasised again and again was that Labour had been fiscally irresponsible and now refused to admit their mistakes. They were deficit deniers. The tough measures which the Coalition Government announced were necessary to restore financial stability and investors' confidence and pave the way for economic recovery. This narrative became as important to the Conservatives as the 'Winter of Discontent' narrative had been in the 1980s,[4] or the 'Hungry Thirties' had been to Labour in the 1940s. One of the reasons the framing of the 2008 crisis as a crisis of the deficit rather than a crisis of banking was so successful was because the Liberal Democrats endorsed this interpretation of events. Nick Clegg justified the abandonment by his party of the economic policy they had advocated before the election by the national emergency which had suddenly arisen after it and obliged the Liberal Democrats to act in the national interest to save the country. The commitment of two of the three main Westminster parties to this message helped to reinforce it and drowned out Labour's response. If the Conservatives had been able to form a majority Government on their own, they would no doubt have sought to implement the same austerity agenda, only this time the Liberal Democrats would have been among their fiercest critics. By being part of the Coalition and supporting the narrative which George Osborne developed the Liberal Democrats enhanced its persuasiveness and its air of inevitability. This was to be a very valuable weapon for the Conservatives in the 2015 election.

The judgement Osborne made was political rather than economic. There was no financial emergency in May 2010, since the Government was still able to fund the national debt with low interest long-dated bonds. The position of the British economy was very different from that of some of the states in the Eurozone, because the British Government had fiscal and monetary autonomy. Since the financial crash it had let the pound devalue by 25% and had provided a major fiscal stimulus, while the Bank of England had used quantitative easing to boost banks' balance sheets and support asset prices, and had reduced interest rates close to zero, a level not seen before in the 300-year history of the Bank. They remained at that level for the whole Parliament. At no point was Britain's creditworthiness seriously questioned. Britain lost its triple-A status in 2013, as several other leading economies were also to do, but this although embarrassing had no impact. Whoever had been the Government after the election in May 2010 would have been obliged to present a clear fiscal plan for the Parliament, but there was no dramatic change in Britain's economic or financial situation which required the shock and awe tactics which George Osborne applied. That was a political judgement, but one which paid handsome dividends by 2015.

---

[4] Hay, C. (1996) 'Narrating Crisis: The Discursive Construction of the Winter of Discontent', *Sociology*, **11**, 87–104.

The policy had its desired effect. It set the terms of the debate on the economy for the entire Parliament, and provided the Conservatives with a narrative which proved very persuasive, and to which Labour never found a reply. In the final television election debate on April 30, Miliband's denials that Labour had overspent when it was in Government were received with derision by a section of the Question Time audience.[5] This reflected the strong lead the Conservatives had established over Labour in terms of economic competence, which by the time of the election in May 2015 was running at 20%. Every Labour minister was continually asked how they justified the overspending of the Brown Government. They were placed so much on the defensive on this issue that having spent most of the Parliament denying that they had overspent, they then used their manifesto to pledge that they would be fiscally responsible if they formed the next Government. Just before the election, they also signed up to the cap proposed by the Conservatives and the Liberal Democrats for total spending on welfare apart from health in the next Parliament. At no stage was Labour able to mount a credible anti-austerity programme as an alternative to the Conservatives. This was in sharp contrast to the success of the SNP in developing such a programme, which proved very popular in Scotland, and was one of the factors in the collapse of the Labour vote north of the border.

Most macroeconomists now agree that the austerity programme pursued by the Coalition Government in its first two years was both too severe and unnecessary and set back the economic recovery which was underway in the first half of 2010. The Office of Budget Responsibility confirmed that the austerity programme reduced GDP, while the Oxford economist Simon Wren-Lewis has calculated that the Coalition Government's austerity programme cost the average household £4000 over the lifetime of the Parliament and severely damaged those public services which were not ring-fenced.[6] Labour at times tried to point this out but the narrative on debt and deficits was much more powerful. Osborne insisted throughout the Parliament when urged to budge from his initial plan that there was no Plan B, and the Government would not be deflected from its path. Ministers claimed repeatedly during the 2015 election that the Government's tough stance had been vindicated, because the deficit had been halved and the recovery was under way with rapidly falling unemployment. What this account ignored was that Osborne's 2010 plan had been to eliminate the deficit in a single Parliament, and to have debt falling as a proportion of national income by 2015, with interest payments coming down. In 2012 faced with the prospect of a double dip recession in the UK and

---

[5] BBC (2015) 'Question Time: Election Leaders Special 30 April', accessed at https://www.youtube.com/watch?v=VE5HFj-qCdg on 11 June 2015.

[6] Wren-Lewis, S. (2015) 'The Economic Consequences of George Osborne', *New Statesman*, 20 April 2015, accessed at http://mainlymacro.blogspot.co.uk on 11 June 2015.

with no recovery in sight, Osborne did adopt a Plan B, easing up on austerity, and postponing many of the cuts in public spending to the next Parliament. This meant that the targets in the original plan were missed and that Osborne ended up implementing a plan which was less draconian than the one proposed by Alastair Darling. By 2015 the deficit was still 5% of GDP, much higher than in most other EU countries, and national debt was still rising, as were interest payments. Osborne's reputation plummeted in 2012, which was also the year of his 'omnishambles budget', but by the time of the election he was riding high again. A series of measures to boost house prices and consumption at last helped to establish a recovery, and this confirmed the view of most voters that the Conservatives had won the economic argument. The Government was able to claim that missing its targets was not a defeat but a triumph, because they had after all made substantial progress towards their goal, and this was evidence that they should be entrusted with a second term of office to finish the job.

The Labour Opposition meanwhile never succeeded in eroding the view which had formed amongst most voters by 2015 that the Coalition Government was fiscally responsible while Labour had been fiscally irresponsible and had led the country to the edge of bankruptcy. Labour struggled to put across a coherent or credible economic message. This was partly because the new Labour leadership elected in 2010, especially after Ed Balls became Shadow Chancellor in 2011, chose to continue Gordon Brown's approach to the deficit rather than Alastair Darling's. They attacked the Coalition Government's plans as too draconian, arguing that they would plunge the country into an unacceptable and unnecessary level of austerity, and threaten the recovery. This may have been true intellectually, but politically Labour failed to convince the electorate that its policies were more likely to succeed than the Government's, and most voters accepted the Conservative narrative that Labour had caused the economic recession and the need for austerity by spending too much and regulating the banks too little. The economy had blown up on its watch, and as in previous great economic crises, the incumbents at the time took the main blame. Liberal Democrats in the Coalition with economic knowledge, perhaps most notably Vince Cable, were uncomfortable at times with the narrative, but most of the Liberal Democrats were enthusiastic converts to the Conservative argument. Labour ultimately was not in a good place. It was seen by the electorate as always dragging its feet on the measures needed to stabilise the economy and this made many of its other economic arguments for example on predator and productive companies unpersuasive.

This perception shaped the debate on the economy in the 2015 election. The actual difference between the Conservatives and Labour in their diagnosis of the problem and what needed to be done was rather small.[7] Both still embraced

---

[7] Craig, 'An Analysis of Crisis Construction in the British post-2008 Context'.

the orthodox explanation of the crisis offered by the Treasury and like the Conservatives, had Labour remained in Government in 2010, it too would have undertaken its own austerity programme and fiscal consolidation. But although both parties had similar diagnoses and would have pursued the same aim of bringing the deficit down, the political narratives were very different, and the distribution of the spending cuts and tax increases would have been different. Because the Conservatives became the Government after 2010, they were in a position to develop a narrative which concealed how much they shared with Labour and instead presented the differences between them as a chasm. This proved very effective politics and by 2015 had delivered the Conservatives commanding leads on economic competence.

In the run-up to the election the Conservatives were boosted by indicators showing that the UK was now performing better than almost any other OECD economy and sought to consolidate their position by making increasingly lavish promises to every section of the electorate in the March Budget and the manifesto. This made it all the more puzzling that the Conservative advantage did not seem to translate into poll leads. In any previous election the position the Conservatives had managed to create by the time of the poll should have been enough to deliver victory. The economic position had stabilised, recovery was under way and so the argument for not risking a change of government was likely to weigh heavily with many swing voters.

2. The General Election campaign

The General Election campaign was fought against this backdrop. The Conservatives tried to make the central issue the deficit, and how only they could be trusted to finish the job, only they had a long-term plan to ensure that the country would once again 'live within its means'. The Conservative economic narrative has often in the past made a simple equation between the finances of households and the finances of the state and 2015 was no exception. Although Keynes exploded this argument 80 years ago, pointing out that the budgets of states are quite different from the budgets of households, this has never dented the political appeal of the household analogy. The tactic the Conservatives employed to force the election debate on to their favoured terrain of the deficit was to publish in the Autumn Statement their spending plans for the next Parliament. The fiscal consolidation achieved in the 2010 Parliament was a reduction of 9% in public spending (£38 billion). The fiscal consolidation needed in the 2015 Parliament to eliminate the deficit altogether was 14% (£51 billion). The Conservatives pledged to achieve this by 2018 and to create a surplus on the public finances by the end of the Parliament, allowing them to promise significant tax cuts in time for the 2020 election, including raising the inheritance tax threshold and raising the higher rate income tax threshold to £50k.

The detail on how the cuts in public spending were to be achieved were vague, especially since the Conservatives promised to continue ring-fencing pensions and pensioner benefits, the NHS, education and foreign aid, spending more on all of them in real terms. They also promised to bind their hands by bringing in legislation prohibiting any increase in the rates of income tax, VAT and national insurance during the next Parliament. The Institute for Fiscal Studies calculated that these commitments meant very large cuts in unprotected areas of spending, principally welfare, housing, defence, transport, justice and local government.[8] Considerable attention in the election campaign focused on where the Conservatives would make their welfare cuts. They had announced a target of £12 billion for cuts in welfare, but did not indicate where the cuts would fall, apart from a few policies included in the manifesto. These were the plan to freeze all benefits apart from pensions for the first two years of the Parliament, saving £1 billion; the proposal to withdraw housing benefit from young adults (16–21), saving £1 million and the proposal to reduce the cap on how much any single household could receive in benefits from £26,000 to £23,000. This would save another £0.1 billion. The IFS pointed out that this still left a shortfall of at least £10.5 billion. They listed options for how that shortfall could be met—among them child benefit, tax credits for working families, housing benefit and disability benefits. All posed severe political difficulties.

The plans of Labour and the Liberal Democrats were also found to lack detail.[9] The difference between Labour and Conservative fiscal plans by the end of the Parliament was £32 billion, because although Labour like the Conservatives was committed to balancing the books and eliminating the deficit, Labour planned to achieve balance in current spending, allowing it to borrow to finance investment. This was an important difference, although it still meant that Labour had to push through major cuts in public spending, while supporting the ring fencing to which the Conservatives were committed, and not announcing any major tax increases. The tax increases to which Labour was committed, such as the mansion tax and raising the top rate of income to 50p in the £, would not be enough. Liberal Democrats received a slightly better rating from the IFS for their fiscal plans, but the IFS noted the same vagueness about where most of their cuts would fall.

All three parties suggested that a major contribution to closing the deficit would be a crackdown on tax avoidance and tax evasion. This would make a considerable difference if it could be achieved, but previous Governments had also made promises which had not been delivered, and the reduction in staffing of the Inland Revenue as part of the austerity drive did not suggest this could easily be changed. What none of the major parties was willing to discuss was whether the

[8] Institute for Fiscal Studies (2015) 'Post-Election Austerity: Parties' Plans Compared', IFS Briefing Note BN170, London, IFS.

[9] IFS, 'Post-Election Austerity: Parties' Plans Compared'.

fiscal base was large enough to accommodate their assessment of what the state needed to spend. Reluctance to confront the voters with the need to raise taxes in order to restore sound finance has become a marked feature of contemporary British political culture and is a sign of the 'privatised Keynesianism' which now dominates Government thinking about how to manage the economy and promote economic growth.[10] There are no fiscal conservatives left in British politics. Instead all three main parties rely on economic growth turning out to be fast enough to generate the resources they need to avoid the need for drastic cuts in spending or large tax increases. None of the three main parties expected if they were in government after the election to have to deliver the scale of the cuts outlined in the 2014 Autumn Statement. All thought that the growth fairy would save them from a series of painful dilemmas. This was also true of the Conservatives. As in the 2010 Parliament they were likely to make judgements about how much to cut based on the actual situation which confronted them. The complexity of managing the public finances made rigid targets and timescales unhelpful, but the Conservatives saw great electoral advantage in proposing such targets and timescales, because it forced their opponents on to the defensive. The other parties could be forced to endorse the same goal as the Conservatives while appearing squeamish about the means of achieving it.

Part of the argument was couched in terms of the size of the state which would result once the fiscal consolidation was complete.[11] Labour accused the Conservatives of having an ideological plan to reduce public spending to a level it had not been at since the 1930s. George Osborne duly adjusted his spending totals in the March Budget and claimed that the state at the end of the process of fiscal adjustment would be slightly larger than it was in 1999–2000, before Labour began expanding public spending again. Public spending had fluctuated around 41% of GDP since 1945, and no move either above or below that level had been sustained for long. The pressures on government to spend more remained intense, as shown by the blizzard of promises all parties showered on the electorate during the election campaign. For the Conservatives these included the pledges on inheritance tax and the 40p tax threshold, but also carefully targeted offers to almost every part of the electorate—help for first time buyers, 30 hours a week free child care, pensioner bonds, the right to buy at a discount for Housing Association Tenants, a freeze on commuter rail fares, £8 billion annually of new money for the NHS, and taking out of tax all those on the minimum wage. Some of these pledges the Conservatives were no doubt expecting to abandon in the negotiations for a new

---

[10]Crouch, C. (2009) 'Privatised Keynesianism: An Unacknowledged Policy Regime', *British Journal of Politics and International Relations*, **11**, 382–399.

[11]Giles, C. (2015) 'Budget 2015: Back to Brown, Beatles or Baldwin?', *Financial Times*, 16 March.

coalition. Finding themselves in Government with a small majority means that potentially all these promises have to be met.

Labour and the Liberal Democrats had their own long lists of promises to spend more, but they tended to be less specific than the Conservatives. Labour in particular with its reputation for overspending around its neck was reluctant even to match the promise of the Conservatives to spend another £8 billion on the NHS. The number of promises all three parties thought it important to make during the election campaign made much of the campaign rather surreal for voters, most of whom were highly sceptical about the ability of politicians, even for the parties they supported, to deliver their promises. The Conservative offer of renewed fiscal austerity, with light at the end of the tunnel in time for the next election, combined with immediate benefits now to every significant electoral interest was the one which seems in the end to have captured most voters' attention and interest. But it is unlikely that particular promises changed many votes. What was more important was the relative trust voters had for particular politicians and parties. Whether voters believed the Conservatives could deliver on all their promises mattered less than the perception that they were less likely to make a mess of the economy than their opponents.

Faced with the Conservative onslaught on the deficit Labour did its best to change the conversation to living standards. As already noted, George Osborne had expected that the tough austerity measures he took in the first two years would spark a sharp recovery in 2012. He was disappointed. The average length of recessions since 1945 had been eighteen months. What no one expected was that the recovery this time would be so slow. It took until 2014, six years after the crash, before UK GDP had reached the level it had been at before the crash. No one expected that interest rates reduced to zero to stop a financial meltdown would still be at zero seven years later. It showed the weakness of demand and the weakness of investment and confidence in the future of western economies.

During the Parliament Labour sought to draw attention to the stagnation of living standards, which can be traced back to the earlier part of the decade, before the crash, but which became much more salient after it. The same trend was observed in the USA and in the rest of Europe. The cost of living issue Labour tried to make its own, through a number of interventions, notably in proposing a freeze on energy prices. Labour began to talk of the 'squeezed middle' and tried to develop a narrative which explained the crash as a banking crash, whose effects had been experienced most sharply by working people and their families. It also launched a major attack on zero-hours contracts, contrasting the insecurity and poverty of those at the sharp end of flexible labour markets with the position of the rich whose wealth had been boosted by quantitative easing. Most investors had received a minimum of 5% per annum increase in their portfolios since the crash. Labour proposed a number of measures to restrict the flow of gains to the rich, including withdrawal of the tax concessions for many individuals claiming non-dom status, raising of the top rate of income tax back to 50p in the £, establishment of a new mansion tax on properties worth more than £2 million. Many of these policies were individually quite popular, but they lacked coherence, and the Conservatives responded with a narrative which suggested that these policies were all evidence of an anti-business approach in Ed Miliband's Labour Party. Labour had no radical anti-capitalist strategy, but it was easy to suggest that it had no sympathy with business and did not understand it, and this became another reason why Labour struggled to convince many voters that it was economically competent and that the economy would be safe in its hands.

3.   Issues that did not feature in the election

As in most elections the economic subjects which the politicians spent most of their time arguing about were often different from the issues and problems which pre-occupied decision-makers and will shape citizens' lives in the future. One of the most glaring omissions from the election campaign was any real concern with where growth was going to come from in the future and whether the British economy needed a fundamental restructuring to make it possible. Rebalancing of the economy had been a topic of some debate since the crash. Both parties advocated that growth should be investment and export led and that the City of London's role in the UK political economy should shrink in favour of other sectors, particularly manufacturing and certain kinds of services where Britain had a clear advantage. Such a policy also involved tackling the increasingly dysfunctional UK housing market, countering the widening chasm between house prices in different parts of the country, and finding a permanent solution to the inadequate supply of new houses. The banks would be reformed so as to contribute more effectively to the development of new industrial and service sectors.

The discrediting of many of the orthodoxies that governed economic policy making immediately after the crash made many feel that this offered an opportunity to effect a long-term reform of the British political economy. But policy soon reverted to the norm. The Government lacked levers and capacity for the full-scale industrial policy envisaged. When the recovery failed to arrive spontaneously in 2012 the Government reverted to the pre-model growth model which had been so successful then, a version of privatised Keynesianism, reliant upon loading more and more debt upon citizens, from University fees to private pensions. Rising house prices and rising immigration were also vital ingredients, both of which helped the UK economy to begin growing again after 2012. The voters who had previously been told that everyone, including the state, should live within their means were now being urged to get their credit cards out again. But although many were uneasy about the return of the previous growth model, no one had any very clear alternative. George Osborne made great rhetorical play of the Northern Powerhouse, giving selected northern cities greater powers over planning, investment and infrastructure. But there was no new money behind this initiative, and some doubts as to whether without other measures it would make much impact on regional inequality in the UK. The SNP developed a strong anti-austerity programme, but because all the three Unionist parties ruled out any role for the SNP in the Westminster Government its proposals were never given detailed scrutiny.

Another major issue which barely surfaced in the election campaign was productivity. Despite the economic recovery, UK productivity remains flat and has been lower than most other OECD economies for the last decade. If productivity does not increase, wages are unlikely to rise, and without wage growth, the prospects for consumption led growth will be weak. There was, however, very little debate between the parties about the causes of low productivity or what might be done about it. The growth in employment was predominantly in low wage, low skill, insecure jobs, many of them part-time. The decline of social mobility and a restriction in the supply of well-paid secure jobs was a signal of major problems ahead for the British economy, but it did not become an election issue. Similarly the balance of payments received no attention. By 2015 the deficit on the balance of payments had reached 5% of GDP, a level which few observers thought sustainable for very long, and which posed some severe risks for the UK economy if investor confidence were at some stage to weaken, and the funds needed to finance it were no longer forthcoming.

Some issues which the main parties did not want to discuss were raised by some of the other parties in the election. UKIP made immigration its core issue, but it was a subject which the two main parties chose largely to avoid. The immigration figures published shortly after the election showed annual net immigration running at a record level, over 300,000, far more than the tens of thousands which the Coalition Government had pledged to achieve. The importance of immigration for so many of the most dynamic sectors of the British economy was recognised in policy circles, but few politicians were prepared to offer a defence. Whenever the issue was raised it was usually dealt with by promising more restrictions.

The Green Party was the one party which focused a great deal on climate change, another elephant in the room which other parties chose to ignore. The long-term implications of climate change and the plans of the different parties for dealing with it were barely raised or discussed. In assessing economic competence, the parties' plans for deficit reduction were much more salient. Similarly, while UKIP wanted to talk about the EU and how Britain could have a better economic future if it voted to leave, the EU was another topic the other parties did not want to talk much about. They colluded in keeping the issue off the agenda before the election, which would determine whether or not a referendum on the issue would have to be held. As for other significant issues of foreign economic policy, such as the negotiations over the Transatlantic Trade and Investment

Partnership, which has profound implications for many aspects of life in Britain, there was much debate among many Green and Labour Party activists, but very little in the national media, and the main parties did not engage. In this as in so much else, as far as the economy was concerned the 2015 General Election followed a well-worn path.

JAMES DENNISON AND MATTHEW GOODWIN[*]

Immigration, Issue Ownership and the Rise of UKIP

On 2 April 2015, in the televised leaders' debate, the UKIP leader, Nigel Farage, used a question to argue that HIV patients from outside of the UK should be excluded from accessing NHS treatment. 'What we need to do', said Farage, 'is to put the NHS there for British people and families, who in many cases have paid into the system for years'.[1] Farage's comments were the most tweeted about moment of the debate and attracted widespread coverage throughout the campaign. The intervention underlined UKIP's decision to target its core supporters at the election— older, white and working-class voters, who mainly reside in England, and were united by anxiety over immigration, opposition to Britain's EU membership and dissatisfaction with the established parties.[2] Farage's comments were quickly condemned by the leader of Plaid Cymru, Leanne Wood, as 'scaremongering', 'dangerous' and 'divisive'. These were echoed by the leader of the Scottish National Party, Nicola Sturgeon, although the Labour leader Ed Miliband said nothing at the time. Yet there was evidence to suggest that some voters took a different view. According to one opinion poll by YouGov, which gave respondents Farage's quotation and asked whether or not they agreed with 'people coming to live in the UK being banned from receiving treatment on the NHS for a period of five years', 50% agreed while 34% disagreed with Farage.[3]

[*]James Dennison, European University Institute, james.dennison@eui.eu; Matthew Goodwin, University of Kent, m.j.goodwin@kent.ac.uk

[1]BBC News, 'Nigel Farage Defends HIV Comments', accessed at http://www.bbc.co.uk/news/election-2015-32176826 on 3 April 2015.

[2]Ford, R. and Goodwin, M. J. (2014) *Revolt on the Right: Explaining Support for the Radical Right in Britain*, London, Routledge; Goodwin, M. J. and Milazzo, C. (2015) *UKIP: Inside the Campaign to Redraw the Map of British Politics*, Oxford, Oxford University Press.

[3]YouGov/*Sunday Times* Survey Results. Fieldwork: 3–4 April 2015, accessed at http://cdn.yougov.com/cumulus_uploads/document/6f4p5p7re7/SundayTimesResults_150404_FINAL_amend.pdf on 3 July 2015.

doi:10.1093/pa/gsv034

On a wider level, the intervention revealed how immigration has remained a highly salient and contentious issue in British politics and raises intriguing questions. How has immigration politics in Britain evolved since the last General Election in terms of issue ownership, party politics and electoral behaviour? Which groups in society have been most receptive to anti-immigration appeals? How did these views influence vote choice at the General Election in 2015? And how did the other parties seek to manage the issue, on which their ability to demonstrate substantial change and competence has been seriously reduced?

Our central argument is that, whilst UKIP won only one seat, by the time of the General Election deeper changes had enabled the insurgent party to secure ownership of one of the most salient issues in British politics. As the urgency of the financial crisis faded, the re-emergence of immigration as an issue of major public concern helped push UKIP from the margins and towards the mainstream, bringing the party its strongest General Election result. UKIP won almost four million votes, or 12.9% of the vote in Great Britain, displacing the Liberal Democrats as the third most popular party. This result was largely, though not exclusively, fuelled by ongoing public concern about immigration, which Farage and his advisors put at the heart of their strategy.[4] For the first time, these unresolved public concerns over immigration allowed a relatively new party to effectively take ownership of this issue in the eyes of many voters, one that the Conservative Party has historically owned. David Cameron and his party won a surprising but small majority in May 2015 in spite of the immigration issue, rather than because of it. The Conservative Party's long-held status as the 'best' or most competent party on immigration came to an abrupt end, although whether this will remain permanently so remains to be seen. If the public had continued to believe that the Conservative Party was the most competent party on immigration, then they may have won a much larger governing majority.

1. Immigration under the coalition government

After the 2010 General Election, and 13 years of Labour Governments, some voters might have hoped that the Conservative Party's return to power, albeit shared with the Liberal Democrats, would usher in a 'harder line' on immigration. To these voters the 2010–2015 Parliament would prove to be a disappointment. As Figure 11.1 indicates, immigration rose substantially. Prior to taking power in 2010, David Cameron had promised to decisively rebalance net migration into Britain by taking it 'back to the levels of the 1990s—tens of thousands a year, not

---

[4]Goodwin and Milazzo, *UKIP: Inside the Campaign to Redraw the Map of British Politics.*

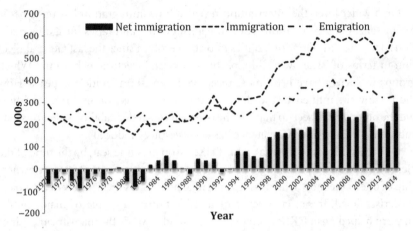

Figure 11.1 UK net migration, 1970–2014. *Source*: Office of National Statistics.

hundreds of thousands'.[5] The pledge had been widely criticised as impossible to guarantee because of free movement rights within the EU.[6] Ultimately, though no cap was included in the coalition agreement, the Tories and the Liberal Democrats did introduce an annual limit on non-EU economic migrants, as well as other 'tough' measures such as the reintroduction of exit checks, minimising abuse of the system through 'student routes' and tougher rules on immigration by spouses.[7] In June 2010, the coalition government brought in a temporary cap on non-EU migrants of 24,100 per annum, which was made permanent the next year at 21,700. Despite the government's attempt to conclusively put the issue to bed, the cap drew fire from both sides of the debate. The Business Secretary and Liberal Democrat, Vince Cable, said the cap was a threat to British business, a view that was echoed as late as 2014 by pro-business Tory backbenchers.[8]

[5]Conservative Party (2010) *Invitation to Join the Government of Britain*, Election Manifesto, accessed at https://www.conservatives.com/~/media/files/activist%20centre/press%20and%20policy/manifestos/manifesto2010 on 3 July 2015.

[6]Newman, C. 'Do 4 Out of 5 Immigrants Come from the EU?', accessed at http://blogs.channel4.com/factcheck/do-4-out-of-5-immigrants-come-from-the-eu/2626 on 3 May 2010.

[7]HM Government, 'The Coalition: Our Programme for Government', accessed at https://www.gov.uk/government/uploads/system/uploads/attachment_data/file/78977/coalition_programme_for_government.pdf on May 2010.

[8]Watt, N., 'Scrap Immigration Cap, Tory MP Tells Cameron', accessed at http://www.theguardian.com/uk-news/2014/mar/25/scrap-immigration-cap-tory-mp-mark-field-tells-cameron on 25 March 2014; also, see Press Association, 'Vince Cable: Migrant Cap Is Hurting Economy', accessed at http://www.theguardian.com/politics/2010/sep/17/vince-cable-migrant-cap-economy on 17 September 2010.

In contrast, the pressure group Migration Watch UK argued that the actual effects on net immigration would be limited.

During the first half of the Parliament, the Immigration Minister, Mark Harper, boasted that net migration had fallen to 'its lowest level for a decade', while also claiming that the Conservative-led government was 'continuing to bring immigration back under control'.[9] The decline was largely the result of tougher immigration restrictions on non-EU migrants, including foreign students, with the number of student visas reduced by 9%.[10] Some, such as the Institute for Public Policy Research, criticised the potential economic effects of a decline in students and warned that future emigration would also fall, as fewer students return home. Attempts to deal with illegal migration also included the controversial 'go home vans', which briefly toured some London boroughs, warning illegal residents to go home or face arrest. The Home Office calculated that the scheme resulted in 11 people leaving Britain, while the vans arguably added to an impression that the government was incompetent.

The Labour opposition mirrored the government's ostensibly tough stance on immigration, with Ed Miliband distancing the Party from the Blair and Brown eras during which New Labour was seen as proactively seeking increased immigration. A former advisor even claimed that Labour's more liberal stance on immigration was an attempt to 'rub the Right's nose in diversity'.[11] But the position also had clear electoral effects, with research showing that Labour's embrace of the 'liberal consensus' on immigration and Britain's EU membership had alienated its traditional, working-class voters. During Gordon Brown's tenure as Prime Minister, Labour voters were more likely to abandon the party because of discontent over immigration than the financial crisis, which they traced to international forces.[12]

Miliband swiftly overhauled Labour's stance on immigration, acknowledging that the Party had mishandled the issue and empathising with public anxiety.

---

[9] *Daily Telegraph*, 'Net Migration to the UK Falls by a Third', accessed at http://www.telegraph.co.uk/news/uknews/immigration/10075761/Net-migration-to-the-UK-falls-by-a-third.html on 3 June 2015.

[10] Cavanagh, M. and Glennie, A. 'International Students and Net Migration to the UK', accessed at http://www.ippr.org/publications/international-students-and-net-migration-in-the-uk on 10 April 2012.

[11] Whitehead, T. 'Labour Wanted Mass Immigration to Make UK more Multicultural, Says Former Advisor', accessed at http://www.telegraph.co.uk/news/uknews/law-and-order/6418456/Labour-wanted-mass-immigration-to-make-UK-more-multicultural-says-former-adviser.html on 23 October 2009.

[12] Evans, G. and Chzhen, K. (2013) 'Explaining Voters' Defection from Labour over the 2005–10 Electoral Cycle: Leadership, Economics and the Rising Importance of Immigration', *Political Studies*, **61**, 138–157.

The Labour leader declared that 'Eastern European immigration is a class issue because it increases competition for jobs, particularly those at lower wages. It looks very different if you are an employee rather than an employer. But we refused to recognise that sufficiently'.[13] Labour continued to view immigration solely through an economic lens, glossing over the more complex concerns over perceived threats to identity, values and ways of life. In 2011, Miliband stated that Labour's decision to allow unlimited numbers of EU migrant workers to settle in Britain had been a mistake and that large-scale migration could undermine wages for low-skilled workers.[14] He would reiterate these messages. In 2014, after UKIP won the European Parliament elections, Miliband claimed that Labour's 'embrace of openness made some people feel we didn't understand the pressures immigration put on them ... they were right'.[15] This more apologetic approach would define Labour's first spell in opposition since the 1990s.

2.   Immigration and the rise of UKIP

Throughout the early years of the post-2010 coalition government, migration into Britain from within the EU had remained stable. Net migration from within the EU was 77,000 for the year ending 2010, and by September 2012 the figure had fallen to 65,000. In 2013 a more strident public debate emerged as Britain headed towards the lifting of transitional controls over migrant workers from Bulgaria and Romania. By this time, Nigel Farage was transforming UKIP from a fringe Euro-sceptic party into a populist radical right party that was campaigning heavily on immigration and a populist critique of established politicians.[16] Farage had developed a fusion strategy, merging Britain's EU membership, traditionally an issue that has been of low salience, with immigration, which since the late 1990s had emerged as an issue of significant public concern. Farage spoke often about the perceived economic and cultural threats from EU migrant workers, referencing 'criminal gangs' and claiming that only by leading the EU could Britain reclaim control over national borders.[17]

---

[13]Miliband, E. (2010) in Fabian Society (2010) *The Labour Leadership: How Important Is It That the Party Has a Distinctive Ideology?*, London, Fabian Society, pp. 55–66.

[14]*Daily Telegraph*, 'Ed Miliband Admits Labour's Immigration Errors Made Britons Poorer', accessed at http://www.telegraph.co.uk/news/politics/ed-miliband/8352458/Ed-Miliband-admits-Labours-immigration-errors-made-Britons-poorer.html on 28 February 2011.

[15]Sparrow, A. 'Ed Miliband's speech in Thurrock: Politics Live Blog', accessed at http://www.theguardian.com/politics/blog/2014/may/27/blair-says-politicians-must-confront-and-expose-ukip-politics-live-blog on 27 May 2014.

[16]Ford and Goodwin, *Revolt on the Right*.

[17]Giannangeli, M. 'Britain to Face New Immigrant', accessed at http://www.express.co.uk/news/uk/366693/Britain-to-face-new-immigrant-wave on 23 December 2012.

The 2013 local elections saw UKIP achieve a significant breakthrough. The party contested 75% of available wards and averaged almost 25% of the vote, whereas four years earlier it had contested 26% of wards and averaged 16%. Its national equivalent vote share increased from less than 5% to almost 20%.[18] The next year, UKIP similarly put immigration at the centre of its campaign at the European Parliament elections, during which Farage suggested that he did not want to live next door to Romanians and that he felt anxious when he did not hear the English language on public transport.[19]

Initially, after the labour market restrictions on migrant workers from Bulgaria and Romania were lifted, Farage's prediction that Britain would attract far more than the 13,000 migrants predicted by the Home Office and could even attract 'many times' more than the 50,000 predicted by Migration Watch, appeared unfounded.[20] The rate of migration among workers from other EU states, however, had begun to increase at an unprecedented rate. Continuing economic problems in the Eurozone combined with Britain's modest economic recovery were significant 'push' and 'pull' factors. For the first time under the coalition government, in 2013 work overtook formal study as the main reason for migrating to Britain, leading to EU and non-EU net migration rising at similar rates, as shown in Figure 11.2.[21] Meanwhile, by the end of 2014 the overall number of migrants from Romania and Bulgaria had doubled to 46,000. Farage was able to claim partial vindication of his original prediction.[22]

The significant increase in net migration was followed by an increase in the perceived importance of the issue among voters, a cycle that had been typical since the turn of the millennium.[23] As public concern over the economy receded following the end of the crisis, immigration moved to the top of the list of important issues. As shown in Figure 11.3, towards the end of 2014, voters saw it as the most important issue of all, a position that it last occupied in May 2008. Those

[18] Goodwin and Milazzo, *UKIP: Inside the Campaign to Redraw the Map of British Politics*.

[19] Phipps, C. 'Nigel Farage's LBC Interview—the Key Moments', accessed at http://www.theguardian.com/politics/2014/may/16/nigel-farage-lbc-interview-key-moments on 16 May 2014.

[20] *The Spectator*, 'Nigel Farage's Speech at the UKIP Conference—Full Text and Audio', retrieved 3/6/2015 from http://blogs.spectator.co.uk/coffeehouse/2013/09/nigel-farages-speech-full-text-and-audio/ on 20 September 2013; BBC News, 'Bulgarian and Romanian Immigration—What Are the Figures?', accessed at http://www.bbc.co.uk/news/uk-politics-21523319 on 14 May 2014.

[21] BBC News, 'David Cameron Won't 'Cave in' on Migration Target Despite New Figures', accessed at http://www.bbc.co.uk/news/uk-politics-32816454 on 21 May 2015.

[22] Worrall, P. 'Fact Check: The Great Trickle from Bulgaria and Romania', http://blogs.channel4.com/factcheck/factcheck-great-trickle-bulgaria-romania/18163 on 14 May 2014.

[23] Duffy, B. (2014). 'Perception and Reality: Ten Things We Should Know About Attitudes to Immigration in the UK', *Political Quarterly*, **85**, July–September, pp. 259–266.

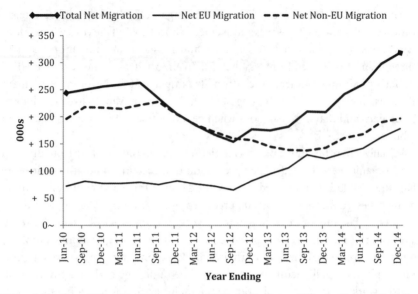

Figure 11.2   UK net EU and Non-EU migration, 2010–2015. *Source*: Office for National Statistics.

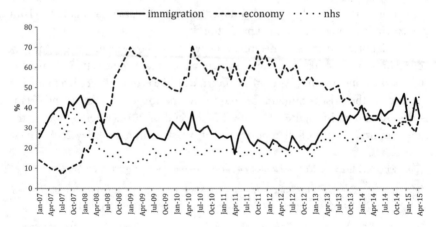

Figure 11.3   Most important issues facing Britain, 2007–2015. *Source*: Ipsos MORI.

who ranked it as a top issue also tended to hold negative views. Among those in the March 2014 wave of the British Election Study (BES) who saw immigration as the most important issue, 78% believed that immigration was bad for the economy, compared with 42% among the full sample. A few months later, the debate over immigration contributed to UKIP winning the European Parliament elections. The party polled almost 28% of the vote, becoming the first new party to win a nationwide election for almost a century. The breakthrough coincided with strong results for other populist radical right parties in Europe that campaigned against immigration, the EU and established parties, and often amidst a financial crisis.[24]

3.   The roots of British public concern over immigration

The British public is not divided on immigration. A large majority of the population wants levels of immigration reduced. This consensus is widespread, so much so that immigration is often thought of as a 'valence' issue—a salient issue on which there is widespread public agreement. In the British Social Attitudes survey, for example, the percentage of voters who want to see immigration 'reduced a little' or 'reduced a lot' increased from 39% in 1995, to 49% in 2003, 55% in 2008, fell to 51% in 2011, and then increased to 56% in 2013. From 2003 onward, less than one in five respondents wanted immigration to 'remain the same as it is'.[25] In the March 2015 wave of the BES, more than 70% of respondents wanted immigration reduced, while only 6% wanted it increased.

There is more disagreement, however, on the perceived effect of immigration. In the more recent BES data, there was a fairly even split between those who believe that immigration is good for the economy (42%) and those who believe that it is bad (39%). There is a more significant gap in terms of the perceived cultural effect of immigration: while 48% think that it has negative effects on British culture, 37% view it as culturally enriching. Greater still was the difference in public attitudes towards whether or not migrants are a burden on the welfare state: while 55% saw them as a burden, 24% did not. These divides are mirrored in other work on how public support for lowering immigration is shaped by the types of migration being considered. While a large majority of Britons oppose immigration *in toto*, they hold more favourable views on groups such as international students and high-skilled migrants.[26] They have been more hostile to low-skilled migrants from Central and Eastern Europe and family reunification migration from 'culturally dissimilar' countries, all types of migration that have been strongly opposed by UKIP. Notwithstanding such nuances, recent research has also shown how unresolved public concerns about immigration can erode trust in politics

[24]Goodwin, M. J. (2014) 'A Breakthrough Moment or False Dawn? The Great Recession and the Radical Right in Europe'. In Sanderlind, C. (ed.) *European Populism and Winning the Immigration Debate*, Brussels European Liberal Forum, pp. 15–39; Kriesi, H.-P. and Pappas, T. (eds) (2015) *European Populism in the Shadow of the Great Recession*, Colchester, ECPR Press.

[25]Data taken from the British Social Attitudes (BSA) surveys. For more information see 'British Social Attitudes 2013: Attitudes to Immigration', accessed at http://www.bsa.natcen.ac.uk/media/38108/immigration-bsa31.pdf on 27 May 2015.

[26]Ford, R., Morrell, G. and Heath, A. (2012) 'Fewer but Better? British Attitudes to Immigration', published as part of the *31st British Social Attitudes Report*. London, NatCen Social Research.

more generally.[27] This, in turn, makes it even more likely immigration sceptics will become receptive to parties like UKIP, which infuse their campaigns with anti-establishment populism. Ahead of the General Election, therefore, while British voters overwhelmingly agreed that immigration should be reduced, they were more divided about its economic and cultural effects.

While overall concern has been fairly widespread, four socio-demographic divides are repeatedly shown to affect the intensity of this concern: generation, class, education and geography.[28] Table 11.1 presents data from the March 2015 wave of the BES, revealing how these divides remain in place. Less than 30% of under-35s viewed immigration as bad for the economy and only 35% saw it as negative for British culture, compared with 58% and 50%, respectively, among the over-60s. The class divide is even more pronounced. More than half of routine and semi-routine workers hold negative views of the effects of immigration while only one-quarter associate migrants with positive effects. Ethnicity has a predictable relationship with attitudes to immigration: large majorities of white Britons saw immigration as having negative economic and cultural effects, while minorities hold the reverse view. University education, which is related strongly to more universalistic and cosmopolitan attitudes, correlates strongly with more positive views of immigration.[29] Finally, Londoners were at odds with the rest of the country in terms of the extent to which they view immigration as beneficial. Overall, and consistent with past research, these findings reveal how it is mainly older, white, less well-educated Britons, those from more insecure lower classes and those who live outside London, who are the most likely to associate immigration with negative effects.

4. Immigration and electoral behaviour

While public attitudes to immigration vary across different social groups, they also vary between and within political parties. Immigration is especially divisive for the Labour Party. According to the British Social Attitudes data, whereas 40% of Labour supporters think immigration is bad for the economy, almost as many—36%—believe that it is good for the economy. A similar divide can be found on the cultural axis: while 40% of Labour supporters think that immigration is bad for national culture, 41% think it is beneficial. We can gather further insight into these divisions and their consequences on the 2015 General Election by looking at

---

[27] McLaren, L. M. (2012) 'The Cultural Divide in Europe: Migration, Multiculturalism and Political Trust', *World Politics*, **64**, 199–241.

[28] Duffy, 'Perception and Reality'.

[29] Bornschier, S. and Kriesi, H. (2013) 'The Populist Right, the Working Class, and the Changing Face of Class Politics'. In Rydgren, J. (ed.) *Class Politics and the Radical Right*. London, Routledge, pp. 10–30.

Table 11.1 Attitudes towards the effects of immigration

	Immigration 'bad for economy'	Immigration 'good for economy'	Immigration 'undermines culture'	Immigration 'enriches culture'
Overall	42.3	38.6	47.5	36.8
18–35	29.4	51.6	34.6	48.4
36–59	46.5	33.8	50.2	34.0
60+	49.8	31.9	57.7	28.5
Routine/semi-routine	55.0	26.0	57.7	26.2
Managers/professionals	34.9	46.7	41.9	42.2
White British	45.0	35.4	50.2	34.3
Non-white	18.2	65.0	22.5	61.1
Degree	24.3	57.1	31.8	51.8
No degree	48.8	32.0	53.2	31.4
London	33.7	49.0	40.6	43.5
Rest of UK	43.6	37.0	48.6	35.8

Source: British Election Study, March 2015.

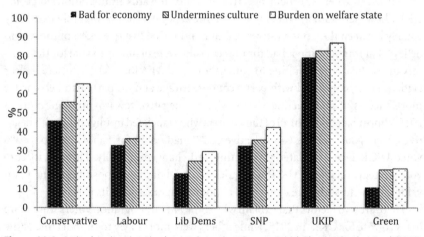

Figure 11.4 Attitude to immigration by vote intention. *Source*: British Election Study, March 2015.

the attitudes of party voters towards immigration in the BES. As shown in Figure 11.4, UKIP's is the only electorate dominated almost exclusively by voters who perceive immigration negatively, confirming how anti-immigration sentiment is a central aspect of its appeal.[30] The only other party with a majority of voters who hold negative views towards immigration is the Conservative Party, with two-thirds of its voters viewing immigrants as a burden on the

---

[30] Ford and Goodwin, *Revolt on the Right*.

Table 11.2 Voting intention of anti-immigration voters ('immigration is bad for the economy') by attitudes to British democracy and the EU

	Proportion of anti-immigration voters opting for UKIP	Proportion of anti-immigration voters opting for another party
Overall	23.9	76.1
Don't trust MPs	32.7	67.3
Not satisfied with British Democracy	33.2	66.8
Britain should leave EU	34.1	65.9

Source: British Election Study, March 2015.

welfare state and significant numbers associating them with having a negative economic and cultural impact. By the time of the 2015 election the only other party besides UKIP with such a homogeneous group of voters on immigration was the Greens—barely 1 in 10 of those voting Green saw migration as having a negative economic effect.

Not every voter who held negative attitudes towards immigration voted for UKIP, however. Rather, voters who held these negative views were divided fairly equally between the Conservatives, Labour and UKIP. Just over 35% of those who believe that immigration is bad for the economy were planning to vote for the Conservatives, 26% were planning to vote Labour and 24% for UKIP. Yet there is clear evidence that, compared with past elections, Farage and his party had become far more successful at attracting voters who are negative towards immigration. In 2010, almost half (47%) of all of these voters who associated immigration with negative effects voted for the Conservatives, 27% had voted for Labour and only 3% voted UKIP. Five years later, this picture had changed radically. Through its core vote strategy, therefore, UKIP was quickly consolidating its position as the main vehicle for voters who are concerned about immigration and its effects.

There are two factors that explain why some anti-immigration voters were more likely to vote for UKIP in 2015, while others were more likely to support one of the other parties. The first concerns the intensity of concern over the issue. Amongst voters who held the most strongly negative views about the economic effects of immigration (those who gave it a '1' on the seven-point scale), 34% favoured UKIP, while 28% favoured the Conservatives. Second, and as shown in Table 11.2, UKIP gain disproportionately large shares of anti-immigration voters both from those who are disenchanted with British politics and those who believe that Britain should leave the EU. The attraction of UKIP, therefore, was its anti-immigration outlook in combination with its anti-political establishment and Eurosceptic stance.

5. Public perceptions of the parties on immigration

UKIP's advance among immigration sceptics has been facilitated by another trend. It is now well documented in political science that certain parties are associated with particular issues and that when this association is positive among voters, parties are able to establish 'ownership' over an issue. Parties will then seek to emphasise issues that they 'own' and demonstrate their competence on them, while avoiding issues that they do not.[31] While issue ownership has tended to be stable over the long-term, not least *because* of the way in which parties seek to reinforce their areas of strength, it also became more important to explaining how voters made their choice.[32] Historical examples of issue ownership include Labour's historic strength on the NHS or the Conservatives' dominance on taxation, crime and, for much of the post-war period, immigration.

While UKIP would fail in its quest to win a handful of seats in May 2015, throughout the 2010–2015 Parliament, the Conservatives lost their historic ownership of immigration, which enabled UKIP to establish a stronger hold over this issue than previously and emerge as a far stronger vehicle for anti-immigration sentiment. As Figure 11.5 shows, in 2010 almost half of all voters saw the Conservative Party as the 'best' party on immigration. The second most trusted party was Labour, on 20%. But from thereon, and while struggling to demonstrate competence on the issue, in the public mindset Cameron and his party steadily lost ground on immigration. This provided an opening for UKIP to establish something that the party had never had before: ownership of a major issue within British politics.

Rather than the Labour Party, it was UKIP that benefited from falling public trust in the Conservative Party on immigration. According to the BES, prior to 2015 a clear majority of respondents, 69%, believed that the coalition government was handling immigration badly. Only 8% believed it was handling the issue well. Meanwhile, a clear minority of only 19% thought that a Labour Government would handle immigration well. Rather than attributing this perceived policy failure to the post-1997 Labour Governments, which presided over the initial influx of EU migrants, a significant number of voters also saw the Conservative Party as part of the 'problem'. Overall, 60% of respondents believe that the Conservative Party in government was to blame for current immigration levels, compared with 34% who blamed the previous Labour Government (Figure 11.6).

Nor does the Conservative Party appear to fare much better on other questions, as shown in Figure 11.7. Only one-third of respondents thought that immigration

---

[31] Green, J. and Hobolt, S. (2008) 'Owning the Issue Agenda: Party Strategies and Vote Choice in British Elections', *Electoral Studies*, **27**, 460–476.

[32] Egan, P. J. (2013) *Partisan Priorities. How Issue Ownership Drives and Distorts American Politics*, Cambridge, Cambridge University Press.

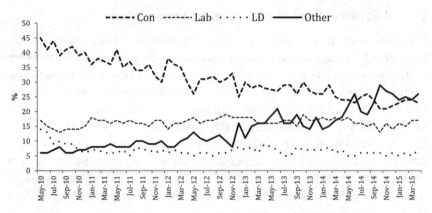

Figure 11.5 Best party to handle immigration, 2010–2015. *Source*: YouGov Issues Tracker.

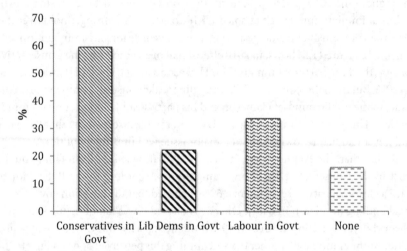

Figure 11.6 Perceived responsibility for levels of immigration, March 2015. Q. What do you think current levels of immigration are the result of? *Source*: British Election Study, March 2015.

was important to the party. The Conservatives are slightly ahead of Labour, whom only one in five voters thought prioritised immigration. Both parties are well behind UKIP, whom 90% of respondents believe would treat immigration as an important issue. Similarly, only 18% believe that the Conservatives could achieve a reduction in immigration, compared with 60% who believe that a UKIP Government would be able to. When taken together, the findings suggest that voters not only attributed blame to the incumbent Conservative Party for high immigration, but also perceived it to be neither interested in the issue nor willing to resolve the perceived problem. Given issue ownership's tendency for long-term, glacial

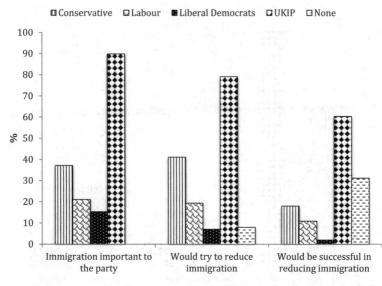

Figure 11.7 Issue ownership of immigration. *Source*: British Election Study, March 2015.

change, we can predict that the Conservatives will go into future elections as they went into the 2015 General Election campaign—as nothing better than the least bad realistic option. In only five years, Farage and UKIP transformed themselves from an afterthought on the issue of immigration into the primary vehicle for voters who felt intensely anxious about this issue and who wanted to see change.

6. Immigration in the election campaign

Despite or perhaps because of UKIP, immigration was less polarised during the 2015 campaign than at any election since 1997. In particular, the Conservatives, who in retrospect had over-promised in 2010, were keen to avoid the issue. Labour, whose supporters are more divided on immigration than those of any other party, also had an incentive to steer clear of immigration, as shown in Figure 11.8. Miliband's attempts to cater to both sides through uneasy vagaries, such as an unspecified commitment to 'control immigration', often did more to stoke controversy than calm the waters.[33] Moreover, the media covered the issue less than they had at past elections. Ultimately, less than a quarter of voters

---

[33]Williams, Z. 'Immigration: The Big Issue that the Left Just Can't Get Right', accessed at http://www.theguardian.com/global/2015/mar/31/immigration-big-issue-left-cant-get-right-labour on 31 March 2015.

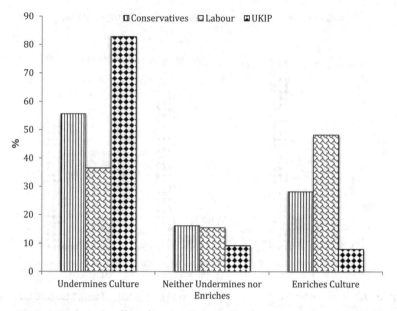

Figure 11.8 Attitudes to the effect of immigration on culture by party vote. *Source*: British Election Study, March 2015.

questioned by Ipsos MORI between March and April of 2015 could remember seeing any media stories on immigration.[34]

Despite being one of the most important issues for voters, the election campaign saw low media coverage of immigration and few policy promises from the main parties that could satiate public demand for a sharp reduction in the number of migrants. The approaches of the parties towards immigration in their campaigns can be placed into three groups. First, UKIP's radical right campaign focused heavily on immigration, continuing Farage's fusion strategy and quest to establish a longer-term niche in the political marketplace.[35] The party often linked immigration to other issues, such as calls to stop the NHS becoming the 'International Health Service', and the claim that Labour had betrayed the traditional working-class in more northern areas. Second, in the mainstream the Conservatives, Labour and, to a lesser extent, Liberal Democrats conveyed a tough approach towards lowering future immigration, while keeping policy specifics to a minimum and avoiding the issue as much as possible. Third, the Green Party and also the Scottish and Welsh Nationalists often sought to depict Labour and

---

[34] Duffy, B. 'Changing Attitudes to Immigration During the Election Debate', accessed at https://www.ipsos-mori.com/researchpublications/researcharchive/3569/Changing-attitudes-to-immigration-during-the-election-campaign.aspx on 5 May 2015.

[35] Ford and Goodwin, *Revolt on the Right*.

the Conservatives as 'UKIP-lite', and themselves as a progressive counter-weight to the populist, anti-immigration backlash.

UKIP's approach to immigration was the most strident. Farage centred his party's manifesto and many policy announcements upon immigration, which he argued could not be controlled so long as Britain remained in the EU. While the party had previous success in fusing immigration and the EU in the public mindset, its repeated attempts to frame the goal of annual net migration of 30,000–50,000 as a 'return to normality' was less successful after a series of communication blunders. In February, UKIP's immigration spokesman, Steven Woolfe, claimed that the party's policy was a strict cap on annual net migration of 50,000. Days later, Farage publicly corrected his colleague, stating that rather than a cap, which he argued was something that the public was 'very sceptical of', UKIP would introduce an Australian-style points system to encourage skilled immigration with tough limits on access to welfare benefits of five years.[36] Then, in April, UKIP decided to introduce a 50,000 per year cap on immigration, in addition to their proposed five-year moratorium on admitting unskilled workers. The muddled approach underlined a sense that, while UKIP's stance on immigration was closest to the views of most voters, its practical policies on the issue were often delivered in an amateurish way.

The Conservative Party went into the campaign having failed to meet their pledge to curb net migration to the 'tens of thousands'. The party kept the target in their manifesto, arguing that they had the ambition to achieve it through reducing pull factors to the UK, such as by curbing migrants' access to welfare benefits. The Conservatives promised to bar EU migrants from receiving tax credits, child benefits and access to social housing, unless they had worked and contributed for four years. In the spring of 2015, Cameron set out his ideas on immigration in an article in the *Daily Mail*, which was typical of his party's campaign in three ways. First, it sought to remind voters of Labour's track record on immigration. Second, when discussing his party's record in government Cameron sought to deflect attention towards the government's employment and economic record. Finally, Cameron mentioned UKIP only once, doing so to warn voters that only his party would offer a referendum on Europe.[37] The Conservative strategy to downplay immigration was also reflected in their tactic of avoiding a one-on-one debate between Cameron and Farage as much as possible. In the end, Farage and Cameron met only once, at the seven party leaders'

---

[36] Mason, R. 'Nigel Farage Drops UKIP's 50,000 Cap on Immigration', accessed at http://www. theguardian.com/politics/2015/mar/04/nigel-farage-drop-ukip-50000-cap-immigration on 4 March 2015.

[37] Chapman, J. 'Miliband Will Bring Back Uncontrolled Migration: Stark Warning from Cameron as He Urges UKIP Voters not to Hand Labour Power', accessed at http://www.dailymail.co.uk/news/article-3053043/Miliband-bring-uncontrolled-migration-Mail-urges-speak-PM-s-stark-warning.html on 23 April 2015.

debate, in which Cameron adopted a low-risk, detached pose, the exact opposite of Farage who courted controversy with his HIV comments. The Conservatives' campaign attempted to divert voters away from immigration and, if forced to discuss the issue, portray their party as the least bad option.

By the time of the General Election, Labour was talking tough on immigration. Its manifesto called for a cap on non-EU workers, banning immigrants from claiming benefits for two years, outlawing child benefits being sent out of the country and banning recruitment agencies from only recruiting from abroad. The manifesto also included a number of measures to give a more social democratic hue to the party's tougher rhetoric on immigration, such as clamping down on people who trafficked and exploited migrants, which it was claimed undercut wages of domestic workers.[38] Shortly before the election and after previously forgetting to mention immigration in his speech to the annual Labour conference, Miliband delivered what was designed to be a keynote speech on the issue, which he hoped would signal his party's departure from the New Labour era. He pledged to deliver a further 1000 border staff, introduce exit checks and stop serious criminals from entering Britain. In doing so, Miliband was attempting to frame Labour as even tougher than the Tories on the issue and went so far as to challenge Cameron to match his pledges, accusing the Prime Minister of 'abandoning the issue to UKIP'.[39] That the speech clocked in at less than seven minutes long was symptomatic of the approach of both of the major parties. The speech was also overshadowed by a leaked document advising campaigners how to deal with immigration on the doorstep. The best approach when dealing with voters who were defecting to UKIP, it was suggested, was to avoid the topic and move on.[40] The document came under fire from Labour MPs who had urged Labour to adopt a more proactive stance on the issue, like Simon Danczuk and Frank Field. Miliband had already attracted public criticism from other MPs after Labour had released its infamous immigration mug, emblazoned with the words 'Controls on immigration' with no further specifics. The mug was said to have 'split' the Shadow Cabinet.[41] The Greens swiftly

[38] Labour Party, 'Britain Can Be Better: The Labour Party Manifesto 2015', accessed at http://www.labour.org.uk/page/-/BritainCanBeBetter-TheLabourPartyManifesto2015.pdf on 3 July 2015.

[39] BBC News, 'Election 2015: Labour Pledges Prompt Immigration Action', accessed at http://www.bbc.co.uk/news/election-2015–32490861 on 28 April 2015.

[40] Riley-Smith, B. 'Revealed: Labour MPs Told Not to Campaign on Immigration in Secret UKIP Strategy Document', accessed at http://www.telegraph.co.uk/news/politics/labour/11293433/Revealed-Labour-MPs-told-not-to-campaign-on-immigration-in-secret-Ukip-strategy-document.html on 14 December 2014.

[41] Eaton, G. 'The Shadow Cabinet Split over Labour's Immigration Mug Reflects a Deeper Divide', accessed at http://www.newstatesman.com/politics/2015/03/shadow-cabinet-split-over-labours-immigration-mug-reflects-deeper-divide on 31 March 2015.

produced their own satirical, pro-immigration mug, with the words 'Standing Up for Immigrants'. With all three of these more minor parties having electoral imperatives to attack Labour and with the parties finding themselves bolstered by recent support from left-wing, ex-Liberal Democrats, putting clear water between themselves and the three centrist parties made sense. Both the Scottish and Welsh Nationalists argued that immigration policy should be devolved, while the Greens offered a 'genuine alternative' in the form of removal of restrictions on foreign students, abolishing family migration rules, more rights for asylum seekers and removing immigration preferences based on resources or skills.[42]

The Green, SNP and Plaid campaigns partly signalled an attempt to outflank Labour. But they also reflected a broader value divide within European democracies between parties that espouse libertarian-universalistic values, who defend minority and immigrant rights, and those with traditionalist-communitarian values, for whom national homogeneity is the foundation of their identity and a well-functioning society.[43] Both New Labour and more socially liberal Conservatives had been influenced by the New Left politics that emerged in the 1960s and saw a stronger emphasis on feminism, environmentalism, minority rights and an embrace of rising ethnic, religious and cultural diversity.[44] Between 2010 and 2015, however, the main parties attempted to win back traditionalist-communitarian voters by toughening their rhetoric on immigration, while, at the same time, trying to keep libertarian-universalist voters happy by backing issues such as gay marriage. By 2015, the most ardent left-wing progressives had mobilised around the three fringe left-wing parties in response to the increasingly anti-immigration rhetoric of Labour and the Conservatives.

7. Conclusion

We have shown that underneath the surface of British politics there is evidence that the radical right has increasingly assumed ownership of immigration. At the same time as the Conservative Party lost its historic advantage as being seen as the most competent party, UKIP deliberately set out to target and mobilise long-standing public anxieties over immigration—putting the issue at the heart of a broader narrative about national loss, threat and abandonment, which was directed strongly to lower middle-class and working-class white Britons. By the General Election in 2015, UKIP was benefiting from a broader and values-driven backlash among these voters

---

[42] The Green Party, 'For the Common Good: General Election Manifesto 2015', accessed at https://www.greenparty.org.uk/we-stand-for/2015-manifesto.html on 3 July 2015.

[43] Bornschier and Kriesi, 'The Populist Right, the Working Class, and the Changing Face of Class Politics'.

[44] Kriesi, H. (1989) 'New Social Movements and the New Class in the Netherlands', *American Journal of Sociology*, **94**, 1078–1116.

to a universalistic and cosmopolitan outlook that had come to dominate British media and politics, and which celebrated change that these voters found most threatening. Against the backdrop of historically unprecedented levels of net migration, voters who felt intensely concerned about the economic and cultural effects of this unsettling demographic change were being increasingly corralled around UKIP. While the electoral system continued to inhibit the rise of a new challenger, the first major domestic success for UKIP was largely down to its transition from a single-issue Eurosceptic party, which it had campaigned as in 2010, to a more fully fledged member of the populist radical right, which campaigns more heavily on immigration and appeals to a socially and attitudinally distinctive electorate.

Ongoing and unresolved public concern over immigration introduces the possibility that UKIP, or a similar radical right party in the future, may establish a more permanent niche on the landscape, similar to populist radical right parties in other democracies. Immigration has not turned out to be a political issue of just the New Labour period and the coalition government certainly did not put the issue to bed. Public angst over immigration remains unresolved and as the Conservatives have lost ownership over the issue, they may have less incentive and less expectation to seriously lessen immigration numbers. It seems unlikely that public anxieties can be resolved by the established parties, who are broadly committed to Britain's continued EU membership and its founding principle of the free movement of migrant workers.

It should be remembered, however, that while immigration is something that the vast majority of Britons agree should be lower, there is less of a consensus on its effects or whether international students and highly skilled migrants are problematic. The efforts of the main parties to win over potential UKIP voters by taking a more negative tone towards immigration since 2010 may have aided the rise of the more actively pro-immigration Green Party, whose support rose from less than 1% to nearly 4%, and possibly the SNP, which campaigned as a radical progressive party and enjoyed an unprecedented landslide north of the border. Henceforth, it seems likely that parties ardently opposed to and in favour of immigration will continue to take votes from Labour and the Conservatives, which both contain blocs of pro- and anti-immigration supporters.

In closing, the General Election in 2015 failed to offer any resolution of the highly contentious immigration issue. The Conservatives won the election in spite of, rather than because of, immigration. The major parties attempted to avoid the issue as much as possible, leaving UKIP in the eyes of a significant number of voters as their preferred vehicle for expressing their often intensely felt concerns over this issue. So long as net migration remains high, Farage and his party or a like-minded successor may entrench their position as the dominant political party within this space. In the upcoming Parliament, all Britons will be faced with a choice that will include the potential for the UK to have greater control over immigration, as Britain decides via a referendum whether to remain in the EU. The General Election suggests that there is a core of older, working-class voters with 'traditionalist-communitarian' outlooks who consider more restrictive immigration a top priority while a smaller number of ardently pro-immigration voters are drawn to the rhetoric of the likes of the Greens. However, most of Britain's voters remain somewhere in the middle—opposed to high levels of immigration, but willing to recognise that immigration has some benefits. Unless a mainstream party can convince these voters that they are able and willing to reduce immigration, we can expect the issue of immigration to continue to exacerbate the breakdown of the British party and political system.

JAMES DENNISON*

The Other Insurgency?
The Greens and the Election

On 24 February 2015, the leader of the Green Party of England and Wales, Natalie Bennett, gave a radio interview that was widely condemned by the media as a 'disaster'.[1] After being unable to specify the financial details of her party's housing policy, she described her own performance as 'excruciating' and 'very bad', later apologising for it.[2] The interview even prompted some journalists to call for the Green Party leader's resignation, blaming her for the party's 'bust' in the polls.[3] Yet the interview began by Bennett celebrating the Greens quadrupling their membership since 2010, up to 54,500 and beyond UKIP and the Liberal Democrats. The party had also shot up in the polls in less than nine months, from around 2% to, at one point, 10% under Bennett's leadership. After the successful completion of the first term in Parliament of the highly popular Caroline Lucas—the Greens' sole MP—the party was targeting up to half a dozen Westminster seats as Bennett predicted that politics at this election would 'break wide open'.[4] Ultimately, the Green Party, benefiting both from the downfall of the Liberal Democrats and the apologetic

---

*James Dennison, European University Institute, james.dennison@eui.eu

[1]Thompson, B. and Aglionby, J. (2015) 'Natalie Bennett interview disaster mars Greens' UK election launch', accessed at http://www.ft.com/cms/s/0/512598a0-bc12-11e4-a6d7-00144feab7de.html on 13 June 2015.

[2]BBC News (2015) 'Election 2015: Green leader Bennett Sorry for 'Excruciating' Interview', accessed at http://www.bbc.co.uk/news/uk-politics-31600324 on 13 June 2015.

[3]Crowcroft, O. (2015) 'Election 2015: Is Natalie Bennett to blame for Green Party Boom to Bust?', accessed at http://www.ibtimes.co.uk/election-2015-natalie-bennett-blame-green-party-boom-bust-1497385 on 13 June 2015. Myers, R. (2015) 'Come Back Caroline Lucas, All Is Forgiven', accessed at http://www.telegraph.co.uk/news/general-election-2015/politics-blog/11519510/Come-back-Caroline-Lucas-all-is-forgiven.html on 13 June 2015.

[4]LBC News (2015) 'Incredibly Awkward Interview with Natalie Bennett', accessed at http://www.lbc.co.uk/incredibly-awkward-interview-with-natalie-bennett-105384 on 13 June 2015.

doi:10.1093/pa/gsv035

stance of Labour towards UKIP, successfully quadrupled their total vote share at the 2015 General Election and consolidated their position amongst the second tier of British parties. The Greens are now a party of choice for those on the left wing who are disenchanted by traditional politics and rally around a commitment to diversity, minority rights and an actively positive outlook towards immigration. With long-term party de-alignment and the on-going transformation of generational values, so long as the political context remains favourable, the Greens can look forward to 2020 with a vastly increased profile and swelling membership ranks.

This contribution asks five questions. How did developments both within and outside the Green Party affect their performance in the 2015 election? Who was attracted by the Green Party's message? How effective was the Green Party's campaign and policy offer? How can we theoretically explain the rise of the Green Party? What does the future hold for the party?

1.   From one hit wonders to professionalised party?

The Green Party that went into the 2015 election campaign was in a completely different position from that of 2010 and was, in many ways, unrecognisable from the same party of just 10 years earlier. The 2015 Green Party, with its single leader and coordinated press strategy, was the result of a painful and long period of transformation that produced a more professionalised and, much to the lament of some of its supporters, more orthodox political party. For nearly 20 years, the Party had lingered in the shadows of its shock 1989 European election performance when the party came from nowhere to claim third place and 15% of the vote. Their success that year resulted from a combination of protest voting and a 'Green Tide' that swept over Europe following post-Chernobyl alarm about environmental degradation, which was exploited in the party's purely ecological and widely acclaimed party political broadcasts.[5] The Greens' particularly large vote share in the UK was also caused by the remarkable collapse of the SDP–Liberal Alliance, the Liberal Democrats' predecessors. However, their success encouraged Labour and the Conservatives to incorporate environmentalism into their own policies and rhetoric, robbing the Greens of their previous monopoly over ecological matters. Moreover, through the 1990s the Liberal Democrats regrouped to become, alongside the Nationalist parties, the natural protest vote in the West Country, Wales and Scotland, a role later played by UKIP in the south and east of England. Such developments forced the Greens to form policies on non-environmental issues and find a political home to the left of the major parties, depriving them of the opportunity to again be the catch-all protest party they were in 1989.

Such squeezing out, both geographically and in terms of policy, led to a long period of electoral underperformance and party infighting. The Greens failed to

---

[5]Curtice, J. (1989) 'The 1989 European Election: Protest or Green Tide?' *Electoral Studies*, **8**, 217–230.

win more than 5% of the vote at European elections again until 2009. However, the proportional electoral system introduced in 1999 allowed the Greens to elect their first two MEPs, re-elected at the 2004 election. The Greens also won seats at the newly created Greater London Assembly and the entirely independent Scottish Greens won seats in the Scottish Parliament. At General Elections, with the First-Past-The-Post system acting as an institutional barrier, Green progress was glacially slow, increasing from a low of 0.3% in 1997 to 1% in 2005. In 2007, in an attempt to increase the party's electoral appeal, the Greens ditched their previous system of two 'Principal Speakers'—one male and one female—and elected Caroline Lucas, the main proponent of the change, as its first party leader. One Green Party London Assembly Member described the move as a 'naïve and forlorn hope'.[6] By the 2010 election, the Greens were able to contest 310 Westminster seats, nearly double the tally in 2005. Although their vote share still dropped to 0.9%, the election saw Caroline Lucas become the party's only MP, offering the party unprecedented exposure and proving that voting Green was not necessarily a waste of time in the First-Past-The-Post system.

One year later, the Greens took minority control of Brighton and Hove City Council. The Green administration in the city proved tumultuous, with in-fighting amongst the party's councillors and a week-long strike by rubbish collectors that pitted Lucas against the head of the council, Jason Kitcat. Some claimed that the Greens were divided between far-left 'watermelons', green on the outside and red on the inside, and 'mangoes', green on the outside and Liberal Democrat orange on the inside.[7] Ultimately, the Greens achieved significant economic and environmental successes in the city, including increased tourism, housing and a strong small and medium-sized enterprises sector.[8] However, the need to impose £26 million in cuts coupled with the lack of a whipping system on council votes exacerbated any internal tensions within the party. At the 2015 local elections, the Greens lost half of their seats on the council and, with them, the only Green controlled council in the country.

It was the 2011 victory in Brighton that increased Caroline Lucas' confidence in her ability to defend her Westminster seat and, in light of the historic opportunity to gain the protest vote of disgruntled Liberal Democrats, increase Green representation elsewhere. 'I want to ensure that we use the leadership of the Green Party in a strategic way', explained Lucas, as she stepped down from the party leadership,

---

[6]Jones, J (2007) 'Leading Edge: No', accessed at http://www.theguardian.com/society/2007/sep/12/guardiansocietysupplement.greenpolitics on 13 June 2015.

[7]Harris, J. (2013) 'Have the Greens Blown It in Brighton?', accessed at http://www.theguardian.com/politics/2013/dec/15/greens-blown-it-in-brighton on 13 June 2015.

[8]Thompson, B. (2015) 'Is Brighton a Far Showground for UK Green Party?', accessed at http://www.ft.com/cms/s/0/850071a-ab9a-11e4-8070-00144feab7de.html#axzz3d4U2ILHW on 13 June 2015.

'to help us build momentum and build up our electoral presence'.[9] Lucas made no bones about her intention to 'take our message to Lib Dem areas in particular' where voters are 'looking for a new home and we want to be able to welcome them'. In her place, Natalie Bennett, an Australian former Guardian journalist, was elected with 42.8% of first preferences—a far cry from the 92.4% of first preferences that Caroline Lucas won when she last ran opposed in 2008. Bennett vowed to fight the government's cuts, describing them as 'economically illiterate'[10] and repeatedly campaigned against the 'pernicious' and 'dangerous' scapegoating of immigrants by both the government and Labour Party, who had followed UKIP in 'a race to the bottom'.[11] By early 2014, the Green Party were still polling between 1 and 3% in the polls but had an increasingly nationally recognised MP, a new leader, a political heartland in Brighton, a virtual monopoly on pro-immigration rhetoric and, in the form of ex-Liberal Democrats, a clear target market for the 2015 election. In short, despite still being considered a fringe party held back by the electoral system, both the Greens' own fundamentals and the political landscape had not before offered the party a better opportunity at a General Election.

2. Media coverage and 'the Green Surge': discovery, scrutiny and decline

In the year prior to the 2015 General Election, no party underwent more dramatic poll fluctuations than the Green Party. How can we explain a party spending over two years at very low poll ratings, then rapidly quintupling its vote share to 10% in just six months, only to see it halved again prior to the election? I argue that, more so than for any other party, media portrayal of the Greens contributed to their notable rise and partial fall. This media coverage followed a pattern familiar to American presidential primary elections, characterised by Sides and Vavreck as 'discovery, scrutiny and decline'.[12] Like many candidates in US primaries, the Green Party and its leader were relatively unfamiliar to the public. Furthermore, there were a significant number of undecided voters, there was a lengthy long campaign and 'the challenge for

---

[9]McCarthy, M. (2012) 'Green Party leader Caroline Lucas Steps Aside to Aid Fight Against Lib Dems', accessed at http://www.independent.co.uk/news/uk/politics/green-party-leader-caroline-lucas-steps-aside-to-aid-fight-against-lib-dems-7743513.html on 13 June 2015.

[10]Jowit, J. (2012) 'Green Party Elects Natalie Bennett as Leader', accessed at http://www.theguardian.com/politics/2012/sep/03/green-party-natalie-bennett-leader on 13 June 2015.

[11]Ramsay, A. (2013) 'Green Party Leader Slams Immigrant Scapegoating', accessed at http://brightgreenscotland.org/index.php/2013/07/green-party-leader-slams-immigrant-scapegoating/ on 13 June 2015.

[12]Sides, J. and Vavreck, L. (2013) *The Gamble: Choice and Chance in the 2012 Presidential Election*, Princeton, Princeton University Press.

reporters [was] that the campaign may not produce newsworthy events or moments every day'[13] These factors combined to create three starkly distinct stages of media coverage of the Green Party—'discovery', 'scrutiny' and 'decline'.

According to Sides and Vavreck the process of discovery begins when a candidate, or in our case, a party, 'who had previously attracted little new coverage did or said something [...] judged to be novel, important and therefore newsworthy'.[14] Three unprecedented events overlapped to offer the Greens a boost in coverage. First, David Cameron insisted in early May 2014 that the Greens should be included in any General Election debates and compared them to UKIP. Second, the number of voters intending to vote Green quickly swelled to 5%. Third, there was some progress in the 2014 European and local elections. At the European contest, the Greens increased their seats from two to three, despite a 1% fall in vote share to 7%. The Greens made modest advances in the local elections, gaining 23 seats, and made a breakthrough in some traditionally Labour areas, becoming the official opposition in Liverpool, Solihull, Islington, Lewisham and Norwich. Most tantalisingly, the Greens also secured over 45% of the vote in two seats in Bristol, opening up the possibility of a second Westminster seat. These three events led to unprecedented media coverage through the summer as news outlets repeatedly described the Greens as a potential 'UKIP of the Left'.[15] Figure 12.1 indicates the growth in numbers in 2014 intending to vote Green.

During the discovery phase 'polls and news coverage reinforced each other, as good poll numbers became a rationale for additional coverage [...] suggesting the candidate's strength and potential viability'.[16] Such positivity was certainly a hallmark of the Green's discovery phase, which increased in intensity throughout the autumn as newspapers proclaimed: 'Potential support for the Greens outweighs potential support for UKIP',[17] 'Rise of Green Party and UKIP [...] have killed the old order and all bets are off', the Greens are the 'third insurgent force',[18] 'A new

---

[13] Sides and Vavreck, *The Gamble: Choice and Chance in the 2012 Presidential Election*, p. 42.

[14] Sides and Vavreck, *The Gamble: Choice and Chance in the 2012 Presidential Election*, p. 43.

[15] Coates, S. (2014) 'Greens Turn into 'UKIP of the Left' as They Steal Protest Vote from Lib Dems', accessed at http://www.thetimes.co.uk/tto/news/politics/article4140426.ece on 12 June 2015; *The Economist* (2014) 'A UKIP of the Left', accessed at http://www.economist.com/news/britain/21616997-green-party-embraces-left-wing-populism-ukip-left on 12 June 2015.

[16] Sides and Vavreck, *The Gamble: Choice and Chance in the 2012 Presidential Election*, pp. 44–45.

[17] Eaton, G. (2014) 'Potential Support for the Greens Outweighs Potential Support for UKIP', accessed at http://www.newstatesman.com/politics/2014/11/potential-support-greens-outweighs-potential-support-ukip on 12 June 2015.

[18] Helm, T. (2014) '2015 General Election Could Be the Most Unpredictable Vote in Living Memory', accessed at http://www.theguardian.com/politics/2014/dec/27/2015-general-election-unpredictable-green-party-ukip on 12 June 2015.

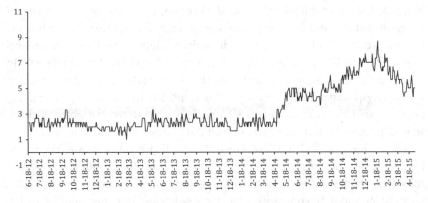

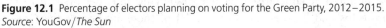

Figure 12.1 Percentage of electors planning on voting for the Green Party, 2012–2015. *Source*: YouGov/*The Sun*

"people's army"? How the Greens could be set to become the new UKIP',[19] 'Here come the Greens'[20] and British politics is now a 'five-party system'.[21] Two further events heightened media interest in the Greens. First, the party's annual conference saw direct attacks by both Caroline Lucas and Natalie Bennett on the Labour Party's left-wing credentials and paid little heed to environmentalism.[22] Despite the Greens' long-standing left-wing economic commitments, commentators such as the Independent interpreted the emphasis on social justice as a 'change of hue' and an 'electoral calculation', adding to the left-wing populist insurgency narrative.[23] Second, the decision by broadcasters to not include the Greens in the General Election debates in October was widely interpreted as a legitimate grievance

[19] Bentley, G. (2014) 'A New "People's Army"? How the Greens Could Be Set to Become the New UKIP', accessed at http://www.cityam.com/1416586707/new-peoples-army-how-greens-could-be-set-become-new-ukip on 12 June 2015.

[20] Payne, S. (2014) 'Green Party Up to 11 Per Cent in Latest Ashcroft Poll', accessed at http://blogs.spectator.co.uk/coffeehouse/2015/01/green-party-on-11-per-cent-in-latest-ashcroft-poll/ on 12 June 2015.

[21] Goldhill, O. (2014) 'Open Thread: Can British Politics Survive in a Five-Party System?', accessed at http://www.telegraph.co.uk/news/politics/11153469/Open-thread-Can-British-politics-survive-in-a-five-party-system.html on 12 June 2015.

[22] Dennison, J. (2014) 'Though the Green Party's Popularity May Continue to Rise, It Is Too Ideological to Become a 'UKIP of the Left", accessed at http://blogs.lse.ac.uk/politicsandpolicy/though-the-green-partys-popularity-may-continue-to-rise-it-is-too-ideological-to-become-a-ukip-of-the-left/ on 13 June 2015.

[23] *The Independent* (2014) 'Turning Red: A Change of Hue Has Helped the Green Party Win Support', accessed at http://www.independent.co.uk/voices/editorials/turning-red-a-change-of-hue-has-helped-the-green-party-win-support-9710056.html on 12 June 2015.

by the media[24] and public alike, with an ICM opinion poll showing 80% in favour of Green inclusion[25] and 280,000 people signing an online petition demanding the Greens' presence.[26] Moreover, the media actively adopted the 'Green Surge' label to describe the Greens improving poll ratings and membership numbers.[27] In short, the last eight months of 2014 saw the Green Party receive unprecedented and largely positive media coverage. This coincided with a subsequent polling boost up to 10% as commentators enthusiastically greeted the potential for a second 'populist' insurgency party in their 2015 General Election narrative.

The enthusiasm did not last. Once the candidate [in our case, the Green Party] seemed 'serious' enough to pay attention to, that candidate was then subjected to increased scrutiny from opponents and the news media.[28] This scrutiny period is characterised by deeper delving into personal histories, issue positions and harsher questioning. All of these applied to the Greens from late January until late March, during which the change of tone right across the media was as rapid as it was uniform. Between 21–26 January, the *Spectator, Financial Times, Independent* and *This Week*—all of which had previously eagerly heralded the 'UKIP of the Left'—described the Greens' policy proposals, respectively, as 'completely bonkers',[29] 'hippie gap year',[30] 'daft',[31] a 'joke'

---

[24]Dunt, I. (2014) 'Why Aren't the Greens in the TV Election Debate?', accessed at http://www.politics.co.uk/blogs/2014/10/13/why-aren-t-the-greens-in-the-tv-election-debate on 12 June 2015.

[25]Wintour, P. (2014) 'Four-Fifths of Public Want Green Party in TV Leaders' Debates—Poll', accessed at http://www.theguardian.com/politics/2014/dec/17/poll-green-party-leaders-election-debates on 12 June 2015.

[26]Change.org (2014) 'Include the Green Party in the TV Leaders' Debates ahead of the 2015 General Election', accessed at https://www.change.org/p/bbc-itv-channel-4-sky-include-the-green-party-in-the-tv-leaders-debates-ahead-of-the-2015-general-election on 12 June 2015.

[27]Harris, J. (2015) 'The Green Surge: Is This the Party That Will Decide the Election?', accessed at http://www.theguardian.com/politics/2015/jan/21/green-surge-party-that-will-decide-election on 12 June 2015.

[28]Sides and Vavreck, *The Gamble: Choice and Chance in the 2012 Presidential Election*, p. 44.

[29]West, E. (2015) 'Welcome to the Completely Bonkers World of the Green Party Manifesto', accessed at http://blogs.spectator.co.uk/coffeehouse/2015/01/welcome-to-the-bonkers-world-of-the-green-party-manifesto/ on 12 June 2015.

[30]Ganesh, J. (2015) 'Greens Contemplate Life Beyond the Fringe', accessed at http://www.ft.com/cms/s/0/529f5f22-a240-11e4-bbb8-00144feab7de.html#axzz3cmU0eQKS on 12 June 2015.

[31]Birrell, I. (2015) 'Labour Should Expose the Greens' daftness—Not Flirt with Them', accessed at http://www.independent.co.uk/voices/comment/labour-should-expose-the-greens-daftness--not-flirt-with-them-10001620.html on 12 June 2015.

and 'loony'.[32] It was during this same four days that leader Natalie Bennett was 'skewered'[33] in a 'car crash interview' on the BBC's *Daily Politics*. Interviewer Andrew Neil focused on the finer details of the Greens' policies of a universal basic income, a wealth tax, the removal of immigration controls, a smaller armed forced and cutting international trade—positions that the Green leader visibly struggled to defend.[34] A month, later, Bennett again struggled to explain Green Party policy in an interview with radio channel LBC, this time regarding the pledge to build 500,000 houses at a cost of £2.7 billion. The leader herself later described the interview as 'excruciating' and explained that she had had a 'mind blank'.[35]

Throughout February and March, the Greens' poll ratings declined and 'the media had a natural incentive to move on and find a storyline that was novel and more exciting'.[36] By the start of the short campaign, on 30 March, the media had already successfully established the narrative that Natalie Bennett was an 'incompetent'[37] leader and that the Green Party's policies were ill conceived. This allowed room for some media outlets to take a more forgiving tone towards the Green Party, despite its leader's now widely recognised shortcomings.[38] Media attention had already begun to turn to the contenders for Prime Minister and the SNP, leaving the post-decline Greens to plateau in the polls at around 5% until the election. Indeed, even the set piece election debates, two of which Natalie Bennett took part in, failed to raise much interest in the Green Party as all eyes were fixed on Nicola Sturgeon and the Scottish

---

[32] Horne, N. (2015) 'Election 2015: How Long Can This Green Party Joke Last?', accessed at http://www.theweek.co.uk/election-2015/62247/election-2015-how-long-can-this-green-party-joke-last on 15 June 2015.

[33] Hutton, W. (2015) 'The Greens, Chaotic as They Are, Give a Lesson to the Main Parties', accessed at http://blogs.spectator.co.uk/coffeehouse/2015/01/watch-natalie-bennett-demonstrates-how-green-policies-dont-add-up/ on 12 June 2015.

[34] Payne, S. (2015) 'Watch: Natalie Bennett Demonstrates How Green Policies Don't Add Up', accessed at http://blogs.spectator.co.uk/coffeehouse/2015/01/watch-natalie-bennett-demonstrates-how-green-policies-dont-add-up/ on 15 June 2015.

[35] LBC (2015) 'Incredibly Awkward Interview with Natalie Bennett', accessed at http://www.lbc.co.uk/incredibly-awkward-interview-with-natalie-bennett-105384 on 12 June 2015.

[36] Sides and Vavreck, *The Gamble: Choice and Chance in the 2012 Presidential Election*, p. 45.

[37] Holehouse, M. (2015) 'Can Natalie Bennett Win Back the Greens?', accessed at http://www.telegraph.co.uk/news/politics/green-party/11453478/Can-Natalie-Bennett-win-back-the-Greens.html on 13 June 2015.

[38] Bennett, A. (2015) 'Natalie Bennett May Be Bad at Interviews, But At Least She Doesn't Think She's Jesus', accessed at http://www.telegraph.co.uk/news/general-election-2015/11534749/Natalie-Bennett-may-be-bad-at-interviews-but-at-least-she-doesnt-think-shes-Jesus.html on 13 June 2015.

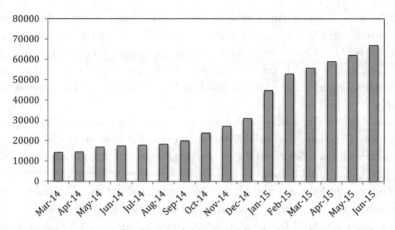

Figure 12.2 Green Party membership, March 2014—June 2015. *Source*: http://www.channel4. com/news/green-party-membership-growth-ukip-natalie-bennett

Nationalists. Perhaps the most active interest that the media took in the Greens during the short campaign was the informal alliance during the televised debates between Bennett, Plaid Cymru leader Leanne Wood and Sturgeon, who urged English voters to vote Green.[39]

Ultimately, the 'Green Surge' in the polls proved temporary. The Green Party performed a useful role for journalists who were eager for another UKIP-esque story of an insurgent party dismantling the traditional political order. Furthermore, media outlets needed political stories between the European elections and the start of the long campaign in late December. After this point, the media dramatically increased their criticism of the Greens, with party leader Natalie Bennett being a favourite target, before losing interest altogether. This pattern can best be described as 'discovery, scrutiny and decline'. The party eventually returned to the same poll ratings it had held just after the European Parliament elections. At the General Election, the Green Party received a still very impressive 3.8% far beyond their 0.9% in 2010. The Greens also had the third best improvement in percentage point gain, with a 2.8% increase, behind UKIP and the SNP, but ahead of Labour and the Conservatives. However, the 'Green Surge' and it accompanying media profile did have one potentially longer lasting legacy. The Green Party saw its membership swell in numbers, throughout the entire year before the election and particularly during December 2014, just before the media began scrutinising the Greens more rigorously (Figure 12.2).

---

[39] Simon, N. (2015) 'Nicola Sturgeon Urges English to Vote Green or "Progressive" Labour', accessed at http://www.huffingtonpost.co.uk/2015/03/16/nicola-sturgeon-urges-english-to-vote-green-or-progressive-labour_n_6876950.html on 12 June 2015.

3. Who votes Green and why: leftists, environmentalists or protest voters?

The Green Party went from unprecedented popularity to unprecedented scrutiny in early 2015. Although the party leadership's long held leftist economic views[40] received criticism, the media failed to mention that the Greens also proposed a range of consistently popular policies, such as renationalisation of the railways, increasing the minimum wage, removing the profit motive from the NHS, as well as opposition to fracking, HS2 and tuition fees. Besides their role as an environmentalist party, they also began to carve themselves a niche as the only party with a clearly non-conciliatory approach to UKIP's anti-immigration rhetoric and an outright rejection of austerity as a fiscal policy. With such an expansive agenda, the Greens had the potential to appeal to a number of different sections of the electorate and indeed their membership and polling figures are in a far better position than they were five years ago. What is less clear is the profile of those voting for Natalie Bennett and Caroline Lucas' party. What is the background of Green voters? Are Green voters of the far-left or are they disgruntled with the mainstream parties? Do they sincerely vote for the Greens' environmental and economic policies or is their vote a protest? And, if the latter, what are they protesting about?

Before turning to the attitudinal drivers of Green Party support at the 2015 General Election, it is worth comparing the socio-demographic background of Green voters with the literature's expectations of the social makeup of Green voters. Supporters of green parties in Britain and elsewhere have long been characterised as relatively young, well-educated and in professional jobs.[41] More recently scholars have noted the disproportionate numbers of socio-cultural specialists and students voting for green parties, as well as green voters' tendency to live in urban areas and identify as non-religious.[42] As shown in Table 12.1, the Green Party's voters at the 2015 General Election seamlessly fit this picture. A majority of Green voters were under the age of 36 and nearly 17% were students, over double the proportion of any other party. The Greens' voters were also the most likely of any party to hold a university degree, though only slightly more so than Liberal Democrat voters. In terms of employment, voters for Natalie Bennett's party were more likely than voters of any other party to be in professional or

---

[40] Dennison, J. (2014) 'Though the Green Party's Popularity May Continue to Rise, It Is too Ideological to Become a "UKIP of the Left"', accessed at http://blogs.lse.ac.uk/politicsandpolicy/though-the-green-partys-popularity-may-continue-to-rise-it-is-too-ideological-to-become-a-ukip-of-the-left/ on 13 June 2015.

[41] Lowe P. and Rudig, W. (1986) 'Political Ecology and the Social Sciences: The State of the Art', *British Journal of Political Science*, **16**, 513–550.

[42] Dolezal, M. (2010) 'Exploring the Stabilization of a Political Force: The Social and Attitudinal Basis of Green Parties in the Age of Globalization', *West European Politics*, **33**, 534–552.

Table 12.1 Socio-demographic background of each party's voters at the 2015 General Election

	Greens	Labour	Lib Dems	Cons	UKIP	Electorate
18–35	54.8	32.3	32.0	27.6	18.8	31.8
36–55	27.9	34.9	30.7	30.2	35.4	32.6
56+	17.3	32.8	37.4	42.2	45.9	53.6
Routine/Semi-Routine workers	13.3	18.9	10.6	11.9	19.2	16.0
Lower supervisory/technical	2.4	8.3	4.2	6.3	9.9	7.2
Professional/management	60.9	44.8	60.6	52.3	42.3	48.5
University degree	42.5	26.9	39.3	26.1	13.4	26.0
If degree, humanities	41.9	39.5	37.2	29.3	21.7	33.9
Not religious	68.6	45.6	50.1	37.2	41.7	44.6
Students	16.8	4.5	7.3	4.1	1.4	5

Source: British Election Study, May 2015.

managerial positions, though again this figure was comparable to that of the Liberal Democrats' voters. The education of the Greens also suggests that they will go on to socio-cultural industries as their university-educated voters were the most likely to have specialised in the humanities. Finally, Green voters were by far the most likely to describe themselves as non-religious, with over two-thirds doing so.

During the 2015 General Election, the Green Party's policies were most commonly described as 'far left'.[43] Indeed, the Green Party's manifesto was clearly far to the left of Britain's centre-left Labour Party. While the Greens called for a maximum wage, a universal basic income and increases in social spending, Labour vowed to cut spending, clamp down on welfare and halt any borrowing in the next Parliament. Yet the clear left-right divide between the parties was not reflected in their voters as both Labour and Green supporters placed themselves very similarly on the left-right spectrum, as shown in Figure 12.3. On specific economic policy issues, those voting Green in 2015 tended to be very slightly *less* left wing than Labour voters: 71% of Greens believed that the government should redistribute incomes, a very slightly lower figure than the 74% of Labour voters, but significantly higher than the 53% of British electors who supported such redistribution.[44]

---

[43] *The Economist* (2015) 'Verdant Pastures', accessed at http://www.economist.com/news/europe/ 21651879-northern-europe-environmental-parties-are-claiming-radical-space-left-vacant-moderate on 13 June 2015. Wigmore, T (2015) '"This Leftwing Label Is Potentially Unhelpful": The Greens on Why They Missed Their Moment', accessed at http://www.newstatesman.com/politics/2015/06/leftwing-label-potentially-unhelpful-greens-why-they-missed-their-moment on 13 June 2015. Hall, Z. (2015) 'The Green Should Lose Natalie Bennett and Appoint Caroline Lucas as Leader', accessed at http:// www.telegraph.co.uk/news/general-election-2015/politics-blog/11619860/The-Greens-should-lose-Natalie-Bennett-and-appoint-Caroline-Lucas-as-leader.html on 13 June 2015.

[44] British Election Study, May 2015.

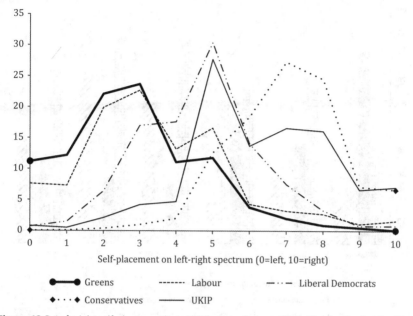

Figure 12.3 Left-right self-placement by vote intention. *Source*: British Election Study, May 2015

Although Green voters are highly similar to Labour Party voters on the trad-itional left-right spectrum, it is when respondents are asked what were once collect-ively designated as post-material issues that a clear divide emerges.[45] Knutsen and, more recently, Kriesi *et al.* [46] have divided these issues between 'new politics' coming from the 1968 movements (environment and liberty-authority) and those on the more recent integration–demarcation divide arising from the cultural and political effects of globalisation (immigration and supranational organisations). Green voters' positions on 'new politics' values are obvious—namely a strong advocacy of environmentalism, the rights of women, ethnic minorities and homosexuals and a disdain for traditional pillars of authority. On contemporary integration–demarcation issues, Green Party voters are expected to support immigration as 'con-trary to the traditional left, whose views of equality were primarily focused on class

[45] Inglehart, R. (1977) *The Silent Revolution. Changing Values and Political Styles among Western Publics*, Princeton, Princeton University Press.

[46] Kriesi, H., Grande, E., Lachat, R., Dolezal, M., Bornschier, S. and Frey, T. (2006), 'Globalization and the Transformation of the National Political Space. Six European Countries Compared', *European Journal of Political Research*, **45**, 921–956; Kriesi, H., Grande, E., Lachat, R., Dolezal, M., Bornschier, S. and Frey, T. (2008) *West European Politics in the Age of Globalization*, Cambridge, Cambridge University Press; Knutsen, O. (1995) 'Party Choice'. In van Deth, J. and Scarbrough, E. (eds) *The Impact of Values. Beliefs in Government Volume Four*, Oxford, Oxford University Press, pp. 461–491.

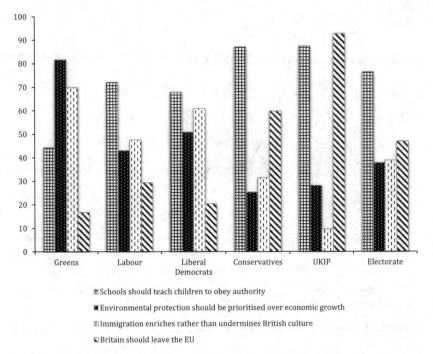

⊞ Schools should teach children to obey authority

■ Environmental protection should be prioritised over economic growth

⊡ Immigration enriches rather than undermines British culture

◩ Britain should leave the EU

Figure 12.4 Percentage agreeing with each political statement, by General Election vote.
Source: British Election Study, March–May 2015

antagonisms, the Green interpretation of equality is related to the welfare of all mar-
ginalised groups, including migrants'.[47] Less clear are Green attitudes towards
supranational governance. Greens should be torn between their decentralised, participatory vision of democracy, which is contrary to the European Union's structure, and their 'cosmopolitan orientation',[48] which underpins support for the
'cultural opening of European societies, as they do not see much importance in
the conservation of their countries' national identities and traditional ways of life'.[49]

How do Green voters' policy attitudes compare to the expectations of the literature? As shown in Figure 12.4, on all issues, those voting for the Green Party express
both more 'New Left' and 'integration' attitudes than Liberal Democrat or, especially, Labour Party voters—who they position themselves alongside on the traditional
left-right spectrum. Only 45% of Green Party voters believe that schools should
teach children to obey authority, compared with a much higher 72% of Labour

---

[47] Dolezal, 'Exploring the Stabilization of a Political Force', p. 542.

[48] Kitschelt, H. (1994) *The Transformation of European Social Democracy*, Cambridge, Cambridge
University Press, p. 227.

[49] Dolezal, 'Exploring the Stabilization of a Political Force', p. 542.

Table 12.2 Issue salience for Green voters and the electorate

Green voters		Electorate		'Old' Green voters		'New' Green voters	
NHS	20.0	Economy	28.7	Environment	20.8	NHS	22.3
Economy	17.7	Immigration	26.8	Economy	17.6	Economy	20.8
Inequality	13.6	NHS	15.8	NHS	16.3	Inequality	13.9
Environment	11.5	Public Services	3.9	Inequality	9.9	Environment	9.3
Poverty	7	Poverty	3.6	Poverty	6.9	Immigration	6.0
Public Services	6.6	Unemployment	2.7	Housing	5.3	Housing	5.1
Immigration	5.4	Housing	2.7	Education	3.8	Unemployment	4.9
Housing	5.1	Inequality	2.5	Public Services	3.7	Education	4.7
Education	2.3	Election	2.5	Immigration	3.2	Public Services	4.3
Unemployment	2.2	Terrorism	2.0	Crime	2	Poverty	2.7
Other	8.7	Other	8.9	Other	10.6	Other	6.1

Q. As far as you're concerned, what is the SINGLE MOST important issue facing the country at the present time?
Source: British Election Study, May 2015.

voters. Indeed, Green Party voters were by far the least likely of each party's voters to agree with this statement. Regarding environmental protection, unsurprisingly, Green Party voters were the most likely to agree that the ecological well-being should be prioritised over economic growth, at 82% with a large divergence from Labour Party voters, less than half of whom thought the same. Regarding immigration, Green Party voters had the most positive outlook, with 7 in 10 believing immigration enriched British culture, which was far higher than Labour voters, on 48%, though not that much higher than Liberal Democrat voters on 61%. Finally, Green Party voters were by far the least likely to believe that the UK should leave the European Union—even less so than the traditionally pro-European Liberal Democrats. It would seem that, for Green voters, a commitment to transnational cosmopolitanism outweighs concerns over any democratic shortcomings of the EU. Overall, despite Green voters not being significantly more left-wing than Labour voters in the traditional sense, on issues of 'post-material', 'new' or 'integration-demarcation' politics, there are consistent and striking divides.

The attitudinal similarities and differences between Green voters and voters of other left-wing parties are apparent. However, it is not clear whether Green voters give certain issues greater significance than others, and if these are classic left-right issues of resources or newer 'post-material' concerns. In Table 12.2, we can see that the Greens' top three most important issues are all classic left-right issues. For Green voters, immigration is only the seventh most important issue facing Britain, whereas for the electorate as a whole it is the second most important issue, just behind the economy. Indeed, over half of Britons see either the economy or immigration as their single most salient topic, whereas Green Party voters' concerns are far more disparate. Interestingly, only 11% of Green voters see the environment as the most important issue, behind the NHS, the economy and inequality. However, when we separate Greens between 'old' Green voters, who were already planning on voting for the Green Party in March 2014, and 'new' Green voters, who, before the European Parliament elections, were planning on voting for another party or had not decided who to vote for yet, there is a clear divide on issue salience. To the Greens' longest-standing supporters, the environment was the most important issue affecting Britain in May 2015, whereas recent recruits to Bennett's party were more concerned by the NHS, the economy and inequality, with less than 1 in 10 considering the environment the most important issue. As the Greens improved in the polls, the most strident environmentalists made up a decreasing share of Green voters. By the time of the General Election, it is fair to conclude that, though Green voters stood out from voters of other left-wing parties in their attitudes towards 'new' political issues, they were still most concerned by the classic left-right struggle for resources.

Green voters are not significantly more left-wing than Labour voters on economic issues nor are they primarily driven by environmental concerns. We have seen, however, that they are distinguished from Labour voters on 'post-material' attitudes. In fact, socially and attitudinally the group of voters closest to the Greens are Liberal Democrats and the similarity does not stop there. Over half of 2015 Green voters supported the Liberal Democrats in 2010 and around one-third voted for the former junior coalition partner in both 2005 and 2010. There are a number of ways of interpreting this. First, Liberal Democrats and Green voters traditionally hold similar socio-demographic profiles. Both are likely to be university educated and to work in professional or managerial jobs, though Green voters are younger and hold more left-wing economic opinions. Second, the Liberal Democrats were, until the 2010 election, the protest vote of many on the left. After entering government, they lost this niche and, subsequently, saw their poll ratings plummet. Third, the Greens entered the 2015 election with certain policy promises that they once owned by the Liberal Democrats—for example, ending university tuition fees. These three issues made the Greens the natural alternative for disgruntled Liberal Democrats who from 2010 onwards had no centre-left party with whom to register their protest.

Indeed, by entering government, the Liberal Democrats almost certainly lost the support of eventual Green Party voters, whose negative attitudes to British democracy and the House of Commons differ sharply with those voting Liberal Democrat in 2015. As shown in Figure 12.5, nearly three-quarters of Green Party voters are dissatisfied with British democracy and over 7 in 10 do not trust MPs. Greens, like UKIP voters, score far higher on both issues than voters of the major three 'governing' parties. The increase in vote share that the Greens secured in 2015 was partially thanks to their ability to win over the most 'post-material', left-wing Liberal Democrat protest voters.

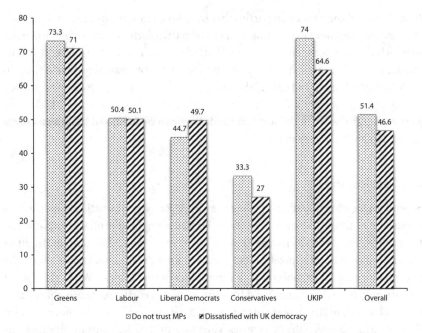

Figure 12.5 Percentage of each party's voters who do not trust MPs in general and who are dissatisfied with UK democracy. *Source*: British Election Study, March 2015

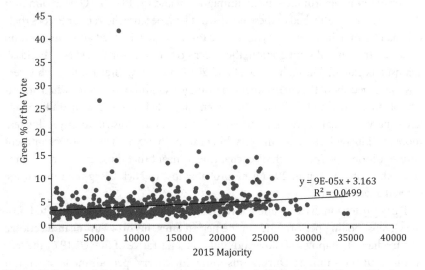

Figure 12.6 Green Party vote share by constituency marginality in the 2015 General Election. *Source*: Author's calculations

Finally, how much did constituency level effects determine one's chance of voting Green in 2015? The most obvious electoral impediment for the Greens has always been Britain's majoritarian electoral system that discourages voters from 'wasting' their votes on parties that have no chance of winning in their constituencies. We would expect this effect to be particularly strong in constituencies in which the race between the top two candidates is close, both because of voters' strategic calculations and because of the increased campaigning that occurs in such 'marginal' seats. Indeed, as shown in Figure 12.6, the effects of constituency marginality negatively affect the Green vote share. A seat with a 10,000 vote greater margin between the top two candidates can be predicted to return a 0.9% higher Green Party vote share.

4. Conclusion

Several forces came together to allow the Green Party to dramatically increase its vote share at the 2015 General Election. First, the ongoing professionalisation of the party coupled with its success in securing its own political fiefdom in Brighton put the party in a stable position that allowed for a greater media profile and the potential to expand its ambitions to other parts of the country. When the golden opportunity of a Liberal Democrat breakdown occurred, the party was able to capitalise. Over half of 2015 Green voters voted Liberal Democrat in 2010 and, even now, the similarities between the two parties' voters are strong. Both parties appeal to students and university-educated professionals with 'post-material' values on authority, minority rights, environmentalism, immigration and the EU. The Greens won over those voters most attached to these norms, not least because the Labour Party's rhetoric had become increasingly sympathetic towards the UKIP-led anti-immigration backlash. In terms of immigration, the Greens could be summarised as a 'backlash against a backlash'. Throughout 2014 and 2015, most new Green voters, who were less concerned about the environment than longer standing Green voters, had originally planned on voting Labour. The Greens appealed to those with traditionally left-wing views that shared Labour voters' attitudes to redistribution yet 'looked' more like Liberal Democrats in everything except their youth and disenchantment with traditional politics. Such disenchantment meant that those ex-Liberal Democrats who voted Green in 2015 were probably lost to Nick Clegg the moment he entered government.

Party professionalisation and a favourable political context combined to boost the Greens' polling performance in the period after the 2014 European Elections. The media were happy to follow and build on a narrative of the 'UKIP of the left' throughout the summer. During this initial 'discovery' period, media attention on the Greens was enthusiastic and positive, with far more regard to their potential electoral performance than their policies. This unprecedented coverage led to a 'Green Surge' in polling. However, by early 2015, the media abruptly took on a far more critical tone, catching the occasionally amateurish party off guard and leading to a number of 'car crash' interviews during this 'scrutiny' period. By

March, support had declined, flattening out at around 5% during the short campaign as media attention turned elsewhere. The main legacy of this cycle in media coverage was a boom in party membership, nearly quadrupling in a year.

Finally, long-term changes to Britain's demographics and politics worked in favour of the Green Party. Not only is generational replacement increasing the number of voters who share the Greens' 'post-material' beliefs but, as partisan de-alignment continues to fragment the party system, those voters who remain engaged have become more critical and their voting behaviour less predictable. For more voters than ever before, in 2015 Natalie Bennett's party was attractive because it provided the best product in an increasingly crowded market. So long as Labour continues to adopt increasingly anti-immigration rhetoric in an attempt to win back its working class support base, there will be growing space for a left-wing and unashamedly pro-immigration, pro-minority rights party like the Greens. Furthermore, so long as the Liberal Democrats remain tainted by their term in government, the Greens should be able to retain a considerable portion of the left-wing protest vote. However, the benefit that the Green Party receives, like UKIP, from being united on issues like immigration may increasingly attract a divided support base on the traditional left-right spectrum. Already commentators have taken opportunities to identify a split between centrist 'mangoes' and far-left 'watermelons'. Overall, depending on what narrative the media sets between now and the 2020 General Election, the Greens may increasingly be seen, in England and Wales at least, as the fifth party of British politics.

ROSIE CAMPBELL AND SARAH CHILDS*

All Aboard the Pink Battle Bus? Women Voters, Women's Issues, Candidates and Party Leaders

1. Introduction

Since at least 1997, the main political parties have made significant attempts to target women voters.[1] New Labour actively sought to undermine the Conservative Party's post-war advantage among women. Labour under Blair and Brown was explicitly liberally feminist in both dimensions of feminisation—the inclusion of women in politics and the inclusion of women's perspectives and issues.[2] The Party enacted legislation designed to further gender equality while using equality guarantees (in the form of all-women shortlists) to ensure the better representation of women on the Labour benches in the House of Commons. As Conservative leader since 2005, David Cameron has adopted the language of liberal feminism, stressing the need for more Conservative women politicians, and fairer access to paid employment for women.[3] To understand how the parties related to women voters during the 2015 election campaign, we situate the election within this context of the interparty competition for women's votes that has gradually brought the parties closer together on 'women's issues' such that all, with the possible exception of UKIP, are competing to be viewed as at least equally liberally

*Rosie Campbell, Birkbeck, University of London, r.campbell@bbk.ac.uk; Sarah Childs, University of Bristol, s.childs@bristol.ac.uk

[1] Lovenduski, J. (1997) 'Gender Politics: A Breakthrough for Women?', *Parliamentary Affairs*, **50**, 708–719; Norris, P. (1999) 'Gender: a gender-generation gap?', In Evans, G. and Norris, P. (eds) *Critical Elections: British Parties and Voters in Long-Term Perspective*, London, Sage, pp. 146–163.

[2] Lovenduski, J. (2005) *Feminizing Politics*, Cambridge, Polity Press.

[3] Childs, S. and Webb, P. (2012) *Sex, Gender and the Conservative Party*, London, Palgrave Macmillan.

doi:10.1093/pa/gsv036

feminist.[4] We trace how women voters were portrayed and targeted throughout the campaign through an analysis of media accounts and party manifestos. We also examine how women voters evaluated the parties and whether the parties' equality rhetoric regarding women's political representation was manifest in their selection of women candidates in winnable seats.

2. The campaign

Considerable attention was paid to women voters in the 2010 election, at least in the long campaign, and some claimed that the contest would be the 'Mumsnet Election',[5] although interest in women voters diminished after the all-male leaders' debates during the short campaign. In 2014, women voters were also a key target group during the Scottish referendum campaign as they were consistently less likely to support independence than men.[6] As a result of the heightened interest in women voters in both contests one might have expected women voters to be a prominent feature of the parties' campaigns and of the press coverage of the 2015 election. Yet, in a *Guardian* blog, Anne Perkins described 2010 as 'not so much as a new dawn as a high water mark' for interest in women voters';[7] arguing that with the exception of the hoo-ha around Labour's pink battle bus women voters were not a central feature of news coverage during the long campaign.

Women voters became more visible during the long campaign when, in February 2015 Harriet Harman, Deputy Leader of the Labour Party, launched the party's special battle bus, intended to reach out to women voters. This bus generated a great deal of publicity, not because the party was targeting women voters *per se* but due to its colour. There was a public debate relating to the colour of the bus which some described as pink and others as magenta. Either way, the colour of the bus generated many column inches that at least touched on the issue of women voters. That said, Harriet Harman and the Labour Party were accused of patronising women and of succumbing to the 'pinkification' of womanhood. However, the colour of the bus may have been a successful strategy as previous

---

[4]Campbell, R. (2015) 'Representing women voters: the role of the Gender Gap and the response of political parties', *Party Politics*, forthcoming.

[5]Campbell, R. and Childs, S. (2010a) 'Wags', 'Wives' and 'Mothers' ... But what about Women Politicians?', *Parliamentary Affairs*, **63**, 760–777.

[6]Campbell, R. (2014), accessed at http://www.psa.ac.uk/insight-plus/blog/you-cannae-shove-your-granny-bus-talk-her-round-instead-women-voters-scottish on 5 June; Kenny, M. and MacKay, F. (2014), accessed at https://genderpoliticsatedinburgh.wordpress.com/2014/11/28/shattering-the-highest-glass-ceiling-in-scotland/ on 28 November.

[7]Perkins, A. (2015), accessed at http://www.theguardian.com/commentisfree/2015/apr/14/why-isnt-anyone-chasing-the-womens-vote on 14 April.

Labour Party women's campaign buses (of other hues) seeking out women voters in previous elections had been largely ignored by the media.[8]

Admirable as this attempt to mobilise women voters and draw attention to women's issues may have been,[9] the bus's deployment was largely publicly justified on the basis of dubious statistics. Harman claimed that there were 9.1 million missing women voters in 2010. This figure was generated by multiplying a percentage of non-voters (calculated by the House of Commons Library using the 2010 British Election Study (BES)) by the number of women in the population. The weighting procedure that was used artificially magnified the gender gap in electoral participation to three percentage points from just one percentage point. In fact, analysis of the 2010 BES post-election face-to-face survey (also the data used by the House of Commons) shows that 77% of men and 76% of women said that they had voted, a gap between men and women of just 1% that is not statistically significant. As well as self-reported turnout, the survey includes a validated vote variable (the survey team used electoral registers to establish whether respondents voted in the election). Using these figures, 57% of men and 56% of women in the survey were found to have voted in the election, producing a gap of just 1% between men and women, again not statistically significant. Thus a good deal of the discussion about women voters that took place during the 2015 election was based on the erroneous belief that women had been less likely to vote in 2010 than men.

There was a perception among some feminist commentators that women voters were less central to the 2015 election coverage than in 2010. However, analysis of UK national newspapers suggests that there was considerable newspaper copy devoted to the subject. In the final three months prior to the election, there were 142 references to women voters in national newspapers compared with 45 references in the same period in 2010. In the campaign's final month there were 37 references to women voters in 2015, compared with 20 in 2010. Thus, at least in terms of newspaper coverage, women voters were arguably given more prominence in 2015 than 2010. In 2015 there was not an easily digestible simple news frame such as the 'Mumsnet Election', or 'Worcester Women', which provided journalistic hooks for articles, but women voters and women's issues were raised during the campaign. From a media perspective this may mean that women were less visible but, potentially, might also suggest that the issue of women voters was more fully integrated into the coverage as a whole. Anne Perkins noted that politicians seemed finally to have realised in 2010 that women make up 52% of voters but then seemed to have forgotten this by 2015; alternatively, perhaps, the 2010 realisation may have led to a

[8]Campbell, R. and Lovenduski, J. (2005) 'Winning Women's Votes? The Incremental Track to Equality', *Parliamentary Affairs*, **58**, 837–853.

[9]Childs, S. (2015) 'Pink Stinks, but Labour's bus is a welcome sight', accessed at http://policybristol.blogs.bris.ac.uk/2015/02/12/pink-stinks-but-labour's-bus-is-a-welcome-sight-on-the-road/ on 12 February.

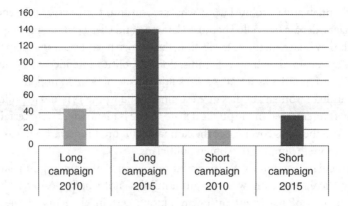

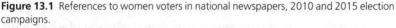

Figure 13.1 References to women voters in national newspapers, 2010 and 2015 election campaigns.
Source: Nexis Search of National Newspapers, 2010, 2015

situation where in 2015 women voters were a central feature of election strategy and not simply another 'minority' target group. Early and preliminary evidence that considers newspaper coverage only is suggestive that women voters were actually a more recurrent feature of the 2015 campaign than in 2010 when the memorable 'Mumsnet' news frame was in play (Figure 13.1).

The trajectory of interest in women in the election campaign appeared to reverse in 2015 compared with 2010. In 2010—the alleged Mumsnet election—women voters were discussed a great deal prior to the leaders' debates but women's issues were largely absent from the debates themselves and after the debates the media's attention shifted from women voters and women politicians to the leaders' wives. The different gender dynamics of the leaders' debates in the two elections explains the reversal of the trend in attention to women voters. In 2015 David Cameron refused to participate in head-to-head debates with Ed Miliband, with just one debate that included the Prime Minister. This instrumental decision, taken by Cameron, had the effect of drawing three women leaders, previously little known to the English electorate, into a prime-time debate watched by 7.4 million Britons. The effect on the campaign was notable: Nicola Sturgeon the leader of the SNP, gave what was regarded by many as an outstanding performance and the three parties with women leaders sought to use gender for electoral advantage. The Green Party produced a video, introduced by a black women, portraying the four male leaders, Cameron, Miliband, Clegg and Farage, as a boy band in cahoots together to preserve the old-boys club;[10] the catch phrase was 'a vote for me is the same as a vote for any of us *guys*'; they also had a poster, picturing

---

[10]Green Party (2015) 'Change the Tune—Party Election Broadcast, accessed at https://www.youtube.com/watch?v=PPgS7p40ERg on 6 June 2015.

Natalie Bennett and Caroline Lucas: 'what are you afraid of, boys?'. At the end of the 'challengers' debate (so-called because Cameron and Clegg did not participate), in one of the key images of the 2015 election, the women party leaders participated in a group hug, again signalling a feminisation of politics intended to symbolise a disruption of 'politics as usual'. As a result the issue of women in politics (the re-presentation of women's bodies in Westminster and women's issues in policy commitments) re-emerged in the public debate.[11] The leaders' wives were certainly not absent from the press coverage of the campaign but on this occasion it was impossible to ignore the impact of women politicians.

The media's reaction to the increased prominence of women politicians, particularly Nicola Sturgeon, was—to put it mildly—not wholly positive. The usual manifestations of persistent misogyny among certain elements of the British Press in their coverage of women politicians intensified to the crudest and most offensive levels in their portrayals of Sturgeon; perhaps the basest of which was a photo-shopped image of the Scottish National Party leader in the *Sun* newspaper swinging in a tartan bikini on a wrecking ball *à la* Miley Cyrus.[12]

3. The manifestos

In order to assess the extent to which the parties were explicitly, and implicitly, targeting women voters, we analysed their election manifestos. Critics will suggest that the manifestos are unlikely to be widely read, but General Election manifestos are broadly comparable documents, containing explicit statements of intent, and reflecting intra- and interparty political debates. Manifesto pledges are frequently implemented too, despite what people might think.[13] We are interested in the policy pledges parties make 'to', 'for' and 'about' women. A women's pledge explicitly names women as women, or as mothers; others may also be included if in their wider consideration they speak implicitly or indirectly to women as a category.[14]

We analysed the manifestos of the seven main parties: Conservative, Labour, Liberal Democrat, Greens, SNP, Plaid Cymru (PC) and UKIP and, through an inductive analysis, identified six main *women's issues*:[15]

---

[11]Lytton, C. (2015), accessed at http://www.telegraph.co.uk/women/womens-politics/11561947/General-Election-2015-What-the-three-women-party-leaders-really-want.html on 27 April.

[12]'Tartan Barmy', *The Sun*, 11 March 2015.

[13]Bara, J. (2005) 'A Question of Trust: Implementing Party Manifestos', *Parliamentary Affairs*, **58**, 585–599.

[14]Childs, S., Webb, P. and Marthaler, S. (2010) 'Constituting and Substantively Representing Women: Applying New Approaches to a UK Case Study', *Politics and Gender*, **6**, 199–223.

[15]Admittedly these are subjective groupings although they are informed by previous research. Campbell, R. and Childs, S. (2015) 'What the Coalition Did for Women: A New Gender Consensus, Coalition Division and

(1) Women and paid work;
(2) Mothers and childcare;
(3) Carers and the 'cared for';
(4) Violence against women and girls (VAWAG);
(5) Public life;
(6) Human rights, development and immigration.

All the main parties had something to say about nearly all of these, except UKIP did not speak to women's role in public life and the SNP to VAWAG.[16] Accordingly, we can note, once again, the broad consensus among the political parties about what constitutes the main terrain of women's issues in the UK, or more precisely, what they consider should be addressed in their General Election manifestos. As in 2010 work–life balance issues were the key focus/battleground, cementing their centrality in UK politics (Table 13.1).

Policy pledges falling outside these broad categories and garnering support by more than one party include: the abolition of VAT on Sanitary Products (SNP, PC, UKIP); the ending of mixed sex hospital wards (Conservatives, Greens); women's imprisonment (Conservatives, PC); and, participation in sport (Conservatives, PC). Issues that only a single party posited as a women's issue include: media sexism (Greens); equal access to the arts (Liberal Democrat); relationship mediation and access to the courts (Liberal Democrat); war widows pensions (UKIP); and the decriminalisation of non-payment of the TV licence (UKIP).

Greater attention to the specifics of the pledges for women by individual parties and the parties collectively is warranted, in addition to noting any shared agenda of women's issues. Here, and again informed by previous research which suggests the possibility of 'safe' women's issues—issues over which all parties might be expected to agree—we are keen to establish whether there are also any *women's interests* that are shared across the parties in 2015. Issues to do with women's bodily integrity or those which incur few financial commitments, or relatively fewer financial commitments, have been found to more likely garner consensus regarding what is 'in the interests of women'.[17] In other words, in 2015, is there evidence of a broad consensus on actions in respect of VAWAG, women and development, and women's international human rights, even as there is significant party differentiation on issues that can be placed on a left/right economic and/or state/market spectrum?

Gendered Austerity', In Seldon, A. and Finn, M. (eds) *The Coalition Effect, 2010–2015*. Cambridge, Cambridge University Press. Childs, S., Webb, P. and Marthaler, S. (2010) 'Constituting and Substantively Representing Women: Applying New Approaches to a UK Case Study', *Politics & Gender*, **6**, 199–223.

[16]This is an issue for the devolved Parliament: accessed at http://www.gov.scot/Topics/People/Equality/violence-women on 10 June 2015. Thanks to Meryl Kenny for confirming this.

[17]Childs and Webb, *Sex, Gender and the Conservative Party*.

Table 13.1 The terrain of women's issues, main British party election manifestos, 2015

Issues	Six out of seven parties	Four or five parties	Three parties
Work, gender pay gap, workplace inequality			
Gender pay gap transparency by big companies	X		
Enhance paternity leave and pay		X	
Careers/segregation		X	
Strengthen law on women's/maternity discrimination			X
Mothers and childcare			
Expand hours of free childcare	X		
Expand provision of childcare	X		
Maternal mental health		X	
Reduction in child benefit			X
Increase numbers of midwives			X
Tax-free childcare			X
Carers and the 'cared for'			
More support		X	
Carer's breaks			X
Increase carer's allowance		X	
Enhance quality of the care			X
VAWAG			
Action on FGM	X		
PSHE education		X	
Better funding		X	
Reform criminal justice system/enhanced training			X
Action on forced marriage			X
Public life			
Enhanced representation in Parliament		X	
Enhanced representation on public boards		X	
Enhanced representation company boards		X	
Support for institutions of gender equality		X	
Women's human rights, development and immigration			
Promote gender equality		X	
Protect women and children in conflict		X	
Immigration and marriage		X	

X indicates presence in manifesto.

Promoting gender equality internationally, via development aid, and in conflict zones is, as we surmised, widespread across the parties (Labour, Conservatives, Liberal Democrats, SNP, Greens). Particular emphasis was placed on action regarding modern slavery and domestic workers (Conservatives, Greens). The one area of conflict is immigration. Here, the Conservatives and UKIP are in opposition to the Greens and PC. The former approve of language tests and income thresholds (Conservatives), seek to abolish the EEA family permit scheme,[18] reinstate the

---

[18] Accessed at https://www.gov.uk/family-permit/overview on 9 June 2015.

'primary purpose rule' (UKIP), and address sham marriages (Conservatives). The latter seek to review (PC) or abolish (Greens) income rules. Here, the Greens presented an explicitly gendered critique suggesting that the arrival of a grandmother might well have no direct economic effect, but the contribution to family life may contribute hugely to society.[19] Labour's contribution on gendered immigration is to end the detention of pregnant women and victims of VAWAG, and review allegations of abuse at Yarl's Wood detention centre.

Shared cross-party sentiment about what constitutes women's interests were also evident in the extensive attention given to various manifestations of VAWAG in all bar the SNP manifesto, which as noted above does not address this issue. There is widespread agreement that there should be better funding (Labour, Conservatives, Liberal Democrats, Greens); better training for advocates and reform of the justice system (Conservatives, Liberal Democrats, Greens). Labour offered additional detailed pledges: reform of gun licensing; retention of DNA data relating to rape; wider access to legal aid; and a right to review police decisions not to proceed with cases. UKIP was an outlier—with far fewer pledges than the others. But the party's manifesto noted that domestic violence is not a specific offence, even if it does not clarify whether it should be. That said UKIP clearly shared the commitment to end Female Genital Mutilation (FGM) and forced marriage, again advocated across the political spectrum. This position arguably sits comfortably with UKIP's wider criticism of immigration. UKIP sided with Labour too, in criticising community or faith-based tribunals for victims of Domestic Violence (DV), even if for different reasons. The one stand-alone UKIP policy pledge that ran in the opposite direction to the other parties, under the banner of VAWAG, was the explicit rejection of compulsory Personal, Health, Social Education (PHSE). Instead, they sought to preserve the parental right to withdraw children and ruled out PHSE in primary schools. In contrast, Labour, the Liberal Democrats, the Greens and PC were all clear that this should be compulsory, so that consent and healthy relationships becomes part of the curriculum. The Tories were quiet on this issue.

Returning to the domestic sphere, there was extensive cross-party agreement over *carers and the cared for*. This appears to be perceived as a gendered 'policy win' for all the parties. Carers should, variously, be in receipt of greater support (Labour, Conservatives, Liberal Democrats, SNP and UKIP). Specific policy pledges included: respite breaks (Labour, Liberal Democrats, SNP); more generous carer's allowance of various types (the Liberal Democrats offered a £250 bonus, for example; SNP, Greens, UKIP). For those being cared for, the quality of care is emphasised (PC). More carers should be recruited, some 5000, the 'new arm' of

---

[19]Green Party (2015) *For the Common Good: Election Manifesto 2015*, available at https://www.greenparty.org.uk/assets/files/manifesto/Green_Party_2015_General_Election_Manifesto_Searchable.pdf, p. 71.

the NHS (Labour); '15-min visits' would be ended (Liberal Democrats, UKIP); there would be better training (PC); and carers' pay should be enhanced (UKIP, Liberal Democrats).

Women's presence in public life is also regarded as a 'good thing' by all the parties bar UKIP, who do not address this issue. In terms of women's presence in Parliament, on public and company boards, there is general agreement that women should be better represented. In respect of parliamentary representation, Labour champion all-women shortlists, and a goal of 50% women in government; the Liberal Democrats wanted to see a more family-friendly House, and the possibility of job-share for MPs; the Greens, an Equality Committee, and 50:50 women and men by 2025. The Tories offered no precise figures or goals. UKIP and the SNP and PC did not address this, the latter two perhaps because of the devolved institutions. Regarding boardrooms, public and private, the parties favour a 'rise' in women's presence (Conservatives), '30%' (Liberal Democrats), '40%' (Greens, PC) or 'parity' (Labour, SNP). Here, though the pledges were lacking in detail: there was talk of a 'push for' (SNP); 'towards at least' (Liberal Democrats); or wanting to 'see [the number of women] rise' (Conservatives). Labour was more pointed, talking of ensuring equal presence. Turning more specifically to the Equality Act 2010, both Labour and the Liberal Democrats defended its provisions: the former in respect of implementing the dual discrimination provisions, and the latter to enact its unimplemented causes. Both the Liberal Democrats and the Greens also emphasise the Public Sector Equality Duty, with the Greens also seeking the reinstatement for the funding of the Equality and Human Rights Commission (EHRC), and lamenting the abolition of the Women's National Commission.

As in 2010 considerable space was given in the manifestos to two issues: *women's work and the work/life balance* and *childcare*.[20] The one work policy pledge on which there was agreement (UKIP-excepted) was that large companies (250+ employees) should be required to publish their gender pay gap data. This is seemingly the minimum/baseline response to the UK's gender pay gap. Thereafter, it is a matter of how far the parties wish to intervene and in what ways. The gender pay gap is a multi-faceted phenomenon, inter alia, implicit and explicit gender discrimination against women; the 'mommy pay gap'; the consequences of a gendered segregated employment market, that leaves women in undervalued and less well-paid employment; and women's greater tendency to engage in part-time work, itself due in large part to the gendered division of labour. Table 13.2 outlines the 2015 party pledges that address the component parts of the gender pay gap and associated party pledges. To this table, one might add under 'gender discrimination', parties' pledges on paternity leave and pay: the SNP wished to enhance; Labour wanted to double leave from two to four weeks and enhance the pay to £260; and

---

[20]These are pledges explicitly linked to women. Hence political parties may address some of these issues elsewhere in their manifestos but we are interested in when they are specifically framed 'for women'.

Table 13.2 The gender pay gap and party election manifesto pledges, 2015

Components of the gender pay gap	Pledge	Parties
Gender discrimination	Enforce Equality Act	Labour, SNP
	Additional pay transparency	Lib Dems, SNP
	Anonymise CVs	Lib Dems, Greens
	Abolish tribunal system	Labour
The 'Mommy' Gap	Back to work support	UKIP, Lib Dems
	Strengthen law on women's/ maternity discrimination	Labour, SNP, Greens
Gender segregated employment market	Better valued women's work,	Labour, PC
	Gender and apprenticeships	Lib Dems, SNP
	Gender and entrepreneurs	Lib Dems, Greens
	Education, careers, segregation	Lab, Lib Dems, SNP, PC, UKIP
	Public sector acceleration programme	Lib Dems
Women's low pay	Raise minimum wage,	Labour, SNP
	Enforce living wage	PC
Women's part-time work/ flexibility	End zero hours,	PC
	Importance of flexible working	Cons, Lib Dems

the Liberal Democrats to introduce a 'use or lose it' provision. Labour's commitment to consult on grandparents sharing some parental leave could work in the same way too. We return to these issues below.

UKIP is once again the outlier on women's work: its focus was limited to two pledges: back to work support for nurses and midwives, and addressing gender segregation in educational and career choice. If the latter seeks to expand young women's career opportunities, the former begs the question of why back-to-work support was not across the board rather than limited to nursing. The Conservative Party was also arguably limited in its efforts to tackle the pay gap, with only one additional pledge on top of its commitment to publication of large company gender pay gaps and this is to do with women's part-time work—'removing barriers that stop women' being included.

Four policy areas address women in their biological capacity as *mothers*. First, there is a commitment to increase the number of midwives—the SNP, Labour and UKIP agreed that there should be more, 3000 more for the latter two parties. Second, the Greens wished to follow the SNP in making it illegal to stop a mother breastfeeding in public spaces and also advocated more support for more home births. The final policy, one that most parties agreed upon 'for mothers', was additional attention to maternal mental health and mothers' well-being (Conservatives, Liberal Democrats, Greens and UKIP). This looks to be a necessary and worthwhile pledge even as it also constitutes another example of the 'safe' women's issues concept discussed above. Table 13.3 lists the policy pledges relating to

Table 13.3 Maternity, paternity and parental leave pledges, 2015 party election manifestos

	Maternity leave	Maternity pay	Paternity leave	Paternity pay	Parental leave
Labour	Strengthen law against maternity discrimination		Double, from two weeks to four weeks	Increase by more than £100 to £260 per week (national minimum wage)	Consult on grandparents' leave'
Conservative		We will freeze working age benefits...with exemptions for disability and pensioner benefits—as at present—as well as maternity allowance, statutory maternity pay...		We will freeze working age benefits...with exemptions for... statutory paternity pay	
Liberal Democrat			'use it or lose it month'; ambition to see paternity leave a 'day one' right		Ambition to see shared parental leave a 'day one' right
SNP	Tighten law on maternity discrimination		Increased		
Greens	Properly enforce discrimination law	Continue receive statutory maternity pay		Continue receive statutory paternity pay	

Table 13.4 Free childcare hours by party, 2015 election manifestos

Party	Free childcare hours
Conservative	30 h, three-and-four-year-olds
SNP	30 h, three and four, and eligible two-year-olds
Labour	25 h, three-and-four-year-olds
Liberal Democrat	20 h, two–four year olds; 20 h all working parents, nine months–two years
Greens	Free but voluntary from birth to compulsory (aged seven)
PC	Three-and-four-year-olds
UKIP	Maintain 15 h three-and-four-year-olds, and two-year-olds on certain benefits

maternity, paternity and parental leave and pay. Note the emphasis given to 'shared' parenting, and the focus by Labour on increasing paternity leave and pay and the Liberal Democrats' 'use it or lose it month'. These are both policies that aim to enhance the likelihood that men will take paternity leave, in practice. The Conservative offering was minimal here—relating to exempting working age benefits caps from maternity and paternity leave; neither PC nor UKIP address this issue.

A single policy—marriage tax allowance (MTA)—addressed the institution of marriage. As in 2010, the Conservatives made what we termed then the 'golden hello' pledge.[21] In doing so, they formally signalled their agnosticism about whether individuals choose to stay home, and arguably, also reveal a preference for 'mother care' and the 1.5 worker model, given that it is mostly likely middle-class and above women who will take up this option. Furthermore, MTA would rise in line with the personal allowance. UKIP agreed with the Tories that MTA should be increased. There was clear division over the policy pledge for the married and civil partnered: labour and the SNP would end the MTA.

On the basis of this manifesto analysis *childcare* has become the most important women's issue for all the main political parties. The Conservatives' commitment to increase to 30 h free childcare, announced prior to the start of the short campaign, was a key moment when the party placed a gender challenge in front of Labour. Unlike the motherhood pledges, childcare is a highly competitive women's issue, underpinned by agreement that this is something that all parties need to address. That said, party differences, at least among the three main parties is largely in terms of degree rather than overall direction (Table 13.4).

Labour's offering centred on the restoration of Sure Start (an intervention praised by the SNP), providing 'integrated early help'. Expanded childcare provision in general was supported by Labour (with wraparound 8 am–6 pm via primary schools), the Liberal Democrats, SNP (free nursery education) and the Greens. PC and UKIP were particularly concerned with children in socially deprived areas

---

[21] Campbell and Childs (2010a) 'Wags', 'Wives' and 'Mothers' . . . But what about Women Politicians?'

(PC also expressed concerns for disabled children). The Coalition partners, along with UKIP, promoted their 'tax-free childcare' policy.

An assumption that UKIP would have little to say on childcare, based on their outlier status on other women's issues, would be mistaken. Previously there was concern that Labour and Conservatives might retreat from this terrain for fear of being perceived as too feminist and, or too 'metropolitan' by UKIP's 'left behind men'.[22] Yet UKIP's childcare pledges are numerous and detailed—four whole pages of its manifesto. Prior to the publication of the manifesto, a search of the party's website yielded little information about policies designed to enable women to combine care with paid employment. Thus, this childcare focus looks to be a recent addition to UKIP's armoury, and perhaps surprising, given previous public sentiment suggesting the party's preference for traditional gender roles. What appears to have occurred is that UKIP has found itself 'infected' by feminisation, at least in this policy area—presumably influenced by their gender gap in voting.[23] The UKIP manifesto was written by the party's deputy chair, Suzanne Evans, who has spoken publicly about the party's need to connect with women voters and take on the 4% gender gap in support for the party. Pledge-wise, UKIP wanted to see childcare provision integrated with planning approval and discussed the conversion of office space into nurseries. UKIP argued that schools should offer 8 am–6 pm childcare (Labour said likewise) and offer an all-day option during school holidays.

The most important strand of the UKIP childcare pledges, however, was deregulation. Deregulation of childcare is the means by which to both expand provision, and reduce the cost of childcare, and arguably differentiated them from the other parties at the election (notwithstanding Conservative efforts to deregulate under the Coalition government).[24] This is a distinct direction about what is perceived to be in the interests of women. UKIP preferred nursery owners 'to be focussed on childcare, rather than drowning in paperwork', while parents would be allowed 'to use any third-party, provided the care can be proven to be genuine' with parents 'free to make their own enquiries as to the suitability of informal providers, in the same way they would check a babysitter' in using care under a voucher scheme.[25]

---

[22] Ford, R. and Goodwin, M. (2014) *Revolt on the Right: Explaining Support for the Radical Right in Britain*, London, Routledge.

[23] Accessed at http://www.britishelectionstudy.com/bes-resources/following-the-pink-battle-bus-where-are-the-women-voters-in-2015-by-dr-rosie-campbell/#.VWbu88_bKUk on 16 February 2015.

[24] Campbell, R. and Childs, S. (2010b) 'Wags', 'Wives' and 'Mothers' … But what about Women Politicians?' In Geddes, A. and Tonge, J. (eds) *Britain Votes: The 2010 General Election*. Oxford, Oxford University Press, pp. 176–192.

[25] UK Independence Party (2015) *Believe in Britain: Election Manifesto 2015*, available at https://d3n8a8pro7vhmx.cloudfront.net/ukipdev/pages/1103/attachments/original/1429295050/UKIP Manifesto2015.pdf?1429295050, p. 26.

Finally, UKIP would give local authorities the responsibility to keep a register of emergency and overnight childcare providers to 'help families who need to access high quality care during unsocial hours, in an emergency, when they are called to a job interview at short notice, or when they are working away from home, for example'. In this, the demand of the women's liberation movement for 24 h child-care springs to mind, posing an interesting challenge to assumptions about which party is making the 'best' offering here.

Although showing variation in the level of commitments, our manifesto analysis thus demonstrates surprising homogeneity about what constitutes women's issues and (to a lesser degree) women's interests. All seven of the parties espoused at least some liberally feminist positions and made explicit commitments to fostering greater gender equality by facilitating women's access to paid employment, for example. Even UKIP, previously considerably more traditional in its attitudes towards gender roles, has shifted to a more liberally feminist position. Importantly, their greater presence in 2015 did not cause the other parties, particularly the Conservatives, to shift from the liberal feminist terrain.

4. Women voters

Since the 1970s in the UK, there has been little in the way of sizeable gender gaps in the vote intentions of women compared with men.[26] Tony Blair's New Labour gained an advantage among women under 45, particularly among middle and high income mothers, but this gap had disappeared by the time of the 2010 General Election—perhaps due to Cameron's attempt to feminise the Conservative Party by addressing issues such as work–life balance and women's representation in Parliament. One area, however, where a gender gap persists is in the timing of the vote choice, as women are consistently over-represented among undecided voters. Using BES early release online survey data, we can see from Table 13.5 that 8.5% more women than men stated that they had not decided how to vote by mid-March 2015. The over representation of women in the undecided group is one reason why they are often among the groups of voters targeted by parties in marginal seats at election time.

Figure 13.2 shows the intended party of vote by sex in the BES online survey conducted in March 2015. The figures in the table reflect the polling figures at the time—which proved to be inaccurate and led to a review of the polling industry. As such we cannot know whether these figures represent an accurate snapshot of the British electorate's vote intention in March 2015 that was followed by a shift to the Conservatives on polling day, or whether the data are biased in favour of the Labour Party; the aggregate figures for the other parties are closer to the

---

[26] Campbell, R. (2006) *Gender and the Vote in Britain*, Colchester, ECPR Press.

Table 13.5 Decisions on General Election vote by gender, March 2015

Decided on General Election vote (%)

	Yes	No	Will not vote	Do not know
Men	72.3	22.5	3.4	1.8
Women	60.3	31.0	5.1	3.6
Total	66.1	26.9	4.3	2.7

n = 11,092.
Source: British Election Study online panel wave four (9–13 March 2015).

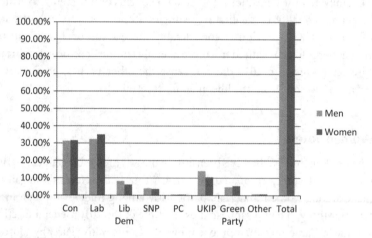

Figure 13.2 General Election vote intention by gender, March 2015. *N* = 10,043.
Source: British Election Study online panel wave four (9–13 March 2015)

actual results. A final analysis of gender and party of vote in 2015 will have to wait until the BES team publish the face-to-face post-election survey with validated voter information. However, on the basis of the March 2015 data, it would seem women were slightly more likely to support the Labour Party than men by three percentage points and slightly less likely to support UKIP, again by three percentage points. If these differences remain in the post-election survey data, then we would see evidence of a modern gender gap (where women support left-leaning parties more than men) at the aggregate level for the first time in a British General Election.

Figure 13.3 breaks down the vote intention data further, by adding age group. It is clear that the modern gender gap is driven by support for the Labour Party among women aged below 55. Again if these results are supported by the post-election study, they would provide support for Pippa Norris's gender generation gap theory: that in many western democracies younger women have shifted to the

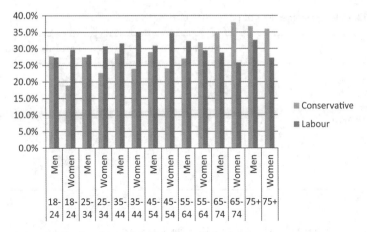

Figure 13.3 Vote intention (party of vote) by sex and age group.
Source: British Election Study online panel wave four (9–13 March 2015)

left.[27] Norris first identified the gender generation gap in the UK in the 1997 election but it was not apparent in the 2010 British General Election.[28] If the gender gap is robust it may result from women's hostility to the Coalition Government's public spending cuts relative to men.[29]

5. Women candidates and MPs

In terms of the representation of women in politics, 2015 saw an increase in the percentage of women in the House of Commons from 22–29%. The Conservative Party increased the percentage of women on their benches from 16–21%, but the overall increase was largely driven by the Labour Party and the SNP who increased the percentage of women among their MPs from 35–43% and 17–36% respectively. The Labour Party delivered this increase through their continued use of party quotas in the form of all-women shortlists. The SNP did not use quotas—although they have recently voted to allow their use—but their landslide victory resulted in the party increasing their representation in Parliament from six to 56 MPs (leaving

[27] Inglehart, R. and Norris, P. (2000) The developmental theory of the gender gap: women and men's voting behaviour in global perspective, *International Political Science Review*, **21**, 441–462. Norris, P. (1999) Gender—A Gender Generation Gap? In Evans, G. and Norris, P. (eds) *Critical Elections: British Parties and Voters in Long Term Perspective*, London: Sage, pp.148–163.

[28] Campbell, R. (2012) 'What do we really know about women voters? Gender, elections and public opinion', *Political Quarterly*, **83**, 703–710.

[29] Campbell, R. and Childs, S. (2015) 'To the Left, To the Right': Representing Conservative Women's Interests', *Party Politics*, **21**, 626–637.

Table 13.6 Elected women MPs by party, 2015 General Election

Party	Number	Percentage (rounded)
Conservative	68	21
Labour	99	43
SNP	20	36
Liberal Democrat	0	0
Green	1	100
UKIP	0	0
Other	3	15
Total	191	29

Table 13.7 Women candidates by party, 2015 General Election

	All seats		Target seats	
	Women candidates %	Men candidates %	Women candidates %	Men candidates %
Conservative	32.2	67.8	28.2	71.8
Labour	33.2	66.8	52.8	47.2
SNP	37.7	62.3	n/a (all seats targeted)	n/a (all seats targeted)
Liberal Democrat	27.6	72.4	35	65
UKIP	13.5	86.5	20	80
Green	37.6	62.4	36.4	63.6
Plaid Cymru	28.9	71.1	0	100

Source: www.parliamentarycandidates.org.

just three seats in Scotland not in SNP hands) creating an unprecedented situation where some candidates elected to Parliament had not even been party members prior to the referendum campaign in 2014. SNP successes also saw the election of the youngest MP (aged 20) since 1832.[30] As such the 2015 General Election in Scotland provided a unique opportunity for women candidates in Scotland to overcome both the incumbency disadvantage and entrenched party practices that discriminate against them in the rest of the UK.[31] Table 13.6 shows the breakdown of women MPs by party.

Table 13.7 reinforces these findings concerning Labour and the SNP. The Labour Party was considerably ahead of the other parties in terms of placing women in

---

[30] Accessed at https://nortonview.wordpress.com/2015/05/08/the-youngest-mp/ on 8 May 2015.

[31] Mackay, F. and McAllister, L. (2012) Feminising British politics: six lessons from devolution in Scotland and Wales', *Political Quarterly*, **83**, 730–734.

target seats (54% of their candidates in target seats were women compared with 33% overall). The Labour Party was followed by the SNP who placed women in 36% of their target seats, although given they took all but three seats in Scotland the notion of target seats might be somewhat redundant in this case. The Liberal Democrats placed women in 35% of their target seats. However, none of these women candidates were returned as MPs. The Liberal Democrats' representation in the House of Commons fell dramatically from 56 to just eight with no women at all among the 2015 cohort. Historically the Liberal Democrats have tended to place men in safer seats than women[32] and this is probably the best explanation for why the residual Liberal Democrat MPs are all men. The Conservative Party placed women in 28% of their target seats, which was an improvement on their historic record but still considerably behind the other main parties. UKIP was by far the least representative party with just 14% women candidates and 20% women in their target seats.

6. Conclusion

Overall 2015 may not have been the 'Mumsnet Election' but gender did play a significant part in the parties' campaigns and in the media coverage. Old fashioned misogyny was also in play, particularly in the coverage of Nicola Sturgeon. Labour's attempts to target women voters brought the issue on to the agenda and the presence of women leaders in the TV debates meant that the interest in women was sustained throughout the short campaign. The seven main parties all offered liberal feminist policy platforms, even if gendered austerity failed to really mark the campaign and it is clear that there remains intense electoral competition for women's votes in the UK. Early evidence suggests that women voters may have voted for the Labour Party in greater numbers than men, but given the wide disagreement between opinion polls prior to the election and the actual result, this finding should be treated with caution prior to the BES post-election face-to-face survey. If post-election data confirm this gender difference in party support then it would seem that the Labour Party won the 'battle' to gain advantage among women voters. The representation of women in Parliament increased by 7% and the three largest parties increased the proportion of women sitting on their benches but the Labour and the SNP side is greatly more representative than the government's.

---

[32] Campbell and Childs. 'What the Coalition Did for Women'.

Britain Votes (2015) 224–240

DOMINIC WRING AND STEPHEN WARD*

Exit Velocity: The Media Election

The previous campaign of 2010 produced electoral firsts in media terms (the televised leaders' debates), drama and unpredictability ('Cleggmania') and memorable moments (Gordon Brown's 'bigoted woman' comments) all of which disrupted the parties' planned scripts. Arguably, the 2015 election seems to have been its very antithesis. The plodding six-week campaign has been widely been portrayed as dull, stage-managed, narrowly focused and lacking in surprise moments, but with a dramatic ending on election night, as the broadcasters announced the shock exit poll. The disbelieving former Liberal Democrat leader Paddy Ashdown declared 'he would eat his hat' if his party suffered the losses predicted by the forecast; in fact the result was even worse. Ashdown like so many of his fellow commentators, whether of the traditional offline or online media varieties, was stunned by the apparent failure of the opinion polls to foresee the Conservative victory. What followed was the political equivalent of 'exit velocity' in the aftermath of a plodding election, with frenetic, intensive debate over the future of the UK sparking the kind of passion lacking in the preceding campaign.

The 2015 campaign as reported in the media was predicated on the assumption that the outcome would be another hung Parliament and, possibly, coalition government. This was constantly reinforced by a stream of experts and opinion-formers fixated on what might happen after the election rather what had just happened in the previous Parliament. This augmented the potential power-broking role of emerging 'challengers' such as UKIP, the SNP and Greens at the marked expense of the Liberal Democrats, clear beneficiaries of the added exposure they had received in 2010. Yet if the campaign differed in terms of its focus on these growing political parties it was also reminiscent of the previous one with its similar emphasis on polls and other aspects of the 'horse race'. This will be explored in more detail together with an evaluation of the role played by broadcasting, particularly

*Dominic Wring, Social Sciences, Loughborough University, D.J. Wring@lboro.ac.uk; Stephen Ward, School of Arts and Media, University of Salford, s.j.ward@salford.ac.uk.

doi:10.1093/pa/gsv037

the leader debates, as well as the partisan press. Consideration will also be given to the influence of social media platforms during the campaign and their place as both a source of additional election news and commentary as well as communication for parties keen to exploit their strategic potential.

1. The traditional media campaign: issues and personalities

The Conservatives' successful campaign was directed by Lynton Crosby, the strategist who helped guide John Howard to power in their native Australia. Crosby subsequently worked for the Tories in the 2005 General Election before overseeing Boris Johnson's successful campaigns to be Mayor of London in 2008 and 2012. The earlier Johnson triumph was set against the backdrop of a rapidly worsening financial crisis that would undermine the then incumbent Labour Government. During the 2015 General Election Crosby aimed to exploit continuing voter anxieties about this economic trauma. The Conservatives ran a focused campaign that remorselessly promoted the substantive issues that would come to dominate the news agenda: the economy, tax and constitutional matters (see Table 14.1).

In contrast, policy areas that might have been more problematic for the Conservatives, such as Labour's favoured theme of the NHS and UKIP's equivalent issue, immigration, received less journalistic attention. Furthermore, there was the now established media fixation with electoral process, particularly the apparent closeness of the two major parties in the opinion polls. Crosby was himself scathing about the proliferation of commentators who viewed the election as 'entertainment'.[1] Yet their speculation helped to reinforce a key Tory claim that dominated the narrative especially in the closing stages of the election: the fear of Labour taking office with SNP support.[2] This was supported by an advertising campaign that depicted a diminutive Ed Miliband as being either in the pocket of or having his strings pulled by the SNP leader.[3] In contrast, there was relatively little media commentary on the possibility or consequences of a majority Conservative Government beyond the Labour supporting *Daily Mirror.*

Media speculation as to the likely nature of a minority or coalition-led government reinforced the already considerable news interest in 'minor' parties whose leaders received unprecedented levels of publicity with Nicola Sturgeon and Nigel Farage among the top five most high profile politicians during the campaign (see Table 14.2). If the attention devoted to Sturgeon underlined the electoral significance of the constitutional issue, the presence of George Osborne and Ed Balls in

[1] Peter Dominiczak (2015) 'Lynton Crosby: Betrayal of British Voters', www.telegraph.co.uk, on 15 May 2015.

[2] Dan Sabbagh (2015) 'How the Tories Won the General Election Air War', www.theguardian.com, on 11 May 2015.

[3] For more on the poster campaign, see Benedict Pringle's blog, www.politicaladvertising.co.uk.

Table 14.1 Top ten campaign issues, by percentage of television and radio coverage, 30 March–7 May[a]

TV	%	Rank	Press	%
Election process	45.9	1	Election process	44.5
Economy	8.1	2	Economy	10.5
Constitutional	6.2	3	Taxation	6.5
Taxation	5.4	4	Standards	3.8
Employment	4.4	5	Constitutional	3.7
Immigration/Race	3.7	6	NHS	3.7
NHS	3.5	7	Immigration/Race	3.5
Business	3.0	8	Europe	3.4
Social Security	2.4	9	Employment	2.9
Europe	2.4	10	Business	2.6

[a]Deacon, D., Downey, J., Stanyer, J. and Wring, D. (2015) 'News Media Performance in the 2015 General Election Campaign'. In: Jackson, D. and Thorsen, E. (eds) *UK Election Analysis 2015: Media, Voters and the Campaign.* Bournemouth, Bournemouth University Centre for the Study of Journalism, Culture and Community.

Table 14.2 Top ten personalities by media (TV and press) appearance[a], 30 March–7 May

Rank	Name	%	Party
1	David Cameron	15.0	Cons
2	Ed Miliband	14.7	Labour
3	Nick Clegg	6.5	Lib Dem
4	Nicola Sturgeon	5.7	SNP
5	Nigel Farage	5.5	UKIP
6	George Osborne	3.8	Cons
7	Ed Balls	2.5	Labour
8	Boris Johnson	1.7	Cons
9=	Tony Blair	0.9	Labour
9	Jim Murphy	0.9	Labour

%, number of individual against all individual appearances.
[a]'Media Coverage of the Campaign (Report 5)', Loughborough University Communication Research Centre, May, http://blog.lboro.ac.uk/general-election/media-coverage-of-the-2015-campaign-report-5/ on 15 June.

the top ten reflected the importance of the economic debate. Tony Blair even made a significant re-appearance warning against the threat of the UK leaving Europe and helping ensure this debate was not dominated by UKIP.

The election campaign itself was a series of largely anodyne, staged-for-camera events usually featuring the party leader that were managed by spin-doctors keen to exert control over the news agenda. Sympathetic audiences of supporters assembled for visiting politicians' speeches, press conferences and photo-opportunities in marginal seats. Popular locations for these events included the kinds of factories and schools populated by members of the 'hard working families' that had become such a clichéd part of the political narrative. Chancellor George Osborne made frequent appearances of this kind kitted out in the requisite high visibility jacket and safety hat in his attempts to identify with what he termed the 'strivers' over the 'skivers'.

There was a dearth of the type of unexpected encounter that so spectacularly derailed Gordon Brown's campaign in 2010 following his meeting with Gillian Duffy. There were, however, a few newsworthy gaffes. In one speech David Cameron expressed support for West Ham and later apologised to his fellow Aston Villa fans, but this was not a career-defining moment for a Prime Minister who had already established his leadership credentials. In contrast, Ed Miliband appeared less self-assured, notably when he partially stumbled whilst leaving the stage of the final live broadcast debate of the campaign. His subsequent unveiling of a huge tablet of stone with six campaign pledges on it, the so-called 'EdStone', provoked considerable mockery compounded when the Vice Chair of Labour's campaign, Lucy Powell MP appeared to suggest to BBC Five Live's Peter Allen that the promises could be broken.

2. The televised debates

In contrast with 2010, negotiations over the format of the leader debates were protracted and nearly ended in failure. This was mainly because David Cameron wanted to avoid participating in the kind of events he claimed had 'sucked the life out' of the previous campaign. The Prime Minister did ultimately participate, but on his own terms with six other party leaders involved. UKIP's case to be included in the leader debates for the first time had been substantially enhanced when broadcast regulator Ofcom afforded them 'major party' status in the aftermath of their 2014 European election triumph and support in the opinion polls.[4] Cameron and his media adviser, Craig Oliver, subsequently tried to minimise rather than challenge Farage's right to participate in the debates through insisting the Greens must also be present on the platform. This forced the broadcasters to abandon their original joint proposal for three encounters in which Farage would appear once, Clegg twice and Cameron and Miliband throughout. What ultimately emerged was a substantially different series of programmes.

The most watched broadcast debate was the ITV programme on 2 April, seen by 5.88 million viewers, the seventh most popular item on the channel that week.[5] Seven party leaders featured, including Cameron in his only face-to-face appearance

---

[4] Ofcom (2015) *Review of Ofcom List of Major Political Parties for Elections Taking Place on 7 May 2015.* London, Ofcom, 8th January.

[5] www.barb.co.uk, data for week ending 5 April 2015.

alongside his rivals (Labour, the Liberal Democrats, the Greens, UKIP, SNP and Plaid Cymru). The SNP had threatened legal action after being excluded from the 2010 debates but entered the 2015 negotiations in a stronger position following the previous year's independence referendum. The SNP's inclusion strengthened the ultimately successful claims of Plaid Cymru leader, Leanne Wood, for involvement. The broadcasters did, however, refuse the Northern Irish parties' attempts to participate.

Leanne Wood was prominent in one of the more newsworthy exchanges of the ITV debate. Wood reprimanded Nigel Farage for his criticisms of 'health tourism' involving migrants with HIV coming to the UK for treatment. But it was Nicola Sturgeon who appeared to gain most momentum when she was judged to have performed well and even 'won', albeit by a small margin, in one of the post-debate polls. Sturgeon appeared in the other face-to-face encounter on 16 April between the opposition 'challenger' parties that attracted 4.35 million viewers.[6] Controversially the Conservatives' refusal to have the Prime Minister participate in another such encounter also led to their negotiators' insistence that the Liberal Democrats not be allowed on to a platform that should be the preserve of opposition politicians.[7] In Cameron's and Clegg's absence, the key exchange occurred when Miliband categorically refused to entertain Sturgeon's proposition that they could lock the Tories out of power. Farage courted more controversy when he criticised the BBC over what he alleged was its selection of a disproportionately 'left-wing' audience. The debate concluded with the three female 'progressive alliance' leaders (Sturgeon, Wood and the Greens' Natalie Bennett) collectively embracing in what proved to be one of the most memorable images of the campaign.

The two leaders' debates were sandwiched between a pair of live programmes that featured leaders making separate appearances. The first of these was a joint venture on 26 March, *Cameron and Miliband Live: the Battle for Number Ten*, involving Sky and Channel 4 that effectively started the election campaign and attracted 2.60 million viewers.[8] This hybrid format had former BBC Newsnight presenter Jeremy Paxman and audience members interrogating the two main party leaders in separate sections of the same broadcast. Paxman appeared to unsettle Cameron with questioning about food banks and zero hours contracts. In contrast, Ed Miliband was judged to have performed well, albeit starting with low expectations born out of poor poll ratings. Miliband memorably responded 'hell yes' when asked if he was tough enough to be Prime Minister.

---

[6] www.barb.co.uk, data for week ending 19 April.

[7] Rosa Prince (2015) 'Nick Clegg Shut Out of Television Debates as Labour Join Minor Parties', www.telegraph.co.uk, on 21 March 2015.

[8] www.barb.co.uk, data for week ending 29 March 2015.

The final live leaders' event was a BBC *Question Time Special* on 30 April involving the Coalition and Labour parties seen by 3.77 million.[9] David Cameron opened the proceedings and came through relatively unscathed whereas Miliband's subsequent denial that the previous Labour Government had spent too much money in office provoked an audible groan from the audience. The incident highlighted the extent to which the Conservatives' had successively established their view as the dominant economic narrative.

The understandable media focus on TV programmes featuring the leaders overshadowed the range of broadcasts involving other party spokespeople. The BBC's *Daily Politics* hosted a series of debates with five of the relevant portfolio holders discussing key policy areas such as the economy, education and welfare. The latter programme featured particularly animated exchanges between Iain Duncan Smith and his Green opponent. The involvement of this and the other challenger parties helped guarantee they were represented in an election campaign to an unprecedented degree.

3. Broadcasting

Throughout the campaign politicians made concerted efforts to try to connect with specific groups of potential voters. While the recent proliferation of niche channels and the fragmentation of audiences may have exacerbated this tendency the trend stretches back further. Party strategists have long prioritised less formal discussion-based formats as a means of engaging viewers believed to be less interested in politics but nonetheless likely to vote. Examples of this in the lead-up to and during the 2015 were appearances by the main leaders on ITV's *This Morning* and by party representatives on the same network's daytime talk show *Loose Women*.

Broadcasters devoted significant airtime to audience-led discussion-based election programming.[10] Most obviously this included familiar strands such as BBC *Question Time* and Radio 4's *Any Questions*. There were also several newer innovations. BBC2 and ITV1 used the campaign to launch two new shows hosted by Victoria Derbyshire and James O'Brien, respectively. More niche outlets provided features tailored to their specific audiences. BBC Three TV and Radio 1 *Newsbeat*, for instance, aired question and answer sessions for young people that were more interactive and often livelier, unpredictable affairs than the more staid and formal debates between the party leaders.

---

[9] www.barb.co.uk, data for week ending 3 May 2015.

[10] That the General Election would definitely occur on 7 May enabled broadcasters to commission topical comedy programmes to coincide with and thereby satirise the campaign. Examples of this include BBC's *Have I Got Election News For You*, ITV's *Newzoids* and Channel 4's *Ballot Monkeys*.

The leaders continued to participate in familiar broadcast rituals such as the BBC series of interrogations by Evan Davis, but other less formal interviews appeared to garner more newsworthy material. A news feature by BBC journalist James Lansdale on David Cameron aired just before the formal campaign elicited the admission that, in the event of a Conservative victory, his next term in office would also be his final one. The BBC ran a corresponding profile of Ed Miliband who could not have predicted the ensuing controversy provoked by the number of kitchens in his house.

Daily Mail columnist Sarah Vine, wife of Chief Whip Michael Gove, described the Labour leader's kitchen as 'bland, functional, humourless, cold' and the Milibands as 'alien'.[11] Vine struggled to defend her insults on BBC's *This Week*, particularly when it transpired—as she herself had speculated in her article—that the space was in fact a utility room. Ed Miliband's 'real' kitchen and him cooking in it featured prominently in another informal profile for ITV's *Tonight* by political editor Tom Bradby. Bradby's was part of a series that gave particular prominence to the leaders' spouses, reinforcing a trend established in the 2010 campaign.

The leaders of the SNP, Plaid and the Greens were profiled by ITV's Julie Etchingham to provide further insights into the personalities of these prominent women including a relaxed Nicola Sturgeon who was shown at home talking about herself and her background. The Green leader Natalie Bennett also fared much better in her appearance in stark contrast to an awkward pre-campaign interview with LBC radio after which she admitted to having felt 'devastated' after failing to explain her party's housing policy.

4.   The press

The campaign experienced the kind of hostile print media coverage of Labour not seen since the 1992 General Election. By 2010, the *Sun* had returned to the Conservative fold with a positive front-page endorsement of Cameron. Ed Miliband's highly-publicised criticisms of *Sun* owner Rupert Murdoch during the hacking scandal of 2011 further soured the already poor relations between the party and the newspaper culminating in the still best-selling paper devoting the front page of its 2015 polling day issue to ridiculing Miliband based on an infamous 2014 photograph of the Labour leader struggling to eat a bacon sandwich. Accompanied by the slogan 'Save Our Bacon', the *Sun* strongly urged readers to endorse the Conservatives as the way to avoid disaster. Table 14.3 provides a guide to which parties were supported by which newspapers.

---

[11] Sarah Vine (2015) 'Why Their Kitchen Tells You All You Need to Know About the Mirthless Milibands . . . and Why There's Nothing to Suggest that Ed and Justine are not, in fact, aliens', www.dailymail.co.uk, on 12 March 2015.

Table 14.3 National daily newspaper declarations and their readerships

Title	Party	Unique browsers	Circulation
Guardian	Labour	7.2	0.18
Times	Conservative/Lib Dem Coalition	Paywall	0.39
Telegraph	Conservative	4.00	0.49
Financial Times	Conservative/Lib Dem Coalition	Paywall	0.21
Independent	Conservative/Lib Dem Coalition	2.33	0.06
Mail	Conservative	13.64	1.63
Express	UKIP	0.78	0.44
The Sun	Conservative	Paywall	1.86
Mirror	Labour	3.74	0.88
Star	None	0.51	0.42

Source: Audit Bureau of Circulation.

Although newspapers have seen a decline in their paper sales, they still appear confident in their own ability to shape the wider news agenda. Roy Greenslade believed this was a decisive factor on polling day:

> I am sure that the relentless ridicule over the six-week campaign may have played some part in the voting decisions of the floating voters who buy the *Sun* and the *Mail* (and yes, there are plenty of them).[12]

The *Sun* and other members of a 'Tory press' that dominates the national newspaper industry (see Table 14.3) published numerous anti-Labour stories during the campaign. Attacks on Miliband were frequent and his adviser David Axelrod, former strategist for Barack Obama, called the British print media more partisan than even his native US television networks.[13] The *Daily Mail* tried to insinuate that a leader it routinely called 'Red Ed' had enjoyed a complex love life when, on its own evidence, this was far from the case.[14] The *Sun* also questioned Miliband's character when he agreed to a high profile meeting with Russell Brand, who had previously used his huge social media presence—including around 10 million Twitter followers—to strongly criticise the newspaper and its veteran proprietor Rupert Murdoch.

The centre-right 'quality' newspapers took a more cerebral approach in their reporting of the campaign. But they nonetheless appeared keen to help Cameron. A letter from 103 business people supporting the current government's

---

[12] Roy Greenslade (2015) 'Yes, Rightwing Newspaper Coverage Did Cause Ed Miliband's Downfall', www.theguardian.com, on 11 May 2015.

[13] Michael Goldfarb (2015) 'The Axelrod Exit Interview', www.Politico.eu, on 6 May 2015.

[14] Andrew Pierce (2015) 'Red Ed's VERY tangled love life', www.dailymail.co.uk, on 9 April 2015.

economic policies was originally printed on the front page in the *Daily Telegraph* before being recycled by the major broadcast news outlets. Furthermore *The Times* and even the normally anti-Conservative *Independent* endorsed the continuation of the Coalition as the best electoral outcome. The possibility of a minority Labour Government being 'propped up' by the SNP led the *Daily Mail* to use its front page to suggest Nicola Sturgeon was the 'Most Dangerous Women in Britain'. Intriguingly while the London version of the *Sun* took a similar line to the *Mail* regarding Sturgeon and her party, the Scottish edition enthusiastically endorsed the Nationalists and campaigned for their victory north of the border. UKIP also secured a notable first with formal endorsement of the party by the *Daily Express*, a longstanding opponent of the European Union.

5. The Internet and social media campaign

If the broadcast and newsprint media campaign followed traditional patterns then the Internet and social media were expected, in some quarters, to produce something different. Yet reporting about Internet campaigning superficially also followed a familiar pattern. The news media once again posed a straw man question of whether this would be an Internet or social media election even though there was little sense of what a social media election might mean.[15] As with the 2010 campaign, 'the Internet election narrative' enabled the news media to hype up the potential of social media often then to dismiss its importance and usefulness as the campaign progressed.[16] However, it was not simply a case of history repeating itself. There was clear evidence this time of considerable activity around popular Twitter and Facebook platforms such as #GE2015. Aside from the nebulous question of whether it was a social media election, broadly three areas of interest emerged around the 2015 campaign and Internet technologies: first, was the Internet/social media challenging traditional campaign styles and becoming a crucial tool for parties? Second, which parties were most active in using Internet tools and where? Third, did Internet activity and competition have much impact in terms of mobilising support or influencing the behaviour of electors and could social media data be used to predict electoral outcomes?

5.1 Internet campaign style

As early as the 2001 General Election, pundits and politicians such as Labour's campaign strategist Douglas Alexander were predicting the end of the so-called

---

[15] See, for example, *Channel 4 News*, 'Is This the First Social Media Campaign?' 6 May, 2015; *BBC News*, 'Will 2015 Be the UK's First Social Media Election? 10 February 2015.

[16] David Fletcher (2015), 'Welcome to the Social Media Election that Never Was', *Guardian*, 27 April.

command and control election campaign.[17] Technology it was suggested would open up more interactive and conversational elections where voters would no longer be passive spectators but could challenge and take a more active role in campaign.[18] One other less highlighted aspect of Internet era campaigns was the continued growth of data-gathering exercises to identify and target key voters with more individualised messages (narrowcasting). Yet, despite these possibilities, the growth of the social media audience and a tidal wave of noise online, the standard response to the 2015 campaign was that it was another dull, stage-managed, risk adverse election both online and offline.[19] Criticism of party online campaigns followed a familiar pattern that they had failed to exploit the channels available and, even when they did so, they (re)produced unimaginative content. For example, most parties restricted themselves to a narrow range of social media channels. Only Labour had an Instagram account (to limited effect) whilst the Greens were the only party to use Reddit. Although the Conservatives dabbled with Buzzfeed it was hardly ground-breaking content. The result was a standard media style interview with David Cameron that generated minimal excitement. Indeed, commentators pointed out that much social media content simply documented campaign events, re-stated basic pledges or attacked opponents rather than necessarily producing anything fresh.[20] There were little or no attempts from leading politicians to interact in online dialogue with voters. In short, social media was deployed as just another broadcast tool with little focus on the social. The idea that the parties did not get it was also underpinned by lack of focus on digital issues in the campaign.[21]

Disappointment with the parties' Internet campaigns has become a recurring theme since 1997. It has some validity but arguably provides an oversimplified portrayal of online electioneering. First, criticism tends to be technology-driven based on what technology can do rather than how it is shaped by the electoral and political environment. Second, it tends to be focused on concerns about stimulating wider democratic conversation and participation which, whilst laudable, sometimes ignore the harsh reality of campaigning from a party perspective. Third, critiques are concentrated mainly on the most public aspects of the online campaign at the expense of the private, data-crunching, drier aspects of modern campaigns.

---

[17] Ward, S and Vedel, T. (2006) 'The Potential of the Internet Revisited', *Parliamentary Affairs*, **59**, 210–225.

[18] See, for example, Norris, P. (2000) *Virtuous Circle*, Cambridge, Cambridge University Press.

[19] Beckett, C. (2015) 'Broadcasting: At the Centre of the Most Managed Election Campaign'. In Jackson, D. and Thorsen, E. (eds) *UK Election Analysis 2015: Media, Voters and the Campaign*. Bournemouth, Bournemouth University Centre of the Study of Journalism, Culture and Community.

[20] Fletcher, 'Welcome to the Social Media Election that Never Was'.

[21] Martha Lane-Fox (2015) @marthalanefox, 23 April 2015.

Whilst the output of the campaign might not have matched idealistic democratic notions of a 'conversational democracy', it is clear that parties were deploying technologies to greater extent than previously and in some cases with much greater level of internal scrutiny. Party campaign officials have subsequently claimed that their parties pursued digital strategies much more seriously than in 2010. In an interview with Channel 4 News, the Conservatives' Creative Director noted the change from the last election campaign:

> [In 2010] We didn't actually stop, we didn't really measure the stats we just did things that we thought would be interesting and exciting at the time . . . Now there's a completely analytical approach to it.[22]

Overall, no single Internet campaigning style emerged amongst the parties despite the two main parties both hiring heavyweight specialists from the Obama campaign team (Jim Messina for the Conservatives and David Axelrod for Labour). The Conservatives' campaign could be characterised as a more top-down, data-driven, targeted marketing approach—spending significant sums of money on Facebook advertising and data mining.[23] Leaked documents to the BBC suggested the Conservatives were spending over £100,000 per month on Facebook and up to £3000 per month in key constituencies in the run up to the campaign. This contrasted with a reported figure of less than £10,000 per month by Labour.[24] Social media videos and posters were then used to drive home Conservative Party messages particularly about the threat of the SNP. Some critics likened these to negative US style attack ads not allowed on UK broadcast media. Perhaps more crucially, the advertising was also combined with a strategy of micro-targeting notably in key marginal seats in South-West England held by the Liberal Democrats. Online data, particularly from Facebook, were mined and combined with private polling and focus groups to identify the concerns of undecided voters and target them with personalised communication through a range of methods (phone, email, letter, in person).[25]

Labour strategy by contrast tended towards a more grassroots, core audience approach seemingly investing much effort in gaining traction through Twitter conversations and mobilising supporters on the ground. Similarly, with regard to Facebook, one party insider was quoted as suggesting that 'we're targeting people we know are Labour supporters . . . to get them to donate and

---

[22] Channel 4 News (2015) 'The Ruthless Reality of the Election 2015 Digital Campaign', 23 May 2015.

[23] Data mining encompasses the collection, automated searching through, and analysing a large amount of data in a database, so as to uncover patterns or relationships.

[24] *BBC News Online*, 16 February 2015.

[25] Tim Ross (2015) 'Secrets of the Tories Election War Room', *Daily Telegraph*, 16 May 2015; Jacob Aron (2015) 'Could Smart Search for Votes Swing UK General Election?' *New Scientist*, 30 April 2015; 'Jim Messina Interview: How the Pollsters Got It Wrong and Why Labour Lost' *The Spectator*, 12 May 2015.

volunteer'.[26] In part, therefore, the differences in approach reflect the state of both the party campaign resources but also their overall campaign strategies. Matthew McGregor one of Labour's key digital advisors commented on the parties' Internet campaigns:

> The fact they [the Conservatives] are outspending the Labour Party many, many times over because of the support from millionaire donors is going to have an impact ... [but] That's something the Labour Party can respond to by out-organising the Conservatives.[27]

That parties adopted different approaches to technology and social media underlines the point that party context is at least as significant as the technology itself in shaping their campaigns.

Whilst much of public content on social media was undoubtedly safe, occasionally parties did try something different although it is not clear that it had much impact or was conducted with much confidence. The Greens' YouTube election broadcast 'Change the Tune' did gain some coverage with over 886,000 views, more than all the mainstream party broadcasts. The most high profile social media event of the campaign was Ed Miliband's meeting with comedian Russell Brand streamed through Brand's Trews YouTube channel. Given Brand's potential audience (around one million) this might been seen as useful means of reaching out to people beyond mainstream politics, although Brand's subsequent endorsement of Labour came at such a late stage in the campaign (the week before polling) that it negated much of its potential impact. Brand's intervention also allowed Conservative newspapers and opponents to accuse Miliband of trivialising the campaign, being obsessed with celebrity and underlining his lack of Prime Ministerial gravitas.

Despite, and perhaps in response to, the supposed dullness of the official election an alternative online campaign sphere of memes, viral videos, Photoshopped posters and satirical hashtags again emerged. Some of these were non-partisan and had minimal political intent. For example, the #dogsatpollingstations, where people took photos of their dog at polling booths, proved to be one of the more popular hashtags on election day. However, many do have more serious intent and are directed at the stage-managed nature of modern campaigns, by targeting and attempting to subvert and ridicule the campaign messages and images of parties. One of the most popular was the Twitter response to Ed Miliband's pledge stone. EdStone led to a rash of Photoshopped images of Miliband with an array of parodied pledges. Whilst the growth of this type of social media content can be seen as a reflection of voter discontent and cynicism with politics, it also

---

[26] Robert Cookson, (2015) 'Parties Hope Their Digital Push Will Click with Britain's Voters'. *Financial Times*, 29 April 2015.

[27] Ross Hawkins (2015) 'Tories £100,000 a Month Facebook Bill', *BBC News Online*, 5 February 2015.

targets the way politics is portrayed through the news media. This was first noted in 2010, with the #NickCleggtoblame hashtag responding to Conservative newspaper attacks on Nick Clegg. In 2015, similar hashtags emerged, notably the rather unlikely #Milifandom where the audience expressed their support (even love) for Ed. Behind the celebrity fan tone was a serious message about countering and ridiculing the negative newspaper attacks on Ed Miliband. As one of creators of #Milifandom argued: '[It] is not a joke. It's young people angry at the distorted presentation of Ed, trying to correct that + make themselves heard'. Similarly, #Dollgate was partially used as a response to the *Sun's* strident attack on Nicola Sturgeon.

Whilst technology might have enabled some voters to move beyond passive spectating, as yet there often appears minimal connection between the official campaign and the lively alternative, satirical campaign sphere. Parties find it difficult to involve themselves with these trends with good reason—as formal, rather staid organisations, it is difficult for the major parties to capitalise on the informal and satirical without both appearing to lack authenticity and also opening themselves up to further attacks from news media about credibility, therefore distracting from serious messages of their campaign.

6. Competition and impact online

A persistent election sub-theme was attempts to declare a winner of the social media battle and try to translate social media activity into electoral outcomes. This raises the question of whether the Internet enables smaller or outsider parties to become more competitive. Further interest was generated by the idea that younger voters, who are traditionally the least likely to vote, could be reached more effectively via social than by traditional media. In the run up to the 2015 campaign, an Ipsos MORI poll suggested that up to a third of younger voters had claimed that social media would influence their voting behaviour.

Looking for winners and losers online, however, proved somewhat confusing, as nearly all the main players in the election were at some point declared to have won something. Labour was repeatedly said to have had the dominant presence on Twitter[28] whilst the SNP's Nicola Sturgeon was declared to have been the most talked about leader on that medium. UKIP and the Conservatives were said to have led the way on Facebook with 15.6 and 12.2 million interactions, respectively (compendium measure of likes, postings, shares and comments) compared with 9.7 million for Labour. It was also suggested at various points that UKIP and Nigel Farage achieved high prominence online particularly through the high volume of Google searches.[29] Perhaps the only relative media consensus was a

---

[28] Arif Durrani (2015), Labour Party Winning Social Media Election Battle', *MediaWeek*, 27 April 2015.

[29] Olivia Rudgard (2015) 'How UKIP Is Winning the Google Election', *Daily Telegraph*, 24 April 2015.

suggested under performance of the Liberal Democrats across the board. This is a significant reversal of traditional patterns of online campaigning where the Liberal Democrats have often been seen as punching above their weight.

More elaborate analysis from the 2015 campaign does suggest that social media allow certain smaller parties a greater competitive presence. Analysis of Twitter data suggests that the SNP outperformed the rest not simply because they had all their candidates using Twitter but that their reach was significantly expanded by the fact that their tweets were mentioned many more times. For example, 100 tweets from SNP candidates generated 10 times more mentions than the same number from the Liberal Democrats.[30] Smaller parties (particularly the Greens and UKIP) also performed well in terms of sharing and likes of online campaign posters leading Campbell and Lee to argue that 'while still not a level playing field to some degree some of the minor parties are outperforming the major parties on social media'.[31]

Following the election, Nigel Farage has claimed that social media was responsible for expanding the party's appeal, enabling it to reach new audiences and changing the party image from one of retired colonels to a younger more female demographic. He stated,

> What is really clear is that the pickup in vote has been due to our success on social media and it's now under 30s that are beginning to vote for UKIP in significant numbers.[32]

Whilst some of this might be hyperbole, UKIP undoubtedly improved its online position from 2010, where it tended to lag in terms of social media presence. Similarly, the SNP has also claimed it reached new audiences in rural Scotland and projected itself beyond Scotland's borders through partly through their well-established online presence.

Nevertheless, although the online world allows some minor players greater presence, exposure and potential competitiveness, it is not a straightforward level playing field. Those minor parties able to compete and benefit were often amplified by their appearance in televised leadership debates and mainstream media coverage. Moreover, in the case of SNP, it is hardly a minor party in the Scottish

---

[30] Oxford Internet Institute (Eve Ahearn, Jonathan Bright, Scott Hale, Helen Margetts, Taha Yasseri), Elections and the Internet, accessed at http://elections.oii.ox.ac.uk/uk-election-2015/ on 15 June.

[31] Campbell, V. and Lee, B. (2015) 'The Slow Shift to the Digital Campaign: Online Political Posters'. In Jackson, D. and Thorsen, E. (eds) *UK Election Analysis 2015: Media, Voters and the Campaign*. Bournemouth, Bournemouth University Centre of the Study of Journalism, Culture and Community.

[32] Seb Joseph (2015) 'Nigel Farage Hails Ukip's Social Media Nous for Ditching 'Old Colonels' Image and Wooing Younger Votes'. *The Drum*, 8 May 2015, accessed at http://www.thedrum.com/news/2015/05/08/nigel-farage-hails-ukips-social-media-nous-ditching-old-colonels-image-and-wooing-younger-voters on 16 June.

context and capitalised on their mobilisation success in the independence referendum eight months earlier. This underscores two potentially key elements in the use of Internet campaign tools. First, the importance of building longer term relationships online in a variety of contexts (not just social media but email also), rather than merely trying to stimulate last minute mobilisation during short election campaigns. Second, the separation of Internet from other media formats is increasingly an artificial divide. Online media, broadcast and newsprint campaigns are increasingly intertwined and interdependent.[33]

The eventual Conservative triumph led to suggestions that social media activity and social media metrics were as inaccurate as the opinion polls in terms of predicting outcome or mobilising voters. For instance, one high profile project combining Twitter and survey data (which had previously correctly predicted the outcome of Greek elections) mirrored almost exactly the inaccurate predictions of most opinion polls. Moreover, as noted above, Twitter, in particular, exaggerated Labour's levels of support and mobilisation. Indeed, post-election day, Twitter seemed awash with left of centre voters expressing their shock and outrage at the result.

'Echo chambers', 'amplification effects' and the potential polarisation of media audiences were themes that received increased attention straight after the election. One intriguing analysis of Twitter during the campaign argued that relatively small numbers of partisan voices from the so-called 'political twitterati' (journalists and party campaigners) can dominate and amplify certain arguments and sentiment. During the televised leaders' debates, a relatively handful of Labour and SNP Twitter accounts, in particular, were successful in providing an apparently dominating response, showing a potentially misleading picture of strength of voter sentiment when magnified by newspapers' uncritical response to social media data.[34]

Disappointment that social media did not provide clear-cut answers to questions of mobilisation or support is perhaps not surprising given the relatively dubious or superficial way that much social media data were reported. The simple use of metrics such as likes or re-tweets is a crude and possibly misleading measure of performance. For example, whilst the number of Google searches might provide a basic indication of levels of interest, a look at the content of the searches makes it difficult to understand the significance of numbers. For instance, a snapshot (on 21 April) of the most popular Google search questions about party leaders seemed to indicate that the British public has an obsession with height and

[33] See, for example, Chadwick, A. (2013) *The Hybrid Media System: Politics and Power*, New York, Oxford University Press.

[34] Adam Parker (2015) 'Twitter May End Up Being "Wot Won It" But Perhaps not for the Reason You Think', accessed at http://www.showmenumbers.com/social-listening/twitter-may-end-up-being-wot-won-it-but-perhaps-not-for-the-reason-you-think on 20 April.

age of its party leaders, along with wanting know who their spouses were. Google data also indicated that over the campaign whilst Cameron was the most searched for politician, the most frequently asked questions about him were whether he was rich, married, dead, left-handed or, indeed, a Labour politician.[35]

If use of raw numbers is problematic, further concerns surround those producing such data. Social media analytic companies with products or services to sell are unlikely to take a sober assessment of social media performance.[36] None of this means that social media analytics in general is worthless, but a more considered analysis of the wealth of data generated in the campaign is required. This is likely to take considerably longer but could generate potentially more interesting findings than trying to answer questions about who won or was it a social media election. Wider consensus is needed both on techniques and how to interpret data. Similarly, such analyses will need to be married to more traditional survey data questions about the role and impact of the social media.

7. Conclusion

After the 2010 televised leaders' debates, electoral campaigning in the UK was supposed to have undergone a seismic shift. Yet in some respects 2015 took us back in time. Whilst still major campaign events, the televised debates did not dominate as they had in the previous campaign. Whilst they were key features of the early part of the campaign and brought the novelty of multiparty campaigning into focus, their impact declined as the race developed. Indeed, the supposedly moribund newsprint media have latterly been seen as playing an important role in agenda setting and magnifying the 'horse race' aspect of the election. Cumulatively, and driven by a surfeit of polling data, they helped to forge a consensus that this was an election race too close to call with one quality newspaper editorial even declaring, without any hint of doubt, that: 'A hung Parliament is certain this week'.[37] This widely-held assumption was shared by online as well as broadcast commentators who were in fact the same opinion-formers whatever the media platform. These were also the pundits who David Cameron's strategist Lynton Crosby dismissed for having treated the campaign as more of an entertainment than critical news story. Publication of the exit poll on election night was a sobering moment, not

---

[35] Rhiannon Williams (2015) 'Google and the General Election: What the UK Wants to Know', *Daily Telegraph*, 28 April 2015.

[36] Anstead, N. (2015) 'Was This the Social Media Election? We Don't Know Yet'. In Jackson, D. and Thorsen, E. (eds) *UK Election Analysis 2015: Media, Voters and the Campaign.* Bournemouth, Bournemouth University Centre of the Study of Journalism, Culture and Community.

[37] *The Independent* (2015) 'Editorial: In Defence of Liberal Democracy', 5 May 2015.

least because the surprise confirmation of a Conservative lead had echoes of the not too distant 1992 campaign denouement.

Lynton Crosby and his Conservative colleagues were focused in their campaigning and exploited the supposed threat of a possible Labour–SNP Coalition Government to raise serious questions of Ed Miliband and his party's economic record. These themes found a ready echo in the once again decidedly 'Tory press' so that Miliband's more distant rather than Cameron's recent record in government appeared to dominate media coverage, particularly in the closing stages of the campaign. This reinforced the Conservatives' Internet campaigning which, though supposed to disrupt the style of modern electioneering by fostering new participatory activism, was arguably most successfully used by the party for a professionalised, top-down marketing approach. This strategy rehearsed their twin campaign themes of economic competency and fear of Scottish nationalism. The latter of course was recognition of a new trend where the 2015 election did differ from previous ones, specifically in the increased media exposure for some of the minor parties. Whilst traditional media are still skewed towards the main parties and their leaders, some minor parties do now appear to have got their foot in the door. This is even more the case in the social media world, which whilst not a level playing field, offers a more accurate reflection of the multiparty nature of British politics.

Britain Votes (2015) 241–254

MATTHEW FLINDERS*

The General Rejection? Political Disengagement, Disaffected Democrats and 'Doing Politics' Differently

In the run up to the 2015 General Election Douglas Carswell, the former Conservative MP who defected to UKIP in 2014, reflected on the growth of anti-politics and argued that British political parties seemed to resemble 'Kodak parties'. He drew from arguments made in his book *The End of Politics and the Birth of iDemocracy* that identified the need for an 'old politics' to keep pace with a 'new politics' that was being driven by exactly those processes of social, economic and technical change that have been identified as 'liquid modernity'.[1] Carswell's argument is that the Kodak brand was once synonymous with cameras and from the moment George Eastman launched the first Kodak camera in 1888 Kodak had a dominant market share. By the 1970s, more than 90% of camera film products sold in the USA were made by Kodak to the extent that people even spoke of taking family photographs as capturing that 'Kodak moment'. Then came digital cameras and in 2012 Kodak filed for bankruptcy. Political parties were once synonymous with democratic politics but their social position and role has clearly changed from the mass-based organisations of the twentieth century. Carswell diagnoses a failure of British political institutions to keep pace with the expectations and demands of an increasingly diverse society and that exists to some extent *beyond the reach* of the public—the *demos*. It is in this context that this chapter reflects on the 2015

---

*Matthew Flinders, Sir Bernard Crick Centre for the Public Understanding of Politics, University of Sheffield, Sheffield, m.flinders@sheffield.ac.uk

[1] Carswell, D. (2012) *The End of Politics and the Birth of Democracy*, London, Biteback; Bauman, Z. (2000) *Liquid Modernity*, Cambridge, Polity.

---

doi:10.1093/pa/gsv038

General Election through a focus on political disengagement and the development of five inter-related arguments.

(1) The 2015 General Election took place in a context that was arguably unique in British political history due to the explicit debate concerning 'anti-politics' and disengagement.

(2) This 'anti-political' climate dovetailed with academic research about 'disaffected democrats'. It was promoted by a number of influential social commentators and it fuelled the rise of the 'insurgent' parties.

(3) A more accurate interpretation of the views of the public, the social commentators and the 'insurgent' parties is that they were more '*anti*-establishment' than '*anti*-politics'.

(4) At the core of the frustration with conventional British representative democracy was a *pro*-political stance and a desire to 'do politics differently'.

(5) The root problem for the future of democracy (in the UK and beyond) exposed by the 2015 General Election was the almost complete lack of any detailed thinking about what 'doing politics differently' actually means.

The argument is that the impact of 'anti-politics' on the General Election was undoubtedly significant, but that frustrations, anxieties and pressures that became entwined beneath the 'anti-political' banner were rarely, if ever, *anti*-politics. They were anti-establishment and *pro*-politics—but *pro*-'doing politics differently'. The chapter's first section focuses on the distinction between anti-politics and anti-establishment, the second section on how this 'anti-something' sentiment played itself out within the election campaign and the final section looks to the future and reflects upon the politics of 'doing politics' differently.

1. Anti-what?

For some commentators the 2015 General Election was the first genuinely 'anti-political' election but at the same time it was one in which the existence of a major debate about the nature of British democracy served to *politicise* huge sections of society. The surge in party membership for the Scottish National Party, for example, with over 100,000 members at the time of the election (i.e. far more members than soldiers in the whole British Army) deserves some explanation in a context dominated by the rhetoric of disenchantment and decline. One element of that explanation lies with a rejection of the term '*anti-political*' as a useful epithet for capturing the sense of public concern about British representative democracy that undoubtedly existed and a sharper focus on the actual existence of an *anti-establishment* atmosphere in the run up to 7 May 2015. It was arguably an *anti-establishment* election (and therefore less novel from a historical position) rather than in any way anti-political.

In *The Establishment: And How They Get Away With It*, Owen Jones provided an influential account of a corrupt political system and a self-perpetuating political elite, largely beyond democratic control.[2] From senior civil servants to media moguls and from politicians, big business and think tanks, Jones provides a view of an insular and inter-woven privileged class and a weak veneer of cosmetic politics that needs to be demolished and rebuilt. Russell Brand, in contrast, adopted the position of a revolutionary populist with a form of celebrity politics with a streak of raw anti-elite, anti-establishment, anti-elections nihilism that was captured in his book *Revolution*.[3] It is notoriously difficult to measure the public influence of celebrity interventions in elections but in the case of Jones and Brand it is difficult to deny that, although they were generally talking to quite different audiences (the former at the educated middle classes, the latter at younger and more disengaged sections of society) they were able to orchestrate a major debate about the nature of British democracy and to cultivate a sense of widespread political failure.

But they were not *anti*-political. They both promoted a *different form* of politics. What is also significant is that Jones and Brand—often working together and citing each other's work (Brand declaring Jones 'our generation's Orwell')—were able to politicise those sections of British society (the young, the poor, ethnic minorities, etc.) that political scientists had branded 'disaffected democrats'. Brand's interview with Jeremy Paxman, for the BBC's *Newsnight* programme in October 2013, sparked a national debate about democracy and raised questions about why certain sections of society felt so disillusioned and disengaged from mainstream politics. Moreover, with 10 million Twitter followers and his own YouTube channel, Russell Brand enjoyed what Douglas Carswell would have termed an 'iDemocracy' capacity that most mainstream politicians could simply not match (Brand's *Newsnight* interview with Jeremy Paxman was watched over 12 million times on YouTube). The perceived influence of Brand was certainly demonstrated in April 2015 when the Leader of the Labour Party, Ed Miliband, allowed himself to be questioned by Brand in what became a highlight of the election—'the Milibrand interview'. The Prime Minister, David Cameron, immediately launched a scathing attack on both Miliband and Brand: 'Russell Brand is a joke. Ed Miliband hangs out with Russell Brand—he is a joke'. Owen Jones denounced Cameron's intervention as yet further evidence of a smug and sneering establishment figure that was out of touch with the public. Brand responded by encouraging his Twitter followers to vote Labour on 7 May. The fact that Brand did so after spending the previous 18 months adamantly encouraging people not to vote and then only urging people to vote three days before the actual election (and long after the deadline for voter registration had passed) should not distract from the simple fact that Brand (and Jones) played a major role in setting the terms of the political debate during the General Election and the debate was firmly focused *not so much on*

[2]Jones, O. (2014) *The Establishment*, London, Allen Lane.

[3]Brand, R. (2014) *Revolution*, London, Cornerstone.

anti-politics but on an anti-establishment standpoint that clearly resonated with large sections of the public and endorsed 'doing politics differently'.

This focus on 'doing politics differently' rather than simply 'doing away with politics' is important in terms of understanding the wider social context because one of the central findings of mass surveys and polling data in advanced liberal democracies around the world is a commitment to democratic principles. The public seems to have a strong normative attachment to the concept of democracy whereas 'politics' is viewed very much as a bad thing wrapped up with dubious practices such as sleaze and skullduggery. Support for democratic politics is therefore strong at the systemic level but weaker at the more specific level of institutions, processes and politicians. Stoker and Evans label this the 'Democracy-Politics Paradox' to suggest that the public crave different forms of politics.[4]

It was this sense of a desire for difference that forged a deep fault-line through the 2015 General Election as 'insurgent parties' such as UKIP and the SNP sought to expose and exploit this gap as part of their critique of the past and promises for the future, while the mainstream parties sought to close and downplay this gap through a mixture of promising limited reforms and focusing on other issues. Like similar parties and movements in the USA, Austria, Denmark, France and Italy, such parties offer a critique of what has gone before and promise new ways of 'doing politics'. They asserted a fundamental divide between the political establishment and 'the people' and positioned themselves as a 'challenger brand' that promises to deliver democracy without the politics.[5] But what *exactly* are these 'insurgent' or 'challenger' parties in the UK really challenging? The value of this question is that it takes us back to a more fundamental question about whether the UK is really facing a crisis of democracy and how the results of the 2015 General Election might be located within an answer to this question.

It could be argued that what is being challenged is a certain understanding of a British political tradition that is institutionally expressed within a constitutional configuration that is essentially elitist, power hoarding and majoritarian.[6] Students of comparative politics will recognise this interpretation from the seminal scholarship of Arendt Lijphart while recent analyses of British politics have revealed a process of 'majoritarian modification' in the UK since 1997 that has sought to implement reforms in response to widespread concern about the over-centralised nature of the British polity.[7] But these reforms have been limited and enacted

---

[4]Stoker, G. and Evans, M. (2014) 'The Democracy-Politics Paradox: The Dynamics of Political Alienation', *Democratic Theory*, 1, 26–36.

[5]Abedi, A. (2009) *Anti-Political Establishment Parties*, London, Routledge.

[6]Flinders, M. (2010) *Democratic Drift*, Oxford, Oxford University Press.

[7]Lijphart, A. (1999) *Patterns of Democracy*, Yale, Yale University Press; Flinders, *Democratic Deficit*.

very much *within* the confines of the Westminster Model. For Richards and Smith it is this British political tradition, and the 'Westminster Model' and notably the failure of obsolete political institutions to adapt to the 'information age'.[8] They start from the assumption that Britain is facing a number of institutional crises that seriously affect the legitimacy of the political system. Although Richards and Smith never use the term 'crisis of democracy' they argue that the problem of decreasing political engagement is a 'supply-side' issue that arises from a failure of decision-makers to properly take into account the electorate's interests and wishes.[9] In this regard they reveal an *anti-establishment* rather than *anti-political* position and their recommendations, in terms of increasing transparency and accountability, offer a modest recipe for how politics might be 'done differently'. The core insight is that the anti-political sentiment that was so prevalent around the 2015 General Election was set against a powerful critique of a very specific model of democracy and complaints regarding:

(1) The manner in which this model perpetuated an elite group (i.e. the *anti-establishment* of Brand and Jones), and
(2) That it had failed to keep pace with societal demands and expectations (i.e. the reformist critiques of Carswell, Richards and Smith).

The question then becomes one of exactly how these complaints affected the 2015 General Election in terms of turnout, inequality and the party system.

2.   A general rejection?

The themes and issues that have so far formed the focus of this chapter are hardly new. They form the backdrop for important works such as that of the Trilateral Commission on 'The Crisis of Democracy' in 1974, through to Anthony Sampson's studies of the British ruling class and William Greenleaf's magisterial three-volume *The British Political Tradition*;[10] through to the more recent work of scholars such as Peter Hennessy, Anthony King and Vernon Bogdanor on British constitutional history, culture and change. But what was significant about the 2015 General Election was that both populist and anti-political (or, as has been argued, *anti-establishment*, *pro-*'doing politics differently') debate formed the backdrop to the election. This section explores how this backdrop influenced both the campaign

---

[8]Richards, D and Smith, M. (2015) 'In Defence of British Politics Against the British Political Tradition', *Political Quarterly*, **86**, 41–51.

[9]Richards and Smith, 'In Defence of British Politics Against the British Political Tradition', p. 42.

[10]Trilateral Commission (1975) *The Crisis of Democracy*, New York, New York University Press; Sampson, A. (2005) *Who Runs this Place? The Anatomy of Britain in the Twenty-First Century*, London, John Murray; Greenleaf, W. (1983) *The British Political Tradition*, London, Routledge.

and results and places these findings against interpretations of crisis and discussions about the future of British democracy. Assessing the impact of 'anti-politics' is difficult due to the simple fact that this umbrella term captures a range of arguments and attitudinal positions and is likely to impact upon different institutions in very different ways. Nevertheless, an argument can be made that the 'anti-political' climate affected the General Election in a number of ways and as such a process of beginning to identify some of these affects and reflecting upon their significance can form the basis for future analyses when more fine-grained data are available. The section is structured around three questions which each in their own ways raise issues and themes that were mentioned in the previous section.

2.1 Did the 2015 General Election suggest a crisis of democracy?

It seems almost inevitable to begin any analysis of the 2015 General Election with the evidence that it provides as to whether Britain is facing a crisis of democracy. But before even beginning to explore this issue it is necessary to state the simple fact that 'crisis' is a very strong and emotive term. It is possibly the most over-used word in the political lexicon and although there is certainly an argument to be made about *the problem with democracy* or *the rise of disenchantment* amongst specific social groups, to talk about a 'crisis' *vis-à-vis* British democracy is something quite different.[11] As Negrine argues 'in carelessly over-using the word "crisis" . . . we may be devaluing its true meaning and change-shifting priorities'.[12]

The 2015 General Election provided little evidence of a polity on the verge of collapse or in which a significant level of systemic support did not exist. There were not accusations of widespread vote rigging or electoral abuse, there were no violent street protests, order did not break down and a smooth transition in power took place. Over two-thirds of those eligible to vote (66.1%, 30.69 million people) engaged in the election, the highest figure for nearly 20 years and just months after 84.6% of Scottish voters voted in the independence referendum.

The argument is not that serious problems and challenges for British democracy do not exist but it is one that is circumspect about the value of narratives of crisis when it comes to understanding both the 'life and death' of democracy.[13] There was no general 'rejection' of representative politics in 2015, but there was evidence of a partial rejection by specific social groups and therefore the real insights offered by recent events are more nuanced and subtle than crude debates that attempt to

---

[11] Flinders, M. (2015) 'The Problem with Democracy', *Parliamentary Affairs*, Advance Access published on 21 April 2015, doi:10.1093/pa/gsv008.

[12] Negrine, R. (2015) 'A Crisis of the Media'. In: Hay, C., Richards, M. and Smith, M. (eds) *Institutional Crisis in Twenty-First Century Britain*, London, Palgrave, p. 221.

[13] Keane, J. (2011) *The Life and Death of Democracy*, London, Simon & Schuster.

link specific scandals to the existence of a broader crisis can ever expose. If anything the 2015 General Election revealed how the nature of the relationships (note the plural) between the governors and the governed are changing and how re-connecting with those currently disconnected elements of society demand that we re-think, re-imagine, re-conceptualise and re-design how we 'do' politics. This, in turn, demands that we drill-down and examine what the 2015 General Election suggests about the nature of democratic inequality in Britain.

2.2   What did the election suggest about democratic inequality in Britain?

The previous section argued that the real insights offered by the 2015 General Election are arguably more concerned with enhancing our understanding of *the extent* of disengagement and its *changing nature* rather than with any definitive statement about systemic collapse. In this regard the Hansard Society's twelfth 'Audit of Political Engagement', published in March 2015, provides an invaluable glimpse into the changing nature of political attitudes and political behaviour and how they did (or did not) read across into the General Election results (Table 15.1).

These findings do not point to the existence of a crisis but do highlight a number of worrying trends, particularly in relation to a sharp social division between certain sections of society and a focus on the generational and economic components of anti-politics in Britain. This is confirmed by the IPPR's *Divided Democracy* report of November 2013 that revealed an increasing polarisation, which, put simply, means that younger and/or poorer people are far less likely to vote than older and/or wealthy people with just 10% of those aged 18–25 stating that they were certain to vote in the 2015 General Election.[14] This gap matters for at least three reasons: first, there is increasing evidence of a 'cohort effect' meaning young people do not get into participatory habits; second, there is a 'policy effect' meaning that politicians cater for those who are most like to vote (the older and wealthier); and, third, those from the most deprived and disengaged communities feel little commitment to broader society, let alone any aspiration to become involved in politics.

Turnout at the 2015 General Election was higher than might have been expected from the results of the Hansard Society's 2015 audit, although the audit was correct in its suggestion that the electorate in Scotland was more likely to vote than other parts of the UK. Turnout was 71.1% in Scotland with two constituencies seeing turnout rise well above 80%. Post-election analysis by polling company Ipsos MORI suggests that overall patterns of turnout remained relatively unchanged with no significant increase in turnout among young people as 18–24s were almost half as likely to vote as those aged over 65 (43–78%).[15] Turnout was

---

[14]Institute for Public Policy Research (2013) *Divided Democracy*, London, IPPR.

[15]Ipsos MORI (2015) *How Britain Voted in 2015: Who voted for whom?* London, Ipsos MORI.

Table 15.1 Key findings of the Hansard Society's 'Audit of Political Engagement, 2015'

	Finding
Certainty to vote	Just 49% of the public said they were certain to vote and the number saying they would be prepared to vote in the event of an election if they felt strongly about an issue had declined to 35% (online voting was identified as the most popular reform).
18–24 year olds	Just 16% of 18–24 year olds said they were certain to vote in an election and 30% said they were certain not to vote. Only 22% said they had undertaken a political activity in the past year but 58% said they would be prepared to do so if they felt strongly enough about an issue.
A Referendum Effect?	Scots were much more likely to vote than other parts of the country (72–49%) and were more interested in politics (62–49%) and more knowledgeable about politics (56–47%). They were also more positive about politics and being able to get involved and deliver change but also more likely to think the system of governing needed improvement.
Party Support	Just 30% claim to be a strong supporter of a political party and the Scots are more likely to say this than other parts of the UK. But only 76% of those that said they were a strong party supporter were certain to vote. Conservative and UKIP supporters were more likely to vote than Labour and Liberal Democrat supporters.
Electoral Registration	The number of people who believed themselves to be registered to vote had declined from 90% to 82%, and almost double the number of respondents claimed that they were not registered to vote had almost doubled from 8% 12 months ago to 15% in 2015.
Satisfaction with the System	Only 61% thought that Parliament was 'essential to our democracy', a decline of six percentage points, and 68% of the public think our system of governing needs improvement. Just 18% think that standards of conduct in office are high.

Source: http://www.hansardsociety.org.uk/launch-of-the-audit-of-political-engagement-12-the-2015-report/.

significantly lower among the working classes, people renting their homes, and Black and Minority Ethnic communities. The question this leaves us with is how this pattern of (dis)engagement affected and was reflected in the party system.

2.3 What was the impact of anti-politics on the party system?

This question really gets to the heart of this chapter and to a focus on the practical impact and implications of the strong 'anti-political', 'anti-establishment', pro-'doing politics differently' context discussed in previous sections. It is possible to distinguish between the impact on mainstream established political parties and on newer or 'insurgent' parties.

For the three mainstream parties (Conservatives, Labour and Liberal Democrats) the available data suggest that the General Election result can be summarised as: the Conservatives did well with voters that turned out while Labour tended to draw its support from low-turnout sections of society. Ipsos MORI polling suggests that 80% of those who had voted Conservative in 2010 did so again in 2015.[16] Amongst voters aged over 65 (the highest turnout group, 78%), the Conservatives saw a 5.5% swing from Labour since 2010. Among AB social groups (the social class with the highest turnout, 75%) they registered a three-point swing from Labour. Amongst those aged 65 and over the Conservatives won 47% of the vote to Labour's 23%; with ABs the Tories captured 45% of the vote, Labour just 26%: in both cases a far greater margin than the overall election result (38–31%). Meanwhile, Labour were only able to secure a substantial swing in their favour among young people—a 7.5% swing from the Conservatives among 18–24 year olds, and a four-point swing among 25–34 year olds and those in rented accommodation.

Labour did have a clear lead over the Tories among voters in social classes D and E (i.e. unskilled and semi-skilled manual occupations, the unemployed, lowest grade occupations) and among black, Asian and minority ethnic voters but turnout for these groups was lower than the overall level of turnout. The democratic in-equality that had been identified before the election in a number of surveys there-fore affected the mainstream parties differently with the Tories retaining the support of those groups that tend to vote most. But beyond the actual voting pat-terns two broader issues demand brief comment. First and foremost, neither the Conservatives nor Labour seemed able to cope with the nature and strength of those public frustrations that became entwined in the 'anti-politics' debate in terms of offering a response or vision of what 'doing politics' might look like. This may reflect that both parties have historically been wedded—for very different reasons—to the traditional Westminster Model, which may, in turn, explain the lack of vision.[17]

The second point, however, is the manner in which the 'anti-political' climate arguably closed-down political debate and discussion and encouraged negative campaigning. It was easier and safer to attack opponents than attempt to defend your own agenda. Debates were to be avoided and replaced by an almost surreal game of fantasy pledges as each of the main parties took turns trying to convince a sceptical electorate that they really could offer 'more for less'. Tax cuts were accompanied by increased spending and the protection of budgets; more teachers, more nurses, more childcare. It was fantasy politics where the figures simply did not stack up. A veteran analyst of political disengage-ment noted that: 'there is something surreal about the way in which British poli-ticians comport themselves at the moment. Few . . . are liars but most of them are

---

[16]Ipsos MORI (2015) *How Britain Voted in 2015: Who voted for whom?*

[17]Flinders, *Democratic Drift.*

living a lie?'[18] Jennings and Stoker suggest that 'Debates about the deficit, austerity and public spending at the core of the General Election are replete with distortions, half-truths and fail to give citizens a sense of the choices they face'.[19]

There was also a more understated response by the mainstream party leaders in the sense that Labour and the Lib Democrats did at least seek to project a more anti-elitist and engaged image while the Conservatives adopted a more distant 'states-manlike' approach that defined the 'anti-political' surge as a threat. This was, for example, the first 'selfie election' as all of the main leaders, with the exception of David Cameron, followed a trend first started by Nicola Sturgeon in Scotland to be snapped by supporters at every opportunity. While the 2015 General Election also saw the 'celebrity-as-interviewer' emerge with greater prominence with, for example, reality TV star Joey Essex 'interviewing' Nick Clegg, Nigel Farage and Ed Miliband. Laudably, Cameron refused to be interviewed by Joey Essex, ridiculed Russell Brand and dismissed the selfie culture as 'frustrating' and as making 'the process of politics quite difficult'. The Conservative response to the rise of the insurgent parties was to label them as a threat and then attach that threat to the Labour Party with, for example, a campaign poster depicting Ed Miliband in Alex Salmond's pocket to scare voters about parties that might form an alliance with Labour in the event of a hung Parliament.

A distinctive feature of the 'insurgent' parties was that they did seem to offer a choice. For the Greens it was a choice focused on sustainability, for the SNP it was anti-austerity platform and for UKIP on taking back 'control'. The Lib Democrats had traditionally played this role but became a lightning rod for anti-political sentiment and was decimated at the polls. The biggest drop for the Liberal Democrats was amongst voters aged below 34.

Taken together the mainstream parties seemed to reinforce a view of Carswell's 'Kodak parties' as out of touch and unable to acknowledge or respond to public frustrations. In their different ways, UKIP, the Greens and notably the SNP thrived against a backdrop of anti-politics. That political parties can thrive in an 'anti-political climate' underlines the main argument of this chapter that the context was one of *anti-establishment* and 'pro-new politics' rather than being anti-political in any nihilistic or anarchic sense. And yet there is no way of avoiding the conclusion that, to some extent, it was by harvesting disillusioned voters that the 'insurgent' parties were able to break through. But even here blanket statements must be replaced with a more specific account of how the different parties deployed anti-political narratives and the challenges they faced in doing so. More

---

[18] King, A. (2015) *Who Governs Britain?* London, Pelican.

[19] Jennings, W and Stoker, G. (2015) 'The Impact of Anti-politics on the UK General Election 2015', http://sotonpolitics.org/2015/01/19/the-impact-of-anti-politics-on-the-uk-general-election-2015/ accessed on 1 May 2015.

fundamentally the Greens, SNP and UKIP had to tread a careful line between, on the one hand, rejecting the actually existing model of politics while, on the other hand, promoting a deeper conviction that democratic politics is not futile, i.e. to nurture systemic support while decrying the existing model. This was arguably more problematic for the SNP who were at one-and-the-same-time a *governing party* (in Scotland) and *challenger party* (in Westminster). However, all the insurgent parties profited from the politicisation of anti-political sentiment based around a condemnation of the Westminster elite, their adoption of 'outsider status' and doses of populism. None of the three mainstream UK parties could offer a convincing response.

Jennings and Stoker highlight the extent of this link between insurgent parties and political disaffection by exploring the determinants of UKIP and Green Party support.[20] Using both the BES Continuous Monitoring Survey (2009–2013) and Internet Panel Study (2014) they reveal that distrust of politicians was almost as big a factor for Greens as for UKIP supporters. The odds of someone intending to vote Green or UKIP were two-and-a-half times higher (and at a minimum 50% higher) if they expressed distrust in politicians. People who intended to vote for UKIP and the Greens were also more dissatisfied with British democracy, disliked both David Cameron and Ed Miliband, and were more likely to agree that 'politicians don't care what people like me think'. Interestingly, Green Party supporters were more likely to accept the view that 'it is difficult to understand government and politics', whereas UKIP supporters disagreed—for them politics was not as complicated as politicians might like to suggest.

One of the most interesting underlying results of the 2015 General Election is that UKIP came second in more constituencies than any other party (120) and achieved nearly four million votes. This may suggest the existence of a latent pool of discontent that was not under the current simple plurality electoral system vented or expressed by the election. UKIP's vote-to-seat ratio was the highest of any party whereas the SNP won 56 seats with just 1.5 million votes—one of the most disproportionate election results in British history. Labour, in contrast, saw their share of the popular vote *increase* by nearly 1.5% but made a net loss of 26 seats. It may well be, therefore, that the 2015 General Election has fuelled political disaffection and that how Britain votes in 2020 *might* be quite different.

3. Conclusion

The 2015 General Election took place in a context that was arguably unique in British political history due to the explicit debate concerning 'anti-politics' and disengagement. This 'anti-political' climate dovetailed with academic research about

---

[20]Jennings and Stoker, 'The Impact of Anti-politics on the UK General Election 2015'.

'disaffected democrats'. It was promoted by a number of influential social commentators and it fuelled the rise of the insurgent parties. And yet a more accurate interpretation of the views of the public, the social commentators and the insurgent parties is possibly that they were more anti-establishment, than 'anti-politics'. This has been the central argument of this chapter—at the core of the frustration with conventional British representative democracy is a *pro*-political stance and a desire to 'do politics differently'. In this regard it could be suggested that British politics is by no means unique. 'The problems Britain faces today are not very different' Gianfranco Baldini argues 'from those of most advanced democracies, regardless of their respective institutional structures'.[21] But this leaves us with the question of what might be distinctive—either comparatively or historically—about how Britain voted in 2015. In answer to this question at least three issues deserve brief comment and all converge to focus attention on what 'doing politics differently' actually means.

First and foremost, if the 2015 General Election was dominated by a form of 'anti-politics' in which 'insurgent' parties could harvest support by framing themselves as somehow beyond conventional mainstream parties then what is striking is the failure of *all the parties* to specify in any level of detail what 'doing politics differently' would actually look like. Indeed the 'mood of the moment' that allowed the challenger brand parties to cultivate their critique was rarely-if-ever-matched by any specific vision of what a re-defined, re-imagined or re-connected political system might look like. Where reforms were promised they tended to be modest, pedestrian and piecemeal rather than offer a coherent vision of how a globalised market economy that was interpreted as running amok in terms of environmental degradation and economic inequality might be restrained. This was equally true of academic prescriptions for change. Richards and Smith, for example, recommend remedies that are either vague, naïve or built on an apparent faith in some form of 'digital democracy' for which little evidence exists.[22] They seem to forget the inconvenient existence of 'stealth democrats' who support democracy but have no interest in getting involved themselves.[23] The participatory assumptions of those who would promote 'doing politics differently' therefore requires interrogation.

This flows into a second deeper point about the relationship between democracy and populism. The insurgent 'challenger' parties in the UK, like many populist anti-establishment parties around the world, are making significant progress on the basis of a simple narrative about a different brand of democratic politics. For

---

[21] Baldini, G. (2015) 'Is British Democracy in Crisis?', *Political Quarterly*, Advance Access.

[22] Richards and Smith, 'In Defence of British Politics Against the British Political Tradition'.

[23] Webb, P. (2013) 'Who Is Willing to Participate? Dissatisfied Democrats, Stealth Democrats and Populists in the United Kingdom', *European Journal of Political Research*, **52**, 547–72.

these parties the traditional institutional frameworks of representative politics are slow, cumbersome, inefficient and tend to benefit a small elite. The anxiety created by this narrative is that although there is no doubt that a different political system could be more equitable and redistributive it is less true that it could be faster, more agile and efficient for the simple reason that democratically politics is inevitably messy. This was Bernard Crick's argument in his classic book *In Defence of Politics* and was more recently captured in Gerry Stoker's definition of democratic politics as 'the tough process of squeezing collective decisions out of multiple and competing interests and opinions'.[24] Democratic politics will grate and grind. It must achieve a delicate equilibrium between democratic participation and governing capacity—too much accountability can be as problematic as too little. Richards and Smith's plea for 'a real era of hyper-democracy' therefore overlooks not only a significant literature on the pathologies of hyper-democracy but also Crick's longer-standing focus on balance and the management of public expectations— 'politics cannot make all sad hearts glad'.[25]

But hyper-democracy is not synonymous with 'doing politics differently', and this brings us to a third and final point and a focus on the nexus. Research by political scientists on democratic participation and engagement suggests not that the public 'hate' politics but that they are increasingly adopting a different repertoire of political activities in order to express themselves. These involve on-line and off-line activities that tend to be more specific and fluid and that chime with Henrik Bang's work on the 'expert citizen' and 'everyday maker' that is typified not only by collective action through individualised modes of behaviour but also through the creation of bottom-up democratic innovations that are captured in the contemporary focus on 'DIY' or 'Pop Up' democracy which reflect a drift away from mainstream democratic processes.[26] What is missing from the manifestos of any of the British political parties is a way of channelling and drawing-this democratic energy into the Westminster model in anything other than a tokenistic way. It's the link between the 'old' and the 'new' politics—the nexus—that offers a new way of thinking about and 'doing' politics in Britain, and beyond.

This brings this chapter full circle and back to the core focus on interpreting 'anti-politics' as more concerned with being 'anti-establishment' than being *anti*-politics. The risk of an 'anti-establishment' narrative is that it focuses on the existence of individuals and specific social groups to the detriment of any greater reflection on the manner in which *the established* way of governing perpetuates

---

[24]Crick, B. (1962) *In Defence of Politics*, London, Penguin; Stoker, G. (2006) *Why Politics Matters*, London, Palgrave.

[25]Richards and Smith, 'In Defence of British Politics Against the British Political Tradition'.

[26]Bang, H. (2010) 'Everyday Makers and Expert Citizens' In: Fenwick, J and McMillan, J. (eds) *Public Management in the Postmodern Era*, London, Edward Elgar, pp. 163–192.

the existence of an elite. The obvious risk is that an anti-establishment reform pro-gramme may simply replace one elite with another, unless it also establishes a quite different institutional structure in terms of institutions, processes and cultures. This is, of course, where the British political tradition enjoys such an entrenched and embedded position. But there are signs that the traditional malleability of the British constitution has been exhausted or, as Andrew Marr recently put it, 'the centre cannot hold'.[27] Such arguments have institutional elements in the sense of the centrifugal forces of devolution (i.e. the 'Untied Kingdom' argument) or the shift from a political to a judicial constitution, but these are symptoms of a deeper issue concerning the values and principles that underpin democracy in Britain. That is, the grand political narrative about the benefits of a majoritarian power-hoarding democracy no longer works and a multitude of differing *populisms* have been unleashed in its place. Many of these are antagonistic and imbued with a desire to attach 'the blame' to a specific social group—'foreigners', 'bankers', 'bureaucrats', 'immigrants', 'politicians', 'the rich' and 'the poor'. But this instability and flux also creates a huge opportunity for any political party with the capacity to see *outside* or *beyond* the established way of 'doing politics', to offer a new political framework or philosophy and through this offer not hyper-democracy but a post-tribal democracy that can close the gap that appears to have grown between the governors and large sections of the governed.

---

[27] Marr, A. 'The Centre Cannot Hold', *New Statesman*, 23 March 2015.

Britain Votes (2015) 255–262

JONATHAN TONGE AND ANDREW GEDDES*

Conclusions: Economic Narratives and Party Leaders

The immediate aftermath of the election saw the construction of much teleological argument based on the inevitability of the Conservatives' win. Much of this assertion appeared starkly at odds with the verities of a 'neck-and-neck' race we were supposedly witnessing throughout the campaign. The failure of the vast majority of journalists, pollsters and academics to predict a Conservative overall majority was perhaps understandable.[1] Even the imported strategists assisting the Conservatives, Lynton Crosby and Jim Messina, were privately predicting the Conservatives would fall just short of a majority, believing that a 312–319 range was probable.[2] What was less excusable was the belief of many academics and pollsters that Labour would win more seats than the Conservatives, given the importance of economic competence and leadership in contemporary elections.[3]

---

*Jonathan Tonge, Department of Politics, University of Liverpool, j.tonge@liv.ac.uk; Andrew Geddes, Department of Politics, University of Sheffield, a.geddes@sheffield.ac.uk

[1] There was the occasional notable exception. The commentator Matthew Parris, for example, declared that 'The Tories are going to win—and win well', *The Times*, 21 March 2015. Even he retreated from this bold position during the campaign, however, and by its conclusion was talking of the Conservatives only winning circa 290 seats.

[2] *The Times*, 'Tories knew they would win three weeks before the vote', 13 May 2015.

[3] The mean seat prediction of political scientists (not the two editors...) in the Political Studies Association's survey was for the Conservatives to win only 277.3, compared with 282.3 for Labour. Pollsters predicted 283.7–284.6, respectively, while journalists at least had the Conservatives as the largest party, at 285.7 to seats to Labour's 281.5. See https://twitter.com/PolStudiesAssoc/status/596599887208292352?utm_source=fb&fb_ref=Default&utm_content=596599887208292352&utm_campaign=PolStudiesAssoc&utm_medium=fb.

doi:10.1093/pa/gsv039

1.   Why did the Conservatives win?

There is no need to over-complicate explanations. The Conservative election victory in 2015, the first case since 1955 of a government increasing its vote share after more than two years in office, was due to two principal factors; greater economic trust invested in the party compared with Labour and, in David Cameron, possession of a leader seen as far more Prime Ministerial than his Labour counterpart. Given that no party has ever overcome rating deficits (and they were large ones) on *both* these issues to form a government, the result ought to have been less of a surprise than the (embarrassingly off-beam) polls suggested. Many commentators did expect the Conservatives to at least be the largest party, a triumph abetted (but not created) by the SNP's demolition of Labour.

The Conservative campaign focus stuck resolutely to its core messages of 'economic competence and strong leadership'.[4] The clue was, after all, in the title of the party manifesto: *Strong Leadership; A Clear Economic Plan; A Brighter, More Secure Future.*[5] There was none of the vagueness of 'invitations to join the government of Britain' that lay in the hazy 'Big Society' civic responsibility appeals of 2010. The Conservatives' 2015 economic message was relatively simple, but had been effectively and endlessly repeated over the previous five years with the Liberal Democrats in chorus. 'The 'other lot' messed up the economy, 'failed to fix the roof while the sun was shining' and the Conservatives 'have fixed it for you. Let us continue the job'. Labour was required to make the argument that it was 'time for change' and failed to do so. In vainly attempting to counter the economic narrative, Labour could highlight the regularity of George Osborne's missed deficit reduction targets. The Chancellor's own forecast suggested only a modest reduction of debt (high under successive governments of different political hues, but lower than the G7 average when Labour left office in 2010) from 80 to 70% of GDP, over the next Parliament. Interest payments would remain huge. Yet, as Andrew Gamble has indicated, perceptions are often more important than reality. Many electors were indeed unconvinced that the previous Labour Government was responsible for the crash—but polls suggested that the largest single category of electors *did* blame the 'debts Labour racked up'.[6]

The leadership message was equally uncomplicated, presenting David Cameron as the only credible Prime Minister. Amid the focus on the economy and the rival

---

[4]http://www.telegraph.co.uk/news/general-election-2015/11608589/Lynton-Crosby-the-so-called-experts-have-lost-touch-with-ordinary-people.html, 15 May 2015.

[5]Conservative Party (2015) '*Strong Leadership: A Clear Economic Plan: A Brighter, More Secure Future*', Election manifesto 2015, accessed at https://s3-eu-west-1.amazonaws.com/manifesto2015/Conservative Manifesto2015.pdf.

[6]See, for example, http://www.theguardian.com/politics/2011/nov/21/gloomy-britons-blame-labour-poll, 21 November 2011.

leaders, other Conservative policies, such as 500 more 'free schools', 30 hours of free childcare and the sale of social housing, were not discussed to anything like the extent of the economy. The same could be said of several Labour policies. While the 'mansion tax' was sometimes dissected, other offerings, such the party's own (25 hours) free childcare promise; a lowering of the voting age to 16; abolition of the 'bedroom tax' and a reduction in university tuition fees, did not perhaps receive the critical analysis they merited.

The rise of the SNP presented the Conservatives with a chance to reinforce core themes. The campaign was marked by inexorable pleas to electors to avoid the 'coalition of chaos' of a weak Labour Prime Minister reliant upon a needy, profligate SNP. No matter that the dire leftist threat posed by Sturgeon and Salmond to *Sun* readers in England was presented positively as Scotland's opportunity by the same paper north of the border. Both portrayals were of course functional for the Conservatives. David Cameron spent the final few days of the campaign attempting to convince voters that a Conservative majority was necessary and *attainable* to avoid this scenario. In bullish performances buoyed by internal polling, Cameron stressed that his party was 'just a few seats short', while steadfastly refusing to answer questions on what a majority Conservative Government might do to the welfare budget in order to satisfy the identified £12 billion of savings required from public expenditure.[7]

The Conservative targeting of Liberal Democrat seats was ruthlessly effective, whilst John Curtice has shown how well the Conservatives defended narrow majorities over Labour. In this respect, as Justin Fisher has demonstrated, the Conservatives had a considerable financial advantage in campaign expenditure. This spending was used fruitfully to mount a combination of nationally promoted messages and sophisticated local operations, including the deployment of 100 paid campaign organisers in target seats and the effective use of social media. The consequences were dramatic as the Liberal Democrats performed far worse than even most of the (already dire) forecasts had indicated.

As the contributions from Tim Bale and Paul Webb and by David Cutts and Andrew Russell have highlighted, the 'black widow effect' of the Conservatives, having lured the (acquiescent) Liberal Democrats into government, was all too apparent, as erstwhile coalition partners were largely destroyed. Guilty of naivety in entering government in 2010 without securing at least a university tuition fees freeze to justify the manifesto grandstanding, the Liberal Democrat leader largely

---

[7] Perhaps, the clearest example of this bullish approach was Cameron's appearance on BBC Breakfast on 2 May. He repeatedly insisted that a Conservative majority was attainable and, apart from rejecting cuts to child benefit, refused to answer any questions from the interviewer, Charlie Steyt, about where cuts would fall. On exiting the studio, Cameron confirmed the deliberateness of this strategy.

ignored his senior Commons team in negotiations with the Conservatives.[8] Cameron needed Clegg far more than Clegg needed Cameron in 2010 and a better bargain was possible. That Clegg was subject to so little internal challenge was surprising, a botched attempted coup in 2014 soon petering out. Liberal Democrat achievements in office—much of the thrust for the raising of tax thresholds for the low-paid came from that direction—were ignored by an electorate which remembered only the broken tuition fees promise and, possibly, the folly of the Alternative Vote referendum. In 2015, the Liberal Democrats' capacity for gullibility stretched to new levels in their belief that a modest incumbency effect could halt a tidal wave.

2. Labour's failings

It is tempting to compare Labour's loss with that in the 1992 election, when the party had significant hopes of office, but lost as a consequence of a lack of economic trust in the party[9] and an unelectable leader. As in 1992, the party led on the 'altruistic' issues, notably the NHS, but trailed on the economy—and there is a clear issue hierarchy. Ed Miliband's alleged threat, prior to the 2015 election, to 'weaponise' the NHS, was always unlikely to shape the outcome, given Labour always leads on the subject. It was also one of the few areas largely protected from expenditure cuts by the Conservative–Liberal Democrat coalition and, amid a brief phase of political cross-dressing, received an (uncosted) extra funding campaign pledge of £8 billion extra per year from the Conservatives.

What Labour had to do instead was 'de-weaponise' the economy as an issue, yet pleading, however objectively valid, that the recovery was not 'one for all' was not tantamount to a clear and sustainable alternative economic strategy. The third big policy issue of the election, accompanying the economy and the NHS, was immigration, but this was, as James Dennison and Matthew Goodwin have shown, infertile territory for both of the main parties, neither of whom the electorate trusted on the subject. UKIP's 3.9 million votes provide ample testimony to the salience of immigration as an issue and demonstrated contempt for the main parties in their handling of the subject. The Conservatives and Labour talked tough on immigration in full knowledge of their lack of control over EU arrivals under current law and a significant section of the electorate remained unimpressed. UKIP harmed the Conservatives and Labour, but it is credible to contend that Labour was hurt more.[10]

---

[8] See David Steel, 'Six ways Nick Clegg steered the Lib Democrats to disaster', *The Guardian*, accessed at http://www.theguardian.com/commentisfree/2015/may/11/nick-clegg-liberal-democrats-disaster-coalition, on 12 May 2015.

[9] Sanders, D. (1993) 'Forecasting the 1992 British General Election outcome: The performance of an 'economic' model, *British Elections and Parties Yearbook*, **3.1**, 110–115.

[10] For the most authoritative arguments on the basis of UKIP support, see the debate in *Parliamentary Affairs*, online, 17 April 2015, Evans, G. and Mellon, J. 'Working Class Votes and Conservative Losses:

As David Denver's review of the polling evidence indicates, Ed Miliband *never* appeared a wise choice of leader, trailing Cameron on 'best Prime Minister' by a very wide margin from the moment he became Labour leader and never threatening to overcome the deficit. The plea in mitigation was that the 2010 leadership contest may not have contained anyone capable of delivering a Labour victory, but that is necessarily speculative.[11] The prospects for Labour ought to have been brighter in 2015 than 1992, when the party struggled to overcome the legacy of its hugely unpopular set of 1980s policies. Labour had at least been popular in office for a decade from 1997; it was not inevitable that the final grim years would eclipse fonder memories of Labour in office.

Yet as Steven Fielding has charted, Miliband's Labour thrashed around, launching three-month wonder ideas: 'pre-distribution'; 'squeezed middle'; 'one nation Britain'; 'predators versus producers' and short-term retail offers, such as a freeze on energy prices. The sum of the parts was never a coherent strategy, although the party was always going to struggle once economic recovery began. Astonishingly, Miliband forgot to mention the deficit at his party's final annual conference before the election, let alone deal with the issue. Labour's 83-page election manifesto was launched with a solemn emphasis upon the need for fiscal responsibility. Yet Miliband issued a flat denial when asked, at the final television showpiece event of the campaign, the BBC's Question Time, whether the previous Labour Government had overspent. Other answers were available: either agreement that Labour was not prudent 'in some areas', or, if feeling obliged to defend the record, the obvious retort was to turn the question to ask the interrogator which Sure Start centre or NHS wards he would like to nominate for closure, given the premise of the question? The importance of Miliband's unsatisfactory response can be overstated: viewing figures were modest. Nonetheless, his responses represented another example of incoherence.

Not that having a different leader in Scotland helped Labour. Ironically, Labour had enjoyed a good 2010 election here, with a swing to Gordon Brown's party. James Mitchell has indicated that the party's choice of Jim Murphy as Scottish Labour leader allowed the SNP to outflank Labour to the left and present itself as the anti-austerity party. The SNP would stand up for Scotland against the 'Red Tories' of Labour. A different choice of Scottish leader might have helped at the margins and it was a mistake to assume that Murphy's high-visibility referendum campaign

---

Solving the UKIP Puzzle'; Ford, R. and Goodwin, M. J. 'Different Class? UKIP's Social Base and Political Impact: A Reply to Evans and Mellon'; 'Class, Electoral Geography and the Future of UKIP: Labour's Secret Weapon?'

[11] For a convincing rebuttal (from a non-left-wing perspective) of the idea that David Miliband represented a 'prince across the water', see Jenni Russell in_The Times_, 'Labour mustn't fall for the myth of David', 11 June 2015.

successes would transfer into a very different form of contest. Yet, the Scottish Labour talent pool did not appear exceptionally deep. An organisational restructuring of Scottish Labour, allowing it much greater autonomy to offer a tailored Scottish message under a federal system, would have taken place much too close to the election to convince and the Scottish party would still have needed a distinctive leader.

3. Onwards to 2020

John Curtice has indicated how winning a majority in our fragmented party system is much more difficult than in previous eras. Without recapturing Scotland—and none of the (English) Labour candidates for the party leadership offered immediate ideas as to how this could be done, seemingly hoping mainly for Scots to tire of the SNP—it is difficult to envisage a Labour majority government. Yet, it is Labour's desperate position in the south of England (London excepted) and abject failure to make any gains in the Midlands in 2015 that provide its biggest problems. Even if Labour had held all its Scottish seats, the party would have won only one more seat than Neil Kinnock managed in 1992.[12]

The election aftermath provoked a measure of introspection and a considerable amount of condemnation of the campaign within Labour ranks. Much of the criticism was concentrated on the party's inability to speak to the majority, instead having focused on small disadvantaged minorities (e.g. the 2% of workers on zero-hour contracts, many of whom indicate they are not dissatisfied with the arrangement)[13] and the lack of association with 'aspiration'. As the former Home Secretary, Alan Johnson, put it, Miliband, 'talked about the squeezed middle but the middle got squeezed out. There was a lot for the very poor and a lot about the very rich not paying their whack but what about all those people in between?'[14] A better leader will broaden appeal and the reputation for economic competence might be restored. A move to the centre, nonetheless, has its own risks. The electorate might spot the existence of an avowedly fiscally responsible, low tax, aspirational, socially liberal, pro-EU, pro-Union party. It is called the Conservative Party. The current move to the Left, however, lacks electoral logic.

Even amid ideological and political incoherence, however, there are significant opportunities for Labour to exploit. Amid the introspection and the 'Must Labour lose?'[15] theses common after a run of election defeats, it is worth remembering that

---

[12]Philip Collins (2015, 22 May), 'Labour's strategy is unfathomably stupid', *The Times*.

[13]http://www.bbc.co.uk/news/uk-25098984, 26 November 2013.

[14]*The Times* (2015, 10 June) 'Labour doomed from the start'.

[15]Such ideas date back many decades. See Abrams, M. and Rose, R. (1960) *Must Labour Lose?* Harmondsworth, Penguin, for perhaps the most famous example.

the Conservatives have only won one more election in the post-war era, the score standing at 10-9. Before the next contest, the referendum on EU membership may have produced significant intra-Conservative friction, which possibly might not heal by 2020. Jostling for position to replace David Cameron as leader is likely to exacerbate internal divisions. There was a significant UKIP 2015 vote from electors who were politically engaged but nonetheless disillusioned. These voters could conceivably return to Labour ranks after the EU referendum. Labour might also interest at least sufficient of that one-third of electors who abstained in 2015, in what Matt Flinders termed the 'general rejection' of politics (although that will require far more than a gimmicky visit seeking Russell Brand's blessing, as undertaken by Ed Miliband). Blaming Labour after 2015 for the economic difficulties of 2007–2010 will not be an adequate election strategy for the Conservatives in 2020, by which time the agenda may be the quality of public services, territory which helped shape the Labour victories of 1997, 2001 and 2005. Moderately regulated neo-liberalism, further cuts in services and rises in, for example, university tuition fees, could wear the patience of the electorate. In 2013, almost two-thirds of the electorate claimed not to have noticed reductions in local council services, but this figure could rise.[16] In 2015, the belief that the Conservatives could be relied upon more than Labour to generate economic growth was not accompanied by much confidence over rises in living standards.

The Conservative victory in 2015 should not disguise the party's continuing structural problems. Swathes of the graduate middle-class (a growing portion of society); black and ethnic minorities and much of northern England, site of the largest public expenditure cuts in local government, eschew the party, while Scotland has been barren territory for years. For all the modernisation of the party's image and outlook under Cameron, exemplified by his social liberalism on same-sex marriage, the party's elected representatives remain overwhelmingly male and, at governmental level, usually the products of an elite private education way beyond the means of most of the electorate they represent. Distaste for Miliband's Labour cannot be conflated with deep affection for the Conservatives. Cameron was discomfited during the campaign when pressed on issues such as zero-hour contracts, food banks and the living wage.[17] That the Conservatives could win an overall majority from a position where approximately two-thirds of electors felt that they 'care more about the rich than ordinary people' and 'are

---

[16] Accessed at https://www.ipsos-mori.com/researchpublications/researcharchive/3123/Public-concerned-about-cuts-to-council-services-but-councils-arent-necessarily-to-blame.aspx, on 30 January 2013.

[17] See d'Ancona, M. 'The Trials of David Cameron', *The Guardian*, accessed at http://www.theguardian.com/politics/2015/may/05/the-trials-of-david-cameron, on 5 May 2015.

too close to big business and the banks'[18] spoke volumes of Labour's inadequacies, but also highlights a continuing need for Conservative change.

Finally, in our second election volume, entitled *Labour's Second Landslide*,[19] so it really does seem a long time ago, we, as editors, used our conclusion to question the concentration upon opinion polls during the campaign, highlighting how they had consistently over-estimated Labour's vote share (even then). Opinion polling and the wider market research industry provide valuable services, data and information, but the conduct of pre-election polling does require close attention and is currently the subject of a review by the British Polling Council (BPC). The BPC review will focus mainly on methodology and ask how the techniques informing the polls could get the result so wrong. Our point is rather different and relates to the impact of opinion polling on the representation of the election and the more substantive content of debate about policy and leadership. In countries, such as France, India, Italy and Spain, there is a brief period during which opinion polls are banned.

Not all contributors to this volume will share our concerns over pre-election polling and its reporting, but, following the 2015 election, we revisit some of the issues we raised in 2001. As Stephen Ward and Dominic Wring have highlighted, much—too much, at nearly half of overall campaign broadcasting—election coverage is of the 'horserace', that is who is winning, at the expense of policy dissection. That imbalance is not the pollsters' fault, but it raises serious questions of the broadcasters. Would they broadcast any other daily 'news' item about which they were unsure of the veracity? Yet they did this nightly in respect of opinion polls which, while far from worthless (they called it right in Scotland and offered clear indications of party leads on key issues and leadership), were incorrect in terms of the 'big race'. An outright ban on opinion polls might justifiably be seen as illiberal and, in an internet age, impractical. We oppose politicians trying to control when and how survey questions are asked of electors, or determine how findings are reported.[20] However, the emphasis upon incorrect polls distorted the election campaign. There ought to have been an inquiry into the reporting of the polls in the 2015 campaign by the broadcasters, to match the inquiry into the seemingly flawed polling methodology undertaken by the pollsters. Ultimately, the overarching contribution of the pre-election polls was merely to make more startling a Conservative triumph, which, although far from inevitable, would otherwise have been seen as a more likely prospect.

---

[18] Accessed at https://yougov.co.uk/news/2012/09/03/big-parties-big-problems/, on 3 September 2012.

[19] Geddes, A. and Tonge, J. (eds) (2002) *Labour's Second Landslide: the British General Election 2001*, Manchester, Manchester University Press.

[20] For these reasons, we regarded the post-election bill of Lord Foulkes, attempting to ban opinion polls, as wrong. Our concern is with the coverage afforded to opinion polls.

INDEX